OXFORD ENGLISH MONOGRAPHS

General Editors

Ireland and Scotland

Literature and Culture,
State and Nation,
1966–2000

RAY RYAN

CLARENDON PRESS • OXFORD

*This book has been printed digitally and produced in a standard specification
in order to ensure its continuing availability*

OXFORD
UNIVERSITY PRESS

Great Clarendon Street, Oxford OX2 6DP

Oxford University Press is a department of the University of Oxford.
It furthers the University's objective of excellence in research, scholarship,
and education by publishing worldwide in

Oxford New York

Auckland   Cape Town Dar es Salaam   Hong Kong   Karachi
Kuala Lumpur Madrid Melbourne Mexico City   Nairobi
New Delhi Shanghai   Taipei Toronto
With offices in
Argentina Austria Brazil Chile Czech Republic France Greece
Guatemala Hungary Italy Japan South Korea Poland Portugal
Singapore Switzerland Thailand Turkey Ukraine Vietnam

Oxford is a registered trade mark of Oxford University Press
in the UK and in certain other countries

Published in the United States
by Oxford University Press Inc., New York

ISBN 0-19-818776-9

For my parents

SEAMUS AND MAEVE RYAN

Acknowledgements

It is a great pleasure to be able to thank those who have helped this book to completion.

At the University of Aberdeen, Terry Brotherstone, Isobel Murray, and Paul Schlicke left a lasting impression. George Watson was an inspiring mentor inside and outside the seminar room during those years, and instrumental in enabling me to pursue postgraduate work.

This study began as part of my doctoral research at St John's College, Oxford. I am extremely grateful to the Carnegie Institute for the Universities of Scotland for the generous award of a scholarship to undertake research. John Kelly was a humane and patient supervisor, providing a formidable example of scholarly rigour and a fund of meticulous criticism and practical advice. My thanks to him and to Christine Kelly for their generous hospitality, support, and forgiveness on many issues over the years.

Sophie Goldsworthy and Matthew Hollis provided valuable advice and friendly guidance at Oxford University Press. Rowena Anketell's expert copy-editing is felt throughout, and thanks to Steve Batchelor for help with the cover design.

I am particularly grateful to the following for comments on sections of the book: Jonathan Allison, Matthew Campbell, Joe Cleary, Catriona Clutterbuck, Cairns Craig, Terry Eagleton, Andrew Hadfield, Hugh Kearney, John Kerrigan, Ben Levitas, Rónán McDonald, Liam McIlvanney. Con Coroneos deserves special mention for his fanatical attention to detail.

For friendship and kindness during the writing of this book, sincere thanks to Ben Levitas and Jen Griggs, Jim O'Hanlon and Mel Thomas, Tony Shaw and Shirley Eccles, John Kerrigan, Dermot Bolger, Emer Ryan, Jim Smyth, Joe Cleary, Martin O'Neill, Bernard O'Donoghue, Máire Ní Mhaonigh, Yug Chaudhry, and Liam McIlvanney.

Julie Costello read this work when it was neither popular nor profitable to do so. It is a great pleasure to acknowledge my debt to her on a wide variety of fronts.

Without countless acts of help and friendship from Lisa McCluskey, this project could not have been completed. My thanks (and apologies) to her for having to live through too much of it with such grace and good humour.

Rónán McDonald was exposed to much graceless bad humour over the years. He dealt with it, as he would be the first to admit, with a special blend of wit and wisdom.

To Joy Porter, and to Muffy, the acknowledgement due for support and inspiration extends far beyond these pages, and is best said 'when you say nothing at all'.

R.J.R.

Contents

Abbreviations

Dermot Bolger,	ASL	*A Second Life* (London, Penguin, 1994)
——	ES	*Emily's Shoes* (London, Penguin, 1991)
——	NS	*Night Shift* (1985; London, Penguin, 1991)
——	TJH	*The Journey Home* (London: Viking, 1990)
——	TWD	*The Woman's Daughter* (1987; London: Penguin, 1991)
Iain Crichton Smith,	AHD	*An Honourable Death* (London: Macmillan, 1992)
——	CTL	*Consider the Lilies* (1968; Edinburgh: Cannongate, 1987)
——	ETA	*An End to Autumn* (Basingstoke: Macmillan, 1978)
——	GMD	*Goodbye Mr Dixon* (London: Gollancz, 1974)
——	MLD	*My Last Duchess* (London: Victor Gollancz, 1971)
——	OTI	*On the Island* (London: Macmillan, 1979)
——	TLS	*The Last Summer* (London: Gollancz, 1969)
——	TS	*The Search* (London: Victor Gollancz, 1985)
Thomas McCarthy,	A&C	*Asya and Christine* (Dublin: Brandon, 1994)
——	TFC	*The First Convention* (Brandon: Dolmen Press, 1978)
——	TLP	*The Lost Province* (London: Anvil, 1997)
——	TNAS	*The Non-Aligned Storyteller* (London: Anvil Press, 1984)

Thomas McCarthy,	*WP*	*Without Power* (Brandon: Poolbeg, 1991)
William McIlvanney,	*AGFN*	*A Gift from Nessus* (1968; Edinburgh: Mainstream, 1990)
——	*D*	*Docherty* (1975; London: Sceptre, 1987)
——	*L*	*Laidlaw* (1977; London: Hodder and Stoughton, 1983)
——	*PTV*	*The Papers of Tony Veitch* (1983; London, Sceptre, 1992)
——	*RIN*	*Remedy is None* (1966; Glasgow: Richard Drew Publishing, 1989)
——	*SL*	*Strange Loyalties* (1991; London: Sceptre, 1992)
——	*STS*	*Surviving the Shipwreck* (Edinburgh: Polygon, 1991)
——	*TBM*	*The Big Man* (1985; London: Sceptre, 1990)
Colm Tóibín,	*BB*	*Bad Blood: A Walk along the Irish Border* (1987; London: Vintage, 1995)
——	*THB*	*The Heather Blazing* (London: Picador, 1992)
——	*TSOTC*	*The Sign of the Cross: Travels in Catholic Europe* (London: Vintage, 1995)

Page references to the above primary sources are given within the text.

Scots steel tempered wi' Irish fire,
is the weapon that I desire.

HUGH MACDIARMID, 'The Weapon' (1930)

Each stage of Scottish political activity has followed the Irish example, right down to the present soporific politics of the Republic of Ireland.

H. J. HANHAM, *Scottish Nationalism* (1969)

A State is always disappointing, especially one that has issued from a high rhetoric of race and nation. It is bound to incur the sardonic note of disillusion.

DENIS DONOGHUE, *The Parnell Lecture, Cambridge* (1997)

Introduction

The Republic of Ireland and Scotland: What Difference Does it Make?

I   A CRITICAL COMPARISON

What is the difference then, between Ireland and Scotland —the difference that makes the difference? I can tell you the answer—Ireland is doing so much with so little while Scotland is doing so little with so much.[1]

ON 1 MAY 1997, the day Tony Blair's Labour Party triumphed in the British general election, the then leader of the Scottish National Party, Alex Salmond, published an article in the *Irish Times* entitled 'Irish Show Scots Road to Success'. The piece strongly criticized Blair's plans for Scottish Home Rule. Salmond quoted Parnell's famous speech at Cork on 21 January 1885, invoking Parnell's declaration that 'No man has the right to fix the boundary to the march of a nation; no man has the right to say to his country—"thus far shalt thou go and no further". We have never attempted to fix the *ne plus ultra* to the progress of Ireland's nationhood, and we never shall.' The SNP leader went on:

Looking across from Scotland we see what a small nation can achieve . . . In Scotland we can only envy Ireland's international visibility, and all the advantages in tourism and investment—not to mention self-respect—which go with it. It is our task, in the SNP, to put Parnell's words into practice: and in attempting to win Scots to our cause, we are aided, not just by the rhetoric of past Irish patriots, but by the more eloquent testimony of the Republic of Ireland's contemporary success

[1] Alex Salmond, Keynote Address, Annual Conference of the SNP, 27 Sept. 1996.

... As a modern, progressive nation, secure in its own identity yet comfortably European, Ireland has much to teach the Scots.[2]

This allusion to Parnell is a potent one for anyone familiar with Irish nationalism, but the politics of the gesture are, this book argues, best understood in relation to the field of culture, a field delineated, in Salmond's case, by the answer given on 10 March 1995 in an interview with the *New Statesman*. Salmond was asked, 'What books and authors have had the greatest effect on your political beliefs?' He replied, 'John Steinbeck for *The Grapes of Wrath* and *Cannery Row*, and William McIlvanney for his range of works.'[3]

At least two themes here are familiar to students of Irish culture. The first is the appropriation of the past for contemporary purposes ('It is our task, in the SNP, to put Parnell's words into practice'), the rewriting of history in the face of present-day anxieties; what in Ireland is called the revisionist controversy. The second is the assumption that literature and culture have a central political significance. Cultural analysis, then, forms part of a wider debate on national politics in a way that has long been taken for granted in Ireland.

A third theme is less familiar: the SNP's invocation of the Republic as a state. It is now widely accepted that the Irish historical experience displays certain affinities with other colonized peoples.[4] The more naive objections to this idea, Joe Cleary argues, seem often to start from the assumption that there is some kind of standard colonial social structure and empirical index to which Ireland should conform.[5] But a claim to

---

[2] For another use of the same Parnell speech, see Salmond, 'Way to Unleash the True Potential of Scotland', *Glasgow Herald* (23 Apr. 1997).

[3] 'Influences', *New Statesman and Society* (10 Mar. 1995), 25.

[4] As examples, see Seamus Deane, 'Introduction', in id. (ed.), *Nationalism, Colonialism, and Literature* (Minnesota: University of Minnesota Press, 1990), 6: Field Day's analysis of the Irish situation 'derives from the conviction that it is, above all else, a colonial crisis'; Declan Kiberd, 'Post-Colonial Ireland: Being Different', in Daltún Ó Ceallaigh (ed.), *Reconsiderations of Irish History and Culture* (Dublin: Léirmheas, 1994), 94–112; and Terry Eagleton, *Heathcliff and the Great Hunger: Essays on Irish Culture* (London: Verso, 1995).

[5] 'Colonial/Post-Colonial Studies and Ireland: A Project in the Making', unpublished paper. I am very grateful to Dr Cleary for making this available to me. Liam Kennedy e.g. disputes the colonial model on the basis of a comparative statistical analysis of Ireland's economic performance with selected African and Asian states: see 'Modern Ireland: Post-Colonial Society or Post-Colonial Pretensions', *Irish Review*, 13 (Winter 1992/3), 107–21. In the same vein, see Kevin Barry, 'Repre-

exceptionalism increasingly underlies the development of post-colonial theory in Ireland.[6] Similarly, in the 'new' subject of British history, Ireland still remains exceptional, an unassimilable element within the emerging British state.[7] The challenge facing Irish studies, given the imperfections of the existing frameworks, is to find comparative contexts that account for the simultaneous experience of colonization and modernization (a combination not unique to Ireland), the backward look and the nervous glance forward, without 'succumbing to the universalising drive of "comparative" studies'.[8] Declan Kiberd's influential book *Inventing Ireland: The Literature of the Modern Nation* emphasized the structural centrality of colonialism in the Irish historical experience.[9] But the discontinuities he cites as characteristic of colonial cultures are also a function of a more general European modernization. Tom Bartlett and Kevin Whelan, for example, both argue that by the eighteenth century Irish social relations reflect this double heritage of fracture with the past and modernization around markets and states.[10]

senting Insurgency: A Critique of Post-Colonial Aesthetic Theory', in *Études irlandaises*, 19 (1994), 10–16, and Stephen Howe's *Ireland and Empire: Colonial Legacies in Irish History and Culture* (Oxford: Oxford University Press, 2000). For a trenchant rebuttal of this critique, see David Lloyd, 'Regarding Ireland in a Postcolonial Frame', in *Ireland after History* (Cork: Cork University Press, 2000), 37–52.

    [6] See Luke Gibbons, 'Introduction: Culture, History, and Irish Identity' in *Transformations in Irish Culture* (Cork: Cork University Press, 1996), 3–22; Desmond Bell, 'Cultural Studies in Ireland and the Postmodernist Debate', *Irish Journal of Sociology*, 1 (1991), 83–95; Liam O'Dowd, 'The States of Ireland: Some Reflections on Research', *Irish Journal of Sociology*, 1 (1991), 96–106.

    [7] See Brendan Bradshaw and Peter Roberts (eds.), *British Consciousness and Identity* (Cambridge: Cambridge University Press, 1998), 1–7; Brendan Bradshaw and John Morrill (eds.), *The British Problem, c. 1534–1707* (Basingstoke: Macmillan, 1996); Hugh Kearney, *The British Isles: A History of Four Nations* (Cambridge: Cambridge University Press, 1989); 'British History: A Review Article', *Bullán: An Irish Studies Journal*, 4/2 (Winter 2000/1), 145–59; Willy Maley and David Baker, 'Introduction: An Uncertain Union', in eid. (eds.), *The British Problem and English Renaissance Literature* (Cambridge: Cambridge University Press, 2002), 1–12.

    [8] David Lloyd, *Anomalous States: Ireland and the Post-Colonial Moment* (Dublin: Lilliput Press, 1992), 9.

    [9] (London: Jonathan Cape, 1997). See Colin Graham, 'Post-Colonial Theory and Kiberd's "Ireland"', *Irish Review*, 13 (Winter 1992/3), 62–7.

    [10] Bartlett, 'Ulster 1600–2000: Posing the Question', *Bullán: An Irish Studies Journal*, 4/1 (Autumn 1998), 1–16; Whelan, 'An Underground Gentry?', in *The Tree of Liberty: Radicalism, Catholicism, and the Construction of Irish Identity, 1760–1830* (Cork: Cork University Press, 1996), 3–56.

The general focus on identity in literary analysis, and the specific achievement of the great writers of the Irish canon, facilitates what Joep Leerssen calls 'the English Hegemony Irish Resistance model' in Irish criticism.[11] Certain themes recur monotonously in that criticism. An essay on Heaney, 'Digging', that 'snug as a gun' simile, and Northern Irish poetry and identity seem an essential rite of passage.[12] The process of self-definition, of engagement with the idea of identity, has been so all-absorbing that our specialist literary journals rarely carry essays on class as a working category of analysis, on geography, on citizenship, on gender, on the idea of civic virtue, on republicanism separated from nationalism, or, to come to the main themes of this book, on space and the state as active agents in Irish cultural life. Irish cultural critics are unaccustomed to seeing the Republic, as a *state*, provide an aspirational model for other emergent groups such as the SNP, a fact that may help explain the primacy of a concept such as 'identity' in our critical lexicon. For, fifteen years on, Terence Brown's wry observation still remains largely accurate:

A historian of the future, if he restricted his researches in the Ireland of the late twentieth century to the pamphlet literature, might gain the erroneous impression that the country consisted of six counties only, and those obsessively and inexplicably concerned with possible unification with a mythical entity variously described as the Free State, the Republic, the South.[13]

Why is 'Digging', for all its merit, so much more attractive to literary and cultural criticism than the Republic, in all its complexity? Partly it is because Heaney's poem provides a good

---

[11] 'Theory, History, Ireland', *Irish Review*, 17/18 (Winter 1995), 170.

[12] 'The statistical curve suggests that, by the next millennium, there will be more foreign doctoral theses than Irish common readers . . . It is already obvious that graduate students "working on Seamus Heaney" vastly exceed the amount of work that Seamus Heaney can hope to put in on himself.' Edna Longley, 'An ABC of Reading Contemporary Irish Poetry', *Princeton University Library Chronicle*, 59/3 (Spring 1998), 518.

[13] 'Letters from Nowhere', *Irish Review*, 3 (Spring 1987), 126. See also his 'Poetry and Partition: A Personal View', *Krino*, 12 (Spring 1986), 17–23; and *Ireland: A Social and Cultural History* (London: Fontana, 1985), a pioneering book in this context. For an attempt to address the Republic as a cultural entity, see Ray Ryan (ed.), *Writing in the Irish Republic: Literature, Culture, Politics 1949–1999* (Basingstoke: Macmillan, 2000).

basis for *unmasking*, for displaying one's critical awareness that both sides in Irish cultural debate critique the racial, linguistic, and religious narrowness of Irish nationalism, and how such ideologies and myths 'infect' literary works. But after thirty years of professional literary and historical scholarship designed to undermine entrenched identities, the competing myths still exist, as implacable as the disputes between the revisionists and their critics. In one sense we are living in a post-sceptical age. These myths and stereotypes are now 'known' to be false. The Famine wasn't simply a pre-orchestrated genocide. Ulster is not immemorially 'British'.[14] We 'know' that the mythologies sustaining them are constructs designed to support political standpoints. This much is 'known' and professionally validated, even as its meaning for the present continues to provoke often fractious debate. But the endurance of these myths, the tenacity with which Irish people cling to these beliefs, suggests both the impossibility of imagining an Ireland wholly expunged of them and the need to move beyond the polarities such a debate generates. As Richard Kirkland despairingly notes, the only point of convergence between Seamus Deane and Edna Longley often seems to be 'the occasional "primary" text unfortunate enough to be caught in the crossfire', a situation that ensures that 'the frameworks of interpretation . . . [are] often so disparate as to make comparative analysis all but impossible'.[15]

The deconstruction of myth and the interrogation of essentialist cultural identities are standard and necessary postmodernist tactics.[16] But they can take their practitioners beyond the point where any coherent politics are left; and their failure to disturb the historical imagination in Ireland, the tenacious adherence to received cultural beliefs on the Famine, 1916, the 'Britishness' of

[14] Cormac Ó Gráda, 'New Perspectives on the Irish Famine', *Bullán: An Irish Studies Journal*, 3/2 (Winter 1997/Spring 1998), 103–16.

[15] Commenting on Seamus Deane and Edna Longley's inability to acknowledge a shared canon, geography or critical practice, Barry O'Seaghdha suggests: 'When it becomes obvious that two people supposed to be engaged in public debate are in fact delivering parallel monologues, it may be time for members of the audience to question the terms of the debate' (quoted in Richard Kirkland, *Literature and Culture in Northern Ireland since 1965: Moments of Danger* (Harlow: Longman, 1996), 111).

[16] Terry Eagleton is a regular commentator on this area. See his 'Revisionism Revisited', in id., *Crazy John and the Bishop and Other Essays on Irish Culture* (Cork: Cork University Press, 1998), 308–27.

'Ulster', might suggest that this point has been reached.[17] For it is arguable that what makes a character stereotypical is less the intrinsic quality of the image—the pleasant peasant, the always devout Catholic, and that always staunch Protestant—than the degree to which a changeable audience, you and I, choose to accept that stereotype as either sympathetic or obnoxious.[18] And that response to the stereotypicality of the stereotype will usually be dictated by an individual's position in a complex matrix of socio-economic power. Analysing the individual's position within that matrix requires directing attention beyond, in the first instance, the very categories of identity and difference. The difference that makes the difference will ultimately be a sense of difference that does not merely rehearse or renounce inherited forms of difference. The Opsahl report on Northern Ireland has captured some of this ambiguity: 'although we are still forced to use the language of stereotypes for analysis, the stereotypes no longer apply'.[19]

But with so much academic prestige and authority invested in the Irish literary canon, compelling professional reasons ensure Irish critics, publishers, journals, syllabuses, and book-length studies remain soldered to its iconic names. As Joe Cleary remarks, developing 'post-colonial' reinterpretations (and, one can add, rereadings of 'Irish identity') of established Irish authors is still the most attractive critical option.[20] For the writing

---

[17] See R. F. Foster, 'History and the Irish Question', in Ciarán Brady (ed.), *Interpreting Irish History: The Debate on Historical Revisionism* (Dublin: Four Courts Press, 1994), 122–45, at 143–5: 'By the 1960s the work of a whole generation of scholars had exploded the basis for popular nationalist assumptions . . . the triumph of revisionism provides a particularly exact instance of the Owl of Minerva flying only in the shades of nightfall. Events in the island since 1969 have both emphasised the power of the ideas of history, and the time it takes for scholarly revolutions to affect everyday attitudes . . . Professional Irish history has turned this corner; but the question which may interest future Irish historians is why the "popular Irish history" took so long to follow it'. See also Tony Canavan, 'The Professsion of the Past: History and the Public', in Ryan (ed.), *Writing in the Irish Republic*, 226–41, and Brendan Bradshaw, 'Nationalism in Ireland: An Historical Overview', *Bullán: An Irish Studies Journal*, 5/1 (Summer–Fall 2000), 5–23.

[18] Joep Leersen, *Remembrance and Imagination: Patterns in the Historical and Literary Representation of Ireland in the Nineteenth Century* (Cork: Cork University Press, 1996), 170–73.

[19] Andy Pollak (ed.), *A Citizens' Inquiry: The Opsahl Report on Northern Ireland* (Dublin: Lilliput Press for Initiative '92, 1993), 95.

[20] 'Colonial/Post-Colonial Studies and Ireland'. See also Eagleton, *Crazy John and the Bishop*, p. ix: 'Scanning the bibliographies, an outsider might be forgiven for con-

addressed here, writing that engages with and to some extent imagines the Republic as a state, Tom Paulin's remarks on Ulster Protestant culture are pertinent: 'In order to establish the distinctive characteristics and values of Ulster Loyalist or Protestant popular culture, it is necessary to abandon conventional ideas of the literary and the aesthetic and consider forms of writing that are often dismissed as ephemeral or non-canonical'.[21] Because the Northern Troubles have produced a literature 'authenticated by crisis',[22] writing whose immediate political and cultural context facilitates the preoccupations of frameworks like postcolonialism and identity politics, the 'South' has been (as Brown notes) largely abandoned by Irish criticism, hidden because its writing did not directly address the conditions of violence.[23] Though this book follows an earlier project, *Writing in the Irish Republic: Literature, Culture, Politics 1949–1999*, in trying to redress this imbalance, the lack of existing criticism will no doubt still make itself felt in the following pages by depriving this study of strategic opposition or alliance;[24] but this absence is partly responsible for the strong historical and political context through which I address this writing.

It is also part of the reason why I introduce the concept of the state to Irish criticism.[25] One aspiration of cultural analysis must

cluding that the Irish literary pantheon was populated more or less exclusively by Yeats, Synge, Joyce, Beckett, Flann O'Brien and Northern Irish Poetry'.

[21] 'Northern Protestant Oratory and Writing 1791–1985', in Seamus Deane (gen. ed.), *The Field Day Anthology of Irish Writing*, iii (Derry: Field Day Publications, 1991), 314. In the current study, a variety of genres are addressed, including journalism, travel writing, literary anthologies, and autobiographical memoirs, as well as fiction, poems, and plays.

[22] John Kerrigan, 'Hidden Ireland: Eiléan Ní Chuilleanáin and Munster Poetry', *Critical Quarterly* 40/4 (Winter 1998), 76–100, at 87. I am grateful to John Kerrigan for making this available to me.

[23] See Sean O'Brien, *The Deregulated Muse* (Newcastle-upon-Tyne: Bloodaxe, 1998), 104–11.

[24] Two important recent books in this area are Conor McCarthy, *Modernisation: Crisis and Culture in Ireland 1969–1992* (Four Courts: Dublin, 2000), and Liam Harte and Michael Parker (eds.), *Contemporary Irish Fiction: Themes, Tropes, Theories* (Basingstoke: Macmillan, 2000).

[25] A recent attempt to refocus attention on the idea of the state is Richard English and Charles Townshend (eds.), *The State: Historical and Political Implications* (London: Routledge, 1999), 1–17. See also Joe Cleary's important study *Literature, Partition and the Nation State: Culture and Conflict in Northern Ireland, Israel and Palestine* (Cambridge: Cambridge University Press, 2000); Emer Nolan, 'State of the Art: Joyce and Postcolonialism', in Derek Attridge and Marjorie Howes (eds.), *Semicolonial Joyce* (Cambridge: Cambridge University Press, 2000), 78–95.

be to address accurately the way things are. This means accepting the Republic as a cultural entity and analysing its various disciplinary formats and designations. Ignoring this dimension ensures that the state remains a static, uncontested concept in Irish cultural debate, instead of being acknowledged as the active participant it is. But for understandable reasons, a study addressing the twenty-six counties as a mature, coherent entity might be accused of promoting a 'partitionist mentality', of prematurely accepting and naturalizing provisional state borders, of acquiescing in a process which perhaps distorts the frameworks and periodizations available for critical debate. In so doing, it to some extent legitimizes and naturalizes the experience of that state, pushes it from the margins of Irish critical attention a little closer to the centre, makes the Republic canonical while, perhaps, marginalizing the experience of smaller groups, such as Northern Nationalists.

> Partitions inaugurate the establishment of new states, and since most historiography is state-centric in its focus, the events that occur after partition tend to be assimilated to the career of one or other of the states involved. In other words, once state borders are established, academic disciplines such as history adapt themselves to them, taking the lineaments of the nation-state as the framework of their own investigations and analysis. As a result, 'after partition', the states thus established are treated as naturalised units of analysis, and the material consequences and functions of their borders tend either to be much less emphasised or to drop out of sight altogether.[26]

This is partly true, but treating the Republic as a mature cultural entity neither accepts nor opposes the constitutional position of the North. It does not necessarily promote a 'partitionist mentality'.[27] Instead, it tries to recognize that all positions are formally learned and all beliefs must be exposed to considered scrutiny. Edna Longley promotes the idea of Northern Ireland as a 'cultural corridor'.[28] At a time when the notion of

---

[26] Cleary, *Literature, Partition and the Nation State*, 60.

[27] See my 'The Republic and Ireland', in Ryan (ed.), *Writing in the Irish Republic*, 1–13.

[28] Review Article, 'What Do Protestants Want', *Irish Review*, 20 (Winter/Spring 1997), 104–20. The intellectual case for Unionism is put in John Wilson Foster (ed.), *Arguments in Favour of the Union* (Belcouver: Belcouver Press, 1995). See also Richard English and Graham Walker (eds.), *Unionism in Modern Ireland* (Basingstoke: Macmillan, 1996).

Britishness seems in terminal decline, it might be timely to ask what awaits the traveller at either end.[29] The construction and legitimization of the state, its inscription through literary and political narratives, its impact on the vocabulary available for critical debate—these themes are most effectively scrutinized in a context which does not return us, again, to the simple affirmation and validation of difference. The structural centrality of the state in writing from the Republic, I argue, requires a language that recognizes questions of power, agency, and space. Peter McDonald, in an attack on the prominence of the concept of identity in Irish criticism, touches on part of my overall objective here: 'Thinking about real problems . . . can often mean thinking around those problems, and finding the language which, rather than plaintively declaring its inability to escape from stereotypes, challenges fundamentally the terms in which the problems have been expressed.'[30]

The comparison with Scotland, a stateless nation, facilitates this fundamental challenge to the terms in which Irish problems are set. As Louis Cullen and T. C. Smout explain, in an introduction to a comparative volume on Irish and Scottish economic and social history, 'even on the most superficial examination, it was clear that both countries have been profoundly affected by a similar geography, by a Celtic heritage, and by a history of close political and economic links with England'.[31] This identifiable historical overlap is important. For as David Lloyd admits, 'suspicion of much contemporary "post-colonial theory" has been justly grounded in the criticism of its easy transferability which,

[29] In his passionate defence of Britishness, Andrew Marr claims 'Ireland and Scotland . . . are multiple detonators bringing us to the point where we do indeed require "the upending of our institutions"' *The Day Britain Died* (London: Profile Books, 1999), 230. On the theme of Britishness and Ulster, see Thomas Bartlett, 'Ulster: 1790–2000', *Bullán: An Irish Studies Journal*, 4/1 (Spring 2000), 1–16.

[30] *Mistaken Identities: Poetry and Northern Ireland* (Oxford: Clarendon Press, 1997), 1–20, at 4. See also (from the opposite end of the political spectrum) Lloyd, *Anomalous States*, 1–11.

[31] Cullen and Smout (eds.), *Comparative Aspects of Economic and Social History 1600–1900* (Edinburgh: John Donald Publishers, 1977), p. v. A second volume on comparative aspects of Ireland and Scotland was published in 1983: T. M. Devine and David Dickson (eds.), *Ireland and Scotland 1600–1850* (Edinburgh: John Donald Publishers, 1983).

like metaphor itself, risks discovering identity at the expense of
significant difference'.[32] The empirical and cultural bases for the
Scottish comparison are easily listed: Scotland and Ireland both
have a Gaelic and English linguistic tradition (with Scots a third
dimension in Scotland), a Catholic and Protestant sectarian
conflict, urbanized centres, and benighted rural hinterlands; and
linked to this last point, the creation of a mystique of Irishness
and Scottishness traceable to these depopulated zones. In both
countries, an Act of Union with the British state still remains contested. And perhaps most importantly, they share an oppressive
relation to the English literary tradition which was at least
partly responsible for the ideological conviction held by Pearse
and Yeats, MacDiarmid and Scott, that a community existed
that had to be recovered and restored. The contrast with the
great English tradition, a tradition endowed with a cumulative
unbroken history supporting an apparently organically growing
literature, is an immediate and obvious one to draw.[33] But if
Ireland is, as Luke Gibbons and Declan Kiberd both put it,
somewhere between the first and third world,[34] a society marked
by colonization and modernization, indeed, colonization *as*
modernization, more complex comparisons are required to
accommodate the findings of historians such as Bartlett and
Whelan.[35] Colonialism is not the single cause of the Irish predicament, any more than is capitalism. The need now is for more
alternative analyses and comparisons, histories and causalities,
than can be produced under a single methodology like post-

---

[32] *Anomalous States*, 9.

[33] See Terence Brown's comments in 'Review Article: New Literary Histories',
Irish Historical Studies, 30/119 (May 1997), 462–70, at 468: 'Part of the interest in
that would, of course, be found in the need to examine the actual conditions in which
the novel developed in England, in a detailed comparison with Ireland and Scotland.
Such an enterprise would complicate the concept of colonialism itself as England
became more visible in the discourse in its own mixed stability and instability. It
might cease to be the fixed entity which allows for Irish dialectics'.

[34] Gibbons, *Transformations in Irish Culture*, 3. See also his 'Identity without a
Centre: Allegory, History and Irish Nationalism', *Oxford Literary Review*, 4 (1992),
358–75. Kiberd, 'Post-Colonial Ireland: Being Different', 108.

[35] In *The Empire Writes Back*, an influential textbook on post-colonial theory and
literatures, 'the subsequent complicity' of Irish and Scottish societies 'in the British
imperial expansion makes it difficult for colonised peoples outside Britain to accept
their identity as post colonial'. Bill Ashcroft, Gareth Griffiths, and Helen Tiffin, *The
Empire Writes Back: Theory and Practice in Post-Colonial Literatures* (London:
Routledge, 1989), 33.

colonialism or a single notion like identity.[36] The claim is not of course, *pace* Lloyd's comments on the 'universalising drive' of comparative studies, that a comparison with Scotland will reveal a perfect knowledge of the Irish predicament, but that it can modify in important, relevant ways what we think we know of ourselves.[37] Discovering significant similarities with Scotland is not enough; retaining the idea of difference so that it makes a difference requires that the different ways in which the same terms—space, state, society, and nation—overlap in two such similar cultures be brought into dialogue.[38]

The new British history inaugurated in 1974 by J. G. A. Pocock offers a relevant example for the comparative framework sought here. 'The premises must be', urged Pocock, 'that the various peoples and nations, ethnic cultures, social structures and locally defined communities, which have, from time to time existed in the area known as "Great Britain and Ireland," have not only acted so as to create the conditions of their several existences but have also interacted so as to modify the conditions of one another's existence . . . There are processes here whose history can and should be studied'.[39] The cultural problems and permutations that flow from this interaction are legion, but one new dimension offered for Irish literary criticism is the broadening of the geographical dimension and comparative perspectives available. Salmond invoked Parnell in the *Irish Times,* as part of a debate on the merits of Home Rule or full Independence, to illustrate what he saw as the 'easy transferability' of Irish historical precedents to contemporary Scottish affairs, the many similar

[36] See McDonald, *Mistaken Identities*, 2: 'As long as the problems of Northern Ireland are framed as problems of identity, solutions will always end up as identity-prescriptions of one kind or another; and these, by offering a fresh sense of identity, will not displace but tend further to entrench the identities already in place.'

[37] See Cairns Craig, 'Twentieth Century Scottish Literature: An Introduction', in id. (gen. ed.), *The History of Scottish Literature*, iv (Aberdeen: Aberdeen University Press, 1987), 5: 'To understand the pattern of development of Scottish literature in the twentieth century we have to see it in relation to the world-wide assertion of cultural independence by peoples who have or have had English as their (imposed) official language.'

[38] David McCrone, *Understanding Scotland: The Sociology of a Stateless Nation* (London: Routledge, 1993), 1–15.

[39] 'British History: A Plea for a New Subject', *Journal of Modern History*, 47 (Dec. 1975), 606; see also id., 'Contingency, Identity, Sovereignty', in Alexander Grant and Keith J. Stringer (eds.), *Uniting the Kingdom?: The Making of British History* (London: Routledge, 1995), 292–302.

political and cultural preoccupations between the Republic, a state that does not correspond with the historically defined nation, and Scotland, a stateless nation. The preoccupations of William McIlvanney and Iain Crichton Smith, two major, critically acclaimed, and widely read Scottish writers, can be illuminated not just through a comparison with Irish writing, but also by utilizing the existing vocabulary of Irish criticism, a process which may also help Scottish cultural debate address the charge that it has yet to fully absorb and reflect developments in cultural studies and literary theory.[40] By introducing the themes of space, republicanism, and colonialism to two canonical writers, the Scottish element of this book hopefully contributes to this process.

Within Scottish cultural criticism, the Irish comparison is now regularly made.[41] Angus Calder's comments (which acknowledge the danger of eliding structural differences or overdramatizing shared tensions) are not just representative of this general trend; they also demonstrate the faintly absurd practice of trying to catalogue the vitality of one culture against another:

It is important that we don't discuss Scottish culture, or judge it, in terms of inappropriate models, taken not to be descriptive, but mandatory. I think the most clearly comparable culture to our own is the Irish, which has an overlapping musical tradition, a partly similar relationship to English culture, and a character marked like ours by waves of seaborne influences, though by even heavier emigration. Set beside Ireland's, our culture competes, but cannot claim precedence in literature, stands more strongly in painting, architecture and the

[40] Robert Crawford, *Identifying Poets: Self and Territory in Twentieth-Century Poetry* (Edinburgh: Edinburgh University Press, 1993), 14.

[41] Colin Kidd, 'The Canon of Patriotic Landmarks in Scottish History', *Scotlands*, 1/1 (1994), 9–10: 'We can learn a great deal from the stimulating debate which these issues [nationalism, revisionism] have provoked in Ireland, where national identity remains a central historical preoccupation . . . Scottish history, with its ethnic diversity, Highland–Lowland divide, borderlands, and regional involvement in Scandinavian and Irish political systems, appears similarly vulnerable.' See also Cairns Craig, *Out of History: Narrative Paradigms in Scottish and British Culture* (Edinburgh: Polygon, 1996); Robert Crawford, *Devolving English Literature* (Oxford: Clarendon Press, 1992), 270–305; Patricia Horton, ' "Bagpipe Music": Some Intersections in Scottish and Irish Writing', *Scotlands*, 4/2 (1997), 66–80; Marilyn Reizbaum, 'Canonical Double-Cross: Scottish and Irish Women's Writing', in Karen Lawrence (ed.), *Decolonizing Tradition: New Views of Twentieth-Century 'British' Literary Canons* (Chicago: University of Illinois Press, 1992), 165–90.

decorative arts, is perhaps weaker in concert music, but at least even-stevens in popular cultural forms.[42]

Whether Calder's last sentence carries any critical value is doubtful. An inventory of significant similarities with another culture is not, ultimately, a very meaningful analytical tool. Calder uses Ireland to retain the idea of cultural difference so that it makes a political difference. A critical comparison, by contrast, will address the different ways in which the same themes and terms—space, state, society, nation, difference—overlap in two such similar cultures.

More tangible expressions of Irish and Scottish connections are now available. Inaugurated by the Irish President Mary McAleese, the Research Institute for Irish-Scottish Studies at the University of Aberdeen is just one part of a network that embraces the universities of Strathclyde, Glasgow, Queen's Belfast, and Trinity College Dublin. The appointment in 1998 by the Irish state of a consul-general to Scotland is welcome evidence that the themes in this book may spill beyond the academy.

Writing in a special supplement of the *Scotsman* devoted to Ireland and Scotland, Ireland's Consul-General expanded on this point:

It is a fortunate coincidence that Scottish devolution has become a reality at a time of hope and opportunity in the evolution of the peace process. The political changes implied by the devolution process were recognised in the negotiations leading to the Good Friday Agreement which included a decision to establish a British-Irish Council . . . When the Council is inaugurated, it will bring Scottish and Irish leaders into formal political dialogue for the first time. This means that the East–West dimension to the peace process can no longer be viewed purely as an 'Anglo-Irish' affair. Scotland and Wales will enrich this dialogue with their own perspectives.[43]

What is happening in Scottish culture is now manifestly impor-

---

[42] 'A Descriptive Model of Scottish Culture', *Scotlands*, 2/1 (1995), 1–14, at 12.

[43] Daniel Mulhall, 'A Changed Perspective on Old Caledonia', 'Scotland and Ireland: A Special Supplement', *Scotsman*, 30 Nov. 1999, p. 3. The relevant passage from the Good Friday agreement is 'Membership of the British-Irish Council will comprise representatives of the British and Irish Governments, devolved insititutions in Northern Ireland, Scotland and Wales': *The Good Friday Agreement* (Dublin, Belfast, London, 1998), 2.

tant for Irish studies simply by virtue of happening.[44] The British-Irish Council gives institutional expression to an informal cultural dialogue with a long historical pedigree: the East–West dimension, in other words, is not being grafted on to Irish studies. Politically and constitutionally, that dimension is now enshrined in the Republic's geographical imagination. T. M. Devine's words on Ireland and Scotland here ring true: 'We cannot know what is distinctive about the society which primarily interests us other than by comparing it with others with similar, but also diverging experiences.'[45] And for Scottish writers, Irish connections are now exuberantly advertised, even celebrated. A recent anthology, *Across the Water: Irishness in Scottish Writing*, explicitly embraces Irish writing as a model Scotland can adopt and adapt:

Dublin and Edinburgh, Glasgow and Belfast seem piquantly alike and yet dissimilar to the point of foreignness. That shared cultural (and biological) DNA, the sense of so near yet so far, the same yet different, makes kinship complex . . . Much about the new Scotland reminds one of the old Ireland the bards once praised . . . [the anthology] is published at a confidently inclusive moment when Scotland seems at last to be healing itself, undergoing its own peace process. May we dedicate *Across the Water* to peace understanding and mutual respect on both shores?[46]

That said, the SNP's seamless invocation of the Republic and Ireland's nationalist past, state, and nation, can sound heavily ironic to certain Irish ears.[47] For its critics, one consequence of the revision of Irish history has been to expunge the Northern

---

[44] An interesting symptom of this is Colm Tóibín's comments in his introd. to *The Penguin Book of Irish Fiction* (Harmondsworth: Penguin, 2000), p. xxxii: 'Most of the work being produced in Ireland now is formally conservative . . . This new conservatism among fiction writers both north and south of the border is most clear when you compare the calmness of contemporary Irish writing with the wildness of contemporary Scottish writing.'

[45] 'Scotland and Ireland', in 'Scotland and Ireland: A Special Supplement', *Scotsman* (30 Nov. 1999), 1.

[46] Jim McGonigal, Donny O'Rourke, Hamish Whyte (eds.), *Across the Water: Irishness in Scottish Writing* (Argyll: Argyll Publishing 2000), 13–23, at 23.

[47] See 'Independent Ireland Prospering at the Heart and Head of Europe: Why Not Scotland?', SNP Research Department, 12 Dec. 1996: 'If Ireland can do it, there is no reason why Scotland can't. Ireland has far fewer resources than Scotland but is achieving more with less because it has Independence.'

conflict from the Republic's collective memory, redefining the Irish nation until it coincides with the twenty-six counties.[48] The comparison with Scotland does not only answer part of Cleary's call for 'a drastic expansion of the field of inquiry in the direction of sustained comparative analysis with other colonial societies and beyond the boundaries maintained by the Irish literary canon'.[49] As Salmond's rhetoric suggests, the Scottish comparison retains one of the most significant aspects of post-colonial discourse: its instinctive alignment with the nation as the logical, correct, even inevitable *telos* of anti-colonial history.[50] In other words, it ensures that the Republic, the state, remains in dialogue with and is potentially modified by historical currents, such as nationalism, which it would prefer to expel. Fintan O'Toole implicitly acknowledged this point recently by suggesting how easily Scotland 'can be imagined as another Ireland, about to follow Ireland's example and restore its rightful freedom'.[51]

What I am suggesting is that an effective critical intervention in Irish debate requires a perspective beyond the (admittedly entertaining) anthology wars of recent years, a totality instead of the occasionally defensive little patch offered by our own fractious and compelling discipline, Irish studies. We need a comparative study with a culture that has both a rich tradition of liberal humanism and a comparable experience of religious and nationalist strife; a comparative context that accounts for colonization and modernization, and colonization as modernization; the nation and the state in order to ensure that the catastrophic dimension to Irish history is neither completely elided or routinely invoked to establish Irish exceptionalism. Or as Flann O'Brien put it in another context, we must keep the wolf from the door, in order to prevent him from getting out. By directing analysis towards the workings of the state, it is possible to supply practical alternatives to current political values, addressing the language of public discourse to pose questions that the state will never ask of itself. So that in this way, criticism becomes not

---

[48] For an eloquent expansion of this idea, see John Waters, *An Intelligent Person's Guide to Ireland* (London: Duckworth, 1997).

[49] 'Colonial/Post-Colonial Studies and Ireland', 13.

[50] Colin Graham, ' "Liminal Spaces": Post-Colonial Theories and Irish Culture', *Irish Review*, 16 (Autumn/Winter 1994), 29–43, at 30.

[51] 'Imagining Scotland', *Granta*, 56 (Winter 1996), 60–76, at 70.

merely an act of scholarship, but has the potential to be an active exercise in citizenship.[52]

II   SPACE: THE FINAL FRONTIER

What terms might account for the qualities in a state's existence; might allow us, in McDonald's terms, to think through the real problems yet still fundamentally challenge the language in which those problems have been expressed? These terms already exist, in the multitude of spatial metaphors running through Irish criticism: the borders, margins, parishes, provinces, cities, counties, places, and regions through which Irish culture is regularly comprehended.[53] The ideological impetus behind this resurgence of regionalism is part of a more general re-evaluation and critical redemption of space. In 1975, for example, Foucault queried the 'critical devaluation of space which has prevailed for generations', one in which 'time was richness, fecundity, life, dialectic' while 'space, on the contrary, was the dead, the fixed, the immobile, the undialectical'.[54] By 1982, he confidently asserts its conceptual centrality to the issue of power: 'space is fundamental in any form of communal life; space is fundamental in any exercise of power'.[55]

In Ireland, the 'form of communal life' associated with regionalism has primarily been post-nationalist, a process, as Seamus Deane describes it, of promoting a 'geniality towards micronarratives . . . in which "Ireland" as the object of study gives way

---

[52] Gearóid Ó Tuathaigh, 'Decolonization, Identity and State-Formation: The Irish Experience', in Rosa González (ed.), *Culture and Power: Institutions* (Barcelona: Promocions y Publicaciones Universitarias, SA 1996), 41: 'The state must and will play a pivotal role in determining the framework and implementing the particular programmes of a language and cultural policy. But it is for the intellectuals to lead in the task of uncovering and discovering, of reclamation and honest interrogation. That interrogation must especially include the role of the state itself.' See also Mary Daly, 'The State in Independent Ireland', in English and Townshend (eds.), *State*, 66–94.

[53] Kevin Whelan, 'The Power of Place', *Irish Review*, 12 (Spring/Summer 1992), 13–20.

[54] 'Questions on Geography', trans. Colin Gordan from the interview in *Hérodote*, 1 (1976), repr. in Michel Foucault, *Power/Knowledge: Selected Interviews and Other Writings 1972–1977* (Sussex: Harvester, 1980), 75.

[55] 'Space, Knowledge and Power', in *The Foucault Reader*, ed. Paul Rabinow (London: Peregrine, 1987), 252–3.

to an analysis of regions, phases, issues . . . there should be no
history of Ireland but a variety of histories of various Irelands'.[56]
The promotion of a cultural regionalism has, as its political
corollary, a decentred pluralism which, Deane implies, plays
amiable host to the partition of the country into political and
spatial categories such as 'North' and 'South'. In this reading, the
restoration and proliferation of discrete places as categories of
understanding, as localist episteme, is a fundamentally pacific
gesture: a carefully coordinated emphasis on 'marginalized' cultures and spaces that undermines any systematic comprehension
of historical narratives like colonialism or capitalism.[57]

   David Lloyd's now famous attack on Seamus Heaney repeated
this charge. For Lloyd, Heaney's bog metaphors sutured place
and nature into an aesthetic that naturalized a speciously unique
space. Always beyond politics and power, this ontologically
whole poeticized territory offers illusory compensation for the
much wider processes of territorial dispossession, political disenfranchisement and cultural homogenization everywhere at
work in a technologically driven society, a society structurally
incapable of allowing Heaney's regionalism the vitality it claims.
In Lloyd's reading, Heaney locks the region and the centre
into an apparently mutually sustaining, continually nourishing
relationship, forging an aesthetic that masks the geopolitical
dependency of the margins on the now imponderable forces of
the centre.[58] But, as David Harvey notes, if it is one thing to

---

[56] *Strange Country: Modernity and Nationhood in Irish Writing since 1790*
(Oxford: Clarendon Press, 1996), 191. See also id., 'The Production of Cultural
Space in Irish Writing', *boundary 2/21* (Fall 1994), 117–44.

[57] See Kevin Whelan, 'The Bases of Regionalism', in Prionsías Ó Drisceoil (ed.),
Culture In Ireland: Regions, Identity and Power (Belfast: The Institute of Irish
Studies, 1993), 45: 'The very idea of regionalism, with its emphasis on inherited
rather than acquired identities forcefeeds the atavistic appetites of tradition . . . The
appeal to regionalism can easily be construed as an appeal to a Burkean sedative to
lull the little platoons into a big sleep'; David M. Jordan, *New World Regionalism:
Literature in the Americas* (Toronto: University of Toronto Press, 1994), 9. See also
Richard Kearney's interview with George Steiner 'Culture: The Price You Pay', in id.
(ed.), *Visions of Europe* (Dublin: Wolfhound Press, 1992): 'Much of regionalism has
a cruel, dark atavism. It lives by hatred: Regions do tend too often to define themselves, not by remembering in joy, but in hatred.'

[58] ' "Pap for The Dispossessed": Seamus Heaney and the Poetics of Identity', in
Anomalous States, 37: 'the celebration of regionalism dulls perception of the institutional and homogenising culture which has sustained its apparent efflorescence at the
very moment when the concept of locality, enclosed and self-nurturing, has become

criticize a politics based entirely on the particularities of environment, collective memory, community, and myth, 'it is quite another . . . to fashion a politics that treats the politics of place as nothing more than a numbing fantasy'.[59] And because historically identity in Ireland has been validated through a relationship to place, the problem becomes one of accounting for these traditional spaces within new designations like the state; of finding a familiar language that does not repeat familiar terms in a fundamentally different space such as the state.[60]

One alternative is offered by Kevin Whelan, who emphasizes the opportunity the region affords for comprehending meta-narratives like the nation at the level of discrete, tactile knowable communities. Region and nation are here not mutually exclusive spatial arrangements, but complementary imaginative and physical configurations each of which contains the other.[61] Whelan's

effectively archaic, and, indeed, functions as such. The pathos which the defenders of high culture and regional identity win from a stance offering to protect the vulnerable and vanishing against imponderable forces of technology and progress is gained in spite of the contradiction that the higher integration, which culture was to maintain beyond the class society, coincides perfectly with that being produced by technological development.' See also John Lucas, *England and Englishness: Ideas of Nationhood in English Poetry, 1688–1900* (London: Hogarth Press, 1991), 7, and 'The Idea of The Provincial', in *Romantic to Modern Literature: Essays and Ideas of Culture 1750–1900* (Brighton: Harvester Press, 1982), 7–29; Peter McDonald, 'History and Poetry: David Mahon and Paul Muldoon', in Elmer Andrews (ed.), *Contemporary Irish Poetry* (London: Macmillan, 1992), 93.

[59] *Justice, Nature, and the Geography of Difference* (Oxford: Blackwell, 1996), 314. See also Brian J. Graham, 'No Place of the Mind: Contested Protestant Representations of Ulster', *Ecumene*, 1/3 (July 1994), 257–82, at 259: 'A representative landscape is one fundamental element in communal identity, whether at the local, regional, national or state scale. Indeed, as the Annales school has shown, regional identities, if less likely to have a political expression are as pervasive and enduring as national ones. Thus, even if a "Europe of the regions" was to replace a "Europe of the nations", that self-same time-space linkage with territoriality would persist'.

[60] See Shaun Richards, 'The Triple Play of Irish History: Progressive Regression in Contemporary Irish Culture', *Irish Review*, 20 (Winter/Spring 1997), 36–43, at 38: 'Inasmuch as identity has been historically validated through a relationship to place it is that dimension of the current debate which remains to be explored.' See also Catherine Nash, 'Embodying the Nation: The West of Ireland Landscape and Irish Identity', in Barbara O'Connor and Michael Cronin (eds.), *Tourism in Ireland: A Critical Analysis* (Cork: Cork University Press, 1993); Seamus Deane, 'Land & Soil: A Territorial Rhetoric', *History Ireland*, 2/1 (Spring 1994), 31–4; Tom Dunne, 'New Histories: Beyond Revisionism', *Irish Review*, 12 (Spring/Summer 1992), 11.

[61] 'The Intellectual and the Region', in Liam O'Dowd (ed.), *On Intellectuals and Intellectual Life in Ireland* (Belfast: Institute of Irish Studies, 1996), 130.

work is just one element in a growing interest in Irish regional perspectives. Postmodernism has made regionalism intellectually respectable again, finding in it one of 'the multiple forms of otherness as they emerge from differences in subjectivity, gender and sexuality, race and class, temporal . . . and spatial, geographical locations and dislocations'.[62] In Ireland, regionalism has been co-opted as a potentially flexible model of political and cultural cohabitation, one that enables entrenched opponents to find common ground by preserving the territorial coordinates of an identity or affiliation without reinscribing the power structures of the nation state. John Hume, for example, calls for a 'Europe of the Regions' that acknowledges the 'synchronic relationship' between each of the European states,[63] while Richard Kearney's *Postnationalist Ireland: Politics, Culture and Philosophy* is the most sustained, optimistic manifesto for the political potential of cultural regionalism. With Hume and Kearney, the region is where the universalist dimensions of republicanism—a civic, classical republicanism that transcends the adversarial extremes of sectarian loyalism and nationalism—can be grounded, made palpable, activated (a notion I shall return to when considering Thomas McCarthy's work).[64] For there is a central and important sense in which regionalism has always existed. Before the emergence of the nation state as, in Benedict Anderson's now famous formulation, an imagined community,[65] the Celtic societies of the British Isles were localized, static, and heavily dependent on kinship for social bonding. Within Ireland and Scotland, regions were so culturally insulated that the concept of a national history is, it is often

---

[62] A. Huyssens, 'Mapping the Post-Modern' in *New German Critique*, 33 (Fall 1984), 5–52. Kenneth Frampton, 'Towards A Critical Regionalism', in Hal Foster (ed.), *Post-Modern Culture* (London: Pluto Press, 1983), 21: 'The fundamental strategy of Critical Regionalism is to mediate the impact of universal civilisation with elements derived *indirectly* from the peculiarities of a particular place . . . it has to "deconstruct" the overall spectrum of world culture which it inevitably inherits in the second place, it has to achieve, through synthetic contradiction, a manifest critique of universal civilisation.' See also Kenneth Frampton, *Modern Architecture* (London: Thames & Hudson, 1992), 315 ff.

[63] 'Europe of the Regions', in Richard Kearney (ed.), *Across the Frontiers: Ireland in the 90s* (Dublin: Wolfhound, 1988), 41.

[64] Kearney, *Postnationalist Ireland: Politics, Culture and Philosophy* (London: Routledge, 1996), 25–38.

[65] *Imagined Communities: Reflections on the Origins and Spread of Nationalism* (London: Verso, 1983).

claimed, an invalid descriptive category. Irish and Scottish social
history, in this reading, then becomes the aggregate and the
interaction of these regional histories, rather than the product
of all-encompassing national movements.[66] The contemporary
reclamation of these discrete regional epistemes attempts to
acknowledge a deeply felt sense of difference without having, as
its inevitable corollary, a culturally homogenous, undifferen-
tiated block.

But it is this very emphasis on discontinuity and hybridity, on
transnational affinities, that animates Brendan Bradshaw's fears
that the 'holistic' conception of the nation's past, a continuous
narrative characterized by frequent crises, is being undermined,
as 'the course of Irish history fragments into a series of more or
less discrete epochs, each representing a unique social, cultural
and political configuration'.[67] This sense of a cultural space that
precedes political nationalism infuses John Hewitt's regional
aesthetic, the best-known example of the regionalist as pluralist
model. In a much-quoted, widely endorsed phrase, Hewitt
defined an Ulster culturally separate from and politically tied to
the British state:

Ulster, considered as a region and not as a symbol of any particular
creed can, I believe, command the loyalty of every one of its inhabitants.
For regional identity does not preclude, rather it requires membership
of a larger association. And whether that association be, as I hope, of a
federated British Isles, or a federal Ireland, out of that loyalty to my own
place, rooted in honest history, in familiar folkways and knowledge,
phrased in our own dialect, there should emerge a culture and an
attitude individual and distinctive, a fine contribution to the European

[66] For this theme in Ireland, see James S. Donnelly Jun., *The Land and the People
of Nineteenth-Century Cork: The Rural Economy and the Land Question* (London:
Routledge & Kegan Paul, 1975); Stephen Ellis, *Tudor Ireland: Crown Community
and the Conflict of Cultures 1470–1603* (London: Longman, 1985); Nicholas Canny,
'The Formation of The Irish Mind: Religion, Politics and Gaelic Irish Literature,
1590–1750', in C. H. E. Philpin (ed.), *Nationalism and Popular Protest in Ireland*
(London: Past and Present Society, 1987), 50–80; L. M. Cullen, *The Emergence of
Modern Ireland* (London: Batsford, 1981), 109. Cullen's book was one of the first to
alert historians to the importance of regional variations. See also the essays in Paul
Ferguson and Kevin Whelan (eds.), *Rural Ireland, 1600–1900* (Cork: Cork Uni-
versity Press, 1987) and T. W. Freeman, *Pre-Famine Ireland: A Study in Historical
Geography* (London, 1957), which is a particularly useful county-by-county guide.
[67] 'Nationalism and Historical Scholarship in Modern Ireland', in Brady (ed.),
Interpreting Irish History, 191–216.

inheritance and no mere echo of the thought and imagination of another people or another land.[68]

Hewitt's regionalism was an understandable response to the complex strata of identities laid down by Ulster's history. But as Seamus Heaney observed, he 'could not include the Irish dimension in anything other than in an underprivileged way'. It was a vision that was 'slightly Nelson Eyed . . . more capable of seeing over the water than over the border'.[69] Here the Catholic 'South' is always in permanent opposition to the denomination-ally mixed North, a scenario that, of course, risked reinscribing religion as the primary and permanent index of regional identity, while Hewitt's poetic use of tropes like soil and blood seemed designed to preclude the loyalty of the Catholic inhabitants of 'Ulster'.

Hewitt's belief in the virtues of rootedness and dialect, a communal memory predicated on the unique contours of locale, recalls Heidegger's notion of 'dwelling', where the work of art comes to know itself as a worldly artefact by communing with the local, immediate 'earth', a term that remains enigmatically ill-defined in Heidegger but connotes a grainy authenticity.[70] In Hewitt, space is fixed and undialectical, permanently inscribed, and immune to the contingencies of history. The gap between the epistemological realm and the practical one, between the mental and the social, is bridged by a set of symbols and a lexicon that is, by definition, tribal and exclusive. The politics it enables is thus primarily defensive: the regional space cannot be radically overhauled or expanded, simply secured against that which it is not. The imaginative basis of his regionalism is finally barely distinguishable from the ethnic, territorial nationalism Hewitt

---

[68] 'Regionalism: The Last Chance', in Tom Clyde (ed.), *Ancestral Voices: The Selected Prose of John Hewitt* (Belfast: Blackstaff, 1987).

[69] 'Frontiers of Writing', *Bullán: An Irish Studies Journal*, 1/1 (Spring 1994), 9.

[70] Heidegger, 'The Origins of the Work of Art', in *Basic Writings*, ed. by David Farell Krell (London: Routledge, 1978), 172: 'That into which the work sets itself back and which it causes to come forth in this setting back of itself we called the earth. Earth is that which comes forth and shelters. Earth, irreducibly spontaneous is effortless and untiring. Upon the earth and in it, historical man grounds his dwelling in the world. In setting up a world, the work sets forth the earth. This setting forth must be thought here in the strict sense of the word. The work moves the earth itself into the open region of a world and keeps it there. The work lets the earth be an earth.'

decried.[71] It forms an ideal topos, where the continuity between past and present is unruptured, and the horizon of expectations commonly shared by all its inhabitants. And what destroys that horizon of expectation is, as in Heidegger's notion of 'dwelling', the intrusion of an Other, a stranger who denudes the soil of its sacral air and reminds the 'natural' resident of his contingent status.

Hewitt's regionalism left Northern Ireland's constitutional status unchallenged, hence Heaney's barely disguised accusation that Hewitt fostered a covert literary unionism.[72] But this Northern example demonstrates the importance of regional cultural activity as a precursor to political identity.[73] The organization of space in this model, the Manichaean division of inside and outside, the reluctance to countenance a genuine dialogue with the rest of the island: these spatial features connect geography very directly with power. Addressing these geopolitical relations in the Republic, the enduring potency of place in the new configuration of the state, requires a more mobile, flexible, and active conception of space. The irrelevance of Hewitt's aesthetic to the urban spaces and consumer capitalism that now comprise part of the Republic hardly needs stressing: there are no Celtic Tigers in the Glens of Antrim.[74] Instead of supplanting history with geography, a more suggestive, productive, and

[71] See Tom Paulin, *Minotaur: Poetry and the Nation State* (London: Faber and Faber, 1992), 190, 194: 'How easily Romantic ideas of authenticity, rootedness, traditional crafts, folklore, take on the stink of power politics and genocide . . . Heidegger celebrates the apparently natural and traditional in order to naturalise a violent politics.'

[72] Hewitt's regionalism and poetry has been well documented and I do not propose to trace it exhaustively here. See Gerald Dawe and John Wilson Foster (eds.), *The Poet's Place: Ulster Literature and Society: Essays in Honour of John Hewitt 1907–1987* (Belfast: Institute of Irish Studies, 1991).

[73] Kirkland, *Literature and Culture in Northern Ireland since 1965*, 28–33. See also on this theme, Seamus Heaney, 'The Regional Forecast', in R. P. Draper (ed.), *The Literature of Region and Nation* (Basingstoke: Macmillan, 1989); Edna Longley, 'Progressive Bookmen: Left Wing Politics and Ulster Protestant Writers', in *The Living Stream: Literature and Revisionism in Ireland* (Newcastle-upon-Tyne, Bloodaxe, 1994), 122–9; see also ead., 'Northern Irish Poetry: Literature of Region(s) or Nation(s)?', in James A. Davies and Glyn Pursglove (eds.), *Writing Region and Nation*, Special Issue of *Swansea Review* (Swansea: Swansea University Press, 1994), 63–83.

[74] Brian J. Graham, 'No Place of the Mind', 259: 'One of the most notable contrasts between the Republic and Northern Ireland is the strength and unity which the former derives from its symbolic universe.'

inclusive way of comprehending the continuing potency of place is provided by Henri Lefebvre's term 'the social production of space'.

Lefebvre showed how space is not just invaded and occupied by a society, as under colonialism, but also something that could be produced at will by and within a society. 'Ireland', to pursue Lefebvre's terms, is not just a space produced by the invader, the product of a colonial relationship with England, and all the sectarian lumber that goes with that.[75] The social space its citizens occupy is also the responsibility of its indigenous residents. There is no plastic 'other' which is permanently external, caught in a frozen partition between inside and outside, Ireland and England, Catholic and Protestant, South and North. Rather, Lefebvre defined a new set of problematics in which the city remained a key determinant:

The problematic of space, which subsumes the problem of the urban sphere (the city and its extensions) and of everyday life (programmed consumption), has displaced the problematic of industrialisation. It has not, however, destroyed that earlier set of problems: the social relationships that obtained previously still obtain; the new problem is, precisely, the problem of their reproduction.[76]

Lefebvre emphasizes the centrality of representation in any conception of space. Physical space was not simply an incidental by-product of built space, but also a human and therefore imaginary and symbolic entity, something to be 'read', mentally grasped, and returned to the realm of discourse, even as it remained a solidly material phenomenon. All forms of cultural activity partook in this production of space and meaning, so that 'even the grossest physical facts of space like railways or warehouses are representational—in their having been planned, designed and built, and in their being used and imagined by

---

[75] David Barker, 'Off the Map: Charting Uncertainty in Renaissance Ireland', quoted in Gearóid Ó Tuathail, *Critical Geopolitics: The Politics of Writing Global Space* (Minneapolis: University of Minnesota Press, 1996), 1–21, at 5: 'Ireland came into being as a "nation" as those who administered it marched across it, mapped it, wrote about it, and, generally speaking, produced and assembled a physical domain which, for them at least, was co-extensive with the space of their own discourse. The country which resulted from their bureaucratic labours was, as much as anything else, a figure of speech—their speech.'

[76] *The Production of Space*, trans. by Donald Nicholson-Smith (Oxford: Blackwell, 1991), 89.

human beings'.[77] Developing this notion, Edward Soja emphasized the occlusion of space by time in social theory, and called
for a recognition of the individual's role not only in the making
of history, but also in the construction of human geographies:
'the social production of space and the restless formation and
reformation of geographical landscapes: social being actively
emplaced in space *and* time in an explicitly historical and geographical contextualization'.[78]

The state, according to Soja, is itself a socially produced space
which is 'also actively engaged in the reproduction of a particular form of social spatialization'.[79] In Part II, I want to address
how the Republic as state not merely exists but becomes known;
in other words how it is reproduced and legitimized through the
production of discrete spaces which then familiarizes its citizens
with, and helps them adapt to, the abstract space inaugurated by
the state. The transformation of social space in the Republic
can no longer utilize Hewitt's redundant tropes, which sound
peculiarly like de Valera's St Patrick's Day broadcast of 1943,
with its call for 'honest history, in familiar folkways, and knowledge phrased in our own dialect'.

But the gravitational pull of group identities and territoriality
remains extraordinarily potent. The elaboration of place-bound
identities has become increasingly important in a world of
diminishing spatial barriers to exchange, movement, and communication.[80] The critical rehabilitation of territory as an
imaginative component of Irish and Scottish writing has also
commenced.[81] What is diminishing is not the importance of place
but the process of historical memory, as place loses its special
sacral significance and the city separates citizens socially from
their neighbour and culturally from their history. The undeniable splintering of collectivities like the nation partly
accounts for the erosion of this palpable sense of place, of what
Lefebvre calls representational space, by the simulated effect

---

[77] Julian Murphet, *Literature and Race in Los Angeles* (Cambridge: Cambridge University Press, 2001), provides a powerful exposition of these themes.

[78] *Postmodern Geographies: The Reassertion of Space in Critical Social Theory* (London: Verso, 1989), 11.

[79] Ibid. 35.

[80] Harvey, *Justice, Nature, and the Geography of Difference*, 246.

[81] Robert Crawford, *Identifying Poets: Self and Territory in Twentieth-Century Poetry* (Edinburgh: Edinburgh University Press, 1993).

of the representations of space through advertising and the systematically random imagery of urban centres.

And yet, it would be naive to assert that the appropriation and adaptation of space is unconnected with Deane and Bradshaw's suspicions that this recuperation of localist episteme is a fundamentally pacific gesture, dedicated to fragmenting a collective like the nation. To demonstrate this, I want to briefly address an essay that could easily be dismissed as 'ephemeral or non-canonical', and show how, as an indigenous cultural text, it produces a form of social space that attempts to account for the Republic's distinctiveness by abandoning traditional notions of the aesthetic and identity of the kind outlined in 'Digging' or John Hewitt. The essay is Ferdia Mac Anna's 'The Dublin Renaissance: An Essay on Modern Dublin and Dublin Writers', a piece which proclaimed the arrival of a new generation of Irish urban writing and identified Dermot Bolger as the leading figure in this movement. Mac Anna programmatically outlines a division of Ireland into three spaces which, in a blatantly partisan fashion, undercuts any 'holistic conception' of Ireland. In Lefebvre's terms, the erosion of a palpable sense of place by the simulated effect of a representation of space, the erosion of an historic Dublin by the advent of consumerism and the semiotics of advertising, works to legitimize the Republic and distance it from the Northern conflict.

Following a routine disavowal of Joyce and of Dublin as a 'literary black hole run by deconstructionists and professors for the benefit of serious students of High Art who would one day go on to become deconstructionists',[82] Mac Anna proceeds to his own folksy literary criticism:

'Ulysses', [*sic*] you could say, is a nightmare from which Dublin is trying to awake . . . Joyce made all other writing about Dublin seem somehow beside the point. In short, he intimidated the bejazus out of the Dublin writers of the 60s, 70s, and 80s . . . but perhaps the real truth revealed by the renaissance in Dublin is that the myth of a single Ireland is no longer true, in either a social or a literary sense. Now there are three very different Irelands, each with its own distinctive literary and

---

[82] See Gerry Smyth, 'The Right to the City: Representations of Dublin in Contemporary Irish Fiction', in Liam Harte and Michael Parker (eds.), *Contemporary Irish Fiction: Themes, Tropes, Theories* (Basingstoke: Macmillan, 2000), 21: 'Denial of Joyce has developed into a minor industry for modern novelists and critics.'

social ethos and traditions: rural Ireland of the prying priest and repressed passions . . . 'The North' of sectarian division and strike [*sic*] and famous poets . . . and now, at last emerging from the shadow of its literary giants . . . the myths and folklore of the other Irelands, the city and environs of Dublin with its urban sprawl and modern plagues and flock of young writers.[83]

Even as he undermines his own or indeed any single person's competence to chronicle this mercurial urban dispensation—a tactic easily legible once remarked upon—this representation of space establishes an essential difference from any historical precedent: this is *the* difference that makes the difference within Irish history. Dublin is not simply externalized, a physical arte-fact cognitively comprehended only when it is travelled upon. 'Dublin' is a mobile cognitive map that connotes a wholly new cultural space. To walk down this version of O'Connell Street is to enter a political jurisdiction unconnected with any palpable sense of place or literary tradition, where this precocious, post-modern revisionist already begins to recognize history as both fictional construct and dramatic spectacle:

When I was growing up in the 60s, Dublin was a dour, unexciting place. The streets were grey, the skies were pale and shifty and the people dressed in dull colours and huddled together as if terrified of being noticed. An exciting afternoon out was to go down to the G.P.O. in O'Connell Street to look for bullet holes left over from the 1916 Rising. Even on a good day, the only relief from the overall bleakness was the horror movies posters outside the Carlton. The sheer seediness of Europe's last great Georgian city was overwhelming. It made you feel that nothing interesting or artistic or original or marvellous had ever happened in Dublin or ever would. No wonder everyone went to pubs.[84]

The human and imaginary aspects to this social space are as important as its pre-existing, physical layers. The tropes of political maturity ('growing up'), and emotional abjection ('bleakness', 'seediness') are bound to the recognition of the GPO as, merely, a pock-marked wall devoid of intrinsic meaning; to the recognition of history as a spectacle, a horror movie from an

---

[83] Ferdia Mac Anna, 'The Dublin Renaissance: An Essay on Modern Dublin and Dublin Writers', *Irish Review*, 10 (Spring 1991), 14–30, at 18.
[84] Ibid. 14.

unfathomable, imponderable past. A fully sober appreciation of Irish history, Mac Anna implies, involves an awareness of this new spatial dimension to Irish life, one in which the aesthetic finally flourishes without the shackles of history. The foreclosure of memory here is synonymous with the erosion of place, the absence of any continuous historical narrative, and the splintering of Bradshaw's holistic nation into three culturally segregated spaces.

This representation of space is not simply derivative or mimetic or empirical: it actively produces a version of Dublin that circulates and acquires meaning in Irish cultural debate. For what the essay produces is a geography of Dublin in which the unrelenting dreariness of the city centre, still scarred by a monologic nationalist history, is renovated by the emergence of new suburbs, 'the bunch of young Dublin writers who do not conform to academic stereotyping and whose inspiration is drawn firmly from the environment around them rather than any literary sugardaddy'. To put this in Lloyd's terms, the ideal register of historical continuity, in which the naming of a place operates symbolically to communicate between the ideal and actual identity, is removed by a cultural reterritorialization that erodes the sacral air surrounding O'Connell Street and the GPO. The city centre is in fact revitalized through the influence of these new deracinated peripheral sites, and there is a corresponding revision of the role 'Dublin' might occupy in a space called 'Ireland' whose troublesome north-east corner this polemical survey encourages it to shed.

The questions posed in this process are predictably bland: 'how would James Joyce have reacted to the Dublin portrayed in Bolger's novels—would he have been able to recognise a single shop front?'[85] But the simple presence of the grossest physical facts, these new shops, are invested with disproportionate representational and spatial impact. This constellation of new names and spaces, and the dizzying array of genres in which they are represented, is meant to figuratively displace the solid centrality of traditional literary and political icons: the Dublin of Joyce and the GPO is appropriated and reimagined to produce a new cultural space outside the narrative of the nation.

---

[85] Ibid. 29.

And it is also outside the aesthetic unity offered by Hewitt's regionalism. In Hewitt's Ulster, the relationship between the individual and community is to be reconciled only through the artist Hewitt, an ideological assumption which, as Richard Kirkland notes, belongs firmly to nineteenth-century nationalist aesthetics.[86] Mac Anna's essay abandons this kind of relationship, claiming instead that 'most of the truly effective writing about modern Dublin that emerged in the 60s and 70s, came from the non-academic types such as the rockstar Phil Lynott'.[87] Journalism, non-fiction, scores of plays, poems, and memoirs—none of which are evaluated according to their aesthetic quality—and, intriguingly, soft-porn vampire lesbian films are now the forms through which Dublin becomes meaningful. It is almost impossible here to propose one language through which these indigenous forms can act as 'a force of unification'. Dublin is the place where what is 'external' is transformed into what is 'internal', as the epistemological space available to individuals seems to resemble the physical, geopolitical space of the renovated city.[88] What was marginal in Irish life—the suburban spaces and ephemeral non-canonical writing and cultural forms produced there—now seeks parity of esteem with Joyce and the GPO.

Mac Anna's essay, accorded a prominent slot in a respected academic journal, contributes to the production and comprehension of space, to the adaptation of social subjects to the spatial transformation of sites like Dublin. But its veiled inscription of the state, its 'three very different Irelands', is legible only if we do not focus exclusively on a notion like identity, a concept which, by configuring politics as a series of personal relations, genially accommodates Mac Anna's polyphony of voices: this systematically random, radical plurality of individual subjects who are, apparently, incapable of unity in any abstract category. There is no doubt this version of Dublin exists in some modified form, but it effectively works here to set the *ne plus ultra* to

[86] Kirkland, *Literature and Culture in Northern Ireland since 1965*, 30: 'The writer becomes saturated with meaning and must mediate the relationship between the individual and the territory in such a way as to propose language as a force of unification rather than division.'
[87] 'Dublin Renaissance', 19.
[88] Con Coroneos, 'History, the Boundary, and the *Third Man*', in González (ed.), *Culture and Power: Institutions*, 81.

the boundaries of the Irish nation. The differences that make the difference are now produced indigenously, by the Irish themselves; the colonialism marking Hewitt's regionalism is, like the scarred walls of the GPO, a remnant of a history Mac Anna tries to fumigate from the public sphere. There is a refreshing insistence that religious markers are now redundant, and difference is no longer the exclusive preserve of the familiar folkways of Ulster as the Irish dimension across the border is emphatically foregrounded. Now, geopolitical categories like 'the South' are exploded, in Bradshaw's phrase, into a series of 'unique social, cultural and political configurations'. This 'Dublin' belongs to a state imaginatively disengaged from the North, one of three mutually exclusive spaces which, in a schematic representation, are structurally incapable of entering into dialogue with one another. In this sense, the essay is part of what Cleary calls the 'political and cultural labour that goes into the maintenance and contestation of partitioning borders'.[89] This theme is explored in Chapter 5 on Colm Tóibín, an influential proponent of the idea of separate cultural and political development for the Northern and Southern states.

What Mac Anna unwittingly demonstrates, however, is that the space of the nation can be synonymous with internal differences. The one stable signifier that contains and makes possible the shifting, variable spaces in his schematic representation is, ironically, the island. Accepting the local as a valid subject for analysis does not necessarily negate the existence of a metanarrative, unless that metanarrative prematurely excludes the emergence of certain forms of difference. Brendan Bradshaw criticizes revisionists for denying the Irish people access to their catastrophic, victimized heritage. 'The communal memory', he claims, 'retains a keen sense of the tragic dimension of the national history.'[90] But this tragic dimension cannot, of course, be a frozen marker of Irish difference. One can deplore Mac Anna's attempts to erase history, lament his limited interest in the political consequences of that history for the North. But for all that, this partisan, present-centred local constituency is one legitimate form of communal memory: the 'catastrophic dimension' to Irish history, Mac Anna's advocates might claim, cannot

---

[89] *Literature, Partition and the Nation State*, 11.
[90] 'Nationalism and Scholarship', 205.

permanently preclude the emergence of other forms of individual
and collective identity. His form of Irish citizenship need not
permanently exhibit psychological scars from the Famine, a fact
which must affect the methodologies used to address writing in
which the state not the nation is a key component. For any
attempt to build unity must have the confidence to face these new
kinds of diversity and difference. We cannot, after all, completely
abandon these concepts; even in an anti-foundational world, we
cannot escape the need for foundations. Deane, Lloyd, and
Bradshaw suspect regionalism of making the local concrete and
the metanarrative of the nation an ever-receding abstraction.[91]
But the nation is the specific product of many regional designations which are constructs, not fixed. And as Doreen Massey
puts it, 'those who conflate the local with the concrete . . . are
confusing geographical scale with processes of abstraction in
thought'.[92] Analysing the local does not amount to fetishizing it,
and grand narratives may equally be required in the study of the
regional space as in the national territory.

The comparison of a west-of-Scotland novelist and a now-
deceased Highland novelist, better known as a Gaelic poet, may,
at first, seem remote from lesbian vampires and Phil Lynott
lyrics. However, the division of Scotland into geographic
regional spaces with connected linguistic and cultural heritages[93]
supports Lefebvre's claim that 'social spaces interpenetrate one
another and/or superimpose themselves upon one another'.[94]
Mac Anna thematizes the city in order to renovate, familiarize,
and legitimize the state by denying this kind of interaction. He
drains the Republic of republicanism, severs its connection with
the geography of the island, and announces an irrevocable split

---

[91] See David Harvey's comments in *The Condition of Postmodernity* (Oxford:
Blackwell, 1989), 303: '"Regional resistances", the struggle for local autonomy,
place-bound organisation, may be excellent bases for political organisation, but they
cannot bear the burden of radical historical change alone'.
[92] 'The Possibility of a Politics of Place', in Linda McDowell (ed.), *Undoing Place:
A Geographical Reader* (London: Arnold, 1998), 317–31, at 320.
[93] Robert Crawford, 'Defining Scotland', in Susan Bassnet (ed.), *Defining British
Cultures: An Introduction* (London: Routledge, 1997), 83–95, at 92: 'Scotland itself
is dynamic, authored through an internal polyphonic process. That authorship
involves a variety of languages (not least English, Scots, and Gaelic) and their atten-
dant traditions; it involves an ongoing regional interaction between parts of Scotland
as different as Glasgow and the Outer Hebrides, St Andrews and Dundee'.
[94] *Production of Space*, 86.

between this contemporary sphere and the history of the 'holistic' nation. There is no doubt this version of Dublin is partially true. But to read this new Dublin space effectively, some other comparative context is required besides the by-now tedious, lame, and self-serving claims that history is, still, a 'nightmare' from which the Irish writer is trying to awake. One compelling comparative context is offered by Scotland, a country where, as George Watson notes, the burden of history and the fragmentation of the nation are for the writer perennial themes.[95] And just as Mac Anna proclaims his irreverance for emblems of Ireland's national past—the GPO and Joyce—Colin Kidd has suggested that 'the Scottish past as an ideological resource is virtually bankrupt'.[96] But if the Scottish historical landscape does indeed lack real contemporary political significance, Ireland's often seems set to engulf the present. What follows brings these separated but related themes into dialogue through five writers who share a common set of thematic preoccupations, in the belief, to revisit T. M. Devine's words, that we cannot know what is distinctive about the society which primarily interests us other than by comparing it with others with similar, but also diverging experiences.

Why these writers? Why bring three youngish Irish writers and two veteran Scots into coalition in a comparative study of state and nation that claims for itself an ambitious title? Chapter 1 is on William McIlvanney, one of Scotland's pre-eminent and best-selling novelists. As an example of his status, on 12 May 1999, presiding over the opening of the Scottish Parliament, the newly elected presiding officer, Sir David Steel, invoked McIlvanney's call that the Scottish lion become a kitten again to learn anew the reality and responsibilities involved in political separateness.[97] And like Iain Crichton Smith, McIlvanney is required reading on

---

[95] 'Scottish Culture and the Lost Past', *Irish Review*, 9 (Spring 1991), 34–44, at 39: 'Scottish writers have felt . . . history as fractured by Calvinism or distorted by Scott's Enlightenment progressivism . . . The regionalism of Scottish literature, its diversity and even fragmentation—if that is what it is—might well function as a strengthening example or ally to us in Ireland as we contemplate our own divided society and its differing imaginative constituencies'.

[96] 'Canon of Patriotic Landmarks', 1.

[97] Report on the proceedings of the Opening of the Scottish Parliament, website: http://www.scottish.parliament.uk/official_report/session99-00/or010104.htm#.

the Scottish Highers syllabus. In a very real sense then, at both a political and popular level, McIlvanney and Crichton Smith come close to being Scotland's contemporary 'national writers', if that dubious category can be deployed momentarily, in a way that few other contemporary writers could manage. Their work is assumed to express the variegated sense of Scottish nationhood that always awaited constitutional expression. From 1966 to the present, a period crucial for the self-definition of the Irish Republic, they not only engaged with the thematics of Scottish cultural and political nationalism, but also in many ways they came to exemplify them. In so doing, they intersect with themes central to Irish cultural life more directly than any other Scottish writer. For the Irish writers chosen, the constitutional expression of Irish nationalism is the state, the aspirational space of a fully independent Scotland. The different ways in which the same themes of region, state, and nation overlap and have been learned anew are here brought into critical dialogue. The claim is that understanding how McIlvanney and Crichton Smith reproduce and represent spaces in the Scottish nation will help us understand the contextualization of similar spaces—Bolger's city, McCarthy's rural nationalism, Tóibín's walk along the border—within the Irish state.

For McIlvanney, the city is where Scotland's submerged republicanism must be made palpable and visible in order to reinvigorate Scotland as a nation, and it is the hard industrial history of west-central Scotland that provides this autonomous zone of republicanism. Like Dermot Bolger, McIlvanney addresses a new Scotland, a region that, as Christopher Harvie puts it, 'is neither rural or urban, this unknown Scotland, not in the guide books, away from the motorway, seen fleetingly from the express, that holds the key to the modern politics of the country',[98] a description that could have been lifted directly from Bolger's manifesto for Dublin. McIlvanney shifted from Labour and socialism to the SNP and nationalism in the 1980s, and that shift, I argue, produces a communal space that erases the Highlands, the region that produced Iain Crichton Smith, the subject of Chapter 2. Through Soren Kierkegaard's philosophy, Crichton Smith's obsessively returns to the category of the indi-

---

[98] Quoted in Craig, *Modern Scottish Novel*, 21.

vidual; and the prominence Crichton Smith accords individuality, I argue, is linked to the 'brokenness' of Scottish history, or to apply Brendan Bradshaw's phrase, its 'catastrophic dimension'. Throughout Crichton Smith's work, the aesthetic provides relief from the kind of national identity pursued through McIlvanney's communalism. But the aesthetic is also, of course, the realm through which the Highlander was configured as an exotic Celtic stereotype. The principal themes in Crichton Smith's novels—history, geography, representation, city and country—are similar to those in McIlvanney. But if Crichton Smith's novels are viewed through the prism of post-colonial theory, if his engagement with the thematics of colonialism are foregrounded, they complicate McIlvanney's republican and nationalist aspirations. They also complicate some of the assumptions of post-colonial theory, a theory which has exerted tremendous influence in Irish cultural affairs. Through their engagement with Republicanism and colonialism, through the sense of expectancy and aspiration with which they surround the idea of the nation, these Scottish writers, I argue, enable us to engage with the cultural themes and politics of Irish post-nationalism, without passively accepting the partisan terms offered by, for instance, Mac Anna's essay.

Part II, Chapter 3 begins by examining the qualities in any state's existence. What distinguishes the state as an imaginative construct from the nation? In the Irish context, how is the state inscribed by literary and political narratives? What role do literary anthologies play in constructing and legitimizing the state? Through the work of Dermot Bolger, I then examine the themes of country and city in contemporary Irish writing. This is not a new theme, but its appropriation and application by Bolger inscribe a public sphere that is hostile to traditional ideologies of Irish nationalism (at least as configured by Bolger). This public sphere Declan Kiberd labels 'Bolgerism'.

Chapter 4 examines the work of Thomas McCarthy, a neglected poet, novelist, and critic from west Waterford and, latterly, Cork. McCarthy's complicated affiliation with Fianna Fáil, the Soldiers of Destiny, the Party, the guardians of the rural nationalist tradition excoriated by Bolger, oscillates between a defensive fondness for its commitment to community and a clearheaded recognition of the tenuous connection between his own brand of civic republicanism and Fianna Fáil's imagined

Ireland. This ambivalence is, like Crichton Smith's doubleness, the dialectic through which meaning emerges in his work. For McCarthy, Irish neutrality in World War Two is a particularly important moment in this process. Caught on the cusp of narratives of state and nation, memory and destiny, the global, national, and the local, McCarthy's interview with Gerry Adams demonstrates his willingness to face the ambivalences laced throughout his own writing.

These same affiliations and ambivalences, I want to argue, are written out of the Irish public sphere by Colm Tóibín's brand of liberalism. The 'End of History' is Francis Fukiyama's phrase for the triumph of a certain brand of liberal democracy in the Western world. In Chapter 5, through his novels, journalism, and travel narratives, I explore the ramifications of this phrase for Tóibín's consistent engagement with Enniscorthy and the 1798 Rising, the foundational moment for the Republicanism of Fianna Fáil and Sinn Féin, the parties of the state and the nation. Tóibín's liberalism, I argue, conscripts the aesthetic to effectively seal the state's borders from any contact or contamination with the politics of the North. Like Mac Anna, his writing produces a regional space that is, in Joe Cleary's phrase, part of the 'political and cultural labour that goes into the maintenance and contestation of partitioning borders'.

Cumulatively, this second part tries to address and critique the regional spaces that comprise the public sphere within the Republic of Ireland: the metropolitan dominance of Dublin through Bolger, the Munster rural nationalism of Fianna Fáil in McCarthy, Tóibín's engagement with the border and partition. But that critique of Irish regions, nation, and state begins, in a stereotypically Irish fashion, with the Scottish nation and the British state.

Part I

Scotland

Region and Nation, Republicanism and Colonialism

The Contours of Republicanism: William McIlvanney and the Geography of Difference

1   GLASGOW, CELTIC, AND SCOTTISH REPUBLICANISM

> Where shall we find the talents which are fit to act with men in a collective body, if we break that body into parts and confine the observation of each to a separate track?[1]

> What books and authors have had the greatest effect on your political beliefs?
> John Steinbeck for *The Grapes of Wrath* and *Cannery Row*, and William McIlvanney for his range of works.[2]

THROUGHOUT WILLIAM MCILVANNEY's work, there is a commitment to the idea of an indigenous Scottish humanism rooted in the industrial, urban experience of the west-central working class. This conflation of geography and justice, space and history, the cultural specificity of Scotland and the universality of civic humanism, is developed in *Surviving the Shipwreck*, a collection of essays written between 1974 and 1990. McIlvanney intends the essays to 'act as reminders of some of the shared ideals that we have that go beyond the self-interest, greed and indifference to others that have so often lately been dressed in intellectual shoddy and presented as political theory' (*STS*, 12). That political theory is Thatcherism. Published in 1991, the collection recovers a tradition of Scottish humanism through which Scottish difference is made visible by shifting attention

---

[1] Adam Ferguson, *Essays on The Intellectual Powers, Moral Sentiments, Happiness and National Felicity* (Paris: Parsons and Galignoi, 1805), 8.
[2] Alex Salmond, 'Influences', *New Statesman and Society*, 10 Mar. 1995, p. 25.

from politics as overtly ideological to nationalism as a form
of recreation, an activity that transgresses the border between
political militancy and popular festivity. In the absence of a
formal parliamentary expression of Scottish nationality, *Surviving the Shipwreck* locates in pubs, greyhound tracks, mines, and
that recurring tragedy of Scottish life, the national team's World
Cup exploits, a means of asserting an enduring Scottish identity.
The nation is discovered in the spectacle of the people at play, a
notion perfectly captured in McIlvanney's centenary history of
Glasgow Celtic, where he (rightly) contrasts Celtic's legendary
style and non-sectarian heritage with that of Glasgow Rangers.
Celtic's historic 1967 European Cup victory over Inter Milan,
the first ever by a British football team, this team of eleven
Scottish men all born within twenty miles of one another is 'a
demonstration of Scottishness at its best'.

The collection begins with an essay on the 1979 Devolution
referendum and ends with an address to the annual conference of
the SNP, where McIlvanney describes himself as a 'John O' the
Commonweal', proclaiming a sermon 'more humanist than
religious' (*STS*, 242). Before a nationalist audience, the language
of civic humanism and classical republicanism defines and legitimizes a common Scottish good. Celtic are, in this sense, the
athletic wing of McIlvanney's provisional Scottish republic, a
notion Bill Shankly memorably captured when he described the
playing style of Celtic under Jock Stein as a form of 'socialism,
without the politics of course'.[3] McIlvanney never clearly defines
whether this humanism is indigenous to the working class as a
class, or is adopted by them, but his loosely defined usage of the
language of civic humanism acts as a means of situating a set of
working-class values within the spectrum of Western thought.
An enduring Scottish ethos exists outside formal intellectual

---

[3] *The Official History of Celtic Football Club 1888–1988*, written and narrated
by William McIlvanney (BBC Enterprises Ltd, 1988). See also Homi K. Bhabha, *The
Location of Culture* (London: Routledge, 1994), 15; Christopher Harvie, *No Gods
and Precious Few Heroes: Scotland since 1914* (1981; Edinburgh: Edinburgh
University Press, 1987), 119–20: 'Yet football was politically important: it defined
class, gender, religion, and nationality, and ritualized and contained all these'. H. F.
Moorhouse, ' "We're off to Wembley!" The History of a Scottish Event and the
Sociology of Football Hooliganism', in David McCrone, Stephen Kendrick, and Pat
Straw (eds.), *The Making of Scotland: Culture & Social Change* (Edinburgh:
Edinburgh University Press, 1989), 207–27.

categories, ideologies, and institutions, achieving the destiny of form through the exemplary performative activities of such characters as Tam Docherty and Jack Laidlaw. Or as McIlvanney puts it,

> You can take the people out of the parliament but you can't take the parliament out of the people . . . one brute fact has been re-enacted again and again: it is the majority who form the opposition, the minority the government. (*STS*, 139)

This lack of statehood generated in Scotland over the last twenty-five years an obsessive quest for cultural self-definition[4] as claims for national distinctiveness were mediated through culture rather than politics.[5] Two political discourses dominated Scottish intellectual life during the period: socialism and nationalism. In 1973 the Kilbrandon commission supported legislative devolution for the three historic nations of 'Britain', while the idea of a separate Scottish Labour Party first voiced in 1974 by Jim Sillars was pushed into being by his resignation from the Labour Party's Scottish executive. This ferment of nationalism and socialism then unaccountably evaporates with the Devolution defeat in 1979 and the apparent reassertion of a British

---

[4] See e.g. Craig Beveridge and Ronald Turnbull, *The Eclipse of Scottish Culture* (Edinburgh: Polygon, 1989), and 'Inferiorism', *Cencrastus*, 89 (Spring 1982), 4–5; Tom Leonard (ed.), *Radical Renfrew: Poetry from the French Revolution to the First World War* (Edinburgh: Polygon, 1990), pp. i–xxvii; Douglas Dunn 'Introduction', in id. (ed.), *The Faber Book of Twentieth-Century Scottish Poetry*, 'Introduction', pp. xvii–xlvi; Harvie, *No Gods and Precious Few Heroes*, p. iv: 'In my chapter divisions . . . I have necessarily accentuated the theme of Scotland's decline'. See also Harvie's *Scotland and Nationalism: Scottish Society and Politics, 1707–1994* (London: Routledge, 1994), and *Cultural Weapons: Scotland and Survival in a New Europe* (Edinburgh: Polygon, 1992), esp. 88 ff; Michael Lynch, *Scotland: A New History* (London: Pimlico, 1992), 422–49; the magazine *Cencrastus* was founded in 1979 after the defeat of the Devolution referendum with the declared aim of promoting Scottish self-awareness and self-determination; Robert Crawford, *Devolving English Literature* (Oxford: Clarendon Press, 1992), 1–16, 271–307; Tom Nairn, *Auld Enemies: Essays from the Nairn on Monday Column in* The Scotsman (Glasgow: Common Cause, 1991); Alasdair Gray, *Why Scots Should Rule Scotland* (Edinburgh: Polygon, 1992); James Kelman, *Some Recent Attacks: Essays Cultural and Political* (Stirling: AK Press, 1992); Paul Scott, 'The End of Britishness', *Cencrastus*, 46 (Autumn 1993), 7–10.

[5] See Angus Calder, *Revolving Culture: Notes from the Scottish Republic* (London: I. B. Taurus, 1994), 11; Neal Ascherson, 'Don't Be Afraid—and Don't Steal!', lecture to the annual conference of the SNP, repr. in *Games with Shadows* (London: Radius, 1988), 62; Murray Pittock, *The Invention of Scotland: The Stuart Myth and Scottish Identity, 1638 to the Present* (London: Routledge, 1991), 145.

political identity.[6] The moment seemed to slide easily into a more
general theme of decline, a movement away from a distinctively
communal value in post-war Scottish culture.[7] In his poem 'The
Cowardly Lion', McIlvanney traced the failure to assert independence to Scotland's ignorance of its own idigenous historical
resources.[8]

This is the political context in which McIlvanney's quest for a
Scottish national identity founded on difference and collectivity,
Celtic with socialism, evolves.[9] *Surviving the Shipwreck* grounds
nationality in a concrete social dimension through the experience
of industrialization. Scottish distinctiveness thus derives from
material resources, always constituting something more than a
mere discursive formation. And the indigenous humanist values,
from which Scottish distinctiveness is derived, are located within
a definable geographic region.

It wasn't the lochs and glens or the west Highland way, though they are
impressive enough. It was the deep commitment of its people, at least
some of the time, to matters beyond the material . . . Their history, I
believe, tells contemporary Scots most clearly where they have been and
who they are. (*STS*, 157)

McIlvanney here discards Walter Scott's romanticized Highland
geography for a political identity based on citizenship; but his
writing, I want to argue, finally reinscribes place as the locus of
an authentic, a truly representative Scottish being. McIlvanney's

---

    [6] See Gavin Wallace, 'Introduction', in id. and Randall Stevenson (eds.), *The
Scottish Novel since the Seventies* (Edinburgh: Edinburgh University Press, 1993),
1–7, for a discussion of the significance of the referendum to Scottish literary life;
William L. Miller, *The End of British Politics? Scots and English Political Behaviour
in the Seventies* (Oxford: Clarendon Press, 1981), 117; Jim Sillars, *The Case for
Optimism* (Edinburgh: Polygon, 1986), chs. 3, 4; Owen Dudley Edwards, *A Claim of
Right for Scotland* (Edinburgh: Polygon, 1989).
    [7] See Douglas Dunn's introd. to id. (ed.), *Faber Book of Twentieth-Century Scot-
tish Poetry*, pp. xvii–xlvi, at p. xlvi: 'It has been a hectic century for Scottish poetry,
one filled with a thrilling turbulence, and in which the stakes have been high—the
survival of a national culture.'
    [8] In *Radical Scotland*, 11 (Oct./Nov. 1984), repr. in *STS*, 23. See also Isobel
Murray and Bob Tait, *Ten Modern Scottish Novels* (Aberdeen: Aberdeen University
Press, 1984), 5: 'Deracination . . . and the need to restore meaningful social bonds,
are [McIlvanney's] recurrent concerns'.
    [9] See 'Big Bill and the Wee Man in the Portaloo', *Aberdeen Press and Journal* (11
Oct. 1991), 12–14: 'The effect of the Thatcher Government has been to colonise a lot
of Scottish attitudes and institutions, so that the social climate here has been changed
by a government we have never voted for.'

political commitment is realizable only under a government, the *res*, that genuinely reflects the will and promotes the good of the community, the *publica*, as a whole. Claiming that though 'Scots would be denied the means of self-government . . . they retained the characteristics of a nation without the political identity of one' (*STS*, 251), he assumes Scottish difference as an inalienable fact that still awaits its final, political consummation. Scotland will achieve independence because in a way it already has it: 'It holds, in suspended animation within itself, an alternative tradition' (*STS*, 248).[10] Hence his writing addresses those traditions already inhering within Scottish life which establish Scotland's irreducible distinctiveness, and the collection acts as a 'reminder' to contemporary Scotland of the history of which it is a guardian. The point is to establish in the present those links with the past that might prefigure the realization of an independent future.

Society, the ideal of the collective, always for McIlvanney a principal determinant of this Scottish identity, is an essential element of these essays, but it is sustained only through the commitment and participation of the individual citizen. Unlike liberal individualism, which gives epistemological and moral priority to the liberty of the individual, and perceives society as a potential threat to this unassailable sovereignty, McIlvanney's civic republicanism establishes the development of public service as the pre-eminent measure of a citizen's private worth.

They [the sixties hippies] didn't seem to realise that to opt out of the materialism and injustice of their society was to strengthen that materialism and injustice. The opting out of a society is the ultimate surrender to society, just as to dismiss history is to give history its total authority over you. (*STS*, 131)

Individual and social freedom in this formulation is detached from behaviour that focuses on self-interest. Scottish citizenship involves actively discharging the full range of civic duties, and the only context in which individual liberty is meaningful is the relationship it makes possible with other members of the *publica*.

---

[10] See 'The Past: Essential Facts of Scottish History', in the 1988 document 'A Claim of Right for Scotland', repr. in Dudley Edwards, *Claim of Right for Scotland*, 13.

If you care for your children, care for the society they will have to live in
. . . Scotland in the past has at least had honourable ambitions in that
direction. But that harmonising thread that has run throughout its hard
history is in danger of being cut. (*STS*, 253)

The distinctive literary element in this social creed is, to
borrow terms from Seamus Heaney, the insistence that the artist
be of 'present use' as 'a citizen of society' to his civic duty.[11] This
is the search for virtue, the classical republican ideal of devotion
to the common good through civic participation. McIlvanney
never deviates from this principle throughout his career, and
the generic and thematic shifts of his writing are all predicated
upon the need to ratify a pre-existing humanist tradition, that
'harmonising thread' buried in Scotland's history. The tension
between a participatory concept of virtue in the civic sphere and
an increasingly nationalist emphasis on Scottish exceptionalism,
runs throughout his work, and in this he reflects a fundamental
strain of Scottish cultural politics during the last twenty-five
years. The global ambitions of civic republicanism collapse into
a militant particularism, the production of a regional space that
admits only those who symbolically embody and reproduce an
ideal continuity between place and *polis*.[12] The *genius loci* that
precedes Scotland's insertion into new forms of conflict and difference becomes not a living republican politics but a nationalist
tradition tied to the tyranny of precedent. 'Matters beyond the
material', in other words, are finally grounded in a predictable
location.

Through Tam Docherty, eponymous hero of McIlvanney's
major novel *Docherty*, there is a figuration of public space—
defined by the struggle to retain nationality as a material
resource—locked into a symbolic battle with an encroaching
privatization of space in which Tam's legacy is for ever excluded.

---

[11] From Seamus Heaney's inaugural lecture as professor of poetry at Oxford, *The
Redress of Poetry: An Inaugural Lecture Delivered before the University of Oxford
on 24 October 1989* (Oxford: Clarendon Press, 1989), 1; for a discussion of
Heaney's sense of public virtue, see Bernard O'Donoghue, *Seamus Heaney and the
Language of Poetry* (Hemel Hempstead: Harvester Wheatsheaf, 1994), pp. vii–ix,
1–24.
[12] 'Militant particularism seizes upon the qualities of place, reanimates the bond
between the environmental and the social, and seeks to bend the social processes constructing space-time to a radically different purpose' (David Harvey, *Justice, Nature
and the Geography of Difference* (Oxford: Blackwell, 1996), 306).

The generic transition between the historical novel of the miner and the detective novels of Laidlaw, both, in their own way, public servants, is part of the attempt to contain, in the fragmented depoliticized spaces of postmodernism, this civic incohesion, the movement away from communal values: the rampant privatization of public space and the waning of nationality as an affective resource. But McIlvanney's replacement of Tam's civic republicanism with a nationalism located in a specific region is, I want to argue, a reterritorialization of political identity, one in which membership is understood as ascriptive, requiring no political choices and no activity beyond ritual affirmation. And the aesthetic wholeness that accompanies this reterritorialization ironically offers a vicarious rather than a practical participation in the ideal of community, the very antithesis of republican virtue.

II   AFTER SCOTTISH VIRTUE

What is this thing called virtue? Described by Cicero as *virtus* and by later Italian theorists as civic virtue or public-spiritedness, virtue denotes 'the capacity that enables us willingly to serve the common good, thereby to uphold the freedom of our community, and in consequence to ensure its rise to greatness as well as our individual liberty'. In classical republican thought, virtue insists on 'the capacity to defend one's community against threat of conquest and enslavement by external enemies'.[13] The ability to defend community, liberty, and independence must be developed, so that the body politic is subject to communal rule, not simply the controlling elite. Crucially, the will of the individual comes to self-knowledge only in its relation to the *patria, res publica*, or common good. Paradoxically, the common good is the realm through which individual liberty is most fully realized, and so the former is always given priority over the latter. Citizenship bisects religious and secular universalism by insisting that, when necessary, priority is allocated to one's political com-

---

[13] See Quentin Skinner, 'The Republican Ideal of Political Liberty', in Gisela Bock, Quentin Skinner, and Maurizio Viroli (eds.), *Machiavelli and Republicanism* (Cambridge: Cambridge University Press, 1993), 303, 307.

munity, so that human identity consists of relationships, not inwardness. As Adrian Oldfield puts it, 'Men develop their humanness not in communion with an extra-terrestrial God, or as discrete individuals, but, on the contrary, only in the company of others.'[14]

For the republican ethos, history tended always to be a movement away from value, a process that only heroic, not social, action could reverse.[15] The masculinity of the virtuous man averts the greatest threat to the republic: corruption. Machavelli explains this process as follows:

In the process of time . . . such a body must of necessity die unless something happens which brings it up to the mark . . . Such a return to their original principles is sometimes due to the simple virtue of one man alone, independently of any bias spurring you on to action.[16]

Fundamentally concerned with the affirmation of moral personality in civic action, the virtuous man conducts his own worship in a setting which is civic where it is not private. Clerical interference in this realm is another example of that corruption—a crucial word in republican thought—which threatens the republic's very foundation.[17] The role of the hero, the man of great virtue, is to inspire citizens to emulate him by engaging in actions which acquire meaning only within the context of society and its institutions.[18] Civic republicanism stresses 'not that which differentiates individuals from each other and from the community, but rather what they share with other individuals, and what integrates them into a community'.[19]

[14] *Citizenship and Commmunity: Civic Republicanism and the Modern World* (London and New York: Routledge, 1990), 32.
[15] J. G. A. Pocock, *The Machiavellian Moment: Florentine Political Thought and the Atlantic Republican Tradition* (Princeton: Princeton University Press, 1975), 486.
[16] *Discourses*, III. i; Pocock suggests that it is 'through military discipline that one learns to be a citizen and to display civic virtue' (*Machiavellian Moment*, 201).
[17] Pocock, *Machiavellian Moment*, 475.
[18] Oldfield, *Citizenship and Community*, 49–51.
[19] Ibid. 145. See also Caroline Robbins, *The Eighteenth-Century Commonwealthman: Studies in the Transmission, Development and Circumstances of English Liberal Thought from the Restoration of Charles II until the War with the Thirteen Colonies* (Cambridge, Mass.: Harvard University Press, 1956), 177–220; Z. S. Fink, *The Classical Republicans: An Essay in the Recovery of a Pattern of Thought in Seventeenth Century England* (1945; repr. Evanston: Northwestern University Press, 1962), 150–8; Nancy Curtin, *The United Irishmen: Popular Politics in Ulster and Dublin 1791–1798* (Oxford: Clarendon Press, 1994), 1–37.

This commitment to the ideal of civic duty, to values beyond the material, places McIlvanney in a context of social thought most fully articulated in Scottish Enlightenment humanism. Neal Ascherson describes this rigid commitment to duty as 'Docherty-ism': the tendency to see social bonds 'described exclusively in terms of duties, never in terms of rights'.[20] The principles of collectivity in *Docherty*, McIlvanney's best-known novel, are traceable to Francis Hutcheson and Adam Ferguson, seminal figures in the Scottish Enlightenment, each of whom explored this concept of virtue in individuals and in the collective. Both insisted that the purely descriptive aspect of moral philosophy was subservient to its prescriptive aspect, and that 'the primary purpose of instruction in moral philosophy was to prepare young men for practising virtue in all spheres of life, religious as well as secular, public as well as private'.[21] Human beings are, in this reading, intrinsically social animals. Their private interests were necessarily connected to the wider society in which they lived[22] and the virtuous citizen should therefore conscientiously carry out these duties.[23] In *The History of the Progress and Termination of The Roman Republic*, Ferguson identified the source of a wider moral corruption in the elevation of the category of the individual, a move that inevitably encouraged selfishness by viewing morality as private, subjective, and therefore relative. For Ferguson, man is 'by nature, the member of a community; and when considered in this capacity, the individual appears to be no longer made for himself. He must forego his happiness and his freedom where these interfere with the good of society.'[24] It is the search for virtue, the insistence on man as a political animal,

---

[20] 'Scottish Contradictions' in *Games with Shadows*, 65–7. Trevor Royle in *The Macmillan Companion to Scottish Culture* (London: Macmillan, 1984), 192–3 describes Tam as 'A man possessed of his own sense of virtue and yet alive to a knowledge of the working man's degraded place in society'.

[21] Richard B. Sher, *Church and University in the Scottish Enlightenment: The Moderate Literati of Edinburgh* (Edinburgh: Edinburgh University Press, 1985), 167.

[22] See John D. Brewer, 'Conjectural History, Sociology and Social Change in Eighteenth-Century Scotland: Adam Ferguson and the Division of Labour', in McCrone, Kendrick, and Straw (eds.), *Making of Scotland*, 13–30.

[23] Sher, *Church and University*, 178.

[24] *Essays on the Intellectual Powers*, 49; Duncan Forbes remarks that 'Ferguson is typical of the Scottish Enlightenment in his emphasis on sympathy, humanity, social solidarity and fellow feeling' in his edn. of Adam Ferguson's *An Essay on the History of the Civil Society* (Edinburgh: Edinburgh University Press, 1966), p. xxvi.

the insistence that each citizen sacrifice self-interest to the common good and fully participate in civil affairs that link the diverse strands of the Scottish Enlightenment. David Allan's magisterial survey summarizes this tendency in terms that can, as we shall see, apply to McIlvanney's whole project. Allan says that 'virtue had to be evinced in Scotland by a sincere and committed orientation towards the service of the public interest'.[25] Through Tam Docherty, McIlvanney offers a foundational myth for Scottish nationality based on a distinctively Scottish civic ideal. And as the carrier of values drawn from the Scottish Enlightenment, Tam establishes the immanent worth and philosophic value of working-class lives.

With *Docherty,* McIlvanney established himself as Scotland's leading man of letters, a position his subsequent career seemed to show him determined to lose.[26] The shift from Tam Docherty to Jack Laidlaw, central character in a series of Glasgow-based detective novels, puzzled critics ready to acclaim an authentic working-class talent.[27] But the public space Tam's values demarcate is what the detective Laidlaw will try to preserve from the civic incohesion fostered by an encroaching, acquisitive, very private, individual space. *Docherty* marks the beginning of a sustained investigation into Scotland's relationship with its industrial past: 'it is the story of a working-class mining family in the West of Scotland in the first quarter of the century . . . but what it was built to reflect is something much bigger' (*STS,* 235).

---

[25] *Virtue, Learning and the Scottish Enlightenment* (Edinburgh: Edinburgh University Press, 1993), 95, 1–16, 93–7; Ian McBride ' "The School of Virtue": Francis Hutcheson, Irish Presbyterianism and the Scottish Enlightenment', in D. George Boyce, Robert Eccleshall, and Vincent Geoghegan (eds.), *Political Thought in Ireland since the Seventeenth Century* (London: Routledge, 1992), 78; see also T. D. Campbell, 'Francis Hutcheson: "Father" of the Scottish Enlightenment', in R. H. Cambell and A. S. Skinner (eds.), *The Origins and Nature of the Scottish Enlightenment* (Edinburgh: John Donald Publishers, 1982), 167–85, esp. 169; Richard B. Sher, 'From Troglodytes to Amerians: Montesquieu and the Scottish Enlightenment on Liberty, Virtue and Commerce', in David Wooton (ed.), *Republicanism, Liberty, and Commercial Society 1649–1776* (Stanford: Stanford University Press, 1995), 368–402.

[26] See Douglas Gifford, 'Scottish Fiction since 1945', in Norman Wilson (ed.), *Scottish Writing and Writers* (Edinburgh: The Ramsay Head Press, 1977), 16: 'With *Docherty* . . . William McIlvanney immediately assured his place at the head of modern Scottish fiction.'

[27] See Fredric Lindsay, 'The Glasgow Novel: Myths and Directions', *Books in Scotland,* 21 (Summer, 1986), 7.

Addressing the SNP, McIlvanney described the party as having 'recognisable features but no coherent identity' (*STS*, 18), a charge levelled repeatedly against twentieth-century Scottish nationalism. By synchronizing the political and cultural into an originary myth, McIlvanney traces the coherence and wholeness of one aspect of the harmonizing thread in this national identity.[28] Tam is thus both man and ideal, and *Docherty* is the foundation upon which McIlvanney's corpus is built.

III   DOCHERTY

At the core of *Docherty* is World War I, economically and socially the major influence on twentieth-century Scotland.[29] Thematically *Docherty* is structured around the axiomatic events of Scottish urban history: Irish immigration, Protestant and Catholic sectarian tension, Marxism, and, primarily, the demise of community and the rise of an acquisitive individualism.[30] Inevitably, Tam's attempt to sustain values predicated on community fail, but his demise is heroic and exemplary, a manifestation of the values contemporary Scotland inherits.[31] The focus throughout is on the reaction to Tam, on the legacy the

[28] H. J. Hanham, *Scottish Nationalism* (London: Faber and Faber, 1969), 146: 'Certainly in the past, the SNP's neglect of the Scottish heritage has been shameful. The party has tended to adopt purely political arguments, which . . . is spiritually bankrupt'. See also *Selected Essays of Hugh MacDiarmid*, ed. with introd. Duncan Glen (London: Jonathan Cape, 1969), 229; Harvie, *Scotland and Nationalism*, 80.

[29] See T. C. Smout, 'Patterns of Culture', in A. Dickson and J. H. Treble (eds.), *People and Society in Scotland*, iii. *1914 to the Present* (Edinburgh: John Donald Publishers in association with the Economic and Social History Society of Scotland, 1991), 261–81. See William Ferguson, *Scotland 1689 to the Present: The Edinburgh History of Scotland* (Edinburgh and London: Oliver & Boyd, 1968), 355; Richard Finlay, 'National Identity in Crisis: Politicians, Intellectuals and the "End of Scotland", 1920–1939', *History*, 79/256 (June 1994), 242–59; Michael Lynch, 'Scottish Culture in its Historical Perspective', in Paul H. Scott (ed.), *Scotland: A Concise Cultural History* (Edinburgh and London: Mainstream, 1993), 15–46.

[30] See Anthony Slaven, *The Development of the West of Scotland: 1750–1960* (London and Boston: Routledge & Kegan Paul, 1975), 235 ff.

[31] 'The hero liberates us into the possibilities of our own nature because he enacts the subjective victory over objective circumstances, and in so doing can teach us that we may do the same . . . He will die, of course. But in meeting death he will transform its significance. He will fill its emptiness with his own humanity. *His spirit will survive his dying*, a part of us that diminishes death' (McIlvanney's introd. to *D*, repr. in *STS*; emphasis added).

life entails, and its continued significance for contemporary Scotland.[32]

The narrator's eloquence is directly related to those values celebrated by the novel, with exuberant similes deliberately imported to commemorate the immanent significance of lives normally excluded from literary discourse. If the flat colourless prose of Alasdair Gray's *Lanark* intensifies that novel's break with the Glasgow linguistic tradition, McIlvanney's narrative eloquence reconciles sophisticated humanist values with the vernacular voice, thereby establishing Scots as an appropriate vehicle for moral value.[33] In James Kelman's novels, the absence of a narrative voice reflects the lack of volition in characters' lives: nothing can be said or explained about events over which characters have no control. 'Character' is thus subordinate to occupations of soul-destroying routine, precariousness, or crushed idealism—the Bus Conductor, the Gambler, the Teacher. Commentary disappears, because existences as arbitrary as any greyhound race defy interpretation. So instead of narrative development there is repetition, 'repetition which becomes a structural principle of Kelman's world in formal repetition of the real world in which his characters are trapped'.[34] In McIlvanney's work, repetition, the reappearance of the same key figures in different novels, emphasizes the persistent durability, the harmonizing, continuous thread of values whose relevance remains undiminished despite the massive social changes within Scottish society. For Tam Docherty's reappearance in *Strange Loyalties,* the last of the Laidlaw novels, testifies to the survival of an indigenous humanist tradition surrounding

---

[32] Isobel Murray and Bob Tait, 'William McIlvanney: *Docherty*', in eid., *Ten Modern Scottish Novels*, 191.

[33] Gray, *Lanark, A Life in Four Books* (London: Paladin, 1987). For 'The Vernacular Basis of Scottish Humanism' see George Davie, *The Democratic Intellect: Scotland and her Universities in the Nineteenth Century* (Edinburgh: Edinburgh University Press, 1961), 203–21.

[34] Douglas Gifford, *The Dear Green Place? The Novel in the West of Scotland* (Glasgow: Third Eye Center, 1985), 13. See also Kirsty McNeil, 'An Interview with James Kelman', *Chapman*, 57 (Summer, 1989), 1–9: 'Getting rid of that standard third party narrative voice is getting rid of a whole value system . . . getting rid of the narrative voice is trying to get down to that level of pure objectivity.' For a comparison of Kelman and McIlvanney, see Cairns Craig, 'Resisting Arrest: James Kelman', in Gavin Wallace and Randall Stevenson (eds.), *The Scottish Novel since the Seventies* (Edinburgh: Edinburgh University Press, 1993), 99–115.

individual lives. The way that history and tradition are encoded in individual lives, I want to argue, is through an anthropological emphasis on ritual.

As the narrator notes in *Docherty*: 'Underpinning the apparent anarchy of their social lives and establishing an order was a code of conduct complex enough to baffle the most perceptive outsider yet tacitly understood by even the youngest citizens of High Street from the time they started to think' (*D*, 32). Independence, the narrator explains, is the code of conduct most fully articulated through Tam's life, a state achieved despite living in 'a penal colony for those who had committed poverty, a vice usually hereditary' (*D*, 31). Tam transcends economic and sectarian division to generate a heavily prescriptive moral code based on the ideal of a common secular commitment to a public civic space. His rage is against 'the *man-made* predestination that loomed over them, his contempt for the acceptance of it in others, his dread that they would have none of them the choice to be what they might have been' (*D*, 89; emphasis added). Tam rails against those forms of corruption—the peeping tom pestering Miss Gilchrist, the cleric claiming young Conn for Catholicism, Angus's individualism—that threaten the mutuality sustaining High Street's communal independence. An essential feature of this is that the private and the public are always porous. No individual exists in the sealed purity of isolation, so that when Angus refuses to marry a girl he has made pregnant, Tam recognizes no individual right to renege on a public obligation. Tam's primary consideration is always the underlying moral axiom in every action.

This insistence on a realm beyond the material then becomes an essential element in Scottish identity. Accepting his father into his home, for example, is an act that makes no economic sense but one that honours the principle of origins.[35] It accords with Seamus Deane's description of Irish nationalism as one way of restoring dignity to what has been oppressed.[36] Throughout McIlvanney's work, a crucial tension exists between the appar-

---

[35] See MacDiarmid's 'Contemporary Scottish Literature and the National Question', in *Selected Essays of Hugh MacDiarmid*, ed. and introd. Duncan Glen (London: Jonathan Cape, 1969), 205–15.

[36] 'Heroic Styles: The Tradition of an Idea', in *Ireland's Field Day* (Notre Dame, Ind.: University of Notre Dame Press, 1986), 47.

ently permanent, universal values of humanism and their use by
Tam and Laidlaw as a point of origin, a natal source that will
restore dignity to an economically oppressed community. And
from this use emerges the sense of difference, the cultural
specificity, the 'special contour lines of experience' around which
the SNP, McIlvanney argues, should organize its political programme. One such special contour line of difference is visible in
Docherty, for instance, when Tam dismisses the possibility of
not taking his father, his origins, into his present, his already
overcrowded house:

> If you want tae be sensible, take yer weans up tae the market oan Friday
> an' sell them. Because that's what we are. Fuckin' cattle. Unless we can
> prove different. Well Ah'm different, an' Ah'm damned if Ah'll leeve ma
> life according tae their sense. Whit's mine belongs tae me. An' Ah'm no'
> askin' Thame tae come an collect him like a bit o' rubbish. (*D*, 101)

But to define the past in familial terms and the future in class
terms ensures that private and public space compete for priority.
In *Strange Loyalties*, the larger spiritual community containing
both elements is no longer civic but national, a nation bound to
the thematics of territory and the ethnic link of family. Humanism is finally subordinate to difference, a difference construed
upon criteria that retain only a tenuous link with Tam's generous, inclusive example.

   The emotional power of the above passage is amplified by the
focus on the reaction inspired: Andra 'thought he understood
why it was he had always liked Tam Docherty so much. He was
more than anything in his life showed him to be . . . Andra sensed
quite simply that Tam was not defeated. And if Tam wasn't,
neither was he' (*D*, 101). *Docherty* is, in this sense, a purposeful
rewriting of a present-centred history, as Tam's legacy, his choice
of origins over economic pragmatism, is re-presented in response
to the anxieties of a valueless present. His towering moral
presence reformulates the choices facing contemporary Scotland:
is the collective self-interest best served by ditching the positive
dynamic his example provides in favour of a genial cultural
depthlessness? Should economic comfort be given priority over
the imperatives of the nation's past? What *Docherty* and the rest
of McIlvanney's corpus does is locate exactly where contemporary Scotland ought to discover answers to these questions.

The usual problem with social realism is that characters can never move beyond the horizon inscribed by an omniscient narrator's interpretative insights. Moral virtue is thus explained by the narrator rather than enacted by characters. The realism in *Docherty,* however, reveals a narrative already implicit in reality itself, a pre-existing, coherent, continuous thread that prevails despite poverty. This is the larger meaning of McIlvanney's point that 'Since their history [i.e. the history of the west-central working class] was largely silence, I would be constructing a communal fabric of myth' (*STS,* 235). The threads in this 'communal fabric' are tradition, identity, essence, and difference, and they are performatively expressed throughout McIlvanney's work in a series of stylized rituals.

Ritual constructs a preverbal pattern of behaviour containing concealed, complex 'codes of conduct'. It reflexively performs what McIlvanney proclaims a characteristically Scottish trait: 'The Scottish tradition, it seems to me, has always insisted that thought and feeling are only happy as a married couple' (*STS,* 13). For a community constrained by articulacy, ritual transgresses the border between political ideology and national identity (between socialism and Celtic) by performatively expressing commonly held values and symbolic codes.[37] As a collective ceremony of solidarity, ritual reinstates cultural unity and wholeness over 'the apparent anarchy of their social lives' by declaring against the indeterminacy and flux poverty generates. In Victor Turner's phrasing, ritual emphasizes 'form and finality, it celebrates *man-made* meaning, the culturally determinate, the regulated, the named, and the explained . . . [every ceremony] seeks to state that the cosmos and social world, or one particular small part of them are orderly and explicable and for the moment fixed . . . Ritual is a declaration against indeterminacy.'[38]

This definition, with its emphasis on a participatory agency constructing for itself a distinctive totality, helps explain the appropriateness of ritual to McIlvanney's mixture of civic humanism and Scottish nationalism. In *Docherty,* the ritualized

---

[37] See Anthony D. Smith, *National Identity* (Harmondsworth: Penguin, 1991), 6: national identity emerges from 'all those who feel they share certain symbolic codes, value systems and traditions of belief and ritual, including references to a supra-empirical reality'.

[38] See *From Ritual to Theater: The Human Seriousness of Play* (New York: Performing Arts Journal Publication, 1982), 82 (emphasis added).

action anticipates and generates social change by inscribing amongst its participants an alternative social order, thereby constructing a meaningful, independent, historical narrative through a profound consciousness of collectivity. Described by the narrator as 'morality by reflex to some extent' (*D*, 33), ritual creates a political space between the lives lived and standards observed. As a performative dynamic permeating individual and collective lives it always emphasizes how both inevitably bond: 'The men gathered compulsively each night at the street corner . . . a parliament without powers' (*D*, 187).

The enormity of the historical forces governing the lives of the inhabitants of High Street are domesticated and absorbed through reflexively functioning rituals; the newspapers, for example, carriers of 'strange demons that haunted the edges of their small lives' are comprehended through a pre-existing cognitive pattern: 'They made a ceremony of it . . . Custom had assigned them distinct roles' (*D*, 64, 65). *Docherty* establishes McIlvanney's method of finding collective value in everyday affairs, as the 'transformation of the ordinary into something powerfully mysterious'[39] occurs through repetitions of behavioural patterns which, in steadfast contrast to Kelman's sterile routine, testify to a complex moral economy already inhering within the culture. Martin's nightly return from the pub to his wife is thus 'a complicated ritual by two people who would never surprise each other again but found pleasure in the repeated patterns of the past—a conversational dance of death, perfected, nicely timed, delicate as a minuet' (*D*, 73); Tam's confrontation with an intruder is 'stylised, with a formal inevitability . . . It was the formality of a duelling challenge' (*D*, 76); while Jenny clears her dead parents' home of dust: 'Ceremonially, as if it represented her parents' past, her own self-pity, Jenny applied the match to the ball of sweepings in the fire' (*D*, 176).

What ritual tacitly communicates, then, are the deepest values of the groups or individuals performing it, expressing wishes which are at odds with conscious experience.[40] Establishing an ontological separateness, a mode of individual and collective being whose deepest coordinates are culturally derivative, it

---

[39] McIlvanney, 'Growing up in the West', in Karl Miller (ed.), *Memoirs of a Modern Scotland* (London: Faber and Faber, 1970), 169.
[40] Edmund Leach, *Lévi-Strauss* (London: Fontana Collins, 1970), 57.

exalts the primacy of place and race because its underlying patterns are accessible only to those within the community. The public and private manifestation of ritual is thus a form of symbolic or idealized experience. Because 'their history was largely silence', ritual in *Docherty* functions not in opposition to thought, but as a performative expression of this otherwise mute cultural formation. It operates as a type of metanarrative surrounding all social activity, so that individual experience and behaviour becomes an isolated example of that communal activity. Through ritual the lives of Tam and his community achieve the destiny and dignity of form, as *Docherty* details an alternative to the social order with which its characters must live, implicitly challenging through their rituals the view that consciousness is deterministically condemned to replicate established social and political structures.[41] And by removing the controlling discourse from the narrator to the narrated, it asserts their independence from the requirements of formal realism. This is how McIlvanney's often-criticized narrative eloquence works; as a part of the process he describes, he is an interlocutor for a community to which he natively belongs. The possibility of change is already implicit in existing social relationships, so that instead of constructing a coherent body of political doctrine, ritual directs attention towards recovering or, to use Seamus Deane's term, restoring an already existing source of value in the lived experience of daily life.

The turning point in *Docherty*, as in Scottish social history, is World War I.[42] Tam's faith in a public, civic space capable of withstanding the war is shattered by the injuries sustained by his son, Mick. Tam's decline marks the disjuncture between an old and new order, and McIlvanney presents this as a public event in a public space to emphasize Tam's representative status in Scottish history:[43]

[41] See Catherine Bell, *Ritual Theory, Ritual Practice* (New York and Oxford: Oxford University Press, 1992), 20–7; Turner, *From Ritual to Theater*, 82.
[42] Ferguson, *Scotland 1689 to the Present*, 355: 'In retrospect it is apparent that the Great War of 1914–1918 was, in fact, the major force in shaping the history of Scotland in the twentieth century'; see also Lynch, 'Scottish Culture in its Historical Perspective', 23.
[43] See T. C. Smout, 'Patterns of Culture', 269: 'The pub eventually became a place of relaxation almost irrespective of sex, age and class, one of the few truly democratic institutions in Scottish life.'

Now he stood at the bar, where before the company of his friends
had approximated to a congregation, a confirmation in mass of his personal conviction, and he felt himself *participating in a useless ritual*,
mechanically lifting and lowering a glass, savouring the sourness of his
past. (*D*, 210; emphasis added)

Tam exemplifies the epic and tragic hero who, by his very
nature, must perish. Jenny is told of his inevitable death: 'It's
happened. It happened, love. It's happened' (*D*, 302). Amongst
Scottish critics, his death saving a workmate is usually seen as a
coded elegy for the disintegration of working-class solidarity,
while the political confusion following Tam's death, the family
schism and fights it generates, represents, in this reading, the
impossibility of traditional forms of political organization being
remobilized.[44] But in a highly stylized death scene, the clenched
fist extending beyond the coalfall is Tam's last image and testa-
ment. As Murray and Tait remark, the confrontation between
Conn and Mick 'points on beyond the covers of the novel'[45]; or
as Mick says, 'Because you an' me's whits left o' ma feyther,
Conn. It's between you an' me. Me wi wan airm an' you in twa
minds, eh?' (*D*, 322). The fist should properly be seen as an
emblem of the lingering potency of the humanism McIlvanney
'considers characteristic of the ways we found of responding to
the industrialisation of our country' (*STS*, 247). In his refusal to
be buried by history, Tam is physically beneath but politically
beyond the coal fall; buried in the coal, he is part of the history
that creates the rituals of resistance and tradition; buried with a
secular funeral ceremony he is testimony to a tradition of
Scottish republican dissent. Organically integrated into the very
fibre of Scottish history, Tam is a natal seam of humanism, part
of the harmonizing thread running throughout Scottish history
that extends into the present and offers Scotland an 'authentic'
means of cultural self-definition. Thus coal mining is not, of
course, just some special economic activity that legitimates
Scottish nationalism. Coal is of the soil and rooted to a sense of

---

[44] See George Watson, 'Scottish Culture and the Lost Past', *Irish Review*, 9 (Spring
1991), 34–44; Murray and Tait (eds.), *Ten Modern Scottish Novels*, 168; See Colin
Milton's 'Contemporary Scottish Fiction', in Peter Zenzinger (ed.), *Anglistik &
Englischunterricht Scotland: Literature, Culture, Politics* (Heidelberg: Carl Winter
Universitatsverlag, 1989), 224.
[45] *Ten Modern Scottish Novels*, 192.

place; this soil, as a physical symbol and rhetorical trope, now forms the territory of the nation, just as the lingering potency of Tam's politics remains a communal possession. Seamus Deane's remarks are suggestive here:

Soil is what land becomes when it is ideologically constructed as a natal source, that element out of which the Irish originate and to which their past generations have returned. It is a political notion denuded, by a strategy of sacralization, of all economic and commercial reference . . . soil is what land had been when it is communally owned, by tribe, community, or nation. Soil is eternally possessed by a community; land is temporarily owned by an individual.[46]

The defiant note on which the novel ends, as it emphasizes the clarity Tam lends to the present day ('When they contemplated Tam Docherty, he helped them to define themselves' (*D*, 324)) amplifies this point.

In this sense, Tam belongs to the iconography of nationalism, effecting what Benedict Anderson describes as 'a secular transformation of fatality into continuity, contingency into meaning'.[47] Because Tam's exemplary, very masculine virtue contains the potential for national regeneration, the novel deliberately aborts the possibility of textually resolving its own most fundamental issues. It does not try to offer imaginary solutions to real historical problems. McIlvanney's realism instead details a social space within which the crises that end his novels might be resolved. *Docherty* thus rejects an aesthetic of resolution, for Tam is proof that Scottish history is not a fiction, and the literary work can never be the imaginary solution to implacable ideological contradictions. Tam provides what Hobsbawm calls a usable past,[48] a knowable origin through which the transition from modern to postmodern, industrial to post-industrial can be comprehended. The values of a Scottish republicanism and humanism have been agnostically lived rather than cognitively articulated through his life, so it is to Tam, this natal source of

---

[46] *Strange Country: Modernity and Nationhood in Irish Writing since 1790* (Oxford: Clarendon Press, 1996), 71.

[47] *Imagined Communities: Reflections on the Origins and Spread of Nationalism* (London: Verso, 1983), 205.

[48] *Invention of Tradition*, 5. For a discussion of this idea, see Timothy Brennan, 'The National Longing for Form', in Homi K. Bhabha (ed.), *Nation and Narration* (London: Routledge, 1990), 50.

political and moral energy, that McIlvanney's *Strange Loyalties* will return, in a narrative loop symbolic of an enduring historical narrative, in a journey that resembles a pilgrimage.

IV   THE CONTOURS OF CLASS

Conn, in many ways the barometer of *Docherty*'s politics, must choose at the novel's end between Mick's Marxism or the humanist values Tam incarnates. But the novel's *telos*, the point at which its central concerns are resolved, is inextricably tied to class. Class is not a descriptive or contingent aspect of Conn's inheritance but a cognitive category never transcended, one fixed stable cultural referent that establishes a geographic demarcation in which a practical autonomy already resides: 'special contour lines of experience invisibly demarcate certain regions from others . . . the west of Scotland, where nature and industry encounter along the seaboard, is such a region'.[49] This paragraph brings into coalition geography and history, and it prefigures the absorption of Tam in death into the iconography of the region, into its 'special contour lines of experience'. David Harvey offers a severe comment on this appropriation of nature in the production of space: 'To write of "the power of place," as if places (localities, regions, neighbourhoods, states, etc.) possess causal powers is to engage in the grossest of fetishisms; unless, that is, we confine ourselves rigorously to the definition of place as a social process.'[50] The social production of space must await Laidlaw, for in McIlvanney's first novel *Remedy is None*, class is an essential category that not only visibly demarcates a regional space, but also provides the basis for an alternative aesthetic to that of the bourgeois metropolis.

After the death of his father, a miner, Charlie is gaoled for a furious, fatal assault on his stepfather Peter Whitmore, a symptom of his inability to reconcile his identity with society's middle-class values. This use of parentage (a notion we will return to in Chapters 4 and 5 on Irish writers) is important, for it is through parentage that an individual begins to locate himself in history. His father's death places Charlie in a 'place outside of place', a

---

[49] McIlvanney, 'Growing up in the West', 169.
[50] *Justice, Nature and the Geography of Difference*, 302.

realm in which even McIlvanney's strong commitment to justice and the common good no longer exists. Whitmore, whose name denotes in Lallans vernacular an attitude of ceaseless consumption ('Whit more do ye want?') cannot be tolerated, only destroyed. Crime, punishment, and culpability are the novel's central concerns, but the idea of the miner as a source of ethical energy and identity already prefigures the later appearance of Tam and Laidlaw.

In the novel, Charlie is beyond any standards of literary or judicial judgement. University encourages the separation of morality from the present, insisting on the dissolution of what McIlvanney sees as the distinctive Scottish trait, the fusion of thought and passion.[51] This leads to a profound distrust of literature as a source of ethical instruction. Shakespeare is taught with an effortlessly patrician blend of caste and class; but the larger point is that a literature based on Charlie's specifically Scottish needs is still to be created:

We must try to appreciate that the very air he breathes has a different texture from that which we inhale at this moment in this room . . . cropper bit and bridle are being dispensed with altogether and the mane of natural instinct to guide the course of life. This is doubtless a sad reflection on the social horsemanship of your elders. (*RIN*, 5–6)

The novel accommodates the self and the world by foregrounding the ethical rather than aesthetic aspects of experience; the point at which the narrative resolves its concerns is always in the context of society.[52] *Remedy is None* anticipates *Docherty* in that the social history of Charlie's father, a former miner, both exhausts and defines him. He shares Tam's private rituals and mythologies: 'The men went through to the kitchen. It was done by ritual, as though the two groups had separate functions to perform' (*RIN*, 34). These rituals possess a liturgical quality which Roy Rappaport calls invariance, a canonical quality of timelessness that enables the participants in the ritual to transmit

---

[51] 'The Scottish tradition, it seems to me, has always insisted that thought and feeling are only happy as a married couple. They should never be divorced' (*STS* 184).

[52] McIlvanney, 'Growing up in the West', 171: '*Remedy is None* and *A Gift from Nessus* are both books which are essentially concerned with an individual's need to be himself and to make that self meaningful through other people. For me self-fulfilment in isolation is meaningless . . . originality is always the result of a compulsive commitment to a truth outside the work itself.'

but not themselves be paralysed by the permanent values it embodies. Here again it is a means of enacting a tradition that functions as an alternative, independent form of order:[53]

He would talk mainly of times far in the past, as if at some point something had happened that negated himself and he had only those things to remember from a better time. *When he talked like that it was like a ritual.* The same stories recurred and Charlie came to learn them, his father's private mythology, the accidental debris of a man that he took out from time to time to look at and be nostalgic over. (*RIN*, 64; emphasis added)

These moments of transmission between father and son embody, reflect, and reinforce deeply embedded cultural values,[54] and their intensely private force does not require ratification by the values of the Whitmores. What Turner calls *communitas*, an almost sacred condition of solidarity expressing the deepest and most basic values of the community, passes between Charlie and his father. And it is this aura of solidarity that the Whitmores' individualism palpably lacks:[55] 'Mrs Whitmore glimpsed herself in the full length mirror as she passed. She passed automatically, making the ritual gestures of arranging her hair, while at the same time being careful not to disturb its lacquered elegance' (*RIN*, 53). The novel dismantles the notion of a shared set of social coordinates, any possibility of cultural space incorporating Charlie and the Whitmores. Where *Docherty* affectionately details the immanent nobility in working-class existence, *Remedy is None* uncompromisingly anatomizes the absolute distance between that identity and a predominantly middle-class society.[56] Charlie's slippage from promising student to unre-

---

[53] See Roy Rappaport, 'The Obvious Aspects of Ritual', in *Ecology, Meaning, and Religion* (Richmond, Calif.: North Atlantic Books, 1979), 176 ff.

[54] See Alan Jenkins, *The Social Theory of Claude Lévi-Strauss* (London and Basingstoke: Macmillan, 1979), 119. The classic work on Lévi-Strauss is still Leach, *Lévi-Strauss*; see esp. pages 54–9: 'the novices of a society who bear myths are being indoctrinated by the bearers of tradition—a tradition, which in theory at any rate, has been handed down from long dead ancestors'.

[55] 'Liminal to Liminoid in Play, Flow, and Ritual: An Essay in Comparative Symbology', in *From Ritual to Theater*, 54.

[56] Cf. Douglas Dunn's comments in 'Divergent Scottishness: The Novel of Damaged Identity', in Wallace and Stevenson (eds.), *Scottish Novel since the Seventies:* 'Inexperience of middle-class Scotland tends to exclude middle- and upper-class characters from fiction by writers like James Kelman and William McIlvanney . . . Could there be pointing-up of accent and dialect, a shade or two of exaggeration

pentant convict poses the question Laidlaw must eventually answer: can the political and social identities forged in a certain place, under an industrial order of a certain sort, survive the collapse or radical transformation of that order? McIlvanney's regionalism combines territory and *communitas,* but this combination, as Harvey notes, is one of the most pervasive bases for progressive political mobilization and reactionary, exclusionary politics.[57] It is precisely this kind of tension that McIlvanney's shift from a civic republicanism to a territorial nationalism involves.

Immediately before his attack on Whitmore, the narrative highlights Charlie's detachment from any specifically Scottish space:

> But within the body's automatism he lived in another place, without a geography that could not take its identity from the town, that had no home. He was given over to a force that denied the demands of time and place, the ties of home, that took possession of him darkly and swallowed his personal identity. (*RIN,* 180)

This profound association between place, memory, and identity repudiates two very powerful theories of communal attachment. One, given influential expression by Benedict Anderson, claims that communities and places are to be distinguished only in the realm of discourse; not by their falsity or genuineness but by the style in which they are imagined. The other treats any attachment to the particularity of a local space as a myopic, politically delusory fantasy.[58] Charlie's alienation from community and history is resolutely linked to this absence of an imaginative geography, any location wherein a political identity could know its own individual agency as part of a community: 'He had immured himself in this place outside of place, where he had existed as the contradiction of himself where everything he

---

as part of the purpose of making a point or exploiting "material"?'. A hostile view of McIlvanney's portrayal of the working class is in Sean Damer, *Glasgow: Going for a Song* (London: Wishart, 1990); see also Roderick Watson, 'Maps of Desire: Scottish Literature in the Twentieth Century', in T. M. Devine and R. J. Finlay (eds.), *Scotland in the Twentieth Century* (Edinburgh: Edinburgh University Press, 1996), 285–305.

[57] *Justice, Nature and the Geography of Difference,* 209. See James Campbell, 'Toughs and Moralists', *The Times Literary Supplement* 8 July 1993, p. 24 for a critical view of McIlvanney's portrayal of violence.

[58] See Elie Kedourie, *Nationalism* (Oxford: Blackwell, 1993).

had been turned against what he now was' (*RIN*, 201). Charlie's imprisonment is thus an ironic response to a consciousness which is already in chains, devoid of any cohesive space where resistance to the values of the Whitmores might begin. And the erasure of the special contour lines of experience means that *communitas*, the almost sacred aura of solidarity, the harmonizing thread running throughout Scottish history, can no longer be transmitted. David Harvey's point is pertinent here: 'If places are the locus of collective memory, then social identity and the capacity to mobilise that identity into configurations of political solidarity are highly dependent upon processes of place construction and sustenance'.[59]

In this first novel, the particularity of a place-bound politics is a necessary prerequisite for any larger transformation of Scottish society. But the constraints preventing the emergence of this civic space are also established: justice is delivered in the deracinated tones of an Anglicized middle class, and a Highland prison officer imprisons Charlie:

His [the prison officer's] alien presence was a strange incursion from a life that had no connection with Charlie . . . having spoken on behalf of all good men and true . . . Charlie's mind was . . . given over to its own turmoil, was caught in a civil war that no extent could influence. (*RIN*, 202)

This 'alien . . . incursion', to which we will return when discussing Iain Crichton Smith, develops the militant particularism of McIlvanney's community. The complicity of 'Anglified' and 'Highland' identities provokes Charlie's repudiation of university for an intense localism and announces the antagonistic relationship between McIlvanney's regionalism and nationalism. For the essence of the transmission of meaning through ritual, the inevitable consequence of the qualities of race and place it exalts, is that it is strikingly non-dialogical: it cannot be expanded to account for the Whitmores and the Highlands. For one leading commentator on Scotland's future role as an independent nation in Europe, regionalism offers individuals the possibility of a localist republican civic culture, 'a citizenry alert and informed enough to make a combination of state and market work in the general interest. As such its prototypes are

---

[59] *Justice, Nature and the Geography of Difference*, 322.

regional rather than national.' The practice of moral action has to be rooted 'in a community which is knowable: the region, the culture, the city state' which can bypass Scotland's subservience to the Westminster parliament.[60] Though McIlvanney is clearly an influential participant in this aspect of Scottish intellectual and cultural life, throughout his work, only Tam's towering moral presence and civic republicanism can transform such cultural specificity into something capable of claiming universal assent, of offering a national culture. But by *Strange Loyalties*, the antagonistic relationship of the region to the nation has reasserted itself, and humanism is once again subordinate to the thematics of place and race.

In McIlvanney's second novel, *A Gift from Nessus*, the representations and commodification of private spaces (the closeted, transient spaces of hotels, cars, and suburbia) colonize and eliminate representational public spaces (the municipality of Glasgow as a civic site and the innerness of emotions, bodies, and senses it supports), so that abstract space dominates and crushes any actively remaining sense of place. Corruption, duplicity, and the corrosive cynicism generated by the segregation of the private and public are the novel's particular themes, and the same erasure of memory by simulation and segregation that Tam will counter in *Docherty* already exists. Glasgow has been denuded of all meaning for Eddie Cameron, a 35-year-old travelling salesman of light bulbs who discovers his wife's infidelity with his boss while revealing details of an affair which led to the suicide of his own mistress. The multiple mediations between individual and community are forever concealed in the novel, as no social event bears the trace of legible human intentions or agency; the spatial and cultural separation of people from their own history means that history becomes an abstraction and Glasgow a simulacrum of itself. The key casualty in this process of segregation is historical memory, so much so that after these two present-centred novels, *Remedy is None* and *A Gift from Nessus*,

[60] Harvie, *Cultural Weapons*, 88, 89. See also id., *Regions and Regionalism* (London: Routledge, 1994). On 'knowable community', see Raymond Williams, 'Region and Class in the Novel', in Douglas Jefferson and Graham Martin (eds.), *The Uses of Fiction: Essays on the Modern Novel in Honour of Arnold Kettle* (Milton Keynes: Open University, 1982), 59–69.

McIlvanney returns to the thematics of time, memory, place, and community in the working class before it was exposed to the endless fragmentation of contemporary life. As the incarnation of a communal history, Tam ensures that history is no longer a disembodied, spectral affair. He hosts the themes that define and destroy him, reorganizing the randomness of history into a substantive and coherent narrative that people like Charlie can in future access. In short, Tam's iconographic status converts Charlie's specificity into an essential enduring political resource, but one whose humanist principles are never hidebound to the local simply as the local.

Yet for all that, McIlvanney retains a lingering attachment to an uncorrupted pre-modern wholeness. The organization of the narrative in *A Gift from Nessus* is around confined spaces: offices, hotels, bedsits, suburban houses, and, most importantly, private transport and hurried telephone calls. Insulated within his car from his fellow citizen, seeking a market for artificial light, this travelling salesman represents an itinerant, place-less, entirely self-interested morality. Though the novel is set exclusively in Glasgow, the city is a flat, deracinated realm. Glasgow exists for McIlvanney only through the intervention of human agency; it requires the constant affirmation of its citizens' participation, an endorsement of one of the defining principles of civic republicanism: 'citizens earn their title to the status of citizens by an effort of will when they attend to the duties and responsibilities which are the defining characteristics of the practice of citizenship'.[61] 'Geography', McIlvanney has said, 'is people', and in the absence of citizens who aspire to virtue, who acknowledge the ideal of the common good, the city itself remains anonymous, depthless.[62] McIlvanney wants to reassert place in order to ensure a zone within which memory is preserved from erasure. The larger claim of contemporary humanistic geography is that the spaces of representation have the potential not only to affect representation of space, but also to act as a material productive force with respect to spatial practices. For McIlvanney, place only emerges through the practice of an identity that always contains this political dimension. By

---

[61] Oldfield, *Citizenship and Community*, 145.
[62] 'Growing up in the West', 172.

Laidlaw and *Strange Loyalties*, however, precisely what that political dimension should contain is defined ever more rigidly.

In *A Gift from Nessus*, one reason for the failure of Cameron's commercial and personal life is its continual definition through a London metropolitan centre. His estranged suicidal lover is, in this sense, part of the complicated social contract he fails to negotiate with Glasgow. The novel insists that Cameron cannot choose to dispense with the political transactions involved in belonging to a community; he cannot choose to abdicate a freedom which is intrinsic to being human. By renouncing the freedom forged through community, Cameron connives at his own alienation: 'To escape from her image, he gave himself a purpose. He would go and collect the car . . . the car was ready. With it he regained routine, welcomed the safety of habit, as if the car would bring him home of its own accord' (*AGFN*, 117). The transposition of these individualistic values to the public realm (the narrator's belief that the 'history of a relationship was a bit like the history of a society') makes impossible the notion of an authentic 'home'. Glasgow possesses a meaningful presence only when it is mediated through this consciousness of collectivity, a republican conception of citizenship that obliges individuals to develop their humanness in communion with and through others.[63] Cameron lacks this moral centre, and so Glasgow is absent from the narrative. Glasgow is not a passive or pre-existing geographical realm or setting. It contributes to history in a specific context by hosting what Neal Ascherson described as 'Dochertyism', the description of social bonds as duties instead of rights:

They didn't even live in the same space, except for the purposes of the census. Cameron's Glasgow was superficially wide, a travelling man's itinerary with known faces to be found in many parts. But the city was essentially something that unreeled across his window, insubstantial as a travelogue. (*AGFN*, 100)

Unlike Jack Laidlaw's affirmation of Glasgow's civic culture, which takes many forms (including the simple but eloquent choice of public transport to detect private injustice), through

---

[63] See Isaiah Berlin, 'The Originality of Machiavelli', in *Against the Current: Essays in the History of Ideas* (Oxford: Oxford University Press, 1981), 53.

habit and choice Cameron denies any interaction between individual and polity. Withholding assent to the idea of a Glaswegian civic consciousness—the *res* of classical republicanism—he erases both Margaret and Glasgow:

Outside, dark, still houses colonised the moonlight, and fenced its acres of mystery into neat order. Within each darkness, people bedded as carefully as planted seeds, imbibing their dreams, sap of tomorrow. All growing in salubrious separation, protected from entanglement with others, drawing sustenance from the roots of their own privacy, the tubers of certainty. Like Cameron himself. (*AGFN*, 156)

The aesthetic consequences of Cameron's zone of privacy are no less significant. His job as a bookseller enables him to attempt to take the past and 'transform it with the future' (*AGFN*, 213), to heal the fissure between self and society by using 'culture' as a transformative and remedial element. But McIlvanney will not allow meaning to be recuperated exclusively through literature or any other private source. In a telling conjunction, Margaret is studying the Scottish literary tradition when Cameron enters her life. The standards which determine literary value, aesthetic criteria, are thus shown to be inseparable from those that evaluate human intentionality, ethical criteria. Literature has to answer to values that correspond to the reality it exists to chronicle. Representation has no priority over that which it exists to represent, and the act of writing depends for its affective power upon an essential realm of shared, civic human values. In renouncing these ethical possibilities through his treatment of Margaret, Cameron dismantles the whole possibility of reliable aesthetic judgements. He cannot have recourse to 'Literature' as an autonomous aesthetic formation capable of transcending the particularities of his social obligations. What Cameron and the novel lack is an internally coherent moral narrative, a harmonizing thread, that serves as a stable point of reference beyond contingency and to which literary representation can refer. The novel exhaustively anatomizes the impossibility of developing character outwith the context of a commitment to one's community. To understand himself Cameron must understand what it is to be involved with another.

Cameron's desperate attempt to retrieve meaning through literature is, in effect, an attempt to invent this community. But

the novel ends with Cameron and his wife living in perpetual discord. Their implacable antagonism establishes that communal
purposes are the ultimate values from which humans' ends as
individuals are identified, and that aesthetic solutions cannot
sanction the evasion of moral responsibility. It is difficult to pin
down the full meaning of this important scene, but one sense of
its meaning is that whatever affective power a truly Scottish
literature can have is linked to its use as a source of ethical
instruction. And politics—the art of living in a *polis*—is not an
activity which can be dispensed with by those who prefer private
life. Cameron discovers that political conduct, a commitment to
one's fellow citizens, is intrinsic to being human.

V   JUSTICE, VIRTUE, AND THE GEOGRAPHY OF
DIFFERENCE

A bemused Isobel Murray greeted *Laidlaw,* the award-winning
detective novel, as 'a step aside if not a step back in the progress
of an important novelist . . . *Docherty* is a great novel, and one
that uniquely articulates and celebrates aspects of working class
life and experience . . . So what was wrong with *Laidlaw?*
Nothing, indeed, except that McIlvanney had just done even
better.'[64] Adding to the mystery of McIlvanney's departure from
his earlier style is the genre's traditionally conservative structure.
Usually viewed as a metaphysical conundrum, the detective
novel focuses on a strict duality: the mind of the killer (absent but
real) and the body of the victim (present but insignificant).[65] In
solving the crime, the detective identifies an individual responsibility and insists on the event's uniqueness, absolving the community of any further culpability by separating the crime from
the surrounding social conditions, the very antithesis of the
republican conception of the common good. The detective's
extraordinary individuality, his unique ability to discover a solution, consolidates this Manichaean division as social change

---

[64] See 'Breaking Out of Crime Writer's Prison', *Glasgow Herald* (23 Apr. 1983).
[65] See J. Stefano Tani, *The Doomed Detective: The Contribution of the Detective Novel to Postmodern American and Italian Fiction* (Carbondale, Ill.: Southern Illinois University Press, 1984), 4 ff; Tzvetan Todorov, *The Typology of Detective Fiction* (Cambridge: Cambridge University Press, 1989), 83.

occurs only through the actions of great men. The reader is assured that the events are unrepeatable and that reason and law, which become synonymous, will prevail.[66]

By restoring order, reasserting rationality, by a rigorously logical recuperation of events prior to the crime, the detective places the 'criminal' beyond rationality, socialization, and, ultimately, humanity, since what is true for the victim, the 'innocent', cannot logically be true for the perpetrator, the 'guilty'. Structurally the genre insists on a formal departmentalization. Because characters have an allotted role which the plot requires them to fulfil, and only the author and reader ever glimpse the murder which generates the narrative, the detective novel appears committed to a fundamentally conservative world-view: '[It] is at bottom one thing only: a conflict of wits between criminal and sleuth, in which the detective is traditionally victorious by outthinking his adversary . . . in basic structure it must never vary from absolute logic. Besides this one simple rule all others pale to relative unimportance. This is the detective story.'[67]

In the Laidlaw novels, however, the formal conventions of the genre are stretched to embody a symbolic social message. The shift from Tam to Laidlaw reflects the actual changes in the relations of power in Scottish society, as the industrial base shrinks and the working class fragments. If geography is people, the dissolution of the working class affects the 'special contour lines' of the region, the ritualistic transmission of values that

[66] See Michael Holquist, 'Whodunit and Other Questions: Metaphysical Detective Stories in Post-War Fiction', in *New Literary History*, 3/1 (Autumn 1971), 141. See Edmund Wilson's seminal articles in *New Yorker* of 14 Oct. 1944 and 20 Jan. 1945: 'And then, suddenly, the murderer is spotted and—relief!—he is not after all a person like you or me. He is a villain . . . and has been caught by an infallible Power, the supercilious and omniscient detective, who knows exactly how to fit the guilt' (14 Oct. 1944); Fredric Jameson, 'On Raymond Chandler', in *Southern Review*, 6 (1970), 624–50; Robin Winks (ed.), *Detective Fiction: A Collection of Critical Essays* (Eaglewood, NJ: Prentice Hall, 1980), 8; Ernest Mandel, *Delightful Murder: A Social History of the Crime Story* (London: Pluto Press, 1984), 47; Richard Bradbury, 'Sexuality, Guilt and Detection: Tension between History and Suspense', in Brian Docherty (ed.), *American Crime Fiction: Studies in Genre* (Basingstoke: Macmillan, 1988), 88; Dennis Porter, *The Pursuit of Crime: Art and Ideology in Detective Fiction* (New Haven and London: Yale University Press, 1981), 85.

[67] Howard Haycraft, *Murder for Pleasure: The Life and Times of the Detective Story* (London: Peter Davies, 1942), 258.

affirm a coherent, distinctively Scottish humanist ethos within a defined territory. The detective genre thus becomes an analytical tool to examine the shift from the modern to the postmodern.[68] Professionally committed to the concept of a public space, the detective constructs a totality from the disparate micronarratives each clue represents. The clues themselves always imply the existence of a greater whole, even as they obdurately resist collation. What Laidlaw does is search a defined geographical public space, the shared, civic territory of Glasgow, for a metanarrative that can totalize the fragmented scraps of information. He is formally committed to the discovery of a residual meaning that binds together the narrative's participants. As a privileged observer of social heterogeneity, the detective is involved in everyday private life, but consistently evaluating it in terms of a return to more secure public origins—the ideal of justice in society. The present time of the narrative must discover how it came to be this way through prior events, through history. Through this dialectical relationship, the detective must somehow comprehend the pastness of the past if the cause of contemporary injustice is to be found.

Gillian Beer claims the detective genre emerged at a time of cultural and political uncertainty: 'The insistence on stable recovery of initiating acts was at odds with (perhaps was an attempt to find comfort against) the lostness of origins figure in nineteenth-century geology and evolutionary theory.'[69] This 'lostness of origins' fuels all McIlvanney's work, but by 1983, with Scotland subjected to Thatcherism, an ideology which garnered most of its support from southern England, an ideology that famously denied the existence of society, the detective emerges as the guardian of social order, a man whose every act insists that meaning is acquired only within the context of the common sphere, the collective, in a word: society. Like a good historian, a good detective communes with the past, sifting the significant from the dross to recover a stable point of order. The

---

[68] John Docker, *Postmodernism and Popular Culture: A Cultural History* (Cambridge: Cambridge University Press, 1994), 219–44.

[69] *Forging the Missing Link: Interdisciplinary Stories*, Inaugural Lecture Delivered 18 Nov. 1991 (Cambridge: Cambridge University Press, 1992). See also her *Arguing with the Past: Essays in Narrative from Sidney to Woolf* (London: Routledge, 1991), 12–33.

detective is the perfect man to investigate corruption; and
Laidlaw is an exemplary citizen, actively practising what it is
to be a member of the *polis*. Laidlaw, then, is no step aside or
back. Mobile and committed, rational and idealistic, this public
servant is uniquely capable of investigating a Scottish public
sphere, of reconstituting, in Deane's term, of restoring the binding rituals of a community stained by Eddie Cameron's work as
a salesman of artificial light.

In *Laidlaw*, the murderer, like Charlie in *Remedy is None*, is
alienated by the criminal act from any conception of community.
A homosexual and a murderer, Tommy's isolation is cultural,
social, and existential, a state again expressed through the
imagery of the car:

> You could walk as long as you liked in this city. It wouldn't know you
> . . . St George's cross was only cars, inventing destinations for people in
> them. The cars controlled the people . . . nothing to do with you . . . You
> would be alone from now on . . . Nowhere in all the city could there be
> anyone to understand what you had done, to share it with you. No one,
> no one. (*L*, 6)

No one, including the narrator, has privileged access to Tommy's
crime. It is an event which defies interpretation, an acute
example of a more general loss of meaning in contemporary
Scotland. Brutalized by his own act of brutality, Tommy is a
marginalized figure Laidlaw reclaims for the centre. The truly
radical element in the novel, one foreign to the genre, is that
Laidlaw's appeal is never just to the text itself. His radicalism
derives at least in part from a larger cultural matrix which
extends beyond the narrative in which the reader sees it
inscribed. Laidlaw shows how the frame that captures the text,
the context for the many micronarratives surrounding Tommy's
crime, offers a zone of meaning and a realm of relative freedom.
Public participation, not private liberty, offers the route to
justice. Laidlaw leaves his family to immerse himself in civil
society in search of meaning, thereby implicitly rejecting the
bourgeois morality and sheltered freedom family life offers. Any
freedom that excludes Tommy but contains Cameron is, this act
implies, always illusory. Laidlaw shares Tam's ritualistic commitment to a wider tradition of public duty: 'He walked back
and forth pacing out his purpose. In the silence of the house it

was like someone doing sentry duty. It was a familiar event and she knew the ritual that he made of it, as if he were doing more than pack a suitcase' (*L*, 65). This symbolic re-entry into history announces Laidlaw's awareness of a public space that exceeds his individual status and to which he must commit in order to secure meaning. The narrative of cool detection here becomes a quest for self-definition, one in which the investigator himself is manoeuvred into discovering his own deepest allegiances. There is a common interpretative community beyond which meaning cannot be secured, and meaning is something already encoded in the culture he examines:

'Your way of life is taught to you like a language. It's how you express yourself . . . there's a lot of languages. All of them human . . . We have to try to crack the code. But what we're looking for is a part of us. You don't know that, you can't begin.' (*L*, 72)

Meaning exists for Laidlaw only insofar as it is produced and reproduced in the contingent contexts of social life in all its generality. What Laidlaw is looking for already exists, whether the text realizes it or not, so social action is not subject to the same interpretative moves as a text; society is an a-priori category whose essential character precedes its representation. Because the text is not the prime vehicle of meaning, Scottish society is not limited to what can be discursively said about it. It is not, as Benedict Anderson would have it, a community realized chiefly through the style in which it is imagined. The narrative is authored by the citizens who inhabit the context the text describes; the meaning behind Tommy's act is discovered only through an interpretation of the 'text' that is Glasgow. In every Laidlaw novel, attention is continually directed towards the cultural formation surrounding the individual act. What is already encoded in Scotland must be discovered in order to arrive at meaning. Amid the contingencies of postmodernism and Thatcherism's acquisitive individualism, Glasgow functions as a stable knowable space in which value and history are determined.

Caught on the cusp of the modern and the postmodern, polarized between inherited working-class values and its post-industrial expansion, Glasgow's essential social unity is recovered by Laidlaw's intuitive link with the values of Tam

Docherty.[70] It is not institutional justice that discovers Tommy but the expansion of the social space within which meaning is locatable. Laidlaw discriminates between doubles that turn out to be opposites in order to offer Glasgow a real and realizable image of itself. John Rhodes and Matt Mason dominate Glasgow's underworld but embody opposing aspects of Scottish identity. Set in the working-class heartland of Glasgow's East End, Rhodes's pub is almost autonomous, existing in 'a kind of separate state. He did the UDI before Ian Smith thought of it.' Rhodes, a remnant of the infamously violent world of *No Mean City*, possesses a casual, brutal, confident egalitarianism and speaks a language Laidlaw instinctively comprehends. His pub is 'the resort of men who hadn't much beyond a sense of themselves and weren't inclined to have that sense diminished . . . just by coming in you had shucked the protection of your social status. In this place your only credentials were yourself.' (*L*, 93)

As Rhodes's double, Matt Mason is a living denial of these values. Where Rhodes hunts Tommy because of the violation of a moral code rooted in the idea of the community, for Mason, the murder threatens to undermine the barriers that cordon off a common history, language, and community: 'The memories threatened this place. They didn't belong here.' (*L*, 76). Mason's preservation of his status in Glasgow means physically and psychologically erasing the history Tommy touches upon. Thus Laidlaw's collaboration with Rhodes to find Tommy performatively insists that any retrieval of value must work through inherited indigenous traditions. Rhodes is 'authentically' Glaswegian ('In the Gay Laddie Formica hadn't been invented' (*L*, 114)) whereas Mason is a simulacrum of an alien identity, and so it is he, Mason, that Laidlaw will finally prosecute in *Strange Loyalties*.

Laidlaw is far more concerned to identify the traditions that properly belong to Glasgow than to rid the city of crime. Mason, as the name suggests, belongs to a secretive, solipsistic world centred on self-advancement. A truly social justice arrives not when gangsters like Rhodes are locked up, but when the individualism that robs the city of its republican virtue are clearly

---

[70] See Margaret Rose, *The Post-Modern & the Post-Industrial* (Cambridge: Cambridge University Press, 1992), 21–39, for a discussion of postmodernism and the waning of class.

identified. Tommy is victimized because Glasgow is incapable
of recognizing its underlying historical unity, and so Laidlaw is
interested in discovering that moment when a public space
emerges within which the apparently deviant is understood as
another irreducible expression of a common humanity. Laidlaw
is, in short, seeking a workable form of virtue, of the kind
Tommy's lover, the suicidal Harry Rayburn, never knew: 'He
knew the viciousness of public virtue, how it subsists through the
invention of its opposite' (*L*, 114).

For virtue to circulate freely, it must subvert the social and
epistemological divisions delimiting the public space. Laidlaw's
Commander is devoted to the concept of the category as an
organizing principle of human experience, whereas for Laidlaw,
'there wasn't one category that he could accept as being
significantly self-contained, from Christian to murderer' (*L*,
104). Laidlaw inaugurates a new form of authority, a brand of
rational humanism that dissects Glasgow's principal conflicts:
Catholic versus Protestant (Tommy and Jennifer against Bud
Lawson), law versus crime (Laidlaw against Rhodes and
Mason), homosexual versus heterosexual (Tommy and Harry
against Bud and John Rhodes), men versus women (Laidlaw and
Harkness against Ena and Mary), family versus society (Laidlaw
and Harkness). Each element in this series is made possible by a
studied determination to acknowledge the other as mutually
exclusive elements, not as oppositions which can still contain the
other. Laidlaw's travels around Glasgow, in the real time of
the novel, direct attention to meaning as dispersed, mobile, and
produced through dynamic human relationships within the context of society. *Laidlaw* thus undermines the authority of textual
representation and interpretation focused solely on the text by
discovering the nature of Tommy's alienation through the social
space that is Glasgow. There is a move beyond language to a
focus upon ordinary human activity as a layered, eloquent,
coded commentary on the novel's search for justice and virtue.
Thus the digression into Glaswegian patter, the choice of a bus
over car, and, importantly, a discussion of Laidlaw's reasons for
leaving university—all these elements are part of a discovery of
meaning in the now disposable remnants of working-class
culture. The wino Eck Adamson and his sister trapped in the
Gorbals, John Rhodes's pub in the East End—Laidlaw scans the

public space which produced Tam Docherty as part of a dialectical relationship with the past. And the symbolic moment that
crystallizes this is Laidlaw's intervention between Lawson's masculine, sectarian certainties and Tommy's confused sexuality.
Straddling both worlds, refusing to demonize even the killer as
beyond society, Laidlaw affects history by complete participation in that history, by being, in other words, an active citizen
vita. Laidlaw rescues Tommy from private vengeance for public
justice in a scene of deliberate epiphanic force:

> It made an arbitrary patch of light in total darkness. Its centre was
> Laidlaw. On his left was Tommy Bryson . . . On Laidlaw's right Bud
> Lawson was slumped, his right hand cradled in front of him . . . Laidlaw
> was the buffer between them, blinking against the manufactured light,
> the mouth that had saved a man's life curled in annoyance at the intru-
> sion. (*L*, 216)

Laidlaw demonstrates that a civic culture is not an incidental
by-product of social life but a moment dependent upon the individual's active intervention. But crucially, Laidlaw is exemplary,
not unique: Minty McGregor, the anonymous Glaswegian dying
of cancer who emerges from the populace then quickly disappears, is equally virtuous. He thwarts Mason by refusing to
victimize Tommy and, in a supremely eloquent statement, hands
Mason's money to a stranger at a bus stop. Minty is a kind of
Glaswegian everyman, defined only through his representative
status. His intuitive connection with Laidlaw's civic republican
values makes Laidlaw the expression of a deeper collective
consciousness. Like Tam, Laidlaw is individuated by humanist
principles already embedded within Glasgow, and his individual
liberty is safeguarded by acknowledging its necessary dependence on the common good.

But because Minty, the Glasgow everyman, is slowly dying,
history is perpetually in decline. This movement away from civic
value, a central element of the republican notion of history, is a
feature of all McIlvanney's work. *Laidlaw* is a clarion call for the
rediscovery of meaning through the humanist values of the
Glasgow working class; 'Minty', as the name suggests, produces
a unique, non-materialist currency that disregards Mason's
money and faces death. Meanwhile Laidlaw disregards conventional notions of justice by entering Tommy's cell. In one

sense, Tommy now shares the existential loneliness of Charlie in
Remedy is None. By questioning the forms of authority one
ought to recognize, the novel already adumbrates McIlvanney's
title, *Strange Loyalties.* For what *Laidlaw* finally asks is whether
necessity and professional obligation can ever outweigh the duty
to one's community, to a larger history, and whether the idealism
anatomized in McIlvanney's next novel, *The Papers of Tony
Veitch,* can ever be given practical application.

> The Puritan Fallacy is that there can be virtue by default.
> You can do the Right thing because you don't know any
> worse. That is society's Woolworth substitute for morality.
> True morality begins in choice: the greater the choice, the
> greater the morality.   (*PTV*, 26)
>
> Everybody's dying should matter to somebody. The more
> people who cared, the closer you came to some kind of
> humanist salvation. There was no other to believe in.
>
>   (*PTV*, 74)

Though Tony Veitch—aristocrat, university drop-out, and
seeker after public virtue—never physically enters the novel that
bears his name, he touches all strands of Glasgow society; from
Eck Adamson, degenerate wino but keeper of the clue to Veitch's
whereabouts, to Milton Veitch, his wealthy father who disowns
him; from Lindsey, daughter of Lord Farren, to Gus Hawkins,
the novel's working-class Marxist intellectual. In this sense,
Tony Veitch represents an idealism everyone knows but to which
no one will admit. Discovering the murderer is subordinated to
the quest for the meaning behind Veitch's death. And though the
labyrinthine complexities surrounding that death are never
completely unravelled, Laidlaw's realization that Veitch 'had,
in a way, died of his own innocence. He hadn't known what
was going on, the complexity of it' (*PTV* 224), poses a more
profound question: how can virtue once discovered and defined
survive?

Laidlaw cannot accept that Veitch poisoned Eck Adamson
before killing himself, for it would mean that idealism connived
in its own corruption, that virtue is easily corruptible. By discovering a prevailing unity beneath apparent contradictions,

Veitch's papers and his alleged actions, the possibility of a public space embracing the privileged Veitch and the pauper Eck is affirmed. This is socialism, certainly, but a culturally specific brand, for this public zone of meaning emerges only when the universal, place-less aspirations of Marxism are repudiated.

Tony Veitch's thoughts are expressed almost wholly through textual analogies. There is, as the title indicates, a consistent literaryness to his attempts at self-definition; it is always an inner experience which acts as the locus of a personal reality. Visible surface signs of the actual must always be traces of a more perfect form, a utopian dimension that renders the untheorizable peculiarity of experience worthless by comparison. Veitch authors a humanism too precious to confront the world it critiques. It collapses under the incessant textualization of his own opinions, making it impossible for him to criticize his father, the most blatant example of the corruption he loathes: 'I was making a note for myself the other day and it was only when I had finished I realised I was trying to say something I believed about you' (*PTV*, 173). But like the Marxism of Gus Hawkins, Veitch's brand of virtue is never inflected by the specificity of place. The possibility of regeneration is always in a place uniquely no place, a time outside time, or as Gus Hawkins says: 'You could show Tony's development geographically. Without going outside Byres Road . . . He spent a year in The Salon in Vinicombe Street. Just down the road there. Seeing some pictures three times. Whatever they were showing, that's what he saw. If it was Tom and Jerry, he was there. He was hiding from the shock of real life' (*PTV*, 105). There is a strict correlation between this imaginative geography and political agency. If nothing exists beyond Veitch's textual analogies, the text is fatally impoverished by speaking to nothing other than itself. Hence his literary legacy, the scraps of paper found by his body, are, in fact, potent and poignant evidence of an external reality he always sought to displace: 'The few words which had survived were worn to meaningless smudges with the water, as accessible as runes' (*PTV*, 176).

Described by his university tutor as 'someone who will re-animate our rituals by attacking them' (*PTV*, 91), Veitch mixes Tam Docherty's commitment to the civic with Laidlaw's icono-clastic distrust of formalist categories. Like Laidlaw he shuns university, for 'such people don't submit too happily to academic categories. They have a refreshing swingeing freedom of mind' (*PTV*, 90). But because Veitch's referent is always imagined, not real, always isolated from the world he purports to describe, he substitutes visionary experience for Glasgow's complex reality. Veitch's idealism lacks the ability to become part of any collective political grouping, never going beyond the text to pose questions the text, lacking effective agency, is always powerless to pose. Thus Veitch, suspended above place and out of time, never physically enters the narrative that bears his name. The detective, by contrast, moves backward as well as forward through narrative in time and space. He does not wage war against or attempt to defeat the past. Accepting but then re-arranging the emplotment bestowed to him, he reveals the possibility of a determinable, significantly different future. The detective's combination of narrative and will makes him capable of understanding, and therefore changing, the meaning of his actions and the context in which they occur. Narrative is used as a means of expression rather than repression, exposing the present to an energy drawn from, but never neurotically repeating, the past. There is no tyranny of precedent because Laidlaw must choose from the available evidence in Scotland's history— Old Jock from Ayrshire, Jinty Adamson from the Gorbals—to construct meaning, to make possible a new narrative which speaks of a consciously designed future.

Gus Hawkins, Marxist working-class intellectual and Veitch's closest friend and interrogator, shares with Tam Docherty a 'refusal to have his vision circumscribed by circumstances' (*PTV*, 102). Though profoundly at odds with his Marxist universalism, Laidlaw's deepest allegiances orbit around the tradition of social justice Hawkins advocates: 'Laidlaw felt immediately two things: that just by standing here he was closer to Tony Veitch, could take the pulse of his comprehensible strangeness, knew a little better where he came from; that he was looking at a lost part of himself' (*PTV*, 102). Hawkins is thematically unimportant to the resolution of the plot, a point that is, obviously, thematically very important indeed. His studied indifference to Eck Adamson, Lindsey Farren, and Milton Veitch—the variegated strands of Glasgow society—makes him irrelevant to Laidlaw's quest. For though Hawkins incorporates elements of

Tam's humanism, Eck and Tony are simply disposable moments in an inevitable historical evolution. For Hawkins, historical truth is fixed, permanent, and hermetically sealed from defined areas of cultural activity. Veitch's papers, which Hawkins tellingly never reads, are necessarily corrupted by the conditions of their production. The search for Veitch, for the tradition of virtue he embodies, is thus organized around two contiguous but distinct intellectual traditions: Laidlaw believes in a meaning produced through the determinate specificity of Glasgow, through the various cultural traditions that compose it, while Hawkins's positivism denies the need or validity of a specifically Scottish agency, a fact emphasized by his distance from the novel's plot. If ineluctable laws govern human behaviour, the individual citizen *vita* is, after all, no longer required.

For Hawkins, as with Mick in *Docherty,* the route to a superior social order must transcend the specific time and space of Glasgow and repress the disparate scraps of meaning Eck and Tony's papers represent. For McIlvanney, Hawkins's Marxism fails to recognize that all societies involve symbolic interaction— the imaginative interaction of individuals encoded in ritual. And this is what Laidlaw forces Hawkins to confront by bringing him to Gina, Eck's sister. The trope of the family is used to emphasize the common, distinct heritage Glasgow shares, and Hawkins is introduced to a narrative embroiled in present time and space. Laidlaw apprehends Veitch's killer at the airport, for example, and returns him to justice within Glasgow, affirming an allegiance to the city as a zone where meaning emerges through conflict. The airport is the gateway to universalism, whereas Laidlaw's conception of citizenship is confined to a defined territorial region. In the novel, Laidlaw sheds his institutional role as policeman to become a citizen of the *polis*, exemplifying a specifically Scottish humanism that enriches those who freely choose it. Citizenship is again a permanent condition, conferring duties as well as rights that cannot be renounced.[71] The novel ends with Gus looking at Laidlaw dance drunkenly with an old woman from a late-night taxi queue. The Marxist universalist gazes as the localist detective discovers a spontaneous Scottish reality that spills beyond any theoretical categories. This is a

---

[71] On this theme, see Edward Shils, 'Nation, Nationality, Nationalism and Civil Society', *Nations and Nationalism*, 1/1 (1995), 93–118.

kinship that arises from a shared common territory and history; in other words, Laidlaw embraces a nationality from which Hawkins remains distant, and in McIlvanney's next two novels, he locates its philosophical foundations in the special contour lines surrounding Tam Docherty's birthplace.

VI   THE STRANGE DEATH OF SCOTTISH VIRTUE

'What I am trying to do', McIlvanney said near publication of *The Big Man*, 'is construct a vision from fragments of reality, to make it all coherent',[72] a phrase that recalls his description of the SNP as having 'recognisable features but no coherent identity' (*STS*, 18). The hero of *The Big Man*, Dan Scoular, dies in *Strange Loyalties*, incidentally helping Laidlaw discover the reasons for the death of his brother Scott (also a character in *The Big Man*), who, as the name suggests, stands in some way for Scotland. Dan Scoular, a 33-year-old unemployed miner, is, like Scotland, negotiating the passage from the industrial to the post-industrial.[73] The replacement of the coalfields by Sulom Voe, an oilfield off Aberdeen, mirrors the displacement of older forms of collectivity by this increasingly narrow individualism. Through the figure of the unemployed miner, what McIlvanney actually asks is how much of Tam's principles a post-industrial Scotland retains.[74]

Dan intervenes between Matt Mason (already familiar from *Laidlaw*) and Vic, the novel's prototype Marxist, to define an ethical terrain previously automatically assumed. Mason brings to Thornbank, an archetypal west of Scotland town, a zero-sum mentality of ferocious competitiveness. Dan, offered quick cash for a bare knuckle fight if he suspends the capacity for ethical discrimination—'You're not being asked to pass judgement on

---

[72] 'Man of the People', *Scotland on Sunday* (21 Sept. 1985).
[73] '*The Big Man* is a metaphor for Thatcher's Britain', McIlvanney quoted in 'Digging Deep to Save a Nation's Culture', *Guardian* (29 Aug. 1985).
[74] See Thomas C. Richardson, 'Reinventing Identity: Nationalism in Modern Scottish Literature', in Horts W. Drescher and Hermann Volkel (eds.), *Nationalism in Literature* (Frankurt am Main: Verlag Peter Lang, 1989), 199: 'Literary character becomes a metaphor for national identity. When external identity is gone there is a need to reinvent identity . . . Metaphors of self appear as metaphors of nation. Historical facts are less important than impressions of truth.'

this—just to participate' (*TBM*, 21)—is required to exemplify a ubiquitous acquisitiveness, where 'it was as if every man and his family were a private company' (*TBM*, 53). Geographically and politically, the novel is strikingly non-dialogical, as McIlvanney aims to reformulate an already encoded political and ethical tradition rather than compromise with the new features of Scottish society. The possibility of national regeneration, of restoration, already exists, therefore, amid the casual confusion of a bleak post-industrial landscape:[75] 'The owner's name was a conundrum of missing letters—Mac—something' (*TBM*, 62). The foundations through which Scotland might know itself stubbornly persist, even as the whole notion of identity, the appendix to 'Mac', is under threat.[76]

The movement away from the singularity of class as a conceptual and organizational category threatens the 'special contour lines of experience', the working-class rituals through which a distinctively Scottish humanism emerges. Dan is caught between a reality for which there is no obvious future, and a set of proffered forms that correspond with nothing he recognizes as real, a dilemma which leads to an estrangement from any notion of a collective identity. Whereas his opponent Cutty Dawson identifies with the terms of the fight, Dan's struggle is with precisely this kind of stoicism. Attempting to inaugurate a conception of selfhood founded absolutely on the individual agency discovered during the fight, he abolishes any connection with Cutty's generation by punching him blind. But Cutty's recovery of his sight in *Strange Loyalties* testifies to one continuous vision in Scottish history: a working-class humanity in the face of brutal, impossible odds:

It went back to something he had felt when they had taught him Scottish history at school. It had been as if nobody wanted to try to link the gaps or find out what they meant. It was almost as if Scotland didn't have any

<hr />

[75] See ' "Fist-Fights and Metaphors for Kilmarnock": D J Taylor on William McIlvanney, a Scottish Storyteller Launching Guerilla Attacks from the Front Line' *Independent* (28 Jan. 1989).

[76] Ian Spring uses the term post-industrial to suggest 'the reconstitution of the image of a city once dependent, both metaphorically and metonymically, on the real industrial mode of production. How this can be done is a central problematic of the New Glasgow' (*Phantom Village: The Myth of the New Glasgow* (Edinburgh: Polygon, 1990), 132).

history or, if it did, not many people knew what it was. And he realised suddenly that was where he felt he was when he was walking through Glasgow, in the truth of Scottish history, the living reality of it. (*TBM*, 130)[77]

Dan's kinship with Cutty resembles nationality in that it cannot be refused. Their fight is actually between an already-authenticated cultural tradition (the only fight Dan had previously lost was with his father), and the promise of continual, depthless, isolated self-creation without any connection to Scottish history or space. At Mason's victory party, Dan recognizes

the desire to happen without history, to escape through a loophole in time and find a new moment where maybe you could begin yourself afresh . . . Realising that, Dan excluded himself from the exclusiveness of the party. Among them, he felt himself more with Cutty Dawson. Just as his will had created his victory, so now it unmade it. (*TBM*, 204)

The pattern of connections and coincidences between all McIlvanney's post-*Docherty* novels detail the non-human authority, the harmonizing thread, underpinning individual lives, supplying them with context and a register of values. This is the narrative of Scottish history. The novels' web of inter-actions—Jack Laidlaw shares the same hotel as Dan, while Scott, Laidlaw's brother and the central character of *Strange Loyalties*, is approached by Dan's wife (who also reappears in *Strange Loyalties*)—suggests a history which, unbidden, unfolds around those inhabiting Scotland. McIlvanney's corpus testifies to its integrity, wholeness, and coherence: its existence is not dependent upon the ratification of its individual citizens.[78]

These continuities undermine the implicit historiographical premiss of *The Big Man*. The title infers that History is the product of individual figures of transhistorical status. But the

---

[77] See Marinell Ash, *The Strange Death of Scottish History* (Edinburgh: The Ramsay Head Press, 1980), 10: 'A general interest in Scottish history had ceased to be the mark of a broadly educated Scotsman and had come instead to be seen as the mark of a narrow parochialism most Scots wished to abandon.' This notion is also discussed in Craig Beveridge and Ronald Turnbull, *The Eclipse of Scottish Culture*, and Colin Kidd, *Subverting Scotland's Past* (Cambridge: Cambridge University Press, 1993).

[78] See Ian Bell, 'McIlvanney: Hunting for Morality in Scotland's Myths', *Scotsman* (16 Apr. 1983).

novel's prevailing irony is that the big man doesn't exist. The mythology surrounding Dan reflects Thornbank's needs rather than the actuality of his achievements, and what the novel wants to establish is the standards by which both can evaluate their lives in the changed time of contemporary Scotland: 'Like the Mount Parish Church clock, he was a familiar fixture by which they checked how things were going. Like that notoriously erratic timepiece, he was misleading' (*TBM,* 23).

Though no solution to the threat posed by Mason is proffered, the point from which resistance must start is identified. Pursued by Mason's violent ideology, Dan walks to the pub at the novel's end for solidarity and defence, testifying to the continuation of public spaces redolent of older forms of social unity in urban life.[79] Dan's death in *Strange Loyalties* is not, therefore, the death of Scottish history, for the restoration of Cutty's sight in that novel testifies to its continuing vitality. Published after the miners' strike and at the height of Thatcherism in 1985, *The Big Man* reactivates a distinctively Scottish tradition of working-class solidarity around which resistance can organize itself. But by 1991 and the publication of *Strange Loyalties,* Mason has murdered Dan. All McIlvanney's post-*Docherty* novels constitute a narrative of decline, a movement away from a cohesive civic value through which Scottish difference is grounded. The impossibility of political action in current circumstances, in the strange loyalties Scotland chooses, produces the emphatically nationalist priorities of the final novel in the Laidlaw series.

In *Strange Loyalties*, the random death of Laidlaw's brother Scott generates an allegorical quest for what constitutes Scotland. In this sense, 'Scott' is a free-floating signifier hovering outside the text who must be reclaimed and grounded in the daily commerce of Scottish life. The search for 'Scott' attempts to re-insert nationality as an active principle of everyday Scottish life and re-establish Scotland as a continuous and cohesive cultural space.

Scott lived in Graithnock, Tam Docherty's home town, Laidlaw's birthplace, his father's adopted home, and close to Dan Scoular's Thornbank. Laidlaw apart, all these figures are

---

[79] 'The pub's a clarifying agent in many folks' lives', McIlvanney quoted in Trevor Royle 'Man of the People', *Scotland on Sunday* (21 Sept. 1985).

dead, emphasizing, again, history as a narrative of decline. Ayrshire contains what Laidlaw calls 'a quintessential Scotland where good people were my landmarks and the common currency was a mutual caring' (*SL*, 142). Graithnock, then, is where an authentic Scottish politics is to be found. The allegorical format, signalled by the epigraph from Keats,[80] links Scott's death to this search for continuity and apostolic succession:

if a man loses his sense of his own continuity, he's had it . . . I needed every scrap of confirmation of life's meaningfulness I could get. My brother, who in my worst times had seemed more substantial to me than myself, my brother had walked into a random car . . . I needed Scott in death as I had needed him in life. I needed a reunion in meaning between us. (*SL*, 10)

The trope of brotherhood, familiar from *The Big Man,* where Dan reaches Cutty's hospital bedside by claiming to be his brother, symbolizes a working-class kinship linking successive Scottish generations. National feeling is an instinctive aspect of social organization, not a formal ideological imposition, and Scott, as brother and national allegory, is a perhaps too pious reinvigoration of the connection between individual and nation. Laidlaw's search for 'Scott' charts an internally coherent geographical space; the region is inscribed as a *polis*, a collective political unit defined by boundaries and organized not vertically but horizontally. Laidlaw's journey is an example of what Anderson calls 'the "national imagination" at work in the movement of a solitary hero through a sociological landscape of a fixity that fuses the world inside the novel with the world outside'. Brotherhood is the appropriate trope for McIlvanney's vision of Scotland because it is democratic, egalitarian, and looks to a common origin. Laidlaw's task is to discover his community as, in Benedict Anderson's overused but useful phrase, a 'deep horizontal comradeship'.[81] But, of course, brotherhood also invokes tropes of blood and ethnicity.

Handsome and charismatic, confident and cosmopolitan, a teacher and an artist, Scott combines the erotic and emotive appeal of nationalism: 'He had plans to live abroad . . . Their children would be Scottish cosmopolitans . . . no matter where

---

[80] 'A man's life of any worth is a continual allegory—and very few eyes can see the mystery.'   [81] *Imagined Communities*, 7, 30.

they might live, any children would have to be born here' (*SL*, 120). Described as 'the most authentic thing that ever happened to me' (*SL*, 80), Scott's predetermined essence and value is further augmented by his painting 'Scotland'. The novel as allegory enables the variegated layers of society to be evaluated by reference to the standards Scott embodied, an inevitably exclusive structure because the boundaries surrounding the region as *polis* are formulated by being within or without Scott's value system. Allegory insists that Scotland can be contained and located within a single narrative form, and that an individual's Scottishness is to be defined solely in terms of his relationship to Scott's paradigmatic nationality. Allegory radically undermines the category of the private to make the psychic and sexual legitimate areas of investigation. The partition between personal and public behaviour is abolished so that everything is evaluated by reference to one overriding principle, 'Scott'. In this sense, *Strange Loyalties* attempts to locate the space within which the philosophical foundations of Scotland might be located, with 'Scott' providing the nation with its imagined unity as a symbolic force. But to achieve this, nationality must continually be on display in everyday experience.

Difference becomes the absolute, defining component of a living Scottish tradition, with 'Englishness' replacing Marxism as the 'other' against which value is defined. Laidlaw's position as arbiter of that value is assured by his blood relationship with Scott, a tactic puzzlingly incompatible with the humanist ideals Tam Docherty incarnated. The novel is premissed on the need to reveal an essence around which new loyalties, new forms of human community, can be arranged. But to do so it must formulate a series of dualities to enable it to calculate this essential value: inside–outside, authentic–inauthentic, male–female, and, ultimately, national and anti-national.

The allegorical structure violently forecloses the geographical and imaginative space within which national identity and gender are organized. Both are always defined in relation to an 'other', but gender is always more rigidly binary than nationality; while femininity and masculinity are mutually dependent, nationality can be defined against a raft of other categories.[82] One key factor

---

[82] See Toril Moi, *Sexual/Textual Politics: Feminist Literary Theory* (London and New York: Routledge, 1988), 104.

preventing the emergence of Scottish identity is Scott's estranged wife Anna. In every sense, she occupies a space always marginal to the needs of the *polis* Laidlaw traces. She is from the Borders, a region described by Laidlaw's father as 'the place that defined Scottishness at its weakest edge, where it meets Englishness, had lost its sense of itself and blurred into anonymity' (*SL*, 150). There, Laidlaw now discovers 'English voices crested like old School ties and native voices in which the confusedly rich broth of Scottishness was passed through strained vowels until it became the thinnest of gruels' (*SL*, 155).

As the negation of everything Scott represents, Anna lives in Edinburgh's New Town, described as 'the most English place in Scotland, built to be a Hanoverian clearing house of Scottish identity . . . anyway you counted it, the result is the defeat of Scottishness . . . I couldn't help wondering how far Anna fitted in with the original premise of the place' (*SL*, 165). Divorced from Scott, she refuses Laidlaw access to her personal memories, insisting on a private space where nationality cannot impinge. Anna is thus epistemologically divorced from the idea of the nation, the category from which all value in the novel derives, and condemned to be a mere object of history. Through his search for Scott, Laidlaw traces the 'recognisable features', the coherent cultural identity the SNP lacks (*STS*, 18); but the special contour lines of experience inscribed by his search become ever more exclusionary, occluding any element that might undermine the transcendent realm of nationalist identity signified by the allegory 'Scott'. 'Authenticity', collectivity, and nationality are merged until they are synonymous, and because Laidlaw the detective conducts a rational search for nationality, the implicit insistence is that to be rational is to be committed to the national.[83]

With Scott as allegory, a national tradition is established, a historic Scottish story which individuals are not free to step outside. It is the central cognitive and evaluative category from which all value arises. Nationality seeps into all aspects of private and public life so that behaviour and belief are constantly apprised in terms of its putative standards. No home or private

---

[83] See Aijaz Ahmad, *In Theory: Classes, Nations, Literatures* (London: Verso, 1992), 95–122 for a discussion of national allegories.

space escapes the reach of Scott as allegory, for Laidlaw does not recognize a libertarian conception of citizenship that reduces it to a mere legal status, setting out the rights the individual holds against the state. In his search for justice and virtue, Laidlaw has the right to invade citizens' private lives. It is not the presence of the rights of citizenship that matters but the way they are exercised, and Laidlaw feels no inhibition about setting down such guidelines. Frankie White's mother's house has 'thick wall-to-wall carpeting, heavy wallpaper, and a lot of ornaments and a fyfe-stone fire-place encasing a very elaborate metal-work gas-fire'. The house is approved because of its representativeness, 'because it pleased the heart. I had seen examples of it all over the west of Scotland' (*SL*, 170). Pleasing because it is representative, it contrasts with Anna's apartment:

All that stunning Edinburgh light poured into the place and made it as bright and sharp and self-delighted as a Hockney painting. The real leather furniture showed off its sheen in the glow. A reproduction mahogany desk against a wall, its green leather surface unmarred by any papers, achieved a cool definition. The three abstract paintings distilled the roofs and the shapes and colours outside and stuck them on the white walls. (*SL*, 180)

Because Scott's paintings are full of concrete images of Scotland, Anna's abstracts are, through the allegorical structure of the novel, facts from which her lack of value is derived, a type of naturalistic fallacy in which her moral degeneracy is refracted through the surrounding landscape.

Laidlaw's physical migration to Graithnock is a symbolic return to the principles Tam and Scott embodied. Laidlaw's closest friend Tom Docherty is a grandson of Tam; and, like Laidlaw, his marriage has failed. Marital breakdown is a recurring theme in all McIlvanney's novels: Laidlaw's already shaky marriage collapses, and an affair ends, because of the search for Scott, while those who have known him remain married only by doggedly denying his memory. This conflation of personal and public discord, the impossibility of discovering the full meaning of 'Scott' while locked into the private contract marriage entails, this inserts male–female relationships as an opposition to be overcome if Scott's death is to be comprehended. Laidlaw and Tom Docherty's virility is impaired or at least suspended because of the state of the nation. In this important sense, national identity is profoundly inflected by gender. Discovering Scott is somehow meant to restore their sexual vitality, as the solution demanded by the novel is a symbolic reinstatement of masculine authority.[84]

As interlocutor and critic, the validity of Laidlaw's interpretation of Scott's painting 'Scotland' is already established by his kinship:

'Scotland' reminded me somehow of my father. I think it was because of the suggestion in the picture that the public reality of Scottish experience was denied in private lives. For my father, the method he hated had been to translate the demotic of Scottish tradition into a bland standard English, losing most of the meaning in the translation (*SL*, 200)

Waverley, Walter Scott's epic tale of Scottish nationhood, ends with a marriage between an English man and a Scottish woman, and a painting that prescribes political reconciliation and cultural harmony through an aesthetic vision realized by 'an eminent London artist'. Alongside the painting hang 'the arms which Waverley had borne in the unfortunate civil war'.[85] Political strife, Walter Scott suggests, can be overcome by submerging differences in a healing aesthetic, a kind of cultural assimilation that threatens the absolute category of difference, masculine difference, which Laidlaw now attempts to establish. For where his humanism previously found a value in the daily experience of human life, 'Scotland' locates the production of meaning only within a determinate and knowable space of signification. It not only represents the Scottish regional space in which history, meaning, and value are produced; it also authorizes the mode of representation through which all three can be articulated. Humanism is now subordinate to certain immanently valuable behaviour and procedures because of the all-pervasive allegory, 'Scott'. 'Scotland', the painting, names and valorizes certain quintessentially Scottish features. And when 'Scotland' is rescued from Anna's rubbish tip, it establishes

---

[84] See R. Radhakrishnan, 'Nationalism, Gender, and the Narrative of Identity', in Andrew Parker (ed.), *Nationalism and Sexualities* (London: Routledge, 1992), 77–95. For a discussion of this area, see Gillean Somerville-Arjat and Rebecca E. Wilson (eds.), *Sleeping with Monsters: Conversations with Scottish and Irish Women Poets* (Dublin: Wolfhound Press, 1990).

[85] *Waverley* (1815; Harmondsworth: Penguin, 1985), 489.

her ethical and aesthetical hostility to what Scott, in both senses of this word, represented.[86]

In this representation, verisimilitude is all. It is as if the reality of the crisis facing Scotland is so urgent that technical innovation is mere distraction: 'the whole thing was rendered in great naturalistic detail, down to the recognisably working-class faces below the bonnets'. The juxtaposition of this 'nightmarish' scene with a typically romanticized landscape expresses the conflict between the 'real' conditions of material existence and the falsified image of Scotland with which it contends. Another part of 'Scotland' 'showed an idealised highland glen with heather and a cottage pluming from the chimney and a shepherd and his dog heading towards it' (*SL*, 210). As 'Scotland' is framed, so too is Scottishness formulated within a determinate geographic space. Any aspect of reality threatening to overwhelm this signifying field, like feminism and the Highlands, is simply elided. As the frame of the painting shifts attention away from what is outside itself to that which constitutes its image, so all McIlvanney's novels direct their gaze towards what is already in Scottish history. The point is to show that conditions of independence and statehood already exist and need to be acknowledged. Laidlaw and realism, both representing Scott, are in conflict with Anna and Romanticism, forms with which Scott could not be reconciled. Only by defeating what does not properly belong to itself can the allegory of the novel, 'Scotland', be mastered. In attempting to shatter the myths of Tartanry and the Kailyard, in responding to Scotland's disenfranchisement under Thatcherism, McIlvanney here comes dangerously close to endorsing an essentialist, unapologetically masculinist, ethnically tinged foundational myth as their replacement. The plot is resolved by locating Matt Mason in a prosperous suburban house. His greed killed the man in the green coat, the representative Scottish Everyman. But this everyman has been defined ever more narrowly until a picture emerges of what attributes he ought to have. The very process of definition is one of exclusion: only those lives which provide national allegories are admitted as authentic examples of what Scottish identity ought to entail.

[86] See Carol Anderson and Glenda Norquay, *Cencrastus*, 15 (1994), 8–10. 'By labelling feminism an alternative and a threat to national identity, men make Scottishness their province. Women are thus forced to choose.'

VII   GLASGOW, CELTIC, AND REPUBLICANISM?

McIlvanney's distinctive contribution to twentieth-century Scottish literature is his insistence that Scotland can enter modernity through its own already encoded procedures and history. *The Kiln,* his most recent and award-winning novel, continues the themes of stoic endurance and ancestral lineage traced above.[87] Exile and alienation offer no privileged vantage point, as they do for George Douglas Brown's clinical narrative voice in *The House with the Green Shutters.* A recurring theme in the Scottish novel is the imaginative evacuation from the city of the controlling consciousness, as in *Mr Alfred MA,* an utterly pessimistic novel of contemporary Scottish society, or Agnes Owen's *Gentlemen of the West,* which takes cruel delight in the miserable lives it chronicles. From George Blake to Archie Hind, Edwin Muir to Gordon Williams and Robin Jenkins, industrialization is the primary obstacle to artistic expression and the source of the continual debasement of the individual consciousness. Hind, Williams, and Muir, for example, all make revealing use of the slaughterhouse in their novels to portray the impossibility of growth in present Scottish conditions.

And yet, the form of modernity McIlvanney offers is not designed to appeal to all members of the nation. The region's special contour lines of experience, for example, are mostly male, as if to specifically rebuke Walter Scott's portrayal of Scotland as feminine. Laidlaw's journey cognitively maps a sovereign source of meaning as the industrial experience of the west-central belt, previously marginalized in Scottish literature, now constitutes the centre. Laidlaw bypasses Scotland's political subservience to the Westminster parliament by cognitively mapping the practical autonomy of Tam's birthplace. But whereas Tam's democratic republicanism resided in a sense of performative virtue, in individuals who unconsciously embodied this humanism, McIlvanney's later work shifts the emphasis to a territorial nationalism grounded in the region. This is the sense in which Cairns Craig understands Scottish regionalism:

[87] (London: Sceptre, 1996).

Regionalism was the means by which Scotland negotiated the complex relationship between its distinctive cultural past, its present incorporation into a greater whole and its possible future submersion in English culture. The value attributed to local identity developed precisely as the counterbalance to the powerful sense that Scotland was disappearing into homogeneous and 'universal' English culture.[88]

The demise of community as a sociological fact leaves Scottish difference bereft of people as a marker: with geography no longer simply people, territory and place emerge as compensatory factors.[89] Any nation or community surely derives strength and unity through diversity, and the aim of a genuinely civic republicanism is a community held together by the loyalty of independent individuals to a common purpose. The allegorical structure of *Strange Loyalties*, however, attempts to fuse many minds into a single purpose; any regional diversity outside the space produced by Laidlaw's migration becomes inherently untrustworthy, potentially hostile to the narrative of the nation. McIlvanney assumes that the terms which apply at the beginning of a historical development remain those which describe it correctly, and that any deviation from these general principles is inevitably a mark of decline. The overarching figure of Tam ensures that nationality is fated not chosen; his strictures must be obeyed, not observed; and those that fall outside the history he represents are an increasingly marginal element of the Scottish experience.

Through ritual, McIlvanney identifies continuity in a period of unprecedented change and a means of preserving consensus, stability, and community. Ritual establishes an already existing alternative form of authority, one which questions the legitimacy of existing modes. It conflates the individual with the community, without losing the definition of either, to produce an ongoing dynamic dialogue between text and context. If the city in Scottish literature has attracted little affectionate treatment, from Mitchison, Gunn, and MacDiarmid onwards (even though

[88] 'Scotland and the Regional Novel', in K. D. M. Snell (ed.), *The Regional Novel in Britain and Ireland, 1780–1990* (Cambridge: Cambridge University Press, 1998), 222.

[89] See John A. Agnew, 'The Devaluation of Place in Social Science', in id. and James S. Duncan (eds.), *The Power of Place: Bringing Together Geographical and Sociological Imaginations* (Boston: Unwin Hyman, 1989), 9–29.

most Scots are urban dwellers),[90] McIlvanney's corpus redresses that imbalance with an affectionate, detailed realism. But like all attempts at myth building, his novels are loose with the historical record. Nostalgia for a golden age of working-class solidarity prevents him from seeing any way of reproducing Tam's values in a post-industrial society. This dissolution of the industrial base, the sense that Scotland was disappearing into homogeneous and universal English culture, leads to the introduction of a nationality based on a narrowly defined regional territory. In *The Modern Scottish Novel: Narrative and the National Imagination*, Cairns Craig expands upon this theme:

The constant erasure of one Scotland by another makes Scotland un-relatable, un-narratable: past Scotlands are not gathered into the being of modern Scotland; they are abolished. Modern Scotland thus has no past, since no past Scotland can be related to the actually existing Scotland, and no narrative can be constructed to constitute its continuing identity. Unrelated and unrelatable, Scotland becomes invisible.[91]

Critics have interpreted *Docherty* as an elegy for the working class, but it is in *Strange Loyalties* that a deeper, disabling pessimism resides. Scott is dead, erased, and Laidlaw, failing to find the source of value he needs, failing to gather Scott into an actually existing Scotland, ends the novel alone, with a bottle of whisky. The state of the nation's politics produces a debilitating psychological impasse. Laidlaw identifies that value which makes Scotland different but it seems too late for it to be exhumed. Writing in 1974, Edwin Morgan identified the malaise still affecting McIlvanney's central character twenty years later:

No country which has once been independent, and is then over-shadowed in Union with a more powerful partner, can develop naturally and happily. Its political history is officially closed but emotionally it remains unfinished. Its cultural traditions soon begin to show a lack of integration . . . either by a sentimental native conservatism or by desperate attempts to imitate the modes of the dominating neighbour culture.[92]

---

[90] Ian H. Adams, *The Making of Urban Scotland* (London: Croom Helm, 1976), 9, 259–69.
[91] (Edinburgh: Edinburgh University Press, 1999), 21.
[92] 'The Beatnik in the Kailyard', in *Essays* (Manchester: Carcanet New Press Ltd, 1974), 166.

McIlvanney's republicanism is one response to the Union of Scotland with England. His much-publicized transfer of allegiance from the British Labour Party to the Scottish Nationalists is another. At the time of that switch, McIlvanney endorsed the principle of a 'mongrel' Scottish nation (a phrase later taken up with some enthusiasm by the SNP leader Alex Salmond):

The reason why I want a separate Scotland is not because of some kind of ethnic purity. Whether Irish or Pakistani or English, all those who make Scotland their home are welcome. Rather it is about the principles that run through our history . . . there has been a right-wing plague across the world, so in the face of that we have to re-trench, regroup, re-establish principles and then try and move out from there. It is important for Scotland to control its own destiny not just for Scotland but for England.[93]

If the fiction seems, in parts, curiously at odds with this honourable statement, also absent from its pluralist vision are the Highlands, the regional space of Iain Crichton Smith, a writer who has throughout a long career strenuously avoided the implications of national categories like Irish, Pakistani, or, indeed, Scottish. For Crichton Smith's imagined constituency, the global phenomenon moulding his 'special contour lines of experience', is not republicanism but colonialism. And it is to that experience I now turn.

---

[93] 'Disaffected McIlvanney Switches Allegiance from Labour for "Pragmatism" of Nationalists: Writer turns to SNP for Socialist Values', *Herald* (6 Apr. 1996), 5. McIlvanney has subsequently denied the wholesale shift to the SNP implied by this headline.

2

Being in Between: Iain Crichton Smith and Scottish Colonial History

IN MCILVANNEY'S *Remedy is None,* the incarceration of Charlie, by a Highland officer who 'spoke for all men good and true', is a mythic version of a civil conflict that peace can never end or redeem. The spatial barriers imprisoning Charlie within an exclusively Ayrshire identity are not simply empirical or derivative or mimetic; the available 'internal' epistemological space mirrors the geopolitical patterns in the 'external' world. The cultural gulf separating the Highland warder and his urban, working-class prisoner (also an image in Scott's painting 'Scotland') repeats some of the historic divisions between the Lowlands and the Highlands, the regional space of Iain Crichton Smith. For Charlie cannot, McIlvanney claims, know justice in a country still defined through predominantly rural, Celtic imagery, and so the quest in *Strange Loyalties* for 'Scott', author of 'Scotland', curtails, even terminates what Lefebvre describes as the inevitable interpenetration and superimposition of social spaces. For McIlvanney, this 'superimposition' is wholly coercive: the political integrity of his region requires the strict segregation of those spaces Scott never (in both senses of this word) represented. Like Charlie, the representative Scottish everyman in 'Scotland' is imprisoned by a series of falsified images that admit no 'authentic' sense of Scotland. McIlvanney's definition of the nation through the hard industrialized history, the 'harmonising thread', the metanarrative that offers Scotland historical continuity—this is the difference that makes the difference.

It is also, in effect, a form of partition: the Highlands are a frozen 'other' against which McIlvanney defines his regionalism.

Though Tam's decline is symptomatic of a more general movement away from value, no single cataclysmic event ruptures
McIlvanney's community. Tam's republicanism is frayed but
never broken by the war, industrial decay, and the rise of an
acquisitive individualism. For Iain Crichton Smith, however, the
'brokenness' of history is always already assumed, traceable to a
series of catastrophic social events and to any representation,
like Scott's 'Scotland', that fixes the individual within a stable,
unchanging identity: 'Behind the haze of falsity imposed on the
islands, both by outsiders and naive exiles, lies the brokenness
which will not allow writers the confidence that others can have,
who when they write do not feel their subject matter disappearing before their eyes.'[1] Scott's allegory 'Scotland', in this reading,
effects what Crichton Smith terms 'an invisible Culloden of the
spirit';[2] it consigns the Highlands to history as an emblem of a
past that change can never affect. The prominence Crichton
Smith accords the category of the individual in his writing, as
the philosophical basis for an aesthetic that evades any supra-
empirical, territorial reality like the allegory 'Scotland', is linked
to this sense of 'brokenness', or to use Brendan Bradshaw's
phrase, this 'catastrophic dimension': the loss of a language,
famine, the Clearances, migration. Throughout Crichton Smith's
work, the aesthetic provides relief from the kind of national
identity pursued through McIlvanney's communalism. But
the aesthetic is also, of course, the realm through which the
Highlander was configured as an exotic Celtic stereotype. As
Christopher Harvie notes, Walter Scott made the Highland
predicament a metaphor for Scotland as a whole,[3] a fact which
partly explains Crichton Smith's ambivalence towards Scotland
as a nation: 'I had no feeling for Scotland at all . . . I did not feel
myself as belonging to Scotland.'[4]

The principal themes in Crichton Smith's novels—history,
geography, representation, city and country—are very similar to

[1] 'Real People in a Real Place', in *Towards the Human: Selected Essays* (Edinburgh: Macdonald, 1986), 35.
[2] Ibid. 35.
[3] Quoted in Charles J. Withers, 'The Manufacture of Scottish History', in Ian
Donnachie and Christopher Whatley (eds.), *The Manufacture of Scottish History*
(Edinburgh: Polygon, 1992), 143–56, at 153.
[4] *Towards the Human*, 80.

those in McIlvanney.[5] But in avoiding the fabrication involved in the very notion of identity, the belief that the individual somehow represents a self and a discrete, ostensibly 'different' history, Crichton Smith engages with the thematics of post-colonial theory: what Edward Said calls the questionable insistence that 'there are geographical spaces with indigenous, radically "different" inhabitants who can be defined on the basis of some religion, culture, or racial essence proper to that geographical space'.[6] Coupled with this, however, is John Agnew's observation that 'political expression in Scotland is intrinsically geographical . . . the product of political behaviour structured by the historically constituted social contexts in which people live their lives: in a word "places" '.[7] Entering the space of the would-be Scottish nation state, then—the public sphere that is principal basis for entry into citizenship and modernity in the global world—actually seems to require the individual to accept being inscribed within a fixed regional space.[8]

In 'Real People in a Real Place', a long, occasionally shrill essay that begins a collection entitled *Towards the Human* (both titles allude to the separate but related concerns of Said and Agnew), Crichton Smith addresses these connected cultural and political layers. From Dunbar through MacPherson and *Ossian* to Walter Scott he criticizes a literary heritage which, he claims, has consistently represented the Highlanders as radically different inhabitants of a defined geographical space.[9] *Consider the*

---

[5] Carol Gow, 'An Interview with Iain Crichton Smith', *Scottish Literary Journal*, 17/2 (Nov. 1990), 56: 'I think there are themes in the novels maybe they haven't been realised yet, but I think the trouble is that though the themes are there, that I'm not really a born novelist in the sense that I think I'm probably a born poet.' Crichton Smith's novels have received very little attention.

[6] *Orientalism* (1978; Harmondsworth: Penguin, 1985), 5.

[7] See the ch. 'Place and Scottish Politics: Aggregate Political Behaviour', in *Place and Politics: The Geographical Mediation of State and Society* (Boston: Allen & Unwin, 1987), 7.

[8] An early collection with Michael Longley and Barry Tebb entitled *Three Regional Voices* (London: Poet and Printer, 1968) carried this caveat on the imprints page: 'Three Regional poets is a title foisted upon the poets and is not meant to qualify the poetry eternally.'

[9] 'It is easy to assign the islander to this misty, rather beautiful world, and leave him there if one first of all succeeds in making that world unreal, and its inhabitants unreal, off the edge of things, a noble savage with his stories and unmaterialistic concerns . . . to dismiss the highlander as being inferior is to make the same mistake as Hitler did: that is, not to see the Highlander as human and real but as a stereotype,

Lilies is one of only two novels to deal explicitly with Highland history, but all his novels engage with the kitsch lumber of this literary tradition. Throughout his novels, Crichton Smith utilizes Kierkegaard's concept of individuality as a reaction against the coercive impact of representation and difference, geography and Calvinism. In 'Real People in a Real Place', he also invokes Daniel Corkery's blast in *Synge and Anglo-Irish Literature* against the effects of an Anglo-Irish education on a native Irish child. Corkery claimed that: 'His education teaches him not to see the surroundings as they are in themselves, but as compared with alien surroundings: his education provides him with an alien medium through which he is henceforth to look at his native land.'[10] Insisting that 'normal and national are synonymous in literary criticism', Corkery's 'monocular vision', in Seamus Heaney's phrase, has been called 'the Irish version of the Dark Ages',[11] a dreary demand for literary orthodoxy. But shorn of its puritanism, and applied to 'a community that has always been broken by history',[12] for Crichton Smith, Corkery's polemic is a plea for a literature that would rescue the mute and humiliated voices of his fellow countrymen from the enormous condescension of an Anglo-Irish literary heritage that had, Corkery argued, consistently portrayed them as 'the freakish, the fanciful, the perverse'.[13]

Corkery insisted that 'interpreters of the nation need to share in the people's emotional background . . . they need to become possessed of a culture based on that emotional subconscious'.[14] The 'emotional subconscious' in Crichton Smith's novels is marked not by republicanism but by a colonial history that has, he claims, robbed the Highlander of any individuality as a real person in a real place. This concept of individuality is a key notion throughout his work, and through it, the apparent contradictions involved in his endorsement of Corkery's

a comic target and not an individual with his own feelings' (Crichton Smith, 'Real People', 32).

[10] (1931; Dublin: Mercier Press, 1966), 15.
[11] Luke Gibbon, 'Introduction', in Seamus Deane (gen. ed.), *The Field Day Anthology of Irish Writing* (Derry: Field Day, 1991), iii. 567.
[12] Crichton Smith, 'Real People', 26.
[13] *Synge and Anglo-Irish Literature*, 18.
[14] Ibid. 16.

nationalism, and disavowal of a single entity called Scotland, become comprehensible. For Corkery's thesis demands an idea of community which is comprehensively not inscribed in Kierkegaardian individualism, and Crichton Smith's commitment to Kierkegaard's notion of the radical individual finally develops into a challenge to it as a negation of true individuality, an individuality located within a community rather than aside from it. But though this might initially seem to share some affinities with McIlvanney's urban republicanism, Crichton Smith's version of cultural recognition does not involve a rational, linear narrative—the harmonizing thread in McIlvanney's republicanism, in which the private individual knows itself through participation in a public history and community. Instead, the 'brokenness' of a colonial history means that the political boundaries between private and public, subject and object, the self and other, must be reconfigured.

The language of post-colonial theory is slowly entering Scottish culture.[15] With Crichton Smith, a major Scottish writer whose novels have been conspicuously ignored, that theory complicates McIlvanney's republican aspirations for the Scottish nation. The novels also complicate some of the assumptions of post-colonial theory. Crichton Smith's individualism is not easily translatable into the familiar categories of liberal self-determination, nationalist anti-colonial and anti-imperial movements, or communitarianism. But before addressing the novels, I want to establish some of the 'emotional subconscious' of his region, some of the special contour lines of the Highlander's colonial experience.

II   REPRESENTING THE HIGHLANDER

The literary representation of the Highlander as barbarian, often thought to commence in the eighteenth century, is traceable to the late Middle Ages. In 'Dance of the Seven Deadly Synnis', for example, William Dunbar presents Highlanders as so beyond the

---

[15] See Berthold Schoene, 'A Passage to Scotland: Scottish Literature and the Postcolonial British Condition', *Scotlands*, 2/1 (1995), 107–21; Michael Gardner, 'Democracy and Scottish Postcoloniality', *Scotlands*, 3/2 (1996), 41.

pale of human civilization that even the Devil himself is forced to banish them from the Highland games that are taking place in Hell:

> Full lowd in Ersche [Irish] begowth to clatter
> And lyk revin and ruke:
> That Devil sa devit wes with thair yell,
> That in the depestpot of hell
> He smorit thame with smoke.[16]

In Sir Richard Holland's 'Book of The Howlat', a Highland bard is identified as Irish, foreign, and unintelligible: 'A bard out of Ireland, with "Banachadee", I said: "Gluntow guk dynydrach, hala mischy doch" '.[17] In Holland's 1697 poem the Highlander is irreligious and dishonest—'Nought like religion they retain I Of moral Honestie they're clean'—and physically repugnant because of dress and habits—'For when they sit their plaids do hang by, I Ye'l see from Navels down each thing fy'.

The immediate political and economic consequences of the 1707 Union of England and Scotland, supported by a minority of the Scottish people, did little to change this. The Scottish privy council, the main agent of crown government for the previous century, was abolished without any arrangement made for Scottish representation in cabinet to replace it. Edinburgh lost both the pomp and ceremony of a parliamentary presence and an effective agency with which to secure the loyalty of individual clan chiefs. Political identity and control suffered. The abolition of the Highland Companies in 1717 meant that Westminster lacked any military and political means of imposing order, and the Highlands were as free from governmental control as they had been for over two centuries.

Economically the benefits of Union were felt by few Scots. The extension of new duties to linen, salt, and malt (the last causing a riot in Glasgow in 1715) helped focus the grievances of Scots on a union which seemed incapable of delivering what it had promised. Worse, it seemed an active agent of economic decline and decay. It is against this background of economic and political uncertainty after the Union that the creation of a Highland

---

[16] *The Poems of William Dunbar*, ed. W. Mackay Mackenzie (London: Faber and Faber, 1970), 123.

[17] Tom Scott (ed.), *The Penguin Book of Scottish Verse* (Harmondsworth: Penguin, 1970), 80.

Jacobite mythology should be seen.[18] As Scottish identity and economic well-being became marginalized and dominated by English concerns in contemporary politics, the myth of the Stuarts became bound up with the idea of Scotland as a unified nation whose essential soul was Celtic. A culture of consolation developed, seeking from the past images of an independent Scottish society organically whole, politically free, and culturally self-confident. Post-Union Scottish society, in other words, sought in the Highlands a compensatory narrative, an explanation or replacement for the palpable sense of loss in cultural identity and political control.

The clans, once thought depraved and foul, now became brave and loyal. Stuart pedigree as devout opponents of the Union and preservers of Scotland's past was unquestioned, in part because Jacobite political culture assiduously cultivated this image. But because their rule was associated with a time when Scotland was free, this past was scrutinized for evidence that Scotland did exist outside the confines of Union. The Highlands, the traditional Stuart hinterland, thus became the region that would redeem the nation.

> Let our brave loyal clans, then,
> Their ancient Stuart race
> Restore with sword in hand, then,
> And all their foes displace.
> All unions we'll o'erturn boys,
> Which caus'd our nation mourn, boys,
> Like Bruce at Bannockburn, boys
> The English home we'll chase.[19]

The Highlander became a paradigm of the noble and free Scot. Nourished by a history of anti-English nationalist struggle, his Celtic vitality made him immune to the treachery of Union, capable of revivifying the Scottish spirit. The passage from Anglicized commercialism to a Highland Celtic Eden was celebrated as a transition from sickness to health, from flaccid pallor to a healthy virility.

---

[18] David Daiches, *The Paradox of Scottish Culture* (London: McMaster University Press, 1964), 13–14.
[19] James Hogg, *The Jacobite Relics of Scotland*, 2 vols. (Edinburgh, 1819–21), i. 55, 100.

No Butter-Box he see'd to be,
    no English-Fop, nor Lowland Laddie,
But by his mein he was well known,
    to be some Gentle Highland Laddie.

O my bonny, bonny Highland Laddie,
    O my bonny, bonny Highland Laddie,
When I am sick and like to dye,
    Thou'lt row me in thy Highland Pladie.

His Quiver hang down by his Thigh,
    his Mein did show his bow was ready,
A thousand Darts flew from his Eye,
    and all fell down before his Lady.[20]

The consummation of lovers here symbolizes a wider political and cultural marriage, one which purifies the Scottish body politic of its unhealthy divisions and restores a lost organic wholeness, as 'the Highlander' becomes an explicitly symbolic force. As William Donaldson puts it, 'The crucial bonding of Highlandry with Jacobitism and love by contemporary song-writers made this available to the creators of national myth and symbol.'[21] The Highlander's potency as a symbol increased with each rebellion, enabling eighteenth-century nationalists to claim that the '15 and the '45 represented an ineradicable Scottish nationality that could never be assimilated into a British state. Both, however, looked to the Highlands as part of that past, and they thus became representative of what the past had produced.

The cultural consequences of the '45 rebellion were at least as important as its causes.[22] The schemes shelved or never fully implemented after the '15 were now imposed with a vengeance. Jacobite estates were forfeited to the crown and bagpipes and kilts were banned as potentially seditious symbols of rebel affection. The aim was 'the forcible incorporation of the Highlands into the social and political system of Great Britain'.[23] Culloden, like the flight of the earls in Ireland in 1603, was a genuine cul-

---

[20] *The Jacobite Song* (Aberdeen: Aberdeen University Press, 1988), 56.

[21] Ibid. 65.

[22] See the chs. 'The Jacobite Challenge' and 'The Disintegration of Clanship', in T. M. Devine, *The Scottish Nation: 1700–2000* (Harmondsworth: Allen Lane, 2000), 31–48 and 170–95.

[23] James Hunter, *The Making of the Crofting Community* (Edinburgh: Edinburgh University Press, 1976), 9.

tural and political landmark. It marked a sustained and massive assault by the British government on the clans as social and political institutions.[24] But this very persecution ensured that Culloden and the Highlander became synonymous. By identifying him as an enemy, the British state also raised the Highlander as the ultimate icon of Scottish patriotism, and, with one further ironic twist, it was this iconic status that Unionist writers and politicians used in the nineteenth century to propagandize in favour of the British link.

To nineteenth-century Unionists like Scott the Highlanders were the dying spasms of a culture history had passed over. Like Scott, MacPherson presented an image of the Highlands safely distanced in antiquity, a history without contemporary political reference. Whether *Ossian* was fake or genuine, MacPherson's 'attempt to create a Gaelic epic was one that drew heavily on existing poetic traditions, of which he made genuine if idiosyncratic use'.[25] His phenomenal popularity—readers included Napoleon and Goethe—brought Scotland, or the Highlands as Scotland, before a pan-European public eye. The dominant tone of the poems is elegiac, the dominant theme loss. Home, country, fame, fortune, and ultimately life are lost against the imposing grandeur of the Highland landscape. The Highlands were sterile terrain incapable of supporting communal life, a rationale not unlike that of the Clearances. Readers responded to 'the vision of a strange remote, exotic ancient world, peopled by grandly heroic characters who move with a kind of stately dignity across wild and barren landscapes of mountains, crags, rivers, seas, clouds and mists'.[26]

In *Ossian*, Highland life is misty, British, and short. The primitive idiom offered an exhilarating contrast to the sophisticated social poetry of the Augustans and their successors. For Tory Romantics it was ideal stuff to convert into pro-Union heroism: 'The poems appeared not in the barbarous language of Gaelic, but in a decorous "translatorese" which harmonised beautifully

---

[24] Ibid. 12.
[25] Murray Pittock, *The Invention of Scotland: The Stuart Myth and Scottish Identity: 1638 to the Present* (London: Routledge, 1991), 73.
[26] Andrew Hook, 'Scotland and Romanticism: The International Scene', in id. (ed.), *The History of Scottish Literature*, ii. *1660–1800* (gen. ed., Cairns Craig) (Aberdeen: Aberdeen University Press, 1987), 311.

with eighteenth-century standards of propriety.'[27] MacPherson provided an immensely convincing and influential typology of the Celt, one which obviously influenced Matthew Arnold's passage on *Ossian*. Often quoted, it is still worth recalling because it represents a strain of criticism which relegated authenticity to a secondary issue.

Make the part of what is forged, modern, tawdry, spurious, in the book, as you will please . . . But there will still be left in the book a residue . . . of the Celtic genius . . . which has the proud distinction of having brought this soul of the Celtic genius into contact with the genius of the nations of modern Europe.[28]

The implications of MacPherson's *Ossian* have been neatly summarized: 'At the height of the Scottish Enlightenment, Scotland was presented as an anti-Enlightenment culture, to the delight of all Europe.'[29] MacPherson's mythopoetic vision of Scotland was related in the voice of the eighteenth-century Highlander and so the two were inevitably conflated. The destruction of the clan's community had the same aura of inevitability as MacPherson's heroes, and the same contemporary political impact.

Scott shared MacPherson's desire to present a typology of the Highlander that was conservative and safely packaged in antiquity. He brilliantly juggled his twin aims of binding Scotland to a Union with England whose advantages he thought obvious, and of creating a common cultural possession for all Scots based on a romantic rendering of Highland history. In part, his novels present an anachronistic Highland world, an obstacle to the inevitable and welcome progress of the age: the polarities are a regressive romantic flirtation with the Highlanders and Jacobitism and a rational calculation of the benefits Union will bring. In *Waverley* Edward's rejection of Jacobite ideology is welcomed as a sign of adult maturity and realism: 'The romance of his life was ended, and that its real history had now commenced'. Scott, as author, editor, and narrator, relates through a perfectly neutral and assured omniscient voice a world he interprets in perfectly neutral and assured footnotes. Scott pur-

---

[27] Robert Crawford, *Devolving English Literature* (Oxford: Clarendon Press, 1992), 35.
[28] *On the Study of Celtic Literature* (London: Smith, Elder, 1867), 116.
[29] Pittock, *Invention of Scotland*, 73.

posefully collapses the distinction between fictional narrative and historical record to impress upon the reader his novel's fidelity to fact. It is not fiction based on history but history imaginatively reconstructed from contemporaneous evidence:

for the purpose of preserving some idea of the ancient manners of which *I have witnessed* the almost total extinction, I have embodied in imaginary scenes, and ascribed to fictitious characters, a part of the incidents *which I then received from those who were actors in them*. Indeed, *the most romantic parts of this narrative are precisely those which have a foundation in fact* [emphasis added].

He is at pains to persuade his reader of the authenticity of his account: 'It has been my object to describe these persons, not by caricature and exaggerated use of the national dialect, but by their habits, manners and feelings.'[30] Having demanded the right to be taken as a trustworthy, informed witness to Scottish history, Scott then emphasizes racial and linguistic divisions, the presence of a fractious past, and the absence of a coherent Scottish future.

Scott's most successful fiction was the immutable racial differences between Highlander and Lowlander. To insist that Scotland's internal strife is racial and absolute rather than political and contingent, the Highlander could only exist for Scott at the level of the symbolic. Colonel David Stewart, a close friend of Scott and with him one of the founders of the Edinburgh Celtic Society, in his 1822 *Sketches of the Character, Manners and Present State of the Highlanders of Scotland,* confirmed Scott's fictional portrayal with a rough mixture of philology and anthropology: '[the Highlander] in many respects, exhibits striking marks of an original and unmixed race . . . their blood uncontaminated by a mixture with strangers'.[31] There is an obsessive concern with the fate and sociological status of the Gaelic language, a theme repeated in all Crichton Smith's work:

The Gaelic bears in its construction the most incontestable proof that it is a primitive language, being for the most part monosyllabic, and, with few exceptions, having no word to express abstract ideas, or such terms of art as are unknown to a primitive people.[32]

---

[30] *Waverley* (1814; Harmondsworth: Penguin, 1985), 493.
[31] (Edinburgh, 1822), i. 12–21.
[32] Ibid. 10.

Scott's political activities paralleled his fiction. An active member of the Celtic Society, an association of lords and lawyers founded in Edinburgh in 1820, he encouraged the wearing of the kilt as a way of restoring the clans to their former glory. Scott organized the tartan pageantry that greeted King George IV during his visit to Edinburgh in 1822, an event that helped transfer vestigial Jacobite loyalties to the Hanoverian administration and assured the king that Scotland was loyal. It also helped create a caricature of Gaelic culture. As a region with pressing political problems that required urgent attention, the Highlands never entered Scott's scheme. He aimed to provide a Scottish identity happily reconciled to membership of the British state, and the price he was willing to pay was to deny the Highlands membership of contemporary Scotland.

Before the Clearances, land was leased to tenants from the clan chief through a tacksman, a middleman who retained a portion of the rent for his services. Dr Johnson described the tacksman's position as 'long considered as hereditary, and the occupant was distinguished by the name of the place at which he resided. He held a middle station, by which the highest and lowest orders were connected.'[33] The pivotal position of the tacksman at the heart of the social framework was taken by estate factors. And it was these men, responsible for implementing the landlord's policy of clearances, who bore the brunt of Highland bitterness. Patrick Sellar, the factor responsible for the Clearances on the Sutherland estate, has emerged as the ogre in this story. Condemned in Highland folk memory by Iain Crichton Smith (in *Consider the Lilies*), amongst others, his views were plain and brutal: the Highlanders possessed

No principle of truth and candour . . . Their obstinate adherence to the barbarous jargon of the times when Europe was possessed by savages . . . places them, with relation to the enlightened nations of Europe in a position not very different from that betwixt the American Colonists and the Aborigines of that Country.[34]

[33] Samuel Johnson and James Boswell, *A Journey to the Western Islands of Scotland and the Journal of a Tour to the Hebrides* (1772; Harmondsworth: Penguin, 1984), 95.
[34] Quoted in Eric Richards, *A History of the Highland Clearances*, ii. *Emigration Protest Reasons* (London: Croom Helm, 1985), 399.

In one sense, the logic behind the Clearances is unassailable. Sellar applied the dogma of laissez-faire capitalism and Malthusian population control with clarity and vigour. Why, he asked, should the Highlands be treated any differently to the rest of Britain? If depopulation and the monoculture of sheep farming resulted from the application of classical political economy, then this was unavoidable and supportable through reference to contemporary classical political economy. Scott and the Tory Unionists differed very little from this view. Warning the landlords of the consequences of continuing the Clearances, Scott inadvertently reveals his limited political vision for the region: 'the Highlands may become the fairy ground for romance and poetry, or the subject of experiment for the professors of speculation, political and economic'.[35] In other words they could conform to the paradigm of tartan pageantry or become a set of agricultural statistics. The choice extended to other parts of Scotland or Britain was never on offer.

By 1841 83 per cent of the entire Scottish population lived in the eastern and western Lowlands. Emigration figures are notoriously difficult to quantify accurately—some figures claim a tenth of the population had left the Highlands before 1775 and a further 20 per cent during the years to 1850[36]—but its impact on Highland society is unquestioned. Those who did not emigrate usually became crofters: small tenants who farmed their land with or without a lease, paying rent directly to their proprietor, and surviving mainly from the cultivation of their holding.

The Clearances, the catastrophic dimension to Scottish history, inscribed a number of themes at the heart of the Highland experience. The replacement of people by sheep on farms resulted in a massive displacement of population and reflected and hardened the dichotomy that existed between the commercialized Lowland mores of the landowners and the traditional Highland concept of *duthchas*, the view that land was held

---

[35] Quoted in G. M. Young, 'Scott and the Historians', *Sir Walter Scott Lectures, 1940–1948* (Edinburgh: Edinburgh University Press, 1946), 107.
[36] See Richards, *History of the Highland Clearances*, ii. 194.; S. G. E. Lythe and J. Butt, *An Economic History of Scotland, 1100–1939* (Glasgow: John Donaldson, 1975), 91–5; R. A. Houston, 'The Demographic Regime', in T. M. Devine and R. Mitchinson (eds.), *People and Society in Scotland 1760–1830* (Edinburgh: Edinburgh University Press, 1988).

in heritable trusteeship. The landlords, having absorbed the commercial ethos of British society, regarded land as any other asset, a commodity ultimately realizable for profit. Highland society divided along new lines: 'the sheep farmers and estate factors indeed became a separate caste, isolated from the population at large with virtually no social and economic connection'.[37] Contemporaries commented on the stark social lineaments that now prevailed: 'There are only two ranks of people— a higher rank and a lower rank . . . The proverbial enmity of rich and poor in all societies has received peculiar development in this simple social structure of the Highlands.'[38]

Dr Johnson described the Highlands in his 1773 tour as 'crushed by the heavy hand of a vindictive conqueror'.[39] He chronicled a culture that was rapidly becoming a relic of the past and delivered the region's obituary, in a narrative that is testimony to the clinical efficiency of the post-Culloden government measures:

There was perhaps never any change of national manners so quick, so great, and so general, as that which operated in the Highlands . . . We came hither too late to see what we expected, a people of peculiar experience, and a system of antiquated life. The clans retain little of their original character . . . their dignity of independence is depressed, their contempt of government subdued, and their reverence for their chiefs abated. Of what they had before the late conquest of their country, there remain only their language and their poverty. Their language is attacked on every side. Schools are erected in which English is only taught[40]

The Clearances, it has been claimed, were made possible partly because the Highlands occupied the kitsch lumber-room of Scottish history: 'this recreation of the rural wilderness of the mythical noble savage cost the livelihoods and houses of most of the real inhabitants of the country'.[41] The crofters' wars, however, between 1882 and 1888, saw the Highlands re-enter contemporary Scottish politics and the Scottish national conscious-

---

[37] Richards, *History of the Highland Clearances*, ii. 352.
[38] Quoted in James Hunter, 'The Emergence of the Crofting Community: The Religious Contribution, 1789–1843', *Scottish Studies*, 18 (1974), 110.
[39] Johnson and Boswell, *Journey to the Western Islands of Scotland*, 97.
[40] Ibid. 73.
[41] Pittock, *Invention of Scotland*, 108.

ness. Responding to renewed agitation of the Irish Land League in 1881, the government set up the Napier commission to inquire into the crofters' condition. Instead of dampening agitation it succeeded only in inflaming it. In 1884, the Highland Land Law Reform Association was established, and in 1886, four MPs who threatened to vote with the Fenians were elected on its ticket. The *Highlander* was founded by John Murdoch, a disciple of Fintan Lalor and a frequent contributor to the *Nation*. A self-conscious and self-referential political community had evolved which quickly became a locus for wider nationalist aspirations.

The victory won at the Napier commission seemed to involve one essential element of generic nationalist struggles: the moral right to ownership of the land by the peasantry was asserted. Intellectuals such as J. S. Blackie, holder of the first chair of Celtic studies at Edinburgh University and a leading member of the Scottish Home Rule Association, saw the crofters as the potential engine of independence. Restoring Scotland's independent past glory did not now mean, *pace* Scott, entering into one long narrative of loss and defeat.

The Home Rule movement attempted to construct a narrative which linked the struggle at Culloden to the crofters. Both were, in this rendering, essentially nationalist events, predicated upon centuries of Scottish history. A revitalized Highlands would reinvigorate Scotland and her latent Celtic identity. This enthusiasm for a Celtic inflection in part reflected the late nineteenth-century Arnoldian distaste for middle-class philistinism. But as in Ireland, its political coloration quickly became nationalist. The preface to Blackie's *The Language and Literature of the Scottish Highlands* unconsciously reveals how nationalists now looked to the Highlands as the pure preserve of Scottishness:

This book is an humble attempt to break down the middle wall of partition which I have found to exist fencing off the most cultivated minds *in England and in the Lowlands of Scotland* from the intellectual life and moral aspirations of the *Scottish* Highlanders. This partition . . . has rudely torn away *one remote limb of the empire* from the sympathy of the rest.[42]

The Highland's status, then, was still primarily as an obvious emblem of the nation. 'The region', as Charles Withers puts it,

---

[42] (Edinburgh: Edmonston & Douglas, 1876), p. ix; emphasis added.

'has national associations precisely because it has been made in the minds of outsiders and because the historiographical creation of how we have *believed* the Highlands to be has been both more enduring and more fascinating (and enduring because it has been fascinating) than our knowledge of changes in Highland life and economy.'[43] That history feeds obliquely into all Crichton Smith's work. The aesthetic realm offers imaginative relief from the deadening impulses of Calvinism; but to escape from this 'real' world through the aesthetic is to enter the fascinatingly 'unreal' realm which produced Scott's Highlander and McIlvanney's allegory 'Scotland'. The work of art asserts difference, but a difference that has made, and continues to make, the difference between the Highlander and the 'real' world of social history. But submitting wholly to that social history denies the aesthetic the opportunity to remove the individual from the world of Mrs Scott in Crichton Smith's best-known novel, *Consider the Lilies*.

III   FROM 'SCOTT' TO 'MRS SCOTT'

I have made the choice. I have forsaken the community in order to individualise myself.[44]

The preface to *Consider the Lilies*, Iain Crichton Smith's famous novel of the Clearances, claims that 'this is not an historical novel . . . it is a fictional study of one person, an old woman who is being evicted'. The 'old woman', however, is a recurring image throughout his early poetry of a personality frozen by the numbing orthodoxies of doctrinaire Calvinism. In the poem 'Old Woman', for example, ageing is an immutable existential element of the communal inheritance, the double-edged emphasis on 'being' conveying the permanence of her psychological stasis: 'And she, being old, fed from a mashed plate | as an old mare might droop across a fence | to the dull pastures of its ignorance'.[45]

---

[43] *Gaelic Scotland: The Transformation of a Culture Region* (London: Routledge, 1988), 155.

[44] Crichton Smith, 'Real People', 12.

[45] From *Thistle and Roses* (London: Eyre & Spottiswoode, 1961).

'Mrs Scott', as her name suggests, has a wider cultural reso-nance than the merely personal. Like McIlvanney's Scott, she incorporates, even exemplifies, a certain aesthetic and ethical regional way of being. To apply Seamus Heaney's evocative phrase, she is an 'indigenous territorial numen':[46] a matriarchal figure who consciously or unconsciously embodies deeply ingrained cultural lineages. For one critic, she 'represents the power of the Calvinist background, the suppression of indi-viduality, of joy, of art'.[47] I want to return to this theme of 'individuality', but part of the aim of *Consider the Lilies* is to retrieve Mrs Scott's experience, as an individual, from the enormous condescension of history. Because she is constitution-ally incapable of comprehending her experience as anything but personal, divorced from any dialectic with the social, the novel invests specific incidents with a significance of which she remains ignorant, thereby excavating a hitherto buried historical narra-tive. When Patrick Sellar, the infamous administrator charged with responsibility for the Clearances, visits her on a white horse, this encounter with economics and power is apprehended through vaguely theological imagery: 'At first she couldn't see him very well, for her sight was beginning to fail a little. All she could tell was that there was a white horse with a man riding on it' (*CTL*, 1). But beyond the myopia Mrs Scott's Calvinist blinkers induce, the horse (often used in Crichton Smith's poetry as an image of instinct and grace) remains at ease, a symbol of the domain beyond the reductive vision of Mrs Scott and Patrick Sellar: 'The horse, however, *relieved of its burden*, was very quiet and began calmly to chew grass though now and then it would toss its head in the air' (*CTL*, 2; emphasis added).[48] The novel is full of such poetic images, with sight a recurring motif through-out. Mrs Scott has for so long averted her gaze from the external that she is now incapable of entering into it: 'Emerging into the day was like entering a hurtful world where the light hurt her eyes' (*CTL*, 16). Like the image of the unburdened horse, light

---

[46] *Preoccupations* (London: Faber and Faber, 1980), 57.

[47] Carol Gow, *The Mirror and the Marble: The Poetry of Iain Crichton Smith* (Edinburgh: Saltire Society, 1992), 31.

[48] Crichton Smith has previously used animals as a symbol of an instinctual, spon-taneous grace that his poetry should try to capture and emulate. See *Deer on the High Hill* (Edinburgh: Giles Gordon, 1962): 'You must build from the rain and stones | till you can make | a stylish deer on the high hills, | and let its leaps be unpredictable.'

here conveys an alternative emotional regime, one open to flux, time, and the chaos of chance. This daylight is secular and generated by human behaviour, the act of participating in the social. But because light is so often used in religious rhetoric, both in sacred texts and here in the novel, its deployment here shows how the spiritual can be customized to incorporate a truth of a fundamentally different order. The quotidian world, in other words, is not completely devoid of its own auratic potential, and a continuous traffic between both realms remains possible. Mrs Scott, however, remains trapped in a temporal realm incapable of shifting from its ancient rhythm: 'She cleaned the grandfather clock and was interrupted once by a terrific boom which seemed to shake its old body to the bones' (*CTL*, 19).

Donald MacLeod, Mrs Scott's cheerfully dissenting agnostic neighbour, a man committed to the idea of civic participation in his community, seems to combine a secular ethic with the political energy endorsed in *Towards the Human*. And at first, the contrast between him and the community is crudely obvious. When McKay, a physically disabled Elder, totally submissive to the Church, passes MacLeod, the agnostic, busy building a wall around his house, the deference demanded by Calvinism contrasts with the participative energy of the freethinker. And of course, Mrs Scott distrusts MacLeod because of his casual dismissal of biblical rules she absorbs as directly analogous to her own life; her Manichaean division of damned and elect cannot concede the possibility of indeterminacy, of betweenness: 'A man who doesn't go to church is an evil man. There's no getting around it . . . A man who didn't go to church wasn't a respectable man, no matter what way you looked at it . . . *You can't serve two masters*' (*CTL*, 43; emphasis added). And yet, MacLeod is no feckless, godless cosmopolitan: ' "Perhaps God is a little boy like me", he thought, continuing with his work' (*CTL*, 37). There is an innerness to MacLeod that values contingency over absolutism, an uncertain, inquisitive attitude to the spiritual over any literal, textual creed; intellectual reflection and physical effort can, he shows, coexist within the community. But *Consider the Lilies* is no mere endorsement of MacLeod and condemnation of Calvinism. It incorporates the possibility of regeneration by pointing beyond the narrative it here recounts.

After Sellar's visit, as Mrs Scott travels to her minister seeking assurance that the Clearances will not happen, she passes a putrefying sheep carcass that seems to contain a 'mute appeal' (*CTL*, 70). But Mrs Scott can offer no ethical response to the decay within her community, the 'brokenness' this mute appeal signifies, because of the premature dismissal of any aesthetic response to the external world: 'you couldn't eat flowers: and as for beauty what was that?' (*CTL*, 71). The void created by this dismissal of the aesthetic is filled by a black crow, an image of a parasitic Calvinism and here the antithesis of what is good and beautiful. Feeding on the remains of the sheep, hovering 'as if it had staked a claim to the place' (*CTL*, 71), the crow that consumes beauty symbolizes the indifference to the aesthetic that corrodes Mrs Scott, both as individual and territorial numen. The journey back towards a fully human realm is, then, fraught with danger. Mrs Scott falls from a bridge returning from a meeting with her minister, after she has been symbolically blinded by the false light of his theological support for the economic logic of the Clearances. But this fall, one small symbol of the region's catastrophic history, is deliberately presented as a rebirth. The journey Mrs Scott finally makes, when she has moved beyond Calvinist dogma and become at least aware of the potential beauty of the world, is towards the human, towards an appreciation of the social world and her place in it.

Crichton Smith is present in all his novels as both author and barely disguised character. As Douglas Gifford puts it, his fiction 'places his own situation into a context where he is only one of countless to suffer repression'.[49] Thus when Iain, Mrs Scott's son in *Consider the Lilies*, emigrates, this physical distance is not just empirical or derivative or mimetic: it enacts in the 'external' world Crichton Smith's imaginative disengagement from her intractable Calvinist orthodoxies, allegorically insisting on an epistemological space in the present separated from all she represents. The trajectory is exactly the opposite of Laidlaw's feverish search for 'Scott', his migration within Scotland in search of the already existing allegory 'Scotland'. But Iain, like Laidlaw with 'Scott', retains an ethnic link with the indigenous territorial

---

[49] 'Bleeding From All That's Best: The Fiction of Iain Crichton Smith', in Gavin Wallace and Randall Stevenson (eds.), *The Scottish Novel since the Seventies* (Edinburgh: Edinburgh University Press, 1993), 38.

numen called 'Mrs Scott', so that she is both an internal moral presence and an external geographical space indelibly marked by Calvinism. In this sense, 'Mrs Scott' is mobile and plastic, a fixed historical referent that continually intrudes, ethically and aesthetically, into 'Iain's' present world. This is one way to interpret the title. The Lily, the funereal flower, is an ironic symbol of purity and also of death. Mrs Scott's fierce ideological purity, her monocular belief that you can't serve two masters, is linked with decay, the redundancy of the aesthetic as a living force in her life and, potentially, in Crichton Smith's. As Iain leaves, she offers her father's gold watch: ' "Take it with you," she said. "It will keep good time for you" ' (*CTL*, 81). The present time of the artist Iain Crichton Smith is, through the allegory of Mrs Scott, continually shadowed by this powerful historical perspective, even as the emigration of her son, Iain, represents the desire to move beyond the idea that an individual can be defined on the basis of some religion, culture, or racial essence proper to a geographical space. Or as Mrs Scott puts it: 'Either you were like that or you weren't. If you weren't there was no way of becoming like that even if you wanted to' (*CTL*, 57).[50]

What MacLeod introduces is an awareness that propriety and morality are not necessarily congruent with the way things are. The most precious sight denied Mrs Scott by her Calvinist blinkers is self-recognition as an individual, a vista essential for the artist. By ignoring Mrs Scott's strict dichotomies, MacLeod touches on aspects of her past she never voiced. Playing at soldiers with his son, his words allude to the departure of her husband to fight for the Duke: 'There are no women soldiers. And that's something. It's the women who tidy things up, isn't it?' (*CTL*, 94). MacLeod discards biblical symbolism and places Sellar firmly in history to view the Clearances as a calculated economic exercise. Asked 'has the man on the white horse come to see you too?', his reply—'Patrick Sellar you mean?' (*CTL*, 97)—strips Sellar of any protective theological associations. MacLeod confronts the past as a text to be decoded, wanting to erase 'not simply those who were bent on destroying the Highlands, not simply . . . the Patrick Sellar, but . . . those

---

[50] This strikes the same paralysing note seen in the poem 'Old Woman' from *Thistle and Roses*.

interior Patrick Sellars with the faces of old highlanders who evicted emotion and burnt down love' (*CTL,* 102). MacLeod is literate, sensitive, and committed to the idea of a narrative in which the history of his community is recorded. And in the novel, MacLeod absorbs the catastrophic dimension of Mrs Scott's history into her story. Eschewing any exclusively intellectual revision of her history, he moves towards an empathetic under-standing of Mrs Scott's narrative, to what Bradshaw in an Irish context advocates as the 'purposeful unhistoricity' of an imaginative engagement with catastrophe: the development of idealism and anachronism in order to accommodate the past to the needs of the present.[51]

MacLeod, then, seems to offer a historical paradigm for the present-day artist Iain Crichton Smith. But a reassuringly liberal fusion of their sensibilities never occurs. Mrs Scott, old and, like a lot of the characters in the village, physically infirm and facing death, is incapable of marrying her mind with another. MacLeod's search for the word that would allow him access to Mrs Scott's history, 'so that he would be united with her and what she was', is ultimately unsuccessful. The interaction of their individual sensibilities is formally achieved not in the novel but *by* the novel itself; it is a 'union' which does not write out their unbridgeable separateness but lives passionately through the dialectic it enables. A profound recognition of the inviolate indi-viduality of each is enacted through the formal unity provided by art, by the physical artefact of the novel itself and by the one character omnipresent throughout—Iain. *Consider the Lilies* resolves some of the questions it poses simply by existing as an example of the aesthetic element Mrs Scott has always ignored in the social world, offering its own existence as part of the cultural solution to the problems within its narrative. In other words, it attempts to bridge the gap between the world of nature and society, art and belief.

Mrs Scott falls from a bridge after her return from her minis-ter, after yet again dismissing the beauty of the external world for the relentless certainty of Calvinist dogma. She fails to tell MacLeod's children a story, an imaginative narrative; but a

---

[51] Brendan Bradshaw, 'Nationalism and Historical Scholarship in Modern Ireland', in Ciarán Brady (ed.), *Interpreting Irish History: The Debate on Historical Revisionism* (Dublin: Four Courts Press, 1994), 211.

narrative is finally completed within her own life *as* her own life. The small steps move towards assuming agency—to refuse the Duke's pension, to betray MacLeod, leave her house, forge a reconciliation with her Church—these acts reclaim an element of her individuality by recognizing the inextricably social dimension to her existence. She is groping towards history, maybe even towards the human, but there is no dramatic victory. The novel ends with a reference to Ecclesiastes—'Another day had passed'—an acceptance of the immutable ebb and flow of human existence, but also of Mrs Scott's new-found acceptance of her self as an individual: 'just the same things came in on the high tide which you could keep when the tide was going out again' (*CTL*, 144). Part of her tragedy is that so small a gain should seem so large a victory. But these tentative steps towards agency are illuminated by Crichton Smith's relationship with Kierkegaard, the philosophical proponent of an individuality that dominates Crichton Smith's novels of the city.

IV   THE INDIVIDUAL WILL

Crichton Smith has long admitted his interest in Soren Kierkegaard's unwavering claim for the ultimate existential, religious and philosophical significance of the individual.[52] Described by Terry Eagleton as an 'apostle of the aporetic and enemy of all totality',[53] Kierkegaard argued that, though the mental and physical went some way towards defining selfhood, it was actually an inviolate element or realm of the self called 'spirit' that enabled man to transcend his natural traits and inherited circumstances.[54] Through a self-conscious act of the will, this spirit was activated and the self consequently animated: 'To be a person is to exist in the mode not of being, but of becoming, and

[52] Gow, 'Interview with Iain Crichton Smith'. See also the poem 'Kierkegaard' in *Thistle and Roses*. The last verse is: 'Till the new category, the individual, | rose like a thorn from the one rose he knew. | The crucifixion of the actual, | by necessary acceptance brought him through | to where his father standing calm and new | cutting his head and life made one from two.'

[53] *The Ideology of the Aesthetic* (Oxford: Blackwell, 1990), 173.

[54] *The Concept of Dread*, trans. Walter Lowrie (Princeton: Princeton University Press, 1973), 38: 'Man is a synthesis of the soulish and the bodily. But a synthesis is unthinkable if the two are not united in a third factor. This third factor is the spirit.'

what a person becomes is his own responsibility, the product of his own will.'[55]

Believing that 'a crowd is the untruth',[56] Kierkegaard reacted against Hegel's universal categories of thought that unfolded according to dialectically necessary laws. Hegel (to whom we will return in Chapter 5) thought that a rationally ordered community would eventually emerge, its institutions so objectively structured they would compel the individual to identify with and ultimately sanction and absorb their moral dictates: 'the framework of rules and duties imposed would be seen by him to coincide with his own essential interests as an agent seeking fulfilment as a free and rational being'.[57] Kierkegaard deplored this abrogation of spiritual power which, he claimed, relieved the individual of his responsibility to intelligently contribute to the historical process, of the 'task of understanding itself in existence'.[58] Such abstraction caused 'individuals [to] fade into humanity', leaving them 'trembling with fear that if they were to become particular human beings they would disappear without a trace, so that even the daily paper couldn't catch a glimpse of them, let alone literary reviews, or the speculative thinkers of world-history'.[59] Hegel's conceptual system explained how individual modes of consciousness were dialectically determined in an immutable sequence; Kierkegaard saw personal development evolving only through a dynamic series of unconstrained personal choices made entirely by a discrete individual: 'The

[55] Patrick Gardner, *Kierkegaard* (Oxford: Oxford University Press, 1988), 106. Compare this to Mrs Scott's view that 'Either you were like that or you weren't. If you weren't there was no way of becoming like that even if you wanted to' (*CTL*, 57).

[56] 'Two Notes about "The Individual"' in *The Point of View of My Work as an Author*, trans. Walter Lowrie (London: Oxford University Press, 1939), 112: 'Hence where there is a multitude, a crowd, or where decisive significance is attached to the fact that there is a multitude, there it is sure that noone is working, living, striving for the highest aim, but only for one or antiearthly aim; since to work for the eternal decisive aim is possible only where there is one, and to be this one which all can be is to let God be the helper—the crowd is the untruth.'

[57] Gardner, *Kierkegaard*, 28. For Kierkegaard on the philosophic category of the Individual see *Soren Kierkegaard's Journals and Papers*, ii. F–K, ed. and trans. Howard V. Hong and Edna H. Hong (Bloomington, Ind. and London: Indiana University Press, 1963), sections 1964–97; *Concept of Dread*, 54–73; *Either/Or Volume II*, trans. Walter Lowrie (Princeton: Princeton University Press, 1971), 159–339. *Concluding Unscientific Postscripts*, trans. David F. Swenson and Walter Lowrie (Princeton: Princeton University Press, 1941), 115–347.

[58] *Concluding Unscientific Postscript*, 314.

[59] Ibid. 317.

communication of the truth can only be by a single individual
... for the truth consists precisely in that conception of life which
is expressed by that individual.'[60] To achieve a sustained, discriminating critique of reality, the individual needed a complete
physical and intellectual disengagement: 'It is impossible to
attack the system from a point within the system. But outside of
it there is only one point, truly a spermatic point, the individual
ethically and religiously conceived existentially accentuated.'[61]
Attempting to comprehend contingency and flux through fixed,
systematic rules inevitably freezes the development of the human
spirit. Resistance and understanding, redress and interpretation,
could only be conceived of in terms of the individual: 'The
category of the individual is and remains the fixed part which is
able to resist the pantheistic confusion. It is and remains the
weight which touches the scale.'[62]

Kierkegaard's oblique presence in *Consider the Lilies* becomes
clearer after considering Crichton Smith's second novel, *The
Last Summer*. But Mrs Scott's attempt to accommodate the wild
reality of the external world, its furious devotion to chance and
contingency, is always through a Calvinist dogma that allows no
space for individual development or digression. The form of
individuality and being allowed in her world are predetermined
and static. And what activates and animates a semblance of
intimacy with and control over an internal realm of her own self,
is the choice—a key term in Kierkegaard—initiated by her fall.
That it is tentative does not lessen its enormous significance in
her life.

In *The Last Summer*, 18-year-old Malcolm, bullied by his
mother into a single-minded pursuit of the village bursary, is
forced to choose between the village and school in a forthcoming
football match, a choice complicated by the fact that 'The world
of the school and the village did not meet.'[63] Set against the

---

[60] 'Two Notes about "The Individual"', 119.
[61] Kierkegaard, 'A Word about the Relation of My Literary Activity to "The
Individual"', in *Point Of View*, 13. See also id., *Journals and Papers*, vol. ii, sect.
1984. [62] Ibid. p. 137.
[63] An essay on his childhood displays the same tension between school and home:
'I moved between two worlds—the world of the school and the world of the village'.
('Between Sea and Moor', in Maurice Lindsay (ed.), *As I Remember* (London: Faber
and Faber, 1979), 115).

background of World War II, the racial and the individual (a dichotomy central to Kierkegaard's thought) and the guilt resulting from the clash, provides the novel's drama and theme.[64] Malcolm defends Dido in a classroom discussion of Virgil's *Aeneid*, insisting that 'Our conscience is equivalent to their Gods'. When a classmate defends Aeneas—'He had his duty to do. The race is more important than the individual'—Malcolm rails against him: 'Fascist . . . What do you think we're fighting for? Isn't that what Hitler says, that the race is more important than the individual?' (*TLS*, 98–9). A society ordered on such principles, Malcolm suggests, is morally indefensible, communally unsustainable, and secretly conspires to destroy its individual citizens: 'What kind of Rome would be founded by an Aeneas who could do that kind of thing?' (*TLS*, 100).

This individual conscience, 'the fixed part which is able to resist the pantheistic confusion', categorically transcends temporal considerations, enabling Malcolm to unconditionally defend Dido's right to choose self-destruction. Like Mrs Scott, she affirms the existence of selfhood by selecting a course that will inevitably destroy it. Malcolm believes that Aeneas' refusal to recognize and engage with Dido as an individual is the cause of her death, and that Aeneas, like Sellar in *Consider the Lilies*, is committed to an abstraction which relegates individuals to secondary importance: 'His responsibility was to the individual, not to Rome' (*TLS*, 101). When pressed, the teacher Collins, the form of authority Malcolm must daily contend with, finally admits an admiration for Aeneas' commitment to duty and Rome.

The plot revolves around a date between Malcolm and Janet that clashes with the school football match. The choice, then, is between duty and desire, the individual and the crowd, conscience and community, and this moment for Malcolm is microcosmic, 'one that went to the roots of his being' (*TLS*, 152). His solution echoes that seen in *Consider the Lilies*. In order to imaginatively engage with his communal inheritance he must first physically disengage from its environs; communicating

---

[64] See Gregor Malantschuk, *Kierkegaard's Thought*, ed. and trans. Howard V. Hong and Edna H. Hong (Princeton and London: Princeton University Press, 1971), 258: 'guilt establishes the new quality which finally leads the individual out of the domain of the race and into the universal'.

aesthetically means evacuating the region physically. The individual's task is not to bring under control the material conditions of life in the region, as it is with the exemplary, performative virtue Tam Docherty offered. Malcolm's task, like that of the author in *Consider the Lilies*, is to incorporate under conscious control the psychological conditions attached to his existence. 'Finite experience', Kierkegaard writes, 'is homeless',[65] and the subject comes alive to the world and being by choosing to be thrust beyond what is given, by recognizing that its 'origin lies beyond its own mastery and [its] end is nowhere in view'.[66] Choosing to enter into the process of becoming, Kierkegaard claimed, must involve the individual physically withdrawing from society: 'We think that by attaching ourselves to society we develop a higher perfection—that is a nice idea, but no, it is regression . . . The single individual is in the medium of becoming—and this earthly existence is the time of testing.'[67]

The Last Summer, the period before this artist as a young man leaves the island for the mainland and university, proposes just such an answer to the question it poses: 'Wasn't the truth far better for people? He was finding out the truth. Why shouldn't others?' (*TLS*, 154). The apparent contradiction between the adolescent's social idealism and the mature artist's consciously sought after individualism is solved by football, as the beautiful game provides, once again, answers to the problem of life and art: 'He knew absolutely instantaneously that this time there would be a goal. He knew this with an intuition that had nothing to do with logic or with weighing odds or with calculation' (*TLS* 154). Success for the team depends on a complete acceptance and expression of his highly individual, immanent talent. The village wins if he is allowed unrestricted access to an instinctual skill. Compare this to McIlvanney's celebration of Celtic, the athletic wing of his republican poetics, where the strength of the European Cup winning side derived, in part, from the fact that all its members were in a sense equal, having all been born within thirty miles of Glasgow. Equality is not, as it was for Kierkegaard, a mere abstract levelling that undermined social bonds and annihilated the pure differences of individual life.

---

[65] Quoted in Eagleton, *Ideology of the Aesthetic*, 190.
[66] Ibid. 180.
[67] *Journals*, vol. ii, sections 2010, 2011.

Celtic's solidarity and teamwork, cohesion and confidence enabled success in Europe of a kind not wholly divorced from the political aims of the SNP. In this reading, Glasgow Celtic incorporate and performatively express a beautiful brand of civic, communal republicanism, as some have long known.

But the form of individuality proposed in *The Last Summer* does not just redeem the present. Mrs Scott, as territorial numen and discrete individual, can in some sense be rescued from the enormous condescension of history if Crichton Smith succeeds as artist. *Consider the Lilies* concludes with Mrs Scott's letter to her son Iain, one example of the historical evidence available to Iain Crichton Smith, the novelist. That it is heavily coded, in parts silent, does not disguise its latent potential for regeneration if one individual can represent with fidelity its coded message: 'It was as if she was relying on his intelligence to work it all out for himself . . . Somewhere it lay concealed under lies and differences, *like the soot in a black house which could be used to fertilise the land*' (*CTL*, 104; emphasis added). A layer of meaning remains recuperable despite the catastrophic dimension to Scottish history; Mrs Scott may remain on one side of a historical divide, but the soot becoming fertilizer challenges the very idea that that division is permanent, immutable, culturally and individually disabling. It proposes a potentiality for regeneration that comes out of 'blackness' (Calvinism) and backwardness (the black house). This is the sense in which Crichton Smith describes history as 'broken'. For McIlvanney, there is one 'harmonising thread' in Scottish history: a singular theme that accounts for the aporia in the nation's narrative and allows direct communication with a single source of virtue such as Tam Docherty. Crichton Smith (following Kierkegaard) acknowledges that there can be no direct, unmediated communication between irreducibly particular individuals, but this does not, of itself, rob the past of meaning. Malcolm's departure for Aberdeen and university resembles Iain's emigration in *Consider the Lilies*. A drunk sings, his mother is in black, and he is alone. But this isolation is, as in Kierkegaard, a liberating point of departure: 'At last he was alone. Free of everything, everyone. Ready to begin' (*TLS*, 192). In 'Real People in a Real Place', Crichton Smith expands upon this sense of belonging:

When I left the community to go to Aberdeen University, I felt paradoxically free since I could walk down Union Street without anyone
knowing who I was. Invisibility became important to me, it was as if I
had cast off chains, as the ship does when it leaves harbour. To leave the
community was to emerge into one's individuality, into a future which
seemed free and unjudged.[68]

V   THE INDIVIDUAL IN THE CITY

This 'future which seemed free and unjudged' belongs to a
radical individualism that dispenses with any supra-empirical
reality like Scotland or religion, any communal notions of
belonging, tradition, and identity, ingredients without which no
society (or individual) can survive. This is an individualism that
can never speak to McIlvanney's republican communalism.
Whatever artistic benefits are gained are wholly mediated
through one individual, a solipsistic tendency that has been
noted in Kierkegaard.[69] But the use of 'seemed' is, I think, important here. Writing in 1986, Crichton Smith is reviewing and
revising his earlier commitment to Kierkegaard's individualism,
and *My Last Duchess,* one of three novels in which this radical
individualism unfolds in the city, scrupulously examines the
shortcomings of Kierkegaard's philosophy. The relocation
dispenses with the kitsch lumber of 'the Highlander' and also of
'Mrs Scott'. For the city—secular, indeterminate, a site open to
becoming—is structurally incapable of accommodating any
'indigenous territorial numen'. The novel's main character
Mark, for example, a lecturer who seeks life through literature,
dismisses the notion that selfhood and identity emerge through
history: 'I can't stand genealogy myself. People who write stuff
about genealogy seem to me to be high-powered gossips and
busybodies' (*MLD,* 13).

   With his marriage disintegrating, Mark seeks out a writer
called Frith who once wrote a good novel about an unhappy

---

[68] 'Real People', 27.
[69] Mark C. Taylor, *Kierkegaard's Pseudonymous Authorship: A Study of Time
and the Self* (Princeton: Princeton University Press, 1975), 253–4: 'A major problem
with Kierkegaard's argument at this point is his refusal to acknowledge the possibility
of a form of human community that enhances and does not abolish responsible individuality.'

marriage. Frith turns out to be banal, possibly senile, while his son is robotic and reflexively right-wing. Kierkegaard's radical individualism is pushed to its logical extremes, as Mark is denied access to any social, artistic, or communal narrative. His potentially liberating rootlessness, the 'paradoxical freedom' offered by the invisibility of city, degenerates into a vapid existential and ethical wilderness. Like Charlie in *Remedy is None*, Mark now lacks any imaginative geography where the self can become aware of its own identity: 'He had no idea where he was going: all places were of equal value and therefore valueless' (*MLD*, 44). Longing for a return to days when 'literature seemed consonant with life and lines of poetry harmonised with the very light itself' (*MLD*, 46), Mark's total intellectual and emotional investment in art now forecloses the possibility of personal growth. The crowd, once simply a metaphor for untruth (a classically Kierkegaardian notion), always constitutionally incapable of recognizing excellence, now acts as the unappointed arbiter of his existence: 'he sensed himself in some way inferior to these people, who didn't seem to work hard and yet lived well'. The distance 'he had moved from his origins' (*MLD*, 68) is now ironically an index of his own unfulfilment.

The philosophical affirmation of subjectivity requires the abolition of all historical connection. Leaving a chapel, and meeting a headmaster who tries to explain a piece of saintly religious lore, Mark reacts violently against this mild social or anthropomorphic connection, a process that inevitably stains the transcendental realm in which aesthetic purity permanently resides: 'I can't stand these bloody people. All these bloody dates . . . why does there always have to be someone like him trying to explain everything and knowing bugger all about it . . . Why do they have to corrupt everything with their dates' (*MLD*, 124–5).

This abuse of history is symptomatic of an increasingly desperate search for a spontaneous and autonomous self-generation. The goal is 'being' sublimely unaware of and uncontaminated by the process of 'becoming' that necessarily preceded it, a condition Mrs Scott in *Consider the Lilies* is constitutionally incapable of ('she had lost the power to be spontaneous'). Yet any inscription that is entirely dependent upon spontaneity for its existence is implicitly an act of erasure. For spontaneity, the instant here and now, is equidistant from both the past and the future, and ineluctably dependent upon the recognition of others before it can know itself. In this sense, it is utterly contingent. Thus to assert the self through an art entirely divorced from history is, ironically, a form of self-erasure, as the identity and individuation achieved comprises nothing other than the visible, external, aesthetic layers:

> The hermit seemed continually under the threat of disintegration by that which composed him, that is the paint itself, or transferred to another plane, time. He was being held in precarious existence by the part which simultaneously threatened also to dissolve and leave nothing at all (*MLD*, 128).

The varying degrees of psychological and emotional intensity in any individual are here abruptly suspended; the abstract individual is deemed irreducibly particular, resistant to all forms of social integration. The 'being held in precarious existence' is, simply, the principle of identity, an utterly contingent realm that avoids the fixed aesthetics of difference that constituted the 'Highlander' and Mrs Scott's frozen selfhood. But the anguished separation this hermit suffers would not be remedied by a dialogue with every other individual, a process which would cause him to 'dissolve'. The form of individuality Mark enjoys makes the universal correspond to the discrete individual rather than vice versa. Instead of travelling 'towards' the human, this transcendental humanism is made palpable through an individuality absolved of any association with locale or community: 'Everything could enter him. He was a mirror open to the doings of the universe. He was as open as a door. Anything, anybody could walk through and take up its place in him. Even the future. Whatever that meant' (*MLD*, 158).

The concept of the individual as a mirror in which the universal not the discrete self is reflected closely follows Kierkegaard's thinking.[70] A phrase such as 'all places were of equal value and therefore valueless' is not, of course, philosophically true or geographically accurate: it takes the concept of equality as merely abstract levelling, a politics that undermines the social bonds

---

[70] Kierkegaard, *Concluding Unscientific Postscript*, 315: 'Abstract thought turns from concrete men to consider man in general; the subjective thinker seeks to understand the abstract determination of being human in terms of this particular existing human being.'

between purely different individuals.[71] To reintroduce Lefebvre's terms, nothing precedes the production of space through the agency of an individual. The crucial element in human consciousness is not history but the present, a present in which the subject emerges into being through the Kierkegaardian notion of 'choice': 'The world of nature can't make choices. Not to make choices is to refuse to live. Hamlet is really a dead man. From the very beginning he is dead' (*MLD*, 54). Perhaps unknowingly, the novel demonstrates the limits of this emphasis on choice, a concept central to Kierkegaard's discussion of the individual, when faced with a complex range of experience. An inarticulate, pathologically violent stage-Irish navvy wanders unannounced into Mark's path spouting nonsense ('A Fine day sor . . . This fellow—Murphy his name was and he came from Donegal—was saying that a hurley pitch was longer than a football pitch. And the other fellow . . . took out a knife and did him' (*MLD*, 118)). In this encounter, Mark's fears seem to result from disinterested observation, his alienation receiving implicit endorsement as the internalization of the city's external chaos.

Contemporary life intrudes only as a parallel to artistic suffering. A black man suffering racial abuse on a train, for example, reflects Mark's cultural isolation: 'sitting in the carriage he had an immense intuition of loneliness, of the black man in front of him, of a life lived in utter loneliness' (*MLD*, 141). Presented as a problem of language and communication—'If I were to pull the communication cord . . . then surely someone would come' (*MLD*, 144)—the incident is then connected to Crichton Smith's status as an artist: Mark visualizes the youths bringing home the black man as a hunter might bring home 'a victim, a deer' (*MLD*, 145). Because the deer is an image scattered throughout Crichton Smith's oeuvre, racism here is somehow analogous to the problem the writer confronts finding an appropriate language and idiom.[72] Politically and artistically, this is questionable. Deployed as an index of artistic angst, it demeans both

---

[71] Id., *Journals and Papers*, ii. 151: 'The new development of the age cannot be political, for politics is a question of the dialectical relation of individual and community in the representative individual, and in our times the individual is in the process of becoming far too reflective to be able to be satisfied with merely being represented'.

[72] See *Deer on the High Hill*: 'You must build from the rain and stones | till you can make | a stylish deer on the high hills, | and let its leaps be unpredictable.'

the problem and the artist and suggests a severe confusion over the demarcation between the social and cultural order. John Carey's comments are instructive on this point:

The mass is the crowd in its metaphysical aspect—the sum of all possible crowds—and that can take on conceptual form only as metaphor. The metaphor of the mass serves the purpose of individual self-assertion because it turns other people into a conglomerate. It denies them the individuality we ascribe to others and to people we know.[73]

Goodbye Mr Dixon, Crichton Smith's next novel, specifically addressed this question of discriminating between cultural and social worth.

In *Goodbye Mr Dixon*, Tom Spence is a middle-aged writer who has never yet 'brought a novel to a successful conclusion' (*GMD*, 8). Writing about the struggle between a civilized and barbarian people, he stops when faced with the question 'How do you learn enough about the "real" world if at the same time in the service of art you remain isolated' (*GMD*, 11). Dixon, the central character in Tom's novel, is the perfect aesthete, 'perched above the battle, immune to the ravages of time and accident, obsessed with the beauties of art and the symmetries of the word' (*GMD*, 12). While Glasgow, Tom's 'real' home, makes meaningful communication almost impossible, Dixon prefers Beethoven to Bob Dylan and meets his women in art galleries, where 'everything was fixed, art gave the illusion of permanence and privacy, it did not flash off and on like neon lighting and was not the half-formed names of ships or on the back of cornflake packets and soup-tins' (*GMD*, 22). For Tom, the contours of a validating personal language must be moulded to account for the landscapes of fact, even as that language observes standards of permanence and privacy utterly divorced from the contingency of the everyday.

The trope used to validate this personal language is music. For Tom, classical music is remote and unappealing, belonging to 'a different race, a larger more solid race' (*GMD*, 72). Jazz, an improvisatory musical form, dependent upon each instrument

---

[73] *The Intellectuals and the Masses: Pride and Prejudice among the Literary Intelligentsia, 1880–1939* (London: Faber and Faber, 1992), 21.

retaining its distinctive individual sound within an overall arrangement, manages to assimilate the city's competing codes. But jazz also offers a combination of origins and artifice, just as the desire to be a real person in a real place emerges in Tom's urgent need to write. As the bastard offspring of several musical genres, and the product of numerous competing soloists, jazz trumpets its own radical impurity, its elaborate, diffuse, and ceaseless musical borrowings. Serenely confident about its own impurity, its questionable musical origins, it is this note of confidence which impresses Tom: he 'thought of the jazz musicians as orphans trying to create music from the fragments of the city' (*GMD*, 94).

A syncopative mesh like jazz is highly un-Kierkegaardian, in that it only exists by directly embracing other idioms. Inevitably remote from the centre, jazz comfortably incorporates, is even dependent upon, its own cultural displacement, thereby offering a possible paradigm for the writer from Lewis, torn between a nostalgia for a romanticized landscape and the cluttered spaces of the city:

In front of him in a corner he saw a pile of records, some Edith Piaf and some folk songs. His eyes moved slowly up to a place where he saw a picture of the deer standing above a swirling river with a green mountain in the background. He suddenly wanted to be wherever it was, away from these people and away from Dixon, somewhere clean and pure and uncorrupted. (*GMD*, 94)

The sealed purity of isolation, Tom slowly realizes, is existentially untenable; one essential element of the self is discoverable through others, and exercising 'choice', fully entering the present time of one's own life, does not necessarily involve an insuperable separateness from other individuals. Watching a bride, Tom realizes the sterility of his relationship with his own double, Dixon:

She had taken a decision . . . she had decided that she would have children by him and populate the world with miniature versions of the two of them. This was in fact the greatest day of her life . . . the only day she would emerge from the crowd, the only day she would be famous. (*GMD*, 114)

The crowd is still a boundary the individual must transgress, but it is something more than a metaphor for untruth; the alternative to community and history is not an isolated, hermetic identity in a continually spontaneous present, an ethical discovery that impacts upon Tom's aesthetic relationship with Dixon.

Tom's wife Ann directs a school play, the invisible pivot in a coherent, unselfconscious arrangement:

The atmosphere of the class was warm, free and relaxed. There was a feeling of emotional growth in the air, a controlled unpredictability. The fact was that there was no script seemed to help . . . Everywhere were bright colours, a higgeldy piggeldy storm of creativity, as if ideas were being picked out of the air in accordance with the laws of life itself. There was no sense of life itself. There was no sense of a forced order, no sense of anyone looking for a theology that would unite the data, that would arrange the world. Everything incomplete, disorderly spawning. (*GMD*, 130–1)

The play repossesses the ability to capture and understand experience by ignoring the audience and deferring to its own internal unity. Tom, by contrast, is reconciled to losing Ann because of Dixon, 'The eternal enigmatic face devouring him' (*GMD*, 139). Drunk, Tom leaves the play, lands beneath a Greek statue in the city, and begins banging it methodically: 'It was Dixon he was hitting, it was Dixon and all he stood for' (*GMD*, 156), before asking a passing lorry driver 'to put me down at the centre . . . The centre.' (*GMD*, 157) What Dixon and the statue represent is a culture so integrated that it can produce an art that will have the impact and perfection of a single image. The perfection of the school play torments because it hints at the objective availability of a formal aesthetic unity, a centre, he seems destined never to realize.[74] Both the statue and 'the centre' are instances of a Grecian perfection attained through wholeness, something Crichton Smith, the self-described 'double man', the writer navigating between Gaelic and English, stereotypical representations of the Highlander and Mrs Scott's Calvinism, can never enjoy. Or as Seamus Deane puts it: 'The dreamy imaginative Celt, unblessed by the Greek sense of form, at home

---

[74] This drunkenness is a variation of the fourth type of madness identified in *Phaedrus*. Plato thought that 'when a man like a bird fixes his gaze on the heights to the neglect of things below . . . that in itself and in its origin this is the best of all forms of divine possession . . . when he is touched with this madness that . . . the man is called a lover.' (*Phaedrus and Letters VII and VIII*, trans. and introd. Walter Hamilton (Harmondsworth: Penguin, 1973), 56.

in wild landscapes, far from the metropolitan centres of modern social and political life, could cure anxious Europe of the woes inherent in Progress.'[75]

The move towards the city, one centre of modern social life and progress, towards the human through Kierkegaard's passionate individualism, attempts to sidestep this legacy. But the believer in Kierkegaard's individuality, Terry Eagleton suggests, will always find a difficulty in being ideologically centred: 'there can be no objective correlative of a subjectivity lived at this pitch of passionate intensity; and the subject is accordingly thrust beyond the world, sustaining a merely ironic relation with it, a permanent thorn in the flesh of all purely institutional life'.[76] What is this Greek sense of form? In both *Phaedrus* and the *Symposium*, a single, originating, uncorrupted transcendental source is identified from which all other forms take their shape, and recovering that essence, that 'original nature' is the single most important task available to the artist and man.[77] As Tom sits drunkenly beneath the Greek statue, unblessed by its sense of form, banging methodically against its calm wholeness, caught between the world of Mrs Scott and Dixon, he is tormented by the 'enormous, mind-breaking' doubleness Crichton Smith has spoken of.[78] Tom now realizes that 'It was Dixon he was hitting, it was Dixon and all he stood for' (*GMD*, 156). The form from which Tom takes his shape is now Dixon; art, the aesthetic, has robbed him of his individuality, reducing him to the status of an artefact in his own life.

[75] 'Arnold, Burke, and the Celts', in *Celtic Revivals* (London: Faber and Faber, 1985), 25.

[76] *Ideology of the Aesthetic*, 190.

[77] Plato, *Symposium*, trans. Robin Waterfield (Oxford: Oxford University Press, 1994), 30: 'We human beings will never attain happiness unless we find perfect love, unless we each come across the love of our lives and thereby recover our original nature. In the context of this ideal, it necessarily follows that in our present circumstances the best thing is to get as close to the ideal as possible . . . if we conduct ourselves with due reverence towards the gods, then he will restore us to our original nature, healed and blessed with perfect happiness.'

[78] Iain Crichton Smith, 'The Double Man', in R. P. Draper (ed.), *The Literature of Region and Nation* (Basingstoke: Macmillan, 1989), 140: 'There are too few openings in Gaelic for me to make a living from writing exclusively in that language. Economic factors govern cultural ones to the extent greater than we often dream of. And thus I am a double man riddled with guilt . . . The complexities are enormous, mind-breaking. Only those who have lived through or are living through them can fully understand them. And it is not even a question of understanding it, it is a question of feeling them on the pulse.'

Aesthetically and biologically, Tom discovers the impossibility of an 'original nature'. The search for his mother's grave, for example, is ongoing and indeterminate, history as a process with no identifiable beginning or terminus: 'He would simply have to walk for a long time till he found it, that was all, for there was no one to tell him where it was . . . he didn't think of himself as belonging to a chain of generations. He didn't have that feeling' (*GMD*, 187). Dixon has, he realizes, always been Richardson, a schoolteacher who was the earliest source of Tom's interest in art. But the source of his literary self remains as profoundly distant as his biological self. As in Kierkegaard, no direct, unmediated communication is possible between two discrete individuals: 'Glad to have seen you. I'd shake hands but I can't, you see, with all these books. You should carry on with your writing. It'd always be something to do. I didn't recognise you at first. It must be the clothes. That's what it must be. Well. Cheerio.' (*GMD*, 164)

Neither 'Mrs Scott' nor 'Dixon'—the marginalized catastrophic dimension to Scottish history or the calm certainty of the centre—can provide what Kierkegaard termed 'spirit': the synthesis that makes the doubleness within Crichton Smith's characters bearable.[79] What the novel finally accepts is the validity of public quotidian experience to participate in the private experience of the aesthetic. Thus Tom paints a room with a stranger, symbolically testifying to this shared public discourse between the artist and everyman, negotiating with rather than transcending the external world for its value: 'He felt as if he were in an art gallery walking from room to room admiring' (*GMD*, 196). When, at the end of the novel, Tom enters the 'real' world of Glasgow with Ann, this ethical relationship flourishes because the role of the aesthetic in that world is established: 'He was ready to be with her. There was about him the gaunt air of beginnings' (*GMD*, 208).

---

[79] Kierkegaard, *Concept of Dread*, 38: 'Man is a synthesis of the soulish and the bodily. But a synthesis is unthinkable if the two are not united in a third factor. This third factor is the spirit.'

VI COLONIALISM AND REPUBLICANISM; CRICHTON SMITH AND MCILVANNEY

This 'gaunt air of beginnings' marks Crichton Smith's slow reconciliation with the catastrophic dimension to Scottish history, the 'brokenness which will not allow writers the confidence that others can have when they write'.[80] This brokenness marks the form of his novels' narratives, the 'purposeful unhistoricity' that blends empathy and imagination in the creative reconstruction of the past that produced Mrs Scott. Literary realism may be possible in sites of settlement and stability, sites which provide the material base for a literary form that can gather individual lives into an integrated whole.[81] But for the Highland writer, especially one who moves freely between Gaelic and English, 'brokenness' and 'doubleness' makes this integrated wholeness profoundly problematic. The 'harmonising thread' in McIlvanney's Ayrshire is part of a realism that aggressively asserts its centrality to Scottish life: the region as the normative centre of the nation's affairs. The centre is a site, however, as Tom illustrates in *Goodbye Mr Dixon*, that is always alien to Crichton Smith. As George Watson notes, Ireland by contrast exemplifies the potentially beneficial effect of a broken tradition.[82] Watson quotes a famous passage from Thomas Kinsella:

Pending the achievement of some total human unity of being, every writer in the world—since he can't be in all the literary traditions at once—is the inheritor of a gapped, discontinuous tradition. Nevertheless, if the function of a tradition is to link us with a significant past, this is done as well by a broken tradition as by a whole one—however painful it may be humanly speaking. I am certain that a great part of the significance of my own past, as I try to write my poetry, is that the past is mutilated.[83]

[80] Crichton Smith, 'Real People', 35.
[81] Terry Eagleton, 'Form and Ideology in the Anglo-Irish Novel', *Bullán: A Journal of Irish Studies* 1/1 (Spring 1994), 17–26.
[82] 'A Culloden of the Spirit', in Colin Nicholson (ed.), *Iain Crichton Smith: Critical Essays* (Edinburgh: Edinburgh University Press, 1994), 37–50, at 49: 'for the Gaelic speaker, the example of Ireland may be depressing; for the writer it must surely be positive'.
[83] 'The Irish Writer', in *Davis, Mangan, Ferguson? Tradition and the Irish Writer* (Dublin: Dolmen, 1970), 57.

A broken history, Kinsella eloquently explains, does not necessarily condemn the writer to a depthless present; the absence or
unavailability of a transparent realism does not make the past
permanently opaque.

The 'gaunt air' of beginnings provided by the ironic absence of
a 'unity of being' pervades *An End to Autumn*, a novel that ends
in spring, with a severing of the maternal bond, a renewed faith
in marriage, a pregnancy, and closes on the word home. When
both their mothers arrive, Tom and his wife Vera find their literate, slightly dull city lives riven by allegiances long thought
buried. Their life together is 'totally free of the past, of relations,
committed only to themselves and the reality of their own, spare
of ancestry' (*ETA*, 29). To please his Highlander mother, Tom
returns to church, a move Vera sees as an attack on order and
meaning. Tom begins to recognize a zone of articulation that lies
beneath the articulable: 'How clearly it [a graveyard] told in
its very dumbness of the continuity of life even in death, of
ancestries that perpetuated themselves through centuries'; Vera's
cognition, meanwhile, remains strictly formalist, assimilating
only what is spoken: 'Her formal world was in danger of destruction, a sentence which would soon lack a verb' (*ETA*, 50). The
doubleness of this existence strains the formal properties of
language and the traditional techniques of realism, but most
importantly, the self. One cannot always be at war with oneself,
and so Tom must discover some other means of accommodating
the familiar to the alien, the broken, and the coherent self: 'He
pushed his face against the glass . . . as if he wished to explode in
front of the mirror, as if he wished both reality and reflection to
merge with each other in the infinite depths of the glass.' (*ETA*,
52). An elaborate fire scene, where Vera chooses to join Tom at
the centre of a blaze started by her mother, merges the real and
the reflected:

The two of them were jumping up and down in the middle of the rings
of fire, dancing and shouting at each other as if they were prancing
round Angela in a primitive form of worship, while on the outside of the
ring the unconsidered Mrs Mallow stood passively suffering what she
was unable to do anything about. (*ETA*, 145)

The scene recalls Kierkegaard's emphasis on the ethical importance of choice. Vera consciously chooses to submit to this

instinctual realm, affirming her individuality through a choice that might involve self-destruction. Tom's mother, clad in all black, remains physically and psychologically distant from the flames; Vera's mother, Angela, dependent on a pure red cloak for warmth, retreats into a solipsistic 'gibberish of her own'. Vera announces her pregnancy to Tom while she is dependent on neither red nor black but a messy, hybrid, and so fertile mix of these very colours: 'her face turning red in the light with spots of dirt from the fire on it, her white dress losing its purity' (*ETA*, 147).

Tom and Vera can never directly know one another or their origins, the red or the black. The continuous collision and medley between past and present generates a novel that revels in a moral and aesthetic impurity, an impurity in which the various forms of 'unity of being' offered by Mrs Scott, the Greek statue, Plato, and Dixon are for ever unavailable. Through Vera's pregnancy, these radical impurities emerge as life enhancing: her 'white dress was flecked with black spots and [her] face was red and dirty'. Simultaneously stained and enriched by the black and the red, this is a doubleness that no supra-empirical term— 'Scott', Scotland, 'Mrs Scott'—can write out. These are the complexities Crichton Smith describes as 'enormous, mind-breaking . . . And it is not even a question of understanding it, it is a question of feeling them on the pulse'.[84]

This pulsating quality resides in the liminal, hybrid spaces elided by McIlvanney's realism, the allegorical search for 'Scott', and Mrs Scott's belief that 'You can't serve two masters' (*CTL*, 43). It is the condition described by post-colonial theory as 'hybridity'. 'Hybridity', according to Robert Young, 'describes the condition of a language's fundamental ability to be simultaneously the same but different', a definition that can seem peculiarly appropriate as well as inappropriate to Crichton Smith's self-description as a 'linguistic double man'. The private world he inhabits may be Gaelic, but the public world he enters as an individual is overwhelmingly English. Gaelic poetry may address themes of global reach, but it can never enjoy the cultural centrality its accomplishment as poetry merits; hence Crichton Smith's need to explain his Gaelic work through English. But

---

[84] 'Double Man', 140.

because Gaelic is a quite different and dissimilar language to English, linguistically, Crichton Smith is, in fact, serving two masters. There is no one difference that makes *the* difference in *An End to Autumn*, *Goodbye Mr Dixon*, and *My Last Duchess*. Their irresolute endings are not just part of Crichton Smith's ambivalence towards the use of history as a metaphor.[85] This form of regionalism is a nomadic quest for a mode of being that navigates between any available descriptive term, including the term 'identity'. The red, black, and white hybrid mix belong to the various 'patchwork identities' Young describes in post-colonial cultures:

Decoding and recoding implies too simplistic a grafting of one culture on to another. We need to modify the model to a form of palimpsestual inscription and reinscription, an historical paradigm that will acknowledge the extent to which cultures were not simply destroyed but rather layered on top of each other, giving rise to struggles that themselves only increased the imbrication of each with the other and their translation into increasingly patchwork identities.[86]

The complicated collision between Tom, Vera, their respective mothers, the productively messy multiplicity which announces Vera's pregnancy—this 'imbrication of each with the other' is an avowedly textual reconstruction of the terms available to describe the very idea of an identity. In McIlvanney, culture is defined within a single geographical, political, and aesthetic frame, whether supplied by Tam or Laidlaw or 'Scott'. The social world beyond the text is immediately comprehended through an instrumental language, a transparent realism, while the construction of subjectivity and cultural identity is always through difference and community. The act of naming—so central to McIlvanney's regional republicanism and so conspicuously absent from Crichton Smith—repossesses place through an act of primordial nomination. Crichton Smith tries instead to discover a space between the tropes of territory, identity, and difference, a space where the individual lives knowing the past to

---

[85] See Colin Nicholson, 'To Have Found One's Country', in id., *Poem, Purpose and Place: Shaping Identity in Contemporary Scottish Verse* (Edinburgh: Polygon, 1992), 121.

[86] Robert Young, *Colonial Desire: Hybridity in Theory, Culture and Race* (London: Routledge, 1995), 174.

be mutilated but still legible: 'How can one be that boy again? How can one walk home from the well with the two pails brimming with water, on paths that are probably now gone, between the cornfields, and the long wet grass?'[87]

This passage recalls Crichton Smith's novel *On the Island,* in which a ghostly old woman accuses a young boy called Iain of actively conniving in his mother's demise: 'I wouldn't do this to you. When you were young I brought you your food but you want me to die . . . In the cracked glass he saw a face not his own, and this face, broken and grained was the face of an old woman with no teeth' (*OTI,* 47–8). While Iain is lying on a mirror, the old woman tries to strangle him. The mirror, an accepted metaphor for literary realism, represents a belief in the ability of a neutral and objectified art to capture and truthfully reflect experience. Realism operates on the presumption of unity, between subject and object, psychological and social, individual and historical, and assumes at least a potential for wholeness.[88] For Crichton Smith this potentiality has always been frustratingly absent, and so the mirror cracks under the strain of a narrative that is both a quest for individual and cultural self-definition, and an exploration of his evolution as an artist. This quest is an impossible burden for realism to sustain, a genre which presumes the artist to be a disinterested observer. Crichton Smith's presence in all his novels, however, allows for a qualified but consistent empathy with the catastrophic dimension of Mrs Scott's history. But the certainties of Mrs Scott are evacuated for a liminal space that never recaptures the past as a totality, for an unstable identity that exists somewhere between Mrs Scott and McIlvanney's 'Scott', between Calvinism and nationalism, between republicanism and individualism: in short, between the idea and actuality of any single tradition. The tradition Crichton Smith originates from is not, as in McIlvanney, the sole source of creativity and the sole context in which the richest meaning is produced and grasped. McIlvanney engages on a purposeful rewriting of the past from the present because the

---

[87] 'Between Sea and Moor', in Karl Miller (ed.), *Memoirs of a Modern Scotland* (London: Faber and Faber, 1970), 109.

[88] 'When one is in harmony with the community then one's identity is reflected back from the others by a plain mirror and not by the exaggerating or attenuating mirrors that one sees in fairs' (Crichton Smith, 'Real People in a Real Place', 28).

tradition he writes from and in, the republican humanism of the
west coast, offers an unbroken 'harmonising thread', a comprehensible metanarrative. Crichton Smith, the double man caught
between two languages, the red and black, writes from the
liminal, hybrid spaces between traditions. The use of ritual in
McIlvanney is because characters have no choice but to inherit
this continuous tradition; the use of choice in Crichton Smith
develops Kierkegaard's belief in the individual. His characters
must choose as individuals how to affiliate with a specific tradition that has multiple fractures: a Gaelic tradition fractured by
Calvinism, the Calvinist world by economic imperatives, the self
by the 'unreal' representations the Highlander has been subject
to. The ultimate denial of individuality is the sense of election
that Calvinism or, indeed, McIlvanney's ritualistic transmission
of tradition, entails; of being specially privileged in terms of
cultural origin or cultural value. Hence his characters struggle to
be released back into an ordinary world which is neither simply
the world of Kierkegaardian choice nor the world of aesthetic
perfection nor the world of 'unity of being' but, to use a term
from Cairns Craig, of persons in relation.[89]

For Craig, Scottish writing in the nineties is part of a larger
cultural effort to assert a national distinctiveness despite the
levelling impact of globalization. The attempt is 'to reconstruct a
mythic identity that is particular to Scotland and so to redeem us
from the banality of a universal economism that would make us
indistinguishable from everyone who lives in a modern industrial
state'.[90] McIlvanney's republicanism and Crichton Smith's
hybridized individualism participate in this general reconstruction of a Scottish past. For neither writer offers any palpable
sense of Britain as a relevant cultural framework; as, in J. G. A.
Pocock's terms, a concept that not only creates the condition
of their several existences, 'but also interacts so as to modify

---

[89] *Out of History: Narrative Paradigms in Scottish and British Culture* (Edinburgh: Polygon, 1996), 187: For Craig, this division and doubleness is endemic to
Scottish culture. Self-division 'is inevitable: the "self", like the nation of which it is a
part, has a double allegiance and a double existence; to dig through language into the
past is to discover not unity and continuity but division and contradiction, and it is
precisely out of the division and contradiction that the poetry is born.'
[90] Ibid. 220.

the condition of each other's existence'.[91] McIlvanney's much-publicized switch from the Labour Party to the SNP,[92] from class to nation, follows the trajectory of his novels: the rediscovery of a national Scottish history is in one sovereign region defined partly in opposition to England.

In Crichton Smith's last two novels, however, the development of his relationship with 'Mrs Scott' is not through the internal dynamics of region and nation but through the international experience of colonialism, a process Patrick Sellar adumbrated when he described the Highlanders as in 'a position not very different from that betwixt the American Colonists and the Aborigines of that Country'.[93] This affiliation with the colonial experience is tentatively acknowledged in *The Search* by Trevor, a Scottish writer-in-residence at an Australian university, searching for his brother, Norman.

He found a book of poems translated from an aboriginal language . . . It seemed to him as he read that he could recognise the images and that they were like pictures of home and that across whatever seas divided him from Scotland this poetry came to him as fresh as if it had been written in his own country. (*TS*, 148)

Lost in the moral underground of Sydney, Norman may have been born on the same day as Shakespeare, a writer indisputably attached to the centre. Trevor now confronts the need for a reunion, some form of wholeness, and this trope of brotherhood is familiar from McIlvanney's *The Big Man* and *Laidlaw*. There, the reunion of brothers signals a higher 'unity of being' that awaits those who directly connect with the epistemology of the nation through the allegory 'Scott'. Such direct communication is one key element in the passage to modernity. For the public sphere in liberal political theory is a moralized conception, not simply a neutrally descriptive realm; and it presumes that transparent communicative reason exists between subject and subject. In this ideal public sphere, a reflective, deliberative, and sovereign citizenry enters into dialogue with a government that is

[91] 'British History: A Plea for a New Subject', *Journal of Modern History*, 47 (Dec. 1975), 606.
[92] 'New Chapter as McIlvanney Endorses Nationalists', *Herald* (6 Apr. 1996).
[93] Quoted in Richards, *History of the Highland Clearances*, 399.

morally bound to reflect their views.[94] In *Docherty*, the nightly gathering of Tam's workmates is one form of this direct communication between individuals. Deliberative, reflective, and rational, the residents of High Street constitute a 'parliament without powers', and the only element preventing their entry into modernity, into the space of the nation state, is the absence of fully sovereign government. But because the detective Laidlaw conducts a rational search for a distinctively Scottish virtue, the origins of 'Scott', the implicit assumption is that the national is rational; that to fully enter modernity and to engage in rational deliberative communication, each individual must enter into the cultural space defined by Scott's life and his painting 'Scotland'.

Yet for Crichton Smith, nothing can create itself until it is first split in two, and in *The Search*, a novel whose form parallels the quest motif of the detective narrative, there is no direct reunion between Trevor and Norman, nor any uncomplicated journey back to a supra-empirical, territorial term called 'Scotland'. Trevor is both subject and object, part colonizer and colonized, linked to an illiterate brother born, possibly, on Shakespeare's birthday. Trevor's closest friend in the novel is Grace, a key term throughout Crichton Smith's oeuvre,[95] and it is she who, like Corkery, insists on the need to share in the people's emotional background,[96] in 'the consciousness of those who have suffered . . . They understand that there are things which belong to the past and things which belong to the future'. Though Trevor finds 'Grace' in Australia, this Australian reality remains an artefact because it cannot be embodied in a style, in a language: 'I suppose as far as an artist is concerned he is the laureate of his own stones or nothing. For myself, I have no language for Australia' (*TS*, 118).

Trevor returns to Scotland through a passage headed 'NOTH-ING TO DECLARE'. For Cairns Craig, this is because 'he carries no

---

[94] Duncan Ivison, 'Postcolonialism and Political Theory', in Andrew Vincent (ed.), *Political Theory: Tradition and Diversity* (Cambridge: Cambridge University Press, 1997), 154–71.

[95] e.g. *The Law and the Grace* (London: Eyre & Spottiswoode, 1961).

[96] Daniel Corkery, *Synge and Anglo-Irish Literature* (1931; Cork: Mercier Press, 1966), 16. Also, 'Real People in a Real Place', 46: 'I found when I visited Australia in 1980, that it is the class consciousness of, especially, the southern English which is most disliked, so that in fact the southern English do not see Australia at all as a country with its own indigenous laws, its own indigenous literature'.

baggage back from the archetypal journey; by not being lost and in need of redemption, Norman has allowed Trevor to return to his normal world and accept it'.[97] Both elements in Crichton Smith's permanent doubleness, 'Grace' and what is 'normal', have to be found in his home. The normative centre to his world is a culture that is, ironically, for ever perched on the periphery, a site where a direct, deliberative communicative reason cannot be assumed. Identity here becomes not so much a self-assured possession as a way of being in the world.[98] Because Australia contains familiar atavisms—'Once he saw a crow pecking out the eyes of a lamb while the exhausted mother looked on helplessly' (*TS*, 25)—the dense particularity of a local cultural memory works not as a simple programme of geography, and the empirical facts of a linear history, but as a migrant hybridization. Trevor, the migrant intellectual, is a symbol of the displaced writer Iain Crichton Smith; and Trevor is recognizably one of Salman Rushdie's 'hybrids':

People who root themselves in ideas rather than places, in memories as much as in material things; people who have been obliged to define themselves—because they are so defined by others—by their otherness; people in whose deepest selves strange fusions occur, unprecedented unions between what they were and what they find themselves.[99]

These 'unprecedented unions' are at the core of *An Honourable Death,* a novel based on the true story of Sir Hector MacDonald, a native Highlander who rose through the ranks of the British army to become one of its most formidable and famous soldiers before, in 1903, after accusations of homosexuality, committing suicide. In one sense MacDonald haunts the margins of *Consider the Lilies,* part of the imperial expansion that enticed Iain's father from the island. The novel's acknowledgement is peculiarly reminiscent of Scott's preface to *Waverley*: 'I would like to stress that although I have done much reading for this book, it is still a novel, and I have used my imagination . . . in elaborating on Hector's thoughts, though within the parameters of his character as I understand it'.

---

[97] 'The Necessity of Accident', in Nicholson (ed.), *Iain Crichton Smith: Critical Essays,* 21.

[98] Declan Kiberd, *Inventing Ireland: The Literature of the Modern Nation* (London: Jonathan Cape, 1997), 164.

[99] *Imaginary Homelands* (London: Granta, 1992), 124.

MacDonald, 'one of those spawned by Culloden who was to serve an Empire which had killed his own people' (*AHD*, 29), is crippled by the doubleness laced throughout Crichton Smith's writing. Colonizer supreme, this hopelessly lonely son of a Highland crofter is incapable of direct communication with either the self or other. His public profile is destroyed by his private homosexuality, for instance, a condition somehow bound up with his inability to incorporate the multiple allegiances his background confers: ' "I have no place, he thought, that is what is wrong. I have no place". And also he had acute sexual urges for which there was no outlet' (*AHD*, 124). Colonizer and colonized, the direct, transparent communication with the self, an essential component in a deliberative, rational citizen, is impossible for this individual broken by history: 'He the son of a crofter from the Highlands of Scotland! That mirror . . . in which he saw himself, looked heavy and rich and imperial' (*AHD*, 1). And just before his suicide, he 'looked into the mirror with an ironic smile' (*AHD*, 135).

The 'harmonising thread' in McIlvanney is a metanarrative that legitimates an autonomous, virtuous citizenry, a citizenry who, if they can only enter into dialogue with the allegory 'Scott', the distant relative of Tam, are poised to possess an independent Scotland. Crichton Smith's version of Kierkegaard's individualism escapes the metanarrative of identity, of 'the Highlander'. But this privileged form of agency never enables direct, transparent connection between the subject and his surroundings. MacDonald never enters modernity; never resolves his sexuality; never fully affiliates with the imperial machine he administers or the colonized subjects he instinctively bonds with; he is never simply inside or outside history. 'Decoding and recoding', in Young's terms, are too simplistic a means of understanding the cultural space MacDonald inhabits. As oppressor and victim, this broken son of a Highland crofter participates in the hybridized patchwork of identities bequeathed by colonialism.[100] Like all Crichton Smith's characters, like Crichton Smith himself, he is being in between.

Clearly visible in Scotland are two of the dominant themes in

---

[100] Young, *Colonial Desire*, 174.

Irish culture: colonialism and republicanism. But the overlap extends beyond broad thematics into specific critical terms. What Neil Ascherson calls 'Dochertyism' recalls Declan Kiberd's 'Bolgerism', a pejorative term Kiberd applies to the politics and subject matter of Dublin writer Dermot Bolger. All Bolger's work accepts, and to some extent legitimizes, the partition of the island into the twenty-six and six county states; and the thematics of country and city provide a crucial element in this process. For Kiberd, 'Bolgerism' implies the definition of a private citizenship that supersedes the historically defined national community; and this is partly the reason, Kiberd contends, why Bolger's generation fails to develop a truly civic culture. Ascherson's charge against 'Dochertyism', McIlvanney's conception of citizenship and nationality, the duties and rights of the individual in the public sphere, are almost exactly the inverse. McIlvanney effectively partitions his urban republic from any contact with a benighted rural hinterland in order to reinvigorate the nation, curbing the claims the individual can make of the polity in order to achieve this. Similar themes preoccupy Thomas McCarthy, a writer who consciously inhabits the intersection between civic republicanism and ethnic nationalism in Fianna Fáil. But discovering such similarities is not enough: instead, the different ways in which the same terms—space, state, society, and nation—overlap in two such similar cultures must be brought into dialogue.

For over and above the specific encounters between these writers is Crichton Smith's general belief that nothing can create itself until it is first split in two. This is, for I hope obvious reasons, a suggestive framework for Irish culture, bringing into focus the space contained within the state, a direct result of the split of the island into two separate spheres. Rushdie described his migrant hybrids as part of the legacy of colonialism, a result of 'unprecedented unions between what they were and what they find themselves'. Writing from the Republic encounters elements of this moment. The writers I now turn to are haunted by what Ireland was in nationalist ideology—a peasantry transmuted, at least in ideal terms, into the thirty-two-county island nation[101]—

---

[101] See the ch. 'The Curse of Rurality: Limits of Modernisation Theory', in Tom Nairn, *Faces of Nationalism: Janus Revisited* (London: Verso, 1997), 90–112, at 91.

and by what it now is: a state that is a socially produced space and as such is, as Edward Soja reminds us, 'also actively engaged in the reproduction of a particular form of social spatialization'.[102]

The work of Duncan MacClean, Irving Welsh, Janice Galloway, and A. L. Kennedy, to name but a handful of current talent on the Scottish literary scene, has redefined contemporary Scotland. But McIlvanney and Crichton Smith—both widely read 'senior' figures in Scottish letters, both recommended reading for Scottish schoolchildren, and both regarded, it seems fair to say, as unofficial spokesmen for Scotland—have addressed Colin Kidd's charge that 'the Scottish past as an ideological resource is virtually bankrupt. Why is the canon of Scottish patriotic cynosures so impoverished?'[103] Tam and Laidlaw, Mrs Scott and Hector MacDonald—the aporia in the narratives of the Scottish nation are filled through figures whose profound difference illustrates that the nation can, in fact, be synonymous with internal differences. In turning to Irish differences, Irish history, the spaces in the state of the Republic of Ireland, I examine three writers who have struggled with an overpopulated canon of Irish patriots, and a history so saturated with ideology that it can sometimes threaten to engulf the present.

---

[102] *Postmodern Geographies: The Reassertion of Space in Critical Social Theory* (London: Verso, 1989), 35.

[103] 'The Canon of Patriotic Landmarks in Scottish History', *Scotlands*, 1/1 (1994), 1–18, at 1.

Part II

Ireland

Region, State, and Nation

3

The Republic and Ireland:
Dermot Bolger, 'Bolgerism',
and Dublin

I STATE AND NATION, ANTHOLOGY AND ONTOLOGY

ONE CONSEQUENCE of the revision of Irish history has been the gradual redefinition of the Irish nation until it becomes almost conterminous with the twenty-six counties. Hence Tom Garvin, professor of political science at University College Dublin, can claim that 'Long before the island of Ireland was partitioned in 1920 . . . the areas that were to become the Irish Republic and Northern Ireland had shown clear signs of developing in different directions and of becoming different societies . . . Partition therefore accelerated or aggravated a process of divergence that had previously existed, and did not artificially instigate it for the first time.'[1] This is refreshingly frank, and 'artificial' is an intriguing term. As Joe Cleary notes, it swaps one mechanistic or deterministic conception of Irish history—the traditional nationalist claim of the island's organic unity—for another that moulds the Irish nation until it is congruent with state borders, thereby enabling the Republic to expunge any traces of the Northern conflict from its collective memory.[2] But the impact of partition

---

[1] 'The North and the Rest', in Charles Townshend (ed.), *Consensus in Ireland: Approaches and Recessions* (Oxford: Clarendon, 1988), 95–109, at 95. See also id. 'A Quiet Revolution: The Remaking of Irish Political Culture', in Ray Ryan (ed.), *Writing in the Irish Republic: Literature, Culture, Politics 1949–1999* (Basingstoke: Macmillan, 2000), 187–203. Also, Thomas Bartlett, 'From Irish State to British Empire: Reflections on State-Building in Ireland, 1690–1830', *Études irlandaises*, 21 (Winter 1995), 25–37.
[2] 'Partition and the Politics of Form in Contemporary Narratives of Northern Ireland', *Ireland and Cultural Studies*, special edn. of *South Atlantic Quarterly*, 95/1 (Winter 1996), 227–8.

on the Southern state, as Todd and Ruane explain, was profound, affecting almost every aspect of the new state and giving
it a 'distinct spatial, economic, demographic, religious and
political profile, shaping its culture, identity, institutions and
sense of community'.[3] Cleary notes how Garvin seems to mecha-
nistically ascribe national feeling or identity entirely to economic
factors; but the states established by partition have experienced
varying degrees of affiliation, legitimacy, and cultural recognition since their foundation.

The state, like any nationalism that claims an immemorial
presence, conceives of itself as *sui generis*. The state does not
exist within the state: it is not a world that can be mapped on the
coordinates given by its laws. In one reading, the idea of the state
is boundless in that it asserts, on certain issues, ultimate claims
over all the lives of those within it. In Hobbes's admittedly
brutal and coercive terms, the state induces the citizen to give up
individual will and act freely having taken this decision not to
disobey. Only when the citizen is prepared to abdicate this right
to disobey can he or she enjoy freedom. Someone unfortunate
enough to be excluded from the rule of the state, a stateless
person, becomes in theory and practice a sort of non-person, a
non-participant in the activity of governing, the activity whereby
the individual is subjected to state power.[4] According to Hobbes,
the state's primary reason for existence is to defend its authority
and sovereignty, to ensure it continues to be. Within the state,
geography acquires a new significance as 'the territorialization of
political obligation'.[5] As Christopher Morris puts it, 'By virtue of
being in a place, circumscribed by lines or markers, people

---

[3] See 'The Republic of Ireland and the Conflict in Northern Ireland', in Joseph
Ruane and Jennifer Todd, *The Dynamics of Conflict in Northern Ireland* (Cambridge: Cambridge University Press, 1996), 249; more generally, see 232–66.

[4] 'Every human agent now alive is held by at least one particular state to be subject
to [a state's] obligations . . . there is no part of the world today in which a human
being can confidently expect to escape the presumption of political subordination
. . . nowhere . . . is there habitable space on earth which lies simply beyond the jurisdiction of state power. Virtually everyone in the modern world accordingly, is
claimed as subject to political obligation.' (John Dunn, 'Political Obligation', in
David Held (ed.), *Political Theory Today* (Stanford: Stanford University Press,
1991), 23). See also Rodney Barker, *Political Legitimacy and the State* (Oxford:
Clarendon Press, 1990), 9.

[5] Christopher W. Morris, *An Essay on the Modern State* (Cambridge: Cambridge
University Press, 1998), 36.

acquire obligations, independently of personal relations, vows, faith or origin ... The territoriality of modern rule means that all who find themselves within the polity's boundaries are, by that fact, governed.'[6] The state then stirs the national imagination by the shape of its territorial remit, by the space in which its public life unfolds.[7] The state is sovereign and perceives itself to be, like the laws of nature, natural, a quality Garvin's analysis unambiguously endorses. Before it emerged with a chrysalis-like shudder in 1920, the twenty-six-county state possessed every quality except the quality of existence, and its borders were conditioned by natural, impersonal, and inevitable processes of economic divergence.

Garvin offers a political context for the literary themes I want to trace in texts from the Republic. In what ways do these apparently inevitable processes of division impact on literary texts? How are they represented? What shape and personality, what social space, does the Republic as a cultural entity, a state, possess? What distinguishes its writing, as opposed to its society, from that of the North? Is there an aesthetic as well as a political division? What role does the aesthetic play in reflecting and enforcing division? The three writers in this part—Dermot Bolger, Thomas McCarthy, Colm Tóibín—are prominent post-nationalists; each has engaged with the problem of representing post-Independence Ireland when the mythic sources of Irish identity have been drained first by economic stagnation, then by the astonishing pace of modernization since the 1960s. Each engages with the idea of the state as propounded by Garvin, and each is at some level involved in the paradox of constructing the Republic's collective memory. For how does an entity like the state, whose sole rational reason for existence is to ensure it continues to be, acquire the value-laden, inevitably selective ballast of memory?

The late Gus Martin indirectly touched on this problem when he said that only a fool would take up where Joyce had left off,[8]

---

[6] Ibid. 37.

[7] Gopal Balakrishnan, 'The National Imagination', *New Left Review*, 211 (1995), 66.

[8] 'Novelist and City: The Technical Challenge', in id. (ed.), *The Genius of Irish Prose* (Dublin: Gill and Macmillan, 1972), 48. See also Declan Kiberd, 'James Joyce and Mythic Realism', in Keith Snell (ed.), *The Regional Novel in Britain and Ireland* (Cambridge: Cambridge University Press, 1998), 136–63.

a point Denis Donoghue elaborated as the peculiar predicament of Irish writers: 'It is my impression that Irish writers sense a rift between experience and meaning, but in reverse; the meaning is premature, already inscribed by a mythology they have no choice but to inherit, and the experience is too narrow to be entirely natural and representative.'[9] One of the most effective ways to naturalize a state in familiar and substantial language, to stir its national imagination, is through literature and, especially, the construction of a canon. The canon now emerging from the Republic, I want to argue, creates the context in which its own work is understood, guaranteeing the naturalness and representativeness of the experience chronicled by establishing a post-mythical landscape; that is, a landscape where meaning is, necessarily, never premature, because no pre-existing or inherited literary tradition has ever accounted for this experience. The absence of a 'natural' and representative Irish identity means that questions of identity, the nation, are subordinate to an examination of the structures of power, the state. All three writers examined here have commented on this aspect of the act of anthologizing. Thomas McCarthy claims that 'Irish politics constantly demands an all-embracing anthology, a single canon, whereas every artistic life rebuffs that demand'.[10] A similar dissonance concludes Colm Tóibín's introduction to *Soho Square*, an anthology of contemporary Irish writing:

This book, then, is a sample of the reactions of forty writers . . . to the sounds and the knowledge that inspired them. They have nothing in common except a beginning under the same sky, the same uncertain weather. And there is no collective consciousness, no conscience of our race, no responsibilities, no nation singing in unison. Instead diversity, the single mind and the imagination making themselves heard.[11]

This, then, is where the Republic's liberal post-nationalism takes up from Joyce: only to the individual imagination is responsibility due. But the most visible proponent of a new interpretative model focused on the Republic's contemporary urban experience is the poet, publisher, playwright, and novelist Dermot Bolger. The division of country and city is not, of course,

---

[9]   'Being Irish Together', *Sewanee Review*, 44/1 (Winter 1976), 133.
[10]   'Documents of Exclusion', *Irish Review*, 4 (Winter 1987), 141–2.
[11]   *Soho Square: New Writing from Ireland* (London: Bloomsbury, 1993), 9.

a wholly new one in Irish writing.[12] But Bolger's is the most sustained attempt to thematize these divisions in order to reconfigure an ethnic Irish identity based on the idea of the island. The model is most obviously new at the level of theme (no fool would try to match Joyce's technical innovations) and geography. A successful, innovative publisher first with the Raven Arts Press then New Island Press, Bolger favoured a demotic poetry and prose that addressed the often grim reality along north Dublin's suburban fringe.[13] Here, a society without the consoling precedent of a literary tradition or historical identity began to find expression:

This was neither country nor city—these streets possessed no place in the school books and poems we learnt at our wooden desks.[14]

This aspect of Irish life, despite being an everyday reality for an increasingly large percentage of the population, was almost totally absent from Irish writing until recently . . . It is only in the post-1968 generation that the confidence to remain true to ordinary modern urban experiences around them finally begins to be displayed.[15]

Bolger formulates a tradition whose main feature is the lack of an underlying tradition. It is not a question of restoring dignity to what has been suppressed—for Seamus Deane, and, as we have seen, William McIlvanney, a liberating effect of nationalism—but of representing for the first time an entirely original Irish formation.[16]

[12] See Terence Brown, 'Dublin in Twentieth-Century Writing: Metaphor and Subject', in *Irish University Review*, 8/1 (Spring 1978), 1–19; Declan Kiberd, 'Irish Literature and Irish History', in R. F. Foster, *The Illustrated History of Ireland* (Oxford: Oxford University Press, 1989), 275–338.

[13] See 'Speaking with . . . Dermot Bolger', *In Cognito*, 1 (1997), 13–14: 'When I formed Raven I had nothing . . . And the illusion of a Dublin thing did come from Raven . . . There was very little about Dublin in Irish writing when Raven came along and certainly Raven made a lot of noises about Dublin . . . Certainly we would regard ourselves as the bold boys of Irish writing and we'd get worried if the *Irish Times* liked the book. We really had this notion that the writer should be an outlaw.' For Peter Fallon, founder of Gallery Press, Bolger exaggerates here the radicalness and originality of Raven Arts. See Peter Fallon, 'Notes on a History of Publishing Poetry', *Princeton University Library Chronicle*, 59/3 (Spring 1998), 547–58.

[14] Dermot Bolger, *Invisible Dublin: A Journey through Dublin's Suburbs* (Dublin: Raven Arts Press, 1991), 12.

[15] Id. (ed.), *The Picador Book of Contemporary Irish Fiction* (1993; rev. and expanded edn., London: Picador, 1994), pp. xviii–xix.

[16] See Seamus Deane, 'Heroic Styles: The Tradition of an Idea', in *Ireland's Field Day* (Notre Dame, Ind.: University of Notre Dame Press, 1984), 47.

This new context generates an incipient post-nationalism, one that emphasizes the fragmenting, alienating experience of the city over pastoral values of wholeness and community. Irish nationalism's imagined community, Bolger claims, cannot incorporate the reality of sites that were 'neither country nor city', a fact which not only denaturalizes the countryside as a locus of moral value, making it no longer an especially virtuous model for the Irish experience; it also excludes these sites from any concept which historicizes their identity as part of any 'collective consciousness', anything remotely resembling a nationalist past.[17]

Modern Irish canons are of course intensely contested and self-conscious constructs.[18] For example, Seamus Deane's introduction to *The Field Day Anthology* claims 'there is a metanarrative here, a story of the island which can accommodate the competing micronarratives it hosts'.[19] This is the metanarrative of history, of the various groups who inhabited the island, the one stable signifier for Deane in Ireland's history of invasion and conquest. The Field Day metanarrative, setting aside its well-documented exclusions, subscribes to the principle of an immemorial historic identity comprised of any group historically resident on the island. It is elastic but systematic, inclusive but bound by a commitment to the idea of the nation and the notion that culture can cooperate with or even sponsor the patterns of political narratives. All writing is ideological, Seamus Deane claims in the introduction; all aesthetic terms are ultimately transposable with political terms in creating our individual and collective self-consciousness. The Irish are a written people as well as a risen people, and the fact and form of the latter are inescapably bound up with the former, whether the writing in question is ostensibly creative or political or religious.

In Bolger's anthology *The Picador Book of Contemporary*

---

[17] See Patrick J. Duffy, 'Writing Ireland: Literature and Art in the Representation of Irish Place', in Brian Graham (ed.), *In Search of Ireland: A Cultural Geography* (London: Routledge, 1997), 64–83, at 74: 'rejection of the city, its secularism and its bourgeois compromises on cultural nationalism, is implicit in the construction of a rural idyll in Ireland'.

[18] See Thomas Kinsella's polemical introd. to *The Oxford History of Irish Verse* (Oxford: Clarendon Press, 1986), pp. xxiii–xxx. See also his *The Dual Tradition: An Essay on Poetry and Politics in Ireland* (Manchester: Carcanet, 1995).

[19] Seamus Deane (gen. ed.), *The Field Day Anthology of Irish Writing*, i (Derry: Field Day, 1991).

Irish Fiction the foundational text is Beckett's,[20] whose language of exhaustion and abjection famously demystified the whole notion of identity and the concept of an indigenous tradition, while the introduction insists that we ditch such frameworks as post-colonialism in favour of an apparently untheorizable range of 'private, fictional, universes'.[21] Bolger's introduction praises *The Field Day Anthology* but, like Thomas McCarthy and especially Colm Tóibín, he dispenses with the idea of a historic national identity, a notion aimed at a 'conservative American university audience'.[22] His writers overcome rather than incorporate history, offering instead a thrilling and, it has to be said, highly unlikely talent for self-generation unconnected to any collective entity called Ireland.

National identities, Anthony Smith claims, emerge from 'all those who feel they share certain symbolic codes, value systems and traditions of belief and ritual, including reference to a supra-empirical reality'.[23] Such identities are importantly negative, that is, formed and affirmed against an oppressive one elsewhere, so that once oppression is withdrawn, that identity is disowned. For Bolger, committed to transcending Field Day's obsessive opposition of Ireland and England, while still asserting the specificity of the Republic, some other 'supra-empirical reality' besides the historic nation is now necessary. This is why a critical framework such as post-colonialism, committed to an ethical evaluation of a historically oppressed Irish national identity, attracts concentrated fire. Instead, each writer's 'unique and private fictional universe' is acknowledged, and 'it is within the contexts of these private worlds that they [the anthologised writers] should be judged'.[24] This is an important formulation, one to

---

[20] In *Strange Country: Modernity and Nationhood in Irish Writing since 1790* (Oxford: Clarendon Press, 1997), 1, Seamus Deane defines this usage: 'A foundational text is one that allows or has allowed for a reading of a national literature in such a manner that even chronologically prior texts can be annexed by it into a narrative that will ascribe to them a preparatory role in the ultimate completion of that narrative's plot. It is a text that generates the possibility of such a narrative and lends to that narrative a versatile cultural and political value'. See also Richard Kearney, 'Beckett: The Demythologising Mind', in id. (ed.), *The Irish Mind* (Dublin: Wolfhound, 1985), 267–93.

[21] *Picador Book of Contemporary Irish Fiction*, p. xxiii.

[22] Ibid. p. xxii.

[23] *National Identity* (Harmondsworth: Penguin, 1991), 6.

[24] Bolger (ed.), *Picador Book of Contemporary Irish Fiction*, p. xvi.

which we will return. Each private consciousness is deemed to
constitute a closed space. Any representation of society as a
totality must bring into coalition these sealed subjective worlds
and their peculiar interaction. This decentring of the individual
in relation to a totality, like the nation, Fredric Jameson
describes as the spatial propensity of postmodernism, 'one
that involves our insertion as individual subjects into a multi-
dimensional set of radically discontinuous realities'.[25] Bolger
repudiates the concept of a totality for the random and undecid-
able micropolitics these new urban sites contain.[26] The notion of
a totality, 'Ireland', seems to be rejected entirely by reference to
the non-essential character of the links uniting the elements of
the presumed totality. But what is uniquely new about this
abstract Irish space is its facility for being, as Henri Lefebvre
describes it, simultaneously homogeneous and fragmented. The
global expansion of industrial capital, Lefebvre claims, bred a
remarkably complex relation to abstract space:

The commodity is a thing: it is in space, and occupies a location . . . the
commodity world brings in its wake certain attitudes towards space,
certain actions on space, even a certain concept of space . . . each location, each link in a chain of commodities, is occupied by a thing whose
particular traits become more marked once they become fixed . . . The
space of the commodity may thus be defined as a homogeneity made up
of specificities . . . Space thus understood is both *abstract* and *concrete*.
This is a space, therefore, that is homogeneous yet at the same time
broken up into fragments.[27]

The political equivalent of this spatial diffusion is, of course,
pluralism. Bolger valorizes difference for its own sake, envisag-
ing no antagonistic relationship between different social constituencies. But the limits of pluralism are its inability to dis-

[25] 'Cognitive Mapping', in *Marxism and the Interpretation of Culture* (Basingstoke: Macmillan, 1988), 353.
[26] See Chris Curtin, Hastings Donnan, and Thomas M. Wilson, 'Anthropology
and Irish Urban Settings', in eid. (eds.), *Irish Urban Cultures* (Belfast: Institute of
Irish Studies, 1993), 1–21.
[27] *The Production of Space*, trans. Donald Nicholson-Smith (Oxford: Blackwell,
1991), 341 (emphasis in original). Gerry Smyth also utilizes Lefebvre's work on these
same themes in 'The Right to the City: Representations of Dublin in Contemporary
Irish Fiction', in Liam Harte and Michael Parker (eds.), *Contemporary Irish Fiction:
Themes, Tropes, Theories* (Basingstoke: Macmillan, 2000), 13–34.

criminate between differences that exist and should not, and those that do not but should.[28] Because liberty is the pre-eminent organizing principle of Bolger's introduction, no confrontation occurs between the principles of equality and the individual's imaginative freedom. The artistic life, then, chooses the exact nature of its relationship to society, is not compelled to reflect the 'real' conditions surrounding it, any pre-existing 'supra-empirical reality', and is not compromised by its aversion towards history or tradition. Bolger's claim that each private universe is equally 'true' allows for no external ethical criteria by which to judge them, since 'truth' has no force unless there is some falsehood present. 'Truth' here seems to imply the writer's ability to evade the claims of any 'supra-empirical' term like the historic nation, and instead claim 'truth' to be something linked entirely to the experience of each private fictional universe. In Bolger's terms, which resonate with Tóibín's introduction to his *Soho Square* anthology, this is 'a generation which is still in the process of forming itself; an anthology of writers . . . whose most remarkable characteristic is to share almost nothing in common except originality; a body of writers who are all working from equally valid, equally true and yet equally different visions'.[29] The rhetoric of pluralism here erases the possibility of a collective cultural difference (and, it might be added, aesthetic discrimination: 'nothing in common except originality'), displacing even the category of Irishness in which we might expect an Irish anthology to invest. It also diminishes any claim for the 'truth' content of these universes, since truth-claims have to somehow measure one's experience against something else. Like Sebastian Barry's 1984 anthology *The Inherited Boundaries: Younger Poets from the Republic of Ireland*, Bolger's anthology inaugurates the tradition it seeks to reflect. But how does this anthology remain a whole if what characterizes its constituent parts is an equal separateness, an inviolate individualism? What is the abstract term that links them, apart from Bolger's rhetoric of pure originality?

---

[28] On this point, see Chantal Mouffe, 'Democratic Politics Today', in ead. (ed.), *Dimensions of Radical Democracy: Pluralism, Citizenship, Community* (London: Verso, 1992), 13.
[29] 'Introduction', in Bolger (ed.), *Picador Book of Contemporary Irish Fiction*, p. xxvii.

A literary canon is a hypothetical image of social diversity, a
kind of mirror in which social groups do or do not see themselves.[30] But Bolger's, Tóibín's, and Barry's anthologies are
not interested in the pathos of admission or exclusion to an
expanded canon of 'Irishness'. The objective is to banish the concept of a historical identity, any special theory of personality
such as the nation or Ireland, and establish a canon that corresponds with Garvin's historiography of the state. And because
the state is not partisan, because it has no rational purpose other
than to exist, the fact that it sponsors this range of 'private
fictional universes', these 'equally valid, equally true and yet
equally different viewpoints and visions', this is proof of its commitment to diversity, its fundamental liberalism, its ability to
sponsor an imagined community capable of incorporating new
urban sites. In this incipient post-nationalism, the state begins to
replace the island as the one stable signifier in Irish discourse.

Sebastian Barry's introduction to *The Inherited Boundaries*,
however, reveals how an ostensibly liberal discourse can be
deformed by the rigidity of its defensive postures, by its commitment to naturalize the state's jurisdiction. Barry's polemical aim
to synthesize a counter-tradition eventually drifts into utopian
proclamations, where Irish identity, having first been banished as
traditionalist, now reappears and finds both a terminus and new
point of departure through writers from the Republic: 'The poets
assembled here . . . they are Irish, the first Irish poets ever in a
way, because that adjective has meant so many things in the past
that it meant nothing . . . this is a first if fragmentary map of the
country.'[31] Just as the state perceives itself to be the terminus of
human development, with no horizon beyond its own existence,
writers are admitted to this canon only when, to reapply Hobbes,
the artist has freely chosen to abdicate the right not to disobey or
contravene the remit of the anthology. Hence the exclusion
of writers who might thematize issues like Catholicism and
nationalism, any history potentially hostile to the state forma-

---

[30] John Guillory, *Cultural Capital: The Problem of Literary Canon Formation*
(Chicago: University of Chicago Press, 1993), 7.
[31] *The Inherited Boundaries: Younger Poets from the Republic of Ireland* (Dublin:
Mercier Press, 1986), 17. The introd. is titled 'The History and Topography of
Nowhere'.

tions, any writer for example, who subscribes to the ideal of Ireland as a historically definable collective entity.

Bolger's partitionism, along with his description of a 'seven hundred year occupation' by a 'foreign army', moved Edna Longley to lament his 'slide between two rhetorics', his 'schizoid separatism'.[32] Yet this rhetoric is consistent with a utopian element in both Barry's and Bolger's anthologies, and the cause of a contradiction in Bolger's. He claims that 1968 is the year when the Republic started to ditch Donoghue's 'premature meaning', a tradition that anchored writers to a socio-political context they had no choice but to reflect. It is the year the Republic introduced free second-level education. By then, emigration had stopped and a generation emerged of 'writers and readers who had nothing to lose by taking apart that state to examine how it worked inside'.[33] This is typical of the relentlessly progressive dynamic of Bolger's introduction, and while it is obviously accurate within its own terms, nowhere does it register the festering civil rights agitation in the North that spawned the Provisional IRA and twenty-five years of armed conflict. Of course, the cataclysmic events of May '68 across Europe actually originated in the universities, as part of a general revolt against the sterility of political and cultural life the nation state sponsored. Inspired by May 1968, Foucault decoded the structures of power through which the state naturalized its authority over social space. If the rapturous political energies of '68 had one guiding theme, it was the challenge posed to all existing forms of political representation in order to liberate the individual into new, as yet unthought-of, forms of community.

Bolger's version of '68 is more modest. As outlined in the anthology, it is egalitarian and heterogeneous, homogeneous yet still fragmented, and implicitly it dissociates nationality from citizenship. The values contained in the social spaces it articulates are irretrievably organized around the idea of the state. With this symbolic opening, Bolger's anthology expunges the North from the Republic's collective memory. The state is enlisted as the guarantor of newly liberated imagination and the traditional constraints of a national tradition no longer apply;

[32] *The Living Stream: Literature and Revisionism in Ireland* (Newcastle-upon-Tyne: Bloodaxe, 1994), 48.
[33] *Picador Book of Contemporary Irish Fiction*, p. x.

the only metanarrative these writers know is the silent, ever-present narrative of the state.[34]

But how different is this 'liberal' formation based on a neutral space like the state from the historically loaded narrative of the nation? Bolger's introduction focuses on the new socio-political structures represented but has little to say about the aesthetic. Again and again he categorizes writers according to the social constituencies they reflect—urban, gay, emigrant, women, etc.—terms which ultimately, of course, do not describe the writing but the society the writing describes. What is new and novel in Bolger's anthology is the state, the steady, relentless, Whiggish maturity of which the anthology describes, naturalizes, and elaborates. The only constant, premature order in Bolger's anthology is the state that permits a systematically random amalgamation of writers no longer gnarled by Irish–English, Catholic–Protestant dichotomies.[35] Bolger's anthology, his work as a publisher, and his many edited collections, sponsor and con-sciously create a youthful, liberally minded, and enthusiastically European constituency. But the justification for the constituency is always made in terms which refer back to the idea of differ-ence; it is just that the difference which makes the difference is no longer ethnic or national but difference from what has gone before, differences within and between the concept of 'the Irish' themselves. The reaction against an 'idea of nationhood which simply could not contain the Ireland of concrete and dual-carriageway (which is as Irish as turf and boreens) that was the reality before our eyes'[36] displaces colonial faultlines, the Anglo-Irish obsessions of Field Day, for the internal divisions of class and geography within the polity. There is still a systematic and elastic metanarrative capable of containing competing micro-narratives; it is just that it is now the metanarrative of the state.

---

[34] See 'Speaking with . . . Dermot Bolger', 15: 'Interviewer: "Do you think there is the foundation for a Dublin literary tradition". Bolger: "I don't think there's such a thing as a tradition"'.

[35] For a general survey of these issues see Henry Louis Gates jr, *Loose Canons: Notes on the Culture Wars* (New York: Oxford University Press, 1992). For the problems in an Irish context see Seamus Deane, 'Canon Fodder: Literary Myth-ologies in Ireland', in Jean Lundy and Aodán Mac Póilín (eds.), *Styles of Belonging: Culture and Ideology in Ireland* (Belfast: Lagan Press, 1992), 22–32.

[36] Bolger (ed.), *The Bright Wave/An Tonn Gheal: Poetry in Irish Now* (Dublin: Raven Arts Press, 1986), 10.

This is not a wholly unprecedented way of organizing experience: it mirrors Field Day's much-criticized schema by retaining a totalizing metanarrative: all that differs is the stable signifier—nation or state—that makes possible meaning. And that, of course, is ultimately a political not an aesthetic choice, if one concedes that the two differ.[37]

Bolger aims to show, correctly in my view, that the North is not emblematic of the contemporary Irish experience, and that the Irish experience is no longer conterminous with the island. The exposure Northern writers received, he claims,

helped reinforce the notion that the North was central to all Irish writing, so that as a writer from the Republic of Ireland—which is three times the size of the North—one frequently felt that you were writing about a society that had been rendered invisible. The genuine changes and struggles and the separate reality of people's lives in the south seemed to count as nothing for academics, editors and critics with their own agenda.[38]

Perhaps it is not surprising, considering this, that Bolger has received many critical reviews and little critical analysis. What criticism there is frequently focuses on the agenda rather than the writing. Declan Kiberd's savage review of *The Woman's Daughter*, for instance, blasted Bolger's appeal to 'the bleeding-heart punditocracy which fancies itself the epitome of a persecuted modernity', all part of 'the current revisionist fad for deconstructing the pious simplicities of the early 1960s, yet in reality, only expressive of a move from clerical autocracy to sticky conformism'.[39] (The delicious sarcasm of 'sticky', a vaguely derogative term for those Marxist republicans who accepted the twenty-six-county state and who now fiercely oppose Sinn Féin's nationalism, makes this worth the admittance price alone.) Kiberd criticized Bolger's private universes, these sites containing multiple narratives and no single, supra-empirical interpretation:

[37] On Field Day see Marilynn Richtarik, *Acting between the Lines: The Field Day Theatre Company and Irish Cultural Politics* (Oxford: Clarendon Press, 1994); Richard Kirkland, *Literature, Culture and Politics in Northern Ireland since 1965: Moments of Danger* (Harlow: Longman, 1996), 121–48.

[38] *Picador Book of Contemporary Irish Fiction*, pp. xi–xii.

[39] Quoted in Shaun Richards, 'Northside Realism and the Twilight's Last Gleaming', *Irish Studies Review*, 2 (Winter 1992), 18–20.

The rising generation did not speak with a single voice: and its members were too mobile to solidify into single schools. Some, such as Dermot Bolger, repudiated Irish nationalism and declared themselves positively uninterested in having a united Ireland. On the most urgent question facing the people, these took a line even more conservative than that favoured by the Dublin government.[40]

A sceptical response to this might ask how Kiberd knows the North to be the most urgent issue facing 'the people', while 'the people' remain obtusely focused on economics, housing, education—all those issues the Dublin government is actually responsible for. But for Kiberd, Bolger, and his confrères Fintan O'Toole and Tóibín, represent the new orthodoxy in Irish cultural life, a state-sponsored elite whose postmodern distrust of any metanarrative undermines the nationalist idea of Ireland, even as they solder themselves to a state they then identify as oppressive.[41] 'Bolgeresque' is Kiberd's adjective for 'the mawkish sentimentality' of this housing-estate realism.[42] Similarly, Shaun Richards urged that 'the same analytical and polemical skills which Kiberd and Deane brought to bear on Yeats should now be brought to bear on Doyle, Bolger and those likely to mine the caustical and comic veins of urban blight rather than celebrate a supposedly apolitical rural idyll'.[43]

Bolger's, Tóibín's, and O'Toole's revival still recognizes the Irish as a written people; it just never wants them again to be a risen people. There is no question that literature still intersects with politics. It might be instructive, however, to ask what alternative model of 'the people' Bolger is deviating from, for it is, surely, undeniable that different social, cultural, and political priorities exist in the Republic and Northern Ireland. To remark on the difference does not make that difference absolute; to admit otherwise is to denigrate the appalling experience of the North. We need to engage with Declan Kiberd's important criti-

---

[40] *Inventing Ireland: The Literature of the Modern Nation* (London: Jonathan Cape, 1997), 610. See also Colbert Kearney, 'Dermot Bolger and the Dual Carriageway', *Études irlandaises* (Autumn 1994), 25–39.

[41] For a brilliantly readable interrogation of the workings of power and the state, see Fintan O'Toole, *Meanwhile Back at the Ranch: The Politics of Irish Beef* (London: Vintage, 1995).

[42] 'Establishment Shots', *Graph: Irish Literary Review*, 13 (Winter 1992–Spring 1993), 6.

[43] 'Northside Realism and the Twilight's Last Gleaming', 20.

cism of Bolger's 'generation's inability to achieve a truly civic discourse'.[44] Kiberd's *Inventing Ireland* ends with a rousing reassertion of the many-coloured quilt of Kathleen Ní Houlihán. This appallingly kitsch metaphor cloaks the credibly liberal claim that Ireland is now 'a quilt of many patches and colours, all beautiful, all distinct, yet all connected too. No one element should subordinate or assimilate the others . . . each has its part to play.'[45] This presumably includes those disaffected from and uninterested in Kathleen and her quilt (such as the yearly gathering of Orange brethren at Drumcree). The idea of the national, as Seamus Deane's introduction to *The Field Day Anthology* acknowledges, must account for those micronarratives uninterested in nationality. Instead of condemning Bolger's project outright, we must acknowledge its potency, analyse its politics and aesthetics, and see what these private fictional universes contain. Bolger's achievements over twenty years deserve serious engagement. And the underlying dynamic of his writing, I want to argue, is the depoliticization of the public sphere it helps brings into existence.

II   DUBLIN AND THE PRODUCTION OF SPACE

We have seen how Bolger's claims for a new cultural order are mediated through the material expansion of Dublin's suburbs, a physical development that mirrors the movement away from a sense of place and identity that precedes the political division of the island into two states.[46] Any discussion of Dublin's literary

---

[44] 'The Children of Modernity', *Irish Times* (22 June 1991), 9. See also Fionnula O'Connor's ch. 'The South: I don't like their attitudes', in *In Search of a State: Catholics in Northern Ireland* (Belfast: Blackstaff Press, 1993), 223–72: 'Brought up to yearn for the greater part of their nation on the other side of an imaginary, arbitrary line on the map, they now feel little more than lack of sympathy with the inhabitants of another country.'

[45] *Inventing Ireland*, 653.

[46] See John Wilson Foster, 'The Geography of Irish Fiction', in Patrick Rafroidi and Maurice Harmon (eds.), *The Irish Novel in Our Time* (Lille: Centre d'Études irlandaises de l'Université de Lille, 1976), 89–102; Seamus Heaney, 'The Sense of Place', in *Preoccupations: Selected Prose 1968–1978* (London: Faber and Faber, 1980), 131–2; Seán Ó Tuama, 'Stability and Ambivalence: Aspects of the Sense of Place and Religion in Irish Literature', in Joseph Lee (ed.), *Ireland: Towards a Sense of Place* (Cork: Cork University Press, 1985), 21–33.

history is dominated by Joyce, of course; but the transformation of Dublin from a small, compact, high-density city into a large sprawling, decentralized 'scarcely comprehensible city-region' means Joyce's city can no longer claim to define the experience of Dublin.[47] His narrow band of petty bourgeois characters are inscribed by an almost exclusively Anglo-Irish history, transforming the streets of *Dubliners*—Hume Street, Trinity College, Duke's Lawn—into an orthographic map of absolute, paralysing certainty. Hence Terence Brown's observation that 'What this Dublin of public buildings suggests is a city of caste divisions and a city where the cultural and social implications of place and name are inevitably etched on the psyches of the various personae. No character is ever allowed more than the merest moment of freedom from a grid plan of a Dublin he knows with an all too impressive familiarity.'[48] The numerous social rituals in *Dubliners* lock citizens into an already internalized, cyclical, suffocatingly intimate history, whereas fragmentation and a pervasive sense of alienation in Bolger's Finglas replace the symbolic sources of Irish identity. Finglas, as 'neither country nor city', acts in Tom Paulin's useful phrase as the 'theoretical location', the actual and symbolic site for Bolger's counter-tradition,[49] a Dublin without a grid or a plan. Joyce's narratives suggest what is often assumed to be a high-modernist fascination with the thematics of time, what Fredric Jameson calls 'the elegiac mysteries of *durée* and memory'. A consequence of the shift from modernism to postmodernism, he argues, is that 'our daily life, our psychic experience, our cultural languages, are today dominated by categories of space rather than categories of time'.[50]

[47] See Arnold Horner, 'From City to City-Region: Dublin from the 1930s to 1990s', in Kevin Whelan (ed.), *Dublin City and County: From Prehistory to Present* (Dublin: Geography Publications, 1992), 327–58. See also Colm Lincoln, 'City of Culture: Dublin and the Discovery of Heritage', in Barbara O'Connor and Michael Cronin (eds.), *Tourism in Ireland: A Critical Analysis* (Cork: Cork University Press, 1993), 203–30.

[48] 'The Dublin of Dubliners', in Bernard Benstock (ed.), *James Joyce: An International Perspective* (Gerrards Cross: Colin Smythe, 1982), 11.

[49] Quoted in Bernard O'Donoghue, ' "The Half-Said Thing is Dearest": Paul Muldoon', in Michael Kenneally (ed.), *Poetry in Contemporary Irish Literature* (Gerrards Cross: Colin Smythe, 1995), 400.

[50] *Postmodernism, or, The Cultural Logic of Late Capitalism* (London: Verso, 1991), 16. See also David Harvey, *The Condition of Postmodernity* (Oxford: Blackwell, 1989), 3–65.

The production and organization of space in Bolger is part of the process of making familiar the experience of unfamiliarity, or in Denis Donoghue's terms, of representing as belonging to Ireland an experience devoid of any mythological meaning. The hierarchical structure of the house in Joyce's 'The Dead', for example, reflects the cultural and social implications of the caste divisions Brown noted. Operating on a vertical spectrum, the self-confident servant Lily on the ground floor, the fading protocols of the sisters' society on the top floor, the social relations unfolding in Dublin are analogously configured through an organization of space that has a narrow but symbolic depth. Those at the sisters' party recall a Dublin which is, literally, beneath them, physically outside on the street; and beneath these streets lie the recidivist memories of the dead that haunt the whole evening. Movement along this vertical spectrum during the night dictates the willingness of individual characters to confront this history unfolding in the public sphere. Miss Ivors, for example, leaves the top floor for the cold reality of the night streets beneath the party; the rest reluctantly disengage at the evening's end when they have no other choice. The house, then, is implicated in the form of time and history experienced by each character, an organization of space that recalls Bergson's philosophy of *durée*, his claim that psychological or organic temporality deviates from the linearity of mechanical and industrial time.

Compare this to Bolger's flat spatialization of history in Finglas's sprawling estates, the chronic disorder that characterizes the expansion of his 'private universe'. One reading of Bolger's repeated blasts against Irish literary critics is to suggest that the persistent historicism of critical frameworks such as post-colonialism, which affirms a historic national identity against an imperial English 'other', obscures the insidious spatialization within Irish society reflected in his writing. The convergence of Dublin's geography and Irish history does not produce depth, collectivity, or any segregated vision of class relations. Bolger's repeated use of illegitimacy as a trope, for example, implies that an individual's contingent existence is always in conflict with an otherwise natural order. Compared to Joyce's fixed grid plan, the absence in new social spaces such as Finglas of any sense of civic cohesion works to subordinate time and erect a spatial system that reflects the new sociological order of contemporary Dublin, an order based not on a narrative of progress and emancipation, but on survival and endurance. What we see in Bolger is the gradual enclosure of memory and its replacement by Lefebvre's 'production of space': the recognition that, as David Harvey and other theorists of space have claimed, the spaces of representation have the potential not only to affect the representation of space, but also to act as material productive forces with respect to spatial practices.[51] The contrast between the diffuse, horizontal space of Dublin's suburbs and the hierarchical structure of the house in 'The Dead' means that, in this 'scarcely comprehensible city-region', a grid-less Dublin, the determinate relationship between individual and environment can be reversed. Or as Jonathan Raban's relentless optimism has it, 'For better or worse, [the city] invites you to remake it, to consolidate it into a shape you can live in . . . Decide who you are, and the city will again assume a fixed form around you. Decide what it is, and your own identity will be revealed, like a map fixed by triangulations.'[52]

The production of space in Bolger is linked with the same problematic as the making of history.[53] Place is never passive; it is recognized and foregrounded as a social process; and the appropriation and transformation of space is inseparable from the wider transformation of Irish society.[54] In such projects as *A New Primer for Irish Schools*,[55] where some of Pearse's most famous visionary poems of an Ireland free and Gaelic are rewritten for Irish schoolchildren, Bolger's incipient, caustic postnationalism deploys Raban's manifesto for the city as a site of

---

[51] Harvey, *Condition of Postmodernity*, 3–65.

[52] Quoted ibid. 5. See also Stephen David Ross, 'Discourse, Polis, Finiteness, Perfection', in Mary Ann Caws (ed.), *Literature, Philosophy, and Film* (New York: Gordon & Breach, 1991), 24–30.

[53] On connections between space and history, see Edward W. Soja, *Postmodern Geographies: The Reassertion of Space in Critical Social Theory* (London: Verso, 1989), 35.

[54] Allan Pred, 'Place as Historically Contingent Process: Structuration and the Time-Geography of Becoming Places', *Annals of the Association of American Geographers*, 74/2 (1984), 279: Pred claims 'place is not only what is fleetingly observed on the landscape, a locale, or setting for activity and social interaction. It also is what takes place ceaselessly, what contributes to history in a specific context through the creation and utilisation of a physical setting'.

[55] Dermot Bolger and Michael O'Loughlin, *A New Primer for Irish Schools* (Dublin: Raven Arts Press, 1985).

revision and reinvention. Poems such as 'Renunciation: P. H. Pearse (after Pearse)' and 'Snuff Movies' foreground the themes of emigration, urban deprivation, the relentless boredom of unemployment, and poverty. These poems cognitively map, to use Fredric Jameson's useful phrase, a social space at odds with an imagined community founded on pastoral, rural values, and they announce his determination to admit the full, grim force of a despiritualized, bureaucratized present to Irish letters. 'Snuff Movie' ends with such abstractions as 'God' or 'heaven' subordinate to the immediacy of televisual information and drained of any wider cultural resonance:

> Long ago I believed in God—now I believe what I am told:
> there is no heaven except that instant when the set comes alive,
> no purgatory except the infinite static bombarding the screen,
> hell could only be if they came for the television or for me.[56]

Throughout Bolger's work, images from the present always discipline any attempt to imagine abstract concepts that might merge contemporary experience into a historical continuum or tradition. *A New Primer for Irish Schools* is actually a good example of Bolger sponsoring a civic identity that counters Pearse's ethno-cultural identity. Another is his use of adoption and absent parents as tropes. For if, as Edna Longley claims, it is through parents that the individual locates himself in history, Bolger's deployment of adoption as a trope ruptures any apostolic ethnic linkage to the past, announcing instead the beginning of a new symbolic order whose integrity is faithful, above all, to the present.[57]

III   A DUBLIN TRILOGY

Bolger emerged as the laureate of the excluded with *The Journey Home*, the third work in a loosely conceived trilogy that has generated high praise as well as considerable rancour. This violent, uncompromising, bitterly critical portrayal of the Plunkett brothers, archetypes of the Fianna Fáil nationalist elite, established his counter-tradition. The Plunketts (named after a leader

[56] Ibid. 21.
[57] Longley, *Living Stream*, 152.

of the 1916 Rising, Joseph Mary Plunkett) control a state still defined through certain immanently valuable, rural imagery. The central theme is the discovery of self-respect in the face of the official denial of Francie Hanrahan's daily, actual home. He works in a voters' register office, administering but never participating in the polity he inhabits, politically and imaginatively disenfranchised and without agency in 'a country in exile from itself'.[58] The historical definition of Ireland allowed by the Plunketts is never inflected by the contemporary.[59]

Francie's narrative unfolds against a general election, an event which emphasizes the overwhelming importance of the present throughout Bolger's writing. The plot of *The Journey Home*—Francie, now known as Hano, fleeing from Dublin to the west of Ireland chased by Gardaí for his murder of Pascal Plunkett—highlights the incompatibility of this present with the sanctified version of history underwriting it, a rupture that generates the novel's tripartite narrative structure. The only strand relayed through a conventional narrator is his escape with Cáit/Kate to Sligo, home of a Protestant woman Hano met as a child. The teleological status of this narrative, the emotional search for value and agency, enhances the shocking discovery that there is, ultimately, no stable concept of home to aspire to. A second narrative has Hano relate the reasons for the journey, his relationship with Shay, Cáit/Kate, and his dealings with the Plunketts. Finally Shay relates his tale from beyond the grave, at last free to narrate experiences suppressed while alive by the Plunketts.

As the novel begins, then, those characters who might aid Francie's self-definition—his father, Shay, an old woman in Sligo—are dead, and each death is evidence of contemporary political corruption and the exhaustion of the historic sources of Irish personal and collective legitimation. Any alternative indices of value are erased by the Plunketts: Shay, the renegade urban

---

[58] 'Who'd be a Northside Playwright?', interview with Bolger, *Irish Press*, 20 Sept. 1989, p. 22.

[59] 'The concept of home in Dermot Bolger has, however, a more extended application: it relates also to the search for an Irish home, or nation, that might answer to the needs of a deracinated, migrant generation still haunted by the assumptions and values of its rural and Catholic parentage and by its Gaelic origins.' Neil Corcoran, *After Yeats and Joyce: Reading Modern Irish Literature* (Oxford: Oxford University Press, 1997), 126.

maverick fired by a vision of Europe; Francie's father, in whom the residual values of rural life are maintained; and the rural Protestant woman's enigmatic (or for some readers, implausible) independence. Anything that collides with the Plunketts' abstract image of Ireland is abolished, as the wholesale transposition of rural idioms onto contemporary urban sites generates a 'perpetual exile', a doubleness caused by the continual intrusion of an irrecoverable rural past into an urban present: 'Whatever world they and my father came from had died among the rows of new streets built here, and I was cut off from that past as surely as if ten generations stood between us' (*TJH*, 121). Shay inaugurates and incarnates Bolger's counter-tradition, helping Hano shed the feeling 'that where you live is not your real home' (*TJH*, 8). Like McIlvanney's Scott, he is primal, sexual, intelligent, charismatic, in a word: cool, an exhilarating glimpse of fresh forms of national affiliation. Shay renames Francie Hano, thereby formally acknowledging the urban component of his self and ensuring Hano is no longer inscribed by any premature urban or rural mythology. Identity is chosen, not fated. For Shay the present self is never simply the result of past actions; the alternative to remembering and acknowledging the past, he shows, is not historical amnesia—Francie still remains Hano—but an ongoing effort at reinvention out of the mixed materials that come with relocation within Ireland or Europe.[60]

This relocation of values starts when Shay introduces Francie/Hano to the city centre, an unambiguously urban site through which more profound dislocations become visible, the realization that he had 'a mother and father I loved but no longer lived or belonged to [because] now it was Shay that I lived for' (*TJH*, 55). Division, separateness, alienation, fragmentation are integral elements in the forms of community Shay makes possible. There is no historical locus that everyone can be presumed to share, so he moves beyond allegiance, solidarity, or commitment as terms of approbation and never attempts to resolve inherent divisions with abstract coherence.

His friendship made no demands. It was simply given, asking nothing in

---

[60] For forceful commentary on the theme of historical amnesia, see Declan Kiberd, 'The Elephantine of Revolutionary Forgetfulness', in Máirín Ní Dhonnchadha and Theo Dorgan (eds.), *Revising the Rising* (Derry: Field Day, 1991), 1–20.

return, making no attempts to conscript you to any viewpoint or take sides in the petty office wars. The discovery that we were from the same suburbs was made not in terms of common links but of shared differences. (*TJH*, 26)

Bolger developed this point in John Waters's book *A Race of Angels*.[61] These finely calibrated social divisions, along with Bolger's observation that the flatness of Finglas made it unsuitable for visual depiction, demands new ways of conveying the *Gemeinschaft*. The traditional attachment to place in the Gaelic genre *dinnseánchas*, or the systematic nomination in Joyce's *Dubliners*, is now redundant in these formless communities. Nature can no longer prefix personal development; there is nothing prior to the promiscuous range of cultural themes shaping Francie and Shay, no existence or being prior to the depthless, shifting forces he and Francie experience. One key theme is Francie's expulsion from his parents' world into a realm where experience now actually exceeds meaning:

As long as I remained among the hens and barking dogs I too could belong, but each walk from school by the new shopping arcades, each programme on the television religiously switched on at half five in every terraced house, was thrusting me out into my own time. I began bringing home phrases that couldn't fit in that house when we still knelt for the family rosary. I hid the photographs of rock stars beneath my mattress like pornographic pictures, wrote English soccer players' names on my copy book, feeling I was committing an act of betrayal. (*TJH*, 7)

This experience, ostensibly presented as apolitical, is, in fact, post-national, in the sense that no abstract term from Irish history—religion, community, nation, territory—can accommodate Hano's identity. This is a space freed from any moral or cultural order inherited from a specifically Irish past, but Hano is never liberated from anxiety or obligation towards that past. There is a strong sense of guilt, betrayal, and transgression in this phrasing: in 'thrusting . . . out', 'like pornographic pictures', 'act

---

[61] *A Race of Angels: The Genesis of U2* (Belfast: Blackstaff Press, 1994), 37: 'The strategy for survival that most people were taught was to say where you were from . . . People who lived a few hundred yards from one another had utterly different descriptions of where they came from. To hear some of the kids from the slightly better houses up the road talk about the Finglas he knew . . . was to hear about a foreign country.'

of betrayal'. This is an active rejection of outmoded shibboleths and a quest for what will fit contemporary experience. But it is never entirely value-free of the nationalism it rejects. What replaces his parents' narrative is an apparently random cannibalization of endlessly varying styles; but these are carefully chosen to highlight both the demise of a coherent, all-embracing, indigenous identity and the civic incohesion left in its wake. Benedict Anderson claims that partitioned states are insufficiently imagined; that is, they lack the kind of *polis* that can command assent.[62] Again and again Bolger deploys conspicuously discordant images to convey this notion, as when children play reggae music round a graffiti-smeared Celtic cross raised to honour the Plunketts. The only constants in this historyless world are alienation and instability:

They were an autonomous world, a new nation with no connection to the housewives passing or the men coming home from work in the factories. And little even in common with me though I was only a few years older than they. Because in those few years the place had changed beyond recognition. I could piece together obscure images that to them would seem from another planet. Corpus Christi processions through these streets; Christmas concerts in the old cinema where shoppers now queued at cash desks. (*TJH*, 227)

What does this counter-tradition, this 'autonomous world' and 'new nation', in Declan Kiberd's phrase, this 'flawed civic discourse', entail? For Fredric Jameson, the alienated city is above all a space in which people are unable to cognitively map 'either their own position or the urban totality in which they find themselves . . . Disalienation in the traditional city . . . involves the practical reconquest of a sense of place and the construction and reconstruction of an articulated ensemble which can be retained in memory and which the individual subject can map and remap along the moments of mobile alternative trajectories'.[63] Through this cognitive map, Jameson claims, each individual understands their own position in a space that is fundamentally unrepresentable as a totality. But this incapacity to map space as a totality is as potentially crippling politically as the paralysis that affects Joyce's *Dubliners*, for the alienated

---

[62] *Imagined Communities: Reflections on the Origins and Spread of Nationalism* (London: Verso, 1983), 10.   [63] *Postmodernism*, 51.

citizen of the city, Jameson argues, can never imaginatively propose a cohesive civic realm or *polis*. By plucking Hano from the Voter's Register Unit, Shay maps, in Jameson's terms, the practical reconquest of the city as a site for political agency by redefining what that concept can entail. Shay deals with a dissolving social unit by detachment and observation rather than engagement and participation. He does not attempt to rise above the private idiosyncrasies on display in the city to cognitively map a prevailing unity, nor look for a more profound solidarity to overcome the absolute differences on display. Shay, with his postmodernist's distrust of innerness, and his willingness to accept the incorrigible pluralness the city offers, embodies the utopian tradition Fintan O'Toole called for in 1985:

> What has been missing [from Irish writing] has been a Utopian tradition, drawing its poetry from the future, taking the city as the ground of transformation to set against the tradition of the Golden Age which draws its poetry from the past taking the country as the ground of timeless, ahistorical innocence. For it is in the nature of the city that it cannot be merely represented without being transformed.[64]

Thus Shay is comfortable in a city-centre bar full of countrymen where 'nobody there was under fifty, no one born in the city that was kept out by the steel door . . . a middle-aged Monaghan man welcomed Shay by name' (*TJH*, 32).[65] Shay embraces city and country, affirming the social divisions in each while cognitively mapping a space in which, as Jameson puts it, the individual subject understands his own position in 'that vaster and properly unrepresentable totality which is the ensemble of society's structure as a whole'.[66]

---

[64] 'Going West: The Country and the City in Irish Writing', in Mark Hederman and Richard Kearney (eds.), *The Crane Bag*, ix (Dublin, 1985), 116. O'Toole claimed that 'It is only now that an urban literature from within the modern city is beginning to develop in the work of Finglas writers Dermot Bolger and Michael O'Loughlin.' See also Conor McCarthy's *Modernisation, Crisis and Culture in Ireland 1969–1992* (Dublin: Four Courts Press, 2000), 152.

[65] Conor McCarthy's useful and highly critical essay on *The Journey Home* interprets this passage as typical in its distaste for the presence of the country in the city: 'the alienation derives from the persistence of the rural, its ability to co-exist with the modern . . . The anguish of modernity is attributable in *The Journey Home* to the domination of a rural culture that is reckoned to be finally monolithic' ('Ideology and Geography in Dermot Bolger's *The Journey Home*', *Irish University Review: A Journal of Irish Studies*, 27/1 (Spring/Summer 1997), 103).

[66] *Postmodernism*, 51.

Shay's delight in irony and ambiguity clashes with the Plunketts' rhetoric of national wholeness, but what motivates Conor McCarthy's strong criticism of the novel is Hano's recourse to a more 'authentic' form of the same tradition.[67] The contingencies marking his existence are erased by his collusion with an apparently natural historical order:

> I could bear to watch no more . . . A tree was glowing by itself in the ditch. I pressed my face against its cold bark, remembering suddenly the old woman's story of the oak tree in her wood that she would embrace to find strength in times of crisis . . . I wrapped my whole body against the base of the tree. I had nobody left to pray to so I prayed to it and to her and to me: and to the living wood itself, to the old woman of the fields, to the memory of someone I had almost been. (*TJH*, 166)

Hano and Cáit/Kate travel to woods in Sligo owned by an old Protestant woman, the former mistress of the local Big House now living in a caravan. This old woman's willingness to accept the ironic permanence of contingency and flux is the most singularly effective means of withstanding the Plunketts' order. She never aspires to the wholeness Hano describes—'Permanency was what he hoped for; life with Shay to continue for ever and ever like bodies trapped in a peat bog' (*TJH*, 181)—a condition he learns through Shay to be a social and metaphysical impossibility. Neil Corcoran describes her as 'a terminal version of the Sean Van Vocht . . . a desolating, virtually apocalyptic image not of the Irish past but of its future as the servile playground of a new European élite, one from which the likes of Hano will be permanently excluded. This is the projected terminal zero to which Irish history and tradition are brought.'[68] This old woman, this indigenous deterritorialized numen, accepts strife as part of her established living pattern, creating an economy of values that is viable to the extent that it is personal and universal:

> she fought a hundred causes . . . The postman brought mail from The Kremlin, Chile, South Africa, and places Hano had never even heard of. The only government she had no correspondence with was her own. Looking back it was impossible to change the Plunketts who carved it up, and she had concentrated on creating her own country instead. (*TJH*, 178)

---

[67] 'Ideology and Geography', 108: 'This does not amount to O'Toole's "critique of received values", but rather an evasion of such a project'.

[68] *After Yeats and Joyce*, 127.

Her exemplary 'private fictional universe', then, is a denational-
ized and deterritorialized realm that transcends rather than
engages, observes rather than participates in the social. Here she
resembles Shay, and offers another indication of Bolger's deep
political pessimism: Ireland is never identified as a place where
change might occur.

Throughout Bolger's work, there is a gradual withdrawal
from the public sphere his work makes such strenuous efforts to
legitimate. His violent antipathy towards the Plunketts makes
any opposition to them necessarily radical, even withdrawal
from the very idea of the *polis*. At one level, this repeats the
contradiction of the Picador anthology, which trades entirely on
the intrinsic radicalism of the writing's context without that
writing subjecting the context it is wedded to, the state, to any
imaginative or political transformation. There is no struggle with
the idea of meaning in these new sites, simply a determination to
preserve them as meaningful in themselves. Without the
exaggerated images of the Plunketts and the existence of *The
Field Day Anthology* respectively, *The Journey Home* and *The
Picador Anthology* would be necessarily less radical. Bolger is
thus wedded to the nationalism he rejects: Shay and Hano are
raped by the Plunketts because one has to accept tradition as
irredeemably and relentlessly hegemonic for his alternative sites
to have the full auratic significance claimed for them. The
Republic in *The Journey Home* is a peculiarly unattractive entity
compared to the Big House and the organic idyll of Leitrim; a
residual nostalgia endures for these sites compared to the suffocating administrative bureaucracy of the Voters Registration
Unit, the symbol of contemporary Ireland.[69]

But if critical and social theory has taught us one thing, it is
that there can be no transcendental realm in the external world
where an essential impermanence reigns, no appeal to a prior
moment in Sligo that evades the instability and contingency of all
things. There is instead only the opportunity to acknowledge,
appropriate, and change it. Richard Rorty describes this opportunity well:

[69] A more optimistic reading is Gerry Smyth's: 'Journeying home is thus a
metaphor of the search for a place that does not exist in modern Ireland, but whose
possibility has to be affirmed as a prelude to the process of spiritual rebirth which will
convert that possibility into a reality' ('Right to the City', 26).

The drama of an individual life, or of the history of the community as a whole, is not one in which a pre-existent goal is triumphantly reached or tragically not reached. It is to substitute a tissue of contingent relations, a web which stretches backward and forward through past and future time, for a formed, unified present self-contained substance, something capable of being seen steadily and whole.[70]

The only thing certain about an organic society is, of course, that it is always dead, and Pascal Plunkett's abuse of Shay in Germany, a highly dubious metaphor for his political power, sours the continent's promise but shows Bolger's awareness that there is no fixed relationship between geography, history, and psychology. Shay still encounters the idiocy of Plunkett's rural hegemony in Europe. The point is that geographical proximity or remoteness does not lessen the intensity of the engagement with history, and so topography is no longer available as a stable symbol for the contemporary. As a basis or index of historical conflict it is redundant. But if Ireland and Europe are both subject to the Plunkett's remorseless dominance, no zone of engagement with a public sphere is ever possible. Change is possible only in a purely private and personal context. You change yourself, not society.

This is why Francie kills Plunkett and embraces Cáit/Kate, forgoing the certainty of tradition for a drug-addicted girl struggling to contain the rural and urban elements of her background. He affirms a reality that cannot be known prior to its experience in the physical world; he cannot know what version of Cáit/Kate will emerge except by immersing himself in her world. Thus as votes are cast in the general election, Hano embraces a form of nationhood that is irreducibly individual, apolitical, and post-democratic: 'It doesn't matter to internal exiles like us. No, we're not exiles, because you are the only nation I give allegiance to now . . . when you hold me, Cáit, I have reached home' (*TJH*, 293). The sanction of society is irrelevant here, for the idea of the *polis* is renounced for the metaphysical certainty of permanent marginalization, for a private universe that never requires or can effect change in its essential alienation. 'Homelessness' has been defined as 'a dramatic loss of power over the way in which one's

---

[70] 'The Contingency of Selfhood', in *Irony, Contingency, Solidarity* (Cambridge: Cambridge University Press, 1989), 41.

identity is constructed, since the house no longer shields the public gaze'.[71] Hano's 'internal exile' is psychological and physical, a consequence of his discovery that history is a process without a subject or goal, origins or terminus. His unfinished journey can never reveal a sovereign source of meaning except what is discovered within himself. For what separates him from all previous Irish society is more profound than any continuities. *The Journey Home* is scarred by rigid class divisions that allow no mobility between classes, and certainly debar access to Plunkett's singular, sovereign source of rural value. If Hano, Shay, and Cáit are 'haunted by their lack of agency, by the way in which all their social, economic and emotional options seem to be mapped out for them in advance',[72] the irresistible conclusion the narrative arrives at is that change is always and only internal.

The Journey Home documents irreconcilable social divisions in the public sphere, Bolger's gravitation towards an entirely 'private, fictional universe', and an irrevocable rupture between present and past—themes that were prefigured in *Night Shift* and *The Woman's Daughter,* the first two novels of the 'Dublin Trilogy'. *Night Shift* offers an emotional history of two Dublin factory workers: Donal, 18 years old, married to the pregnant Elizabeth, and Dan, single, elderly, from Mayo. They are separated by the urban, industrial routine they share, a theme introduced in the first pages as Dan works behind Donal: 'he squeezed the twin handles of the machine downwards as if he were drawing two long invisible threads towards his body . . . Donal knew he was neutral in everything, as if he existed in a parallel world to the rest of the factory . . . His body adjusted quickly to the pace of the work. The hardest part was in the mind' (*NS*, 9, 13). This alienated city is a space where people are unable to mentally map either their own physical positions or the total urban sphere they inhabit, hence Jameson's claim that 'Disalienation' involves the 'practical reconquest' of a sense of place and the reconstruction of a flexible, cognitive map retained as personal memory for

[71] Neil Smith, 'Homeless/Global', in John Bird et al. (eds.), *Mapping the Futures: Local Cultures, Global Changes* (London: Routledge, 1993), 127–42.
[72] Gerry Smyth, *The Novel and the Nation: Studies in the New Irish Fiction* (London: Pluto Press, 1997), 78.

public usage.[73] Donal is Irish for Dan, so the young man's fate is somehow implicated in the elder man's life. Donal inhabits the faultline between an emergent urban culture and a displaced rural tradition, inscribed, through his name, within a linguistic contour at variance with the social facts of his life. Conquering the social division within the city involves constructing a cognitive map that somehow incorporates Dan's memories. In this sense, Donal is one of Bolger's characters who, as Corcoran puts it, is 'haunted by the assumptions and values of [his] rural and Catholic parentage and by its Gaelic origins'.[74] The connection between Donal's name and his identity is derivative of a historical relation, but the task of forging a reciprocal relationship between the ambiguous continuity of old and new is defeated by the city's violent disregard for any unified, stable self. Despite their shared social space,[75] what separates Donal from Dan is far more profound than any continuities connecting them.

The beginning of the end of a certain type of history, a theme we will return to in Colm Tóibín, is already apparent in *Night Shift*. Donal copes with the city's all-pervasive alienation by initiating an ongoing process of segregation, so that Elizabeth meets Frankie, an urban cowboy with the alluringly named 'The Snots', but not Dan. What the novel's central image dramatizes, however, as a white horse is gratuitously hauled onto a bonfire, is the coarsening of emotions such demarcation entails. The animal's suffering results from the absent 'tissue of contingent relations', the minimal commitment Rorty deemed necessary for civic cohesion:

A sickness went through him in a shudder: at the minds of the well-dressed boys who refused to admit feelings, at the horse for refusing to attack them, at his own cowardice . . . the scene could be seen clearly from the roadway. Occasionally somebody passing would stop in shock for a moment then hurry on. But most walked on the far side of the road with a staged deliberateness, casualness, blatantly avoiding the scene with their eyes. No police car came. Dan remained in the shadows. (*NS*, 51)

[73] *Postmodernism*, 51: 'The cognitive map is not exactly mimetic in the older sense; indeed, the theoretical issues it poses allow us to renew the analysis of representation on a higher and much more complex level.'
[74] *After Yeats and Joyce*, 126.
[75] Lefebvre, *Production of Space*, 86: 'Social spaces interpenetrate one another and/or superimpose themselves upon one another.'

Dan remains in the shadows of his own life and the urban totality because, in the absence of the traditional markers of rural
Ireland, he is unable to cognitively map any other aspect of the
city. Obsessed by women whose faces resemble the Virgin Mary,
his desire for a physical replica of an imagined spiritual perfection damages all forms of human interaction and leads to a
fascination with violent pornographic images. Dan singularly
fails to occupy the physical space of the city, and he shares with
Donal a trauma borne of the evacuation of values founded on
wholeness and purity. Dan's homelessness, his expulsion from
numerous flats, is a physical and spiritual condition, a reflection
of his impossible metaphysical expectations. As the scarred,
'oriental' girl who most closely resembles his religious vision
demonstrates, no form of human community can be entirely
reliant on divine revelation. Donal's isolation, the loss of his
childhood friendship with Frankie, now hooked on heroin, is
part of the ceaseless renewal and recreation the city demands, as
its gaps, contradictions, and discontinuities disrupt any seamless
linkage to the past:

He had grown up in the city and yet had never really bothered to
examine it and now it was moving past him and he felt strangely homeless. As he stared at the new neon displays over the fast food huts and
video arcades he seemed no longer certain of the sense of place he had
taken for granted. (*NS*, 128)

Without Jameson's 'cognitive map', urban space is fundamentally unrepresentable as a totality, inducing a crippling inability
to map any cohesive realm where agency might be located.
The Journey Home ends with Cáit/Kate's pregnancy, Hano's
impending imprisonment or death, and a general election.
'Home' for Hano and Cáit/Kate will for ever be divorced from
the surrounding social protocols, with them unable and unwilling to participate in the general elections the Plunketts routinely
win. In *Night Shift*, Bolger's first novel, this same sense of alienation is so total that Elizabeth's emotional growth is enabled
only by the termination of her pregnancy. Any bond with
husband, child, and, by implication, the wider public sphere is
severed, as she shows an exemplary willingness to confront the
crippling dependence afflicting every other character in the
novel. Elizabeth refuses to give assent to the space Donal demar-

cates through the exclusion of Dan, thereby transforming her termination of her pregnancy into a positive assertion of individual will: 'But at least I did something. It may have been something wrong, but at least I did it. And in one way I did it for you Donal. And now I've done it and it's for me to be able to live with' (*NS*, 143). The abortion ensures, in one reading, that otherness is an internal and permanent component of the self, that estrangement and alienation are essential components of the city. John Wilson Foster, commenting on a range of rural poets, noted Irish writing's preoccupation with place as 'an unseverable aspect of self',[76] a phrase that echoes Denis Donoghue's claim that Irish writers are 'already inscribed by a mythology they have no choice but to inherit'. Elizabeth terminates her pregnancy because of the separation and severance the city demands, its refusal to allow any easy choice between flux and stability, caravan and house, Donal and Dan. As the novel ends, Donal discards doorkeys, wedding ring, company pen, keyring—anything, in short, connecting him to a stable social unit to re-enter the city because, in this first novel, self-awareness involves a recognition of the full extent of an individual's irreducible isolation and alienation. In an essay entitled 'Cities without Maps', Ian Chambers describes the emotional and physical terrain Donal and all Bolger's characters now confront: 'The city suggests a creative disorder an instructive confusion, an interpolating space in which the imagination carries you in every direction, even towards the previously unthought.'[77] *Night Shift* begins Bolger's gradual disaffiliation from an imagined, abstract category called Ireland.

But why does the absence of single, substantive, commonly accepted public sphere in *Night Shift* and *The Journey Home* make a complete, irrevocable break with the past an obligatory component of each characters' private universe? These urban sites host a second, ulterior order of consciousness which the title, *Night Shift*, attempts to convey. Its realism probes the older rural economies still shadowing contemporary social life, producing the divisions between and within individuals. Donal and Dan, Francie and Hano, are separated by volatile deposits of

---

[76] 'Geography of Fiction', 89.
[77] In Bird et al. (eds.), *Mapping the Futures*, 189.

historical memory that continually irrupt into their inner lives, generating the dreams and surreal imagery disrupting all Bolger's narratives. Characters are as fragmented as the context they inhabit, and the stable cultural order realism requires is everywhere absent. The formal qualities of Bolger's second novel, *The Woman's Daughter*, represent these unsystematic, indeterminate patterns of historical memory, as it moves between a first-person, omniscient narrator, a sexually wrought lyricism, and a tough-minded vernacular.[78]

The quotations prefacing *The Woman's Daughter* exemplify this radical contingency. From P. W. Joyce's *The Origin and History of Irish Place Names*, Bolger lifts a definition of Finglas as a little stream, or in its Victorian form, the Crystal Rivulet, and combines this with a quote from *Finnegans Wake*: 'They're the best relics of Conal O'Daniel and writing *Finglas since the Flood.* That'll be some work in progress.' James Joyce's apocalyptic vision of a Finglas packed full of an Irish and universal history mixes with P. W. Joyce's characteristically Victorian desire for order and definition. What the shared surname suggests, however, is that enduring contradictions, the apocalyptic and the specific, are containable within the same imaginative universe. 'Finglas' does not nominate or inscribe an unvarying essence; it does not, in Harvey's terms, subscribe to the gross fetishism of 'the power of place'.[79] Finglas instead finds it possible to be one thing and another.[80] The novel's tripartite structure, in which each section unfolds independently of the rest, mirrors this quality as it traces Finglas's history from the Druids to the Beatles and beyond. All three parts are set in Finglas. The first part is the story of Sandra O'Connor, her family's move from a

---

[78] For Fintan O'Toole, a leading theoretical advocate of the Republic's post-nationalist culture, 'the more all-embracing a term—nation, spirit, nature, history, Ireland—appears to be, the more rigidly it is excluding someone from its embrace' ('The Southern Question', in Dermot Bolger (ed.), *Letters from the New Island* (Dublin: Raven Arts Press, 1991), 23; see more generally, 15–43).

[79] *Justice, Nature and the Geography of Difference* (Oxford: Blackwell, 1996), 302.

[80] See Seamus Deane's comments in 'Brian Friel: The Name of the Game', in Alan Peacock (ed.), *The Achievement of Brian Friel* (Gerrards Cross: Colin Smythe, 1994), 104: 'If a name necessarily belongs to a place—or a place a name—that is, in some sense embodies the essence of the place and therefore indicates, even ostensibly, some radical aspect of that place's meaning, we are dealing with metaphysics not history.'

rural community to Finglas, her incestuous relationship with her brother, and the secret growth of her child. Part II, 'Victoriana', set in the latter half of the nineteenth century and the 1980s, concerns Johnny, a young man from humble origins who tutors in Latin and Classical Greek at a Big House in Finglas, and another young man who is working in a mobile library on the outskirts of contemporary Dublin. Part III, 'The Crystal Rivulet', chronicles Finglas's unwritten history through Turlough, an old Gaelic seer.

Unravelling the tortuously complex plot reveals a historical dimension excluded from Irish conventional history, a constant Bolger theme. But because the connections between individual sections never imply any greater reconciliation, Bolger questions the very idea of historical narrative itself. The past is never fully recaptured in the text; like the river which appears and disappears throughout the novel, and gives Finglas its name, it is glimpsed at random, unpredictable intervals. No single concept of historical time adequately accounts for the layers of reality within this world, the inextinguishable recidivist history that never quite reveals itself as either coherent or unified. Thematically and structurally, the novel invokes a temporal dimension that is constantly double-edged and non-linear; its sites of memory are also sites of mourning, places where the history is glimpsed even when, like the river, it suggests that there is, after all, nothing there.

The river appears on page 1, where Johnny and Sandra, incestuous brother and sister, whose story dominates the first part, try to locate its origins, the source that names their home. Yet the refusal of constancy is the river's only consistent feature; it is persistently volatile, incapable of being contained within one single source. Within the novel, Henry VII, Cromwell, the recovery of buried Celtic Crosses, and the arrival of the Beatles are welded together: no distinction is made between invasive and indigenous, authentic and inauthentic history. The apparent degeneration of the river—flowing from purity to a promiscuous mixture of blood and dirty water—is enabling to the extent that such impurities are acknowledged. This is the only heritage Finglas knows:

A few feet below me the stream was polluted by oil and scraps of debris but just here where it had become a crystal rivulet, I broke the water

with my cupped palms and raised it, dripping, towards my lips. It
tasted sweet like clear water and blood mixed together. I felt calmed
and strengthened by its taste. (*TWD*, 241)

This heavily stylized rite of passage is laden with ironic imagery.
Johnny Whelan, traumatized by the sight of Sandra in part I,
reappears in part III to use 'an abandoned washing machine to
cross the stream' before 'join[ing] my people walking in the
anonymous after-hours' (*TWD*, 242). The stream is bridged by
an image that suggests perfect purity can never be captured. The
'reconciliation' with his people is similarly ironic; they remain
remote, anonymous, socially and emotionally distant even as he
re-enters their world by crossing the stream.

The catastrophic dimension to Irish history—the loss of a
language, Cromwell, famine, the displacement of a rural-based
family unit by an encroaching city—each element is absorbed
through stylized images of alienation and isolation. If, as
Benedict Anderson claims, communities are to be distinguished
not by any reference to authenticity but by the style in which
they are imagined,[81] dualisms such as P. W. and James Joyce, the
preliterate Bridget and the tutor Johnny, Bolger's sexualized
lyricism and tough Dublin vernacular—these, to use Anderson's
terms, enact a conflictual model of Irish history in which no
single element ever predominates. The one character who seems
to symbolize an organic Celtic society, Turlough, is dead by the
novel's end, yet his existence throughout the narrative validates
one loyal component of the Irish community. The numerous
competing elements in this historical novel lack any foundational
myth through which they might be mediated and reconciled. The
narrative is framed by the 'real' time of contemporary Ireland—
Sandra on page 1, the crossing of a dual carriageway in Finglas
at the end—because history provides no refuge from the
implacable divisions in the contemporary public sphere. Unlike
McIlvanney's Glaswegian and west-coast rituals, the historical
patterns Bolger excavates in Dublin possess no single narrative
structure of the kind myth requires to validate substantive,
supra-empirical, all-embracing terms like 'Ireland', 'territory', or
'nation'. And it is this harmonizing thread which Malinowski
identified as one crucial component of myth:

[81] *Imagined Communities*, 6.

myth acts a charter for the present-day social order; it supplies a retro-spective pattern of moral values, sociological order, and magical belief, the function of which is to strengthen tradition and endow it with a greater value and prestige by tracing it back to a higher, better, more supernatural reality of initial events.[82]

Part I of *The Woman's Daughter* is based on a true story from Finglas first used in a 1981 poem.[83] Sandra, named Bridget by the Nuns, has a child by a brother forced to emigrate after violent rows with their widowed father, a man unable to accept the move from the city centre to the suburbs. This deeply dysfunc-tional family conveys Bolger's disaffection with one founda-tional myth of Irish life: the stable nuclear family unit, one source of symbolic identity for the new Irish state. For incest as a theme wrests the family as a symbol from the quarantine of political rhetoric and diminishes its implied cultural force.[84] Sandra's incestuous relationship results, in part, from the denial of the ele-mental features of her identity, her name and place. In Bolger's reworking of the actual story, the imposition of an image at odds with her real experience generates (as it did with Elizabeth and Dan) an intense introspection and a distorted notion of physical love. But because this heightened realism is grounded in actual historical events and geography, Sandra is not a historical or psychological aberration but a consequence of social and politi-cal choices.[85] Incest is at some level a quest for likeness, a desire to see the self in the sexual partner chosen. It obliterates the otherness of the partner, and in its quest for a perfectly identical partner, paradoxically chooses isolation over the communion and community any relationship entails. Sandra is what Eavan Boland describes as 'the unseen inner life that the nation occludes

---

[82] Quoted in Timothy Brennan, 'The National Longing for Form', in Homi Bhabha (ed.), *Nation and Narration* (London: Routledge, 1990), 45.

[83] Dermot Bolger, 'The Woman's Daughter', in *Finglas Lilies* (Dublin: Raven Arts Press, 1981), 32–6.

[84] See De Valera's eloquent advocacy of the family as the basis for the nation: 'We can have our own people united as a family—a nation of brothers each working in industrial harmony, not for himself only but for the good of all.' Quoted in Gearóid Ó Crualaoich, 'The Primacy of Form: A "Folk Ideology" in De Valera's Politics', in J. P. O'Carroll and J. A. Murphy (eds.), *De Valera and His Times* (Cork: Cork University Press, 1983), 47–61.

[85] In the 1981 notes to *Finglas Lilies*, the collection in which the poem 'The Woman's Daughter' first appeared, Bolger states 'While researching the poem I was surprised to discover that such an event is not totally uncommon in Ireland.'

from its history when defining itself'.[86] Dramatizing the consequences of this occlusion through incest, against the rhetoric of a 'people united as a family—a nation of brothers', attempts to convey the implausibility of founding a cohesive public sphere on this kind of rhetoric.

Only Turlough comes close to comprehending the novel's multiple narratives. Named from the Irish for 'a lake that wells up during the winter rains to disappear in springtime again', he somehow embodies the persistence of the region's history, its durability and its inconstancy. Emphatically Gaelic, Turlough also knows loss; his father's streets are 'torn apart now, the carriageway has sliced open its soul' (*TWD*, 204), but his endurance proves that the transition from *Gemeinschaft* to *Gesellshaft* does not necessarily mean the sacrifice of difference, identity. Turlough is, like Finglas/the Crystal Rivulet, original and capable of being something else, part of a tradition that challenges the notion of a stable, constant tradition, a figure whose enigmatic endurance undermines the Plunketts' belief in a single rural stable origin. His confrontation with Sandra, a contemporary suburban outcast, involves this degree of equivalence, a mutual recognition of a shared emotional plight that does not have priorities based on purity or, in Donoghue's phrase, prematurity: 'Only the lonely, withered figure of Turlough, who never speaks, seems to recognise her, seems to tell her she is not alone in her story, that she is part of something greater, that there are others abandoned as her' (*TWD*, 46). This 'something greater' is a community in which identities are multiple, variable, continuously fluid, and always relational. The novel does not harmonize experience so that each event becomes a version of something else, so that the divisions between Turlough and Sandra cohere into some greater, all-embracing whole. None of the three narratives makes sense in isolation; the juxtaposition of the Joyces, P. W. and James, order and flux, is one enduring contradiction throughout the novel. Simultaneity (used again in *The Journey Home*) is an important structural device in this difficult novel. The narrative is organized to emphasize the importance of the voices or perspectives of the individual narrators in their relations with each other. It diminishes the importance of

---

[86] 'Outside History', in *Object Lessons* (Manchester: Carcanet, 1995), 123–53.

temporal succession as a medium of narrative. Different versions of events turn out to be complementary rather than mutually exclusive so that time transcends the individual without obliterating it. The novel leaves the reader with a spectrum of possible developments rather than a single plot line, one effect of which is to project into the narrative present and past an experience of time as unassailably random, forever dividing and subdividing into multiple possibilities.[87]

The 'Victoriana' part added to the Penguin 1991 edition expands on this theme of simultaneity through two parallel narratives. A schoolteacher called Johnny, Seán in the Irish, moves from the tenements to a Big House near Finglas Bridge; meanwhile in contemporary Finglas a librarian has an affair with Joanie, a girl infatuated with Victorian times, in a tale of moral blackmail and sexual revenge. The teacher is caught between classes and cultures—a learned papist ministering to the Protestant ascendancy while secretly having an affair with the preliterate peasant Bridget—as the librarian's loyalty to Joanie clashes with his duty to the fellow workers she steals from. The self, like the nation of which it is part, has multiple allegiances.

The city crystallizes an emerging linguistic and class conflict, as the tutor's ties to his family, still longing for their native Sligo, are loosened by the creeping individualism his mentor introduces: while his family 'gave to each other . . . Hegarty taught me to withhold, to gather the strength to master the books and not fall asleep . . . I lived in a world without rich or poor, a sphere of cold rigid letters' (*TWD*, 107). With Hegarty 'in the city he encountered words'. This juxtaposition of learning and intuition, textuality and (through Bridget) sexuality, restores dignity to a tradition of thought that does not seek to reconcile contradictions. Bridget's obsessive belief in the supernatural overwhelms the tutor's innerness and rational precision; the reality and meaning she recognizes always exceeds his ability to describe through mere language her physical and spiritual experience. This is why no one in the novel fully understands Bridget's fears. The tutor has 'a strange sense of absolute power as though I could mould this frightened figure into anything that

---

[87] See Ursula Heise, *Chronoschisms: Time, Narrative, and Postmodernism* (Cambridge: Cambridge University Press, 1996), 50–5.

I wished' (*TWD*, 116), but she remains beyond his cognitive reach. Their relationship is tied to the transition from an oral to textual culture: the tutor prospers from a system that penalizes his parents while his infatuation with Bridget's intuitive grasp of the non-rational certainties of his own parents' world breeds an eroticized guilt. A corollary of his private, economic, and social advancement is the transmission of a sanitized Gaelic heritage, of which Bridget is one highly erotic representative:

Five guineas I received for my first work of translation, the tales from the west of Ireland which my mother spluttered out to us in that tenement, now set down in stiff, antiquated English. They are praised in a small way as long as I curtail them, take out the native sweat and dirt and put in noble peasants with flighty words. I was born at the tail-end of a famine nobody wants to be reminded of. Instead I give them heroic vassals as sour and forced as Bridget's set smile. (*TWD*, 191)

This triumph of style over deprivation is the beginning of Anglo-Irish literature, but Bridget's belief in the supernatural is a rejection of the inherently progressive concept of time upon which this world, as presented in the novel, is based. Like Joanie, Bridget comprehends time as simultaneous, of this world and another. Buried with Bridget and resurrected through Joanie, this facet of the Irish experience is what the tutor and librarian glimpse through each woman, and what they choose to avoid:

I felt suddenly one of a long line that stretched behind me and before me, I as much a speck in their minds as they were in mine, that if I could only grasp them this would all make sense to me. Then I shook the feeling. I wished I could believe in ghosts, that I did have some connection with that place, but I know it was just drink and physical signals from my body that this madness would have to stop. (*TWD*, 189)

These multiple connections, disconnections, and repeated doubling of names capture what Oliver McDonagh calls the contemporaneity of the past in Irish culture, 'an absence of a developmental or sequential view of past events',[88] the tendency to collapse that past into an ever-receding present which is shadowed by a mythic history. Bolger's narratives never enable any unmediated access to this past; catastrophic memories of the 'storm of progress' never proceed seamlessly between pre-

[88] *States of Mind: A Study of Anglo-Irish Conflict 1780–1980* (London: Allen & Unwin, 1985), 6.

ordained points. Like the history it symbolizes, the river secretes an unstable and porous sediment without distinguishing between indigenous and invasive, authentic or artificial terrain. Access to the past is too limited for such evaluative judgements—Joanie, Bridget, and the tutor never know of each other's existence—and history is always riddled with uncertainty and irresolution even as it continues to engulf the present. *The Woman's Daughter* imagines that history through a style which enacts these enduring contradictions and divisions, constantly emphasizing the unassailable randomness and unpredictable repetitiveness of history. Though it appears less focused on contemporary Ireland than *Night Shift* or *The Journey Home*, this systematic randomness has important consequences: it is almost impossible for the reader (this reader, at least) to infer a coherent image of the action that underlies the repetitions, since there are no overarching criteria for evaluating the reality of the version each section presents. The repetitions in these three novels create a temporality ruled not by cause and effect, a medium of comparative stability and continuity, but by contingency and dispersion,[89] a narrative technique that bequeaths a series of contradictory accounts without any overarching psychological or political motivation.

Hence the organization of Bolger's novels around intense explosions of energy that halt an already gapped narrative. Moments like Turlough's death by fire reveal time and memory as private and cyclical rather than public and linear, laid out in a private mental geography that can never be directly mapped. In *The Sense of an Ending*, Frank Kermode suggests that narrative endings reflect the human need for a temporality shaped by the regulating force of the ending.[90] Turlough's importance to Johnny, for example, is revealed only at the old man's destruction, but even this does not bestow retrospective meaning on the plot. For to do so would, in Bakhtin's definition of the chronotope, cause time to thicken, take on flesh, become artistically visible, the very antithesis of Bolger's counter-tradition.[91]

[89] See Heise, *Chronoschisms*, 56–9, for a discussion of repetition and the novel.
[90] (London: Oxford University Press, 1967), 3–32.
[91] M. M. Bakhtin, *The Dialogic Imagination: Four Essays*, trans. Caryl Emerson and Michael Holquist, ed. Michael Holquist (Austin: University of Texas Press, 1981), 84.

In 'The Dublin Trilogy', this counter-tradition involves an escape from the very idea of a tradition. To adapt Donoghue, Bolger's characters have no choice but to inherit a post-mythological landscape. The concept of a single tradition accommodating Finglas's unassailably random history is wholly anachronistic, and chronicled in all its (for this reader) bewildering complexity in *The Woman's Daughter*. This is the basis, it seems to me, of Declan Kiberd's charge that Bolger's generation is incapable of imagining a civic discourse. Kiberd refurbishes a national tradition through his invocation of Kathleen Ní Houlihán, a move Bolger's private fictional universes, devoid of any external suprahistorical horizon, are structurally incapable of duplicating. For Bolger, history consists of a radical indeterminacy which causes him to abandon any hope of affirming a general and substantive unity. And it is this fundamental opposition that generates Kiberd's charge: 'When he accepted the Irish past as a basis on which to know the Irish present, Bolger impressed as a writer: but when he went to war against the past, he was left dependent on his own resources, which could never equal the challenge.'[92]

Kiberd's point, however, is also relevant to *The Journey Home*, where the tradition the Plunketts personify produces some implausible characterization and rhetoric. But Bolger's principled belief that new communities like Finglas know only a rupture with the past animates the 'Trilogy'.[93] Part of the difference between Kiberd and Bolger is the belief that a historical community existed which can be recovered and restored, for Kiberd, as for Deane (and William McIlvanney), a requisite basis for any emancipatory politics. For Bolger, this principle is essentially, uniquely, relentlessly, oppressive. In its stead, a history that escapes the consolation of an all-embracing narrative is imagined. Each novel in Bolger's trilogy ends with a young

---

[92] *Inventing Ireland*, 610.

[93] See unpublished interview with Dermot Bolger by Alexander Downes: 'I am from a place where only 1000 people lived up to 1945, and where now 50,000 people live . . . If you take the suburb, you have people who are living in a place and their lives have no connection with those people who were living there before . . . I don't see myself in any tradition of Irish writing . . . Ireland is like a big mirror that has been dropped and there are a thousand pieces of it, and all those pieces are giving a true reflection but they are giving a different reflection.' I am grateful to Jim O'Hanlon for making this available to me.

citizen of the Republic—Donal, Francie, Kate, Johnny—embarking on journeys, an anti-Eden myth in which destination rather than origin provides the true repository of identity. The first question asked is not 'who am I?' but 'where am I?'. The task of *Emily's Shoes* and *A Second Life* is to locate the physical space within society that these three novels had begun to cognitively map.

IV   CITIZENSHIP IN THE CITY: THE POSSESSOR CLASS

All Bolger's novels contain a strong autobiographical element, and by 1991 and *Emily's Shoes,* with Bolger and Bolgerism firmly established, his familiar themes of allegiance, origins, and alienation were explored through a newly arrived member of the Irish middle class. Successful and literate, Michael inhabits the world from which Bolger's previous characters are excluded. He struggles with a dual allegiance, the Ireland of his longed-for dead mother and his aunt Emily's England. A desire for Emily as surrogate mother develops into a fetish for her shoes; they replace not just maternal and romantic love, but also family, spirituality, nation, and, ultimately, a portion of the self. Because each pair is the same, the shoes provide uniformity and the illusion of change extending through time, for they symbolically admit Michael's inability to create his own history: he literally walks in the footprints of others, unable to register an impression on the external world, lacking an 'authentic' origin and inhabiting an emotional realm devoid of the mythic idioms of collective identity.

As a child Michael intuitively absorbs the wider sense of dislocation his mother's death generates. The Fianna, one legendary source of Irish identity, are used as an emblem on his boy scout's jumper: 'Next year I was a Fianna warrior emerging from the forests to be confronted by bewildering drips and hospital charts. I was a Fianna warrior stranded without a spear to fling at them' (*ES*, 30). Alienated from any inherited historical patterns, Michael cannot articulate a narrative through which the present achieves the destiny of form, a fact evoked through a key trope in recent Irish writing (one which reappears in Tóibín): Michael stutters. In 'An Open Letter', a poem provoked by his inclusion in an anthology of British verse, Seamus Heaney included this preface from Gaston Bachelard: 'What is the source of our first suffering? It lies in the fact that we failed to speak.'[94] The poet silently participates in the anthology's erasure of difference if his reservations are not voiced. Speech here has the dual mandate of willing the individual self and collective culture into existence through a freely exercised act of advocacy. This same theme is appropriated, somewhat schematically, by Ferdia Mac Anna (one of the first to proclaim a new Dublin urban renaissance) in *The Last of the High Kings*.[95] A fiercely Republican, rural mother, prone to often implausible anti-Protestant diatribes, so intimidates her Dublin-born son that he stutters. Incapable of addressing his immediate urban context, he works as a hapless customs officer at Dublin airport, unable to decide if he is coming or going, participating in or evacuating Irish soil. Bolger and Mac Anna's tropes and images dramatize fragmentation, not coherence. For if speech combines freely chosen concepts to describe an individual's understanding of his world, Michael's impediment enacts the distance between the individual self and the public zone, making it impossible to interpret or describe and disallowing any possibility of changing it.

His response is to expel history, suppress the social, and estrange himself from any category of Irishness, of identity, through a willed, strategic amnesia. Renting a flat from a woman he never meets, surrounded by anonymous neighbours—he escapes being mauled by the condition of Irishness by severing all connections with it, happy to be neither in passive flight from nor in active conflict with the idea of society. Like Mac Anna's customs officer, he is suspended above any possible engagement. Like Shay, who confronted the Plunketts' corruption with a post-modern indifference, Michael rejects the tissue of contingent relations in 'conventional society', finding instead an affinity with Dublin's transvestites, a community where membership is optional and no style of belonging stipulated: 'And yet those half glimpses of lives at night seemed to grant me some kind of fulfilment, as though I were now merely an observer, no longer a participant in life' (*ES*, 197).

---

[94] In *Ireland's Field Day*, 23–32.
[95] (London: Penguin, 1991).

Emily's Shoes develops themes in Bolger's play *The Lament for Arthur Cleary*, a contemporary version of an eighteenth-century poem called 'Caoineadh Airt Uí Laoghaire', 'The Lament for Art O'Leary', in which an Irish nobleman returns from exile to an Ireland he can no longer comprehend, a fact which eventually causes his death.[96] In *Emily's Shoes,* the emotional submission to the principle of home by Nick and Maggie represents a particular narrative response to the Irish condition. Maggie, Michael's childhood sweetheart, returns to Ireland from Canada and rekindles their relationship. Suffering a series of mental breakdowns each time she leaves home, when her mental state is described as 'a pattern of ever decreasing circles', since childhood she has sought an 'island in the river' (*ES*, 28), an impossibly stable terminus suspended above history. Nick, an old man who chose to remain and work on the housing estates of contemporary Ireland, invokes King Lear to claim that 'a man without his own home was not a man' (*ES*, 160). The teleological purpose to Nick's life, the destiny of form it enjoys, stems from his decision to endure economic depression and participate in the substantive idea of Ireland, a fact Michael acknowledges. 'It was the arc of years moving on to an inevitable conclusion . . . Nick was eighty-seven yet I envied him. His life added up, it made sense' (*ES*, 161).

For Neil Corcoran, *The Lament for Arthur Cleary* defiantly locates contemporary experience in a historical continuum.[97] This is true, yet despite Nick's immersion in this same historical continuum, he dies alone, unloved. And this is partly the reason for Michael's pathological attempt to displace the very notion of a historical continuum through the shoes, through a wholescale devotion to inner needs. Because the shoes are generic and customized, various and uniform, functional and a changeable marker of a personal style, they are an intimate, personal possession which simultaneously remains functional and, therefore, at some level, alien. They symbolize the contradictions in the cultural moment Bolger's 'post-trilogy' characters now occupy. Michael belongs to the post-'68 generation of the Picador

---

[96] *The Lament for Arthur Cleary*, in *A Dublin Quartet* (Harmondsworth: Penguin, 1992). Bolger's contemporary version of the poem is contained in *Internal Exile* (Dublin: Raven Arts Press, 1986), 69–79.
[97] *After Yeats and Joyce*, 126.

anthology, enjoying a remorselessly progressive history that banishes the concept of a historical identity, the idea of Ireland, to enjoy the well-heeled existence of the 'possessor-class'.[98] Yet even for this class, culture not cash, a realm which remains imaginary, is desirable. Michael controls his stutter to enter the possessor-class, but ironically is dispossessed of any individuating voice. The prestige Nick accords origins is replaced by a self-conception based entirely on an authentic state of absence. Likewise, at the core of Maggie's ever-decreasing circles is a void, a place devoid of placeness. And it is at such a site that Michael renews his relationship with her, as the disappearance of place becomes a metaphor and a context for the kinds of relationship possible in this new Ireland: 'Clonsilla. I knew nothing about the place. It was a new suburb still in the process of forming. Unfinished houses, unfinished roads' (*ES*, 114).

Michael neutralizes the emotional force of home by continually reinventing himself in terms which are anti-humanist. He fumigates his private universe of any historical connection, distilling it into a permanently mobile set of signifiers in which a plastic, sterile sameness erases all antagonistic differences. The social is solidly suppressed, yet it must still account for one unalterable reality of Irish life. The 1984 European commission on spiritual values reported that, when it comes to belief in 'the soul', in 'life after death' in heaven and in prayer, Irish beliefs are so different from the rest of the Western world that comparisons are totally irrelevant.[99] Michael may insist on a prior secular space—'I am a private citizen . . . I have the right to be left in peace' (*ES*, 212)—but religion remains part of any private Irish universe. The foundations of his ultra-modern flat contain 'the dried up bed of a stream in which a neat procession of eight adult skeletons were laid out in a row' (*ES*, 187). He cannot choose to ignore the historical dimension this stream represents, but the form of citizenship it provokes is predicated entirely on the need to protect his individual status from the community. In

---

[98] J. J. Lee's phrase for 'that aspect of the Irish middle-class where performance broadly took second place to possession as a criterion of status' (*Ireland: 1912–1985: Politics and Society* (Cambridge: Cambridge University Press, 1989), 392).

[99] Michael Fogarty, Liam Ryan, and Joseph Lee (eds.), *Irish Values and Attitudes: The Irish Report of the European Value Systems Study* (Dublin: Dominican Press, 1984).

McIlvanney's civic republicanism, the community offered the individual the fullest potential to know himself as an individual; the community constituted the very identity of the individual, which was recognized through a participation in the idea of a political community, a *polis*. In the actually existing Republic of Ireland, Bolger's freedom is made manifest when there is definitive recognition of the distinction between the private and public domain, the realm of morality and the realm of politics. Michael's sacrifice of his individual free will would be patently absurd here, for the common good is configured in such totalitarian terms that notions like republican virtue appear nostalgic relics of a bygone era. Active political participation is incompatible with the idea of liberty. Individual liberty is defined purely as the absence of coercion by the millenarian Catholicism rampant across the land.[100]

Bolger acknowledges through the imagery of the skeletons the state's need to account for the subterranean energies of the nation. But the religious imagery seeping through his apartment's lock, ironically transforming a private space into a public shrine and propelling him into conflict with an external world he calculatedly avoids, allows no possible proportion or measure. Again and again Bolger's imagery suggests that even the definition of a common purpose will inevitably lead to the category of the individual being overwhelmed. *Emily's Shoes* and *A Second Life* acknowledge that it is not a question of whether history can be confronted by Michael but how and how much is to be absorbed, a singular advance on *The Journey Home*. But both suggest that no conclusive answer awaits this question. History may be watched and described but it is never subject to transformation or intervention. Liberty is conceived as the absence of impediments to the realization of the individual's chosen ends, a credible plank of liberal pluralism; but what Bolger constitutes as an impediment in *Emily's Shoes* is any engagement with the world beyond his status as an individual. Why is this? What is so different, now, about Irish society that makes it so resistant to reform?

The religious fervour in early 1980s Ireland was generated in part by the notorious phenomenon of the 'moving' statues,

---

[100] For an expansion of this general idea, see Mouffe, 'Democratic Citizenship and the Political Community', in ead. (ed.), *Dimensions of Radical Democracy*, 225–39.

events which register in the narrative when Bolger, not Michael, speaks in awkward literary analogues.

I thought of Jim Jones and his cult of followers out in the jungle, how they had come forward eagerly to receive the poison from his hand. It is said that they were smiling as they shot their children and calmly waited arm-in-arm for their turn . . . I have always found something vaguely obscene about first communion dresses, the girls like miniature brides and children in the windows of a Bangkok brothel. I remembered suddenly Graham Greene's review of Shirley Temple's sexual innuendoes in *Wee Willie Winkie*, and the venom with which they sued him. (*ES*, 235)

The social is perched precariously on the cusp of salvation or damnation, as the narrative reflects the priest's rampant millenarianism, his strict division of society into the elect or damned. The obvious symbolism of the lighthouse that ends the novel must be read against this categorization. When Michael discards the shoes in daytime, after a visionary experience in which he acknowledges the death of his mother, and Clare, rescued from the priest, is lodged within the lighthouse her father used to operate, they finally enter a geographically recognizable Ireland, as Howth is described with notable precision. This liminal zone between sea and land, night and day is, prosaically, the present, a realm which is never fully knowable and therefore implicitly unalterable: the lighthouse can, after all, only provide imperfect illumination.

The *telos* of *Emily's Shoes,* and *A Second Life,* is a private space sufficiently distant from a fractious public sphere for change to be an exclusively personal process. Each novel inserts the main protagonist ambiguously but firmly into a social space that is, to inelegantly adapt Bakhtin, completely *un*-chronotopic, completely devoid of the sudden irruptions of the forgotten space-times that make *The Woman's Daughter*, for example, such a difficult novel to comprehend as a totality (always assuming one would want to). Stability is the goal in these novels of the possessor-class, a coherent, utterly private universe that unreservedly accepts the discipline of a present. Geographically Michael and Clare are on the margins of Ireland; imaginatively Bolger is marginalized from a culture that defines depth and interiority with an ability to completely absorb the full emotional impact of the historical dimension the skeletons beneath the flat represent. This is still a form of internal exile, a consciousness tangential to any collective cultural expression in Ireland. *Emily's Shoes* continues what Corcoran described as the defiant location of contemporary experience in a historical continuum, one not indelibly marked by history and religion; but this present defiantly polices the distinction between private and public rights, and only in the former does the individual find a realm of freedom. It is a variant of the liberalism John Rawls proposed in *A Theory of Justice*: each person, Rawls claims, possesses an inviolability founded on justice that even the welfare of society as a whole cannot override. The rights secured by justice, he argues, are not subject to political bargaining or the calculus of social interests. And at the risk of imposing too orderly a sequence on Bolger's oeuvre, *A Second Life*, I want to argue, represents the culmination of this aesthetic, political, and cultural preoccupation.

V SWEENEY, SHELBOURNE, AND THE PLACE OF POST-NATIONALISM

This reluctance to predicate the present entirely on an understanding of the past is central to *A Second Life*, where Seán Blake, christened Paudi Sweeney, mourns the limited access to his past his adopted state allows. Seán learns of his 'real' mother's death, for example, weeks after she dies, an individual symptom of a more general and permanent partition between history and the present. Yet Seán discovers that even a fractured tradition can be commemorated, as publicly burying the mother he never knew, attended by her brother, the priest responsible for her betrayal, inscribes, to adapt Donoghue's phrase, a rural Catholic mythology he has no choice but to inherit. The use of the Sweeney myth suggests this partial compromise with Irish lore, but it is a mythology founded on an authentic sense of absence, not presence, one with an ironic sense of its distance from any governing horizon of meaning. The public burial legitimates one veiled strand of Seán's history, but only after the return from rural Ireland to Dublin. The consolation of historical understanding, of comprehending a rural past that has substantial depth, is abandoned, as his present self irresistibly propels him back towards the city, the social space containing his present life. Historical understanding arrives only as history fades from view, perceived most fully when part of a different epistemological order to which the contemporary has no immediate facility. A profound but never absolute gulf exists between the present, the time of the state, and the immemorial identity the nation construes as its own. The priest who betrayed Seán's mother, for example, offered himself as his substitute father, so that Seán's biography is entwined with a narrative of rural Catholicism which, if comprehended fully, would mean that history had made the present, and space, intolerable.

The novel's plot revolves around Seán's near fatal car crash outside the Botanic Gardens. Badly injured, he experiences important moments from his life, faces of people long dead, and resolves to discover their relevance to his own adopted state. His search is told in the first person, while the background information on his mother, Elizabeth, is relayed in a third-person narration. The two narratives never meet. Complete knowledge of the second life is not just an existential impossibility; the novel maps a social space which does not require the ratification of historical depth. Seán is fated to discover a liberating failure to fully comprehend history. The proposition the reader is invited to meditate upon is the Nietzschean one: 'the unhistorical and the historical are necessary in equal measure for the health of an individual, of a people, and of a culture'.[101]

Seán Blake, born Paudi Sweeney, blends the visionary and the nomadic: a Blakean desire for social justice with the frenzied Irish Sweeney, a figure from Celtic lore driven half-mad by the battle against a priest and forced to live a miserable life in exile away from his home and the comfort of his family. Sweeney is, in the original Irish version of the poem, finally reconciled to Christianity through the ministry of a priest. Seamus Heaney's recent adaptation (one of many in contemporary Irish writing) emphasized Sweeney as an artist at odds with society. Bolger appropriates the poem's central conflict, the clash of pagan and Christian values, to emphasize the maddening absence of a stable

---

[101] Friedrich Nietzsche, 'On the Uses & Disadvantages of History for Life', in *Untimely Meditations*, trans. R. J. Hollingdale (Cambridge: Cambridge University Press, 1983), 63.

social unit.[102] Seán Blake, a photographer looking to develop, wanders through rural Ireland in search of his real mother but is driven to distraction by a society that refuses to solidify into one fixed image. Photography is another carefully chosen trope full of political implications. Seán's present is bankrolled by his adopted father's postcard business; materially and emotionally, he is mortgaged to a series of idealized Irish images. As a child he posed as an archetypal Celtic peasant in a rural scene based, ironically, on an English pastoral idyll. This is still, as in *The Journey Home*, a state that defines itself through certain immanently valuable rural images. Like the culture to which he belongs, Seán's referential frame is entirely at odds with the real conditions of his urban, metropolitan existence. Luke Gibbons describes these postcards, which were enormously popular in 1950s Ireland, as 'not simply an evocation of an idealised past, but a distinctive form of longing: *nostos* to return home, *algos*, a painful condition—the painful desire to restore the sense of belonging that is associated with childhood and the emotional resonance of the maternal.'[103] This 'emotional resonance of the maternal' is for Bolger always fabricated and imposed. For Seán, the corrosive influence of postcards destroys any meaningful attachment to the present, so he leaves his wife to wander like the Gaelic Sweeney through a barren emotional landscape in search of authenticity, a 'real' origin that is necessarily historical and rural. Dublin is a city (to adapt Terence Brown's description of *Dubliners*) where the cultural and social implications of place and name cannot yet be etched on his psyche because of this premature meaning. Inserted into the cultural grid of the present by his adopted father, this is sustained only by the expulsion of his 'real' mother to Coventry, a place of proverbial exile and social ostracism. Photography, the provision of a material record of a transient present, thus supplies a political and psychological compensation for this elision, as its fixed borders establish the referential frame absent from the social world, while his

[102] See Corcoran, *After Yeats and Joyce*, 20: Sweeney is described as a 'compelling self-image for the modern Irish writer'.

[103] *Transformations in Irish Culture* (Cork: Cork University Press, 1996), 39; 'To criticise these postcards for ignoring the real Ireland, for masking over the social realities of the time, is to miss the whole point of the genre . . . what it is often trying to say is "*Wish I was home*" . . . they are less about our climate and more about our desire to establish or maintain social contact' (ibid., 38).

photojournalism possesses a verisimilitude missing from the kitsch postcards.

The present, however, cannot know itself as the present in *A Second Life*. Seán has 'a phobia about being drawn into the present' (*ASL*, 53). He is unable to photograph himself or reveal his adopted state to his wife because the meaning in that liminal region beyond his own life, his mother's suppressed history, remains permanently inaccessible and continually intrusive. Photography thus duplicates the worst aspects of his adopted state by being both indelible and malleable, a lasting, potentially forgeable record of events, a product of a possibly dubious perspective. Seán cannot memorialize his image, fully enter the frame of his own present life, without condoning a culture distorted by the exclusion of his mother.

This antagonistic relationship generates the quest for *logos*, the emotional resonance of the maternal home; but it is a quest that never extends beyond the Republic. Bolger's sole reference to the Northern Troubles in his novels describes the Republic's paranoid response to the IRA. Frank Conroy, accused of being an IRA sympathizer by a drug-crazed British soldier in Ennis (de Valera's old constituency), cannot cope with the state's suspicion that he is, in fact, a Republican. An exemplary, active citizen, he kills himself and his young son to escape this relentless probing, but no reasons for the deaths emerge. This symbolic death of innocence is masked by a tradition comprised of postcards, priest, and the IRA—by landscape, Catholicism, and nationalism. No legible trace of social conflict remains from Conroy's encounter with contemporary Irish politics, as the present is a dimension that the Republic, because of the North, can never fully enter.

It is not simply that beneath untroubled surfaces—the lake that hides Conroy's body, the postcard's romanticized landscape, the church's imperious façade—hidden energies lie. Rather it is that a profound and general amnesia ensures the past never defaces a present which is thus never fully complete. The postcard's depthless surface converts history into bathos not because that past is unknown, but because the enormity of that legacy is unbearable as history. Seán's adopted state is in this sense a ubiquitous symptom of a more general condition. Everyone in this culture, regardless of whether they have 'real' parents, is exposed to this surfeit of experience over meaning; the demand for postcards is one symptom of this condition as they displace this enormous cultural freight. No one can testify to the experience the postcards actually represent because that history is all too fully known, and so an amnesia is willed into being in order to protect the Republic from its own 'inauthentic' past, the feeling that it is always incomplete, incompetent, unpunctual.

Linked to this is the ostentatious parade of rural place names Seán briefly passes through. Dotted across every page of his journey, they function as a kind of framed group of animated particles in complex relation with one another and the idea of a totality. These transitory place names contain no mythic significance (especially if compared with the use of naming in Brian Friel's great play *Translations*) and impose no greater pattern; their quick, spontaneous randomness instead supplies a form of order without any shaping intention, lacking any deterministic relation between these places. The Republic's 'separate reality' is evoked—he crawls along but never crosses the border—through a cognitive map that shifts the paradigm through which Ireland is understood. The border becomes an incidental not a malign feature of Irish life, as accepting the political divisions within the island enables the cultural divisions to exert ever greater force.

Seán's surrogate identity, the 'deeper' history and origins he is driven to discover, lie not in the public, political world but within an already observable self; this is history as a private, psychic force, a mental geography rather than a connected narrative of public events. The second life Seán seeks to verify, in other words, already exists, in both senses of this term, within his adopted state, within his own private universe. This is why, to adapt Tom Paulin's phrase, the Botanic Gardens is Seán's theoretical context, the site that nurtures and records the varying elements in his life. There, his life ceases to be an approximation of one he wanted to live. There, 'he had learned to walk', discover a historical precedent: 'I knew that I had to track him down before I could fully re-enter my life again. Here, in the library of the Botanic Gardens, seemed as good a place as any to start' (*ASL*, 177). Seán intuits a link to a nineteenth-century figure called Austin Davitt, but no apostolic succession is possible because, as one key image exemplifies, the identity sought is not exclusively historical.

Denis Donoghue described the digging trope in Heaney's earlier poetry as 'a sense of time [that] circumvents the immediacies of historical event by recourse to several different levels of experience, the accretion of culture'. The archaeological recovery of human and political history involves 'the dream of full and immediate presence, time at once historical and perennial, in which the dichotomy between self and other is obliterated'.[104] Beneath surface events resides a richer, residual meaning that mediates an unruly and fractious present. The absence at the core of Seán's life makes impossible this type of innerness. The dichotomy between self and other is obliterated because otherness, his estranged mother, is already one essential element of the self. An irreducible gap exists between the self and the otherness of that self's origins, a fact which detaches Seán from all things Irish, including, of course, his self. Certain layers of historical meaning always remain irrecoverable and unknowable. In the following passage, soil functions as the mediating agent for knowledge of the past but is never infinitely permeable. Seán asks the keeper of the Botanic Gardens if original Famine graves still exist, somewhere presently veiled that might contain a precedent: 'No. Definitely not . . . The soil down there though, it's not the original soil. That soil was too shallow really for an arboretum. I believe they did a lot of replanting after the destruction on the night of the Big Wind. They would have dug fairly deep trenches and brought good loam in' (*ASL*, 168).

Seamus Deane describes soil as 'what land becomes when it is ideologically constructed as a natal source, that element out of which the Irish originate and to which their past generations have returned. It is a political notion denuded, by a strategy of sacralization, of all economic and commercial reference.' Soil, Deane says, precedes land; it is a symbolic medium prior to ideology, bureaucracy, and economy, through which the nation is imagined as a cohesive, internally unified entity.[105] In McIlvanney's *Docherty*, 'coal' is an example of Deane's 'soil', a commodity that by burying Tam, the natal source of Scottish difference, becomes, in the novel, more sacred than economic. In

---

[104] *We Irish* (Berkeley and Los Angeles: University of California Press, 1986), 267–71.   [105] *Strange Country*, 71, 77.

A Second Life, the replacement of the original soil with loam, a crumbly mixture of clay, silt, and sand, is a similarly political gesture. There is no sacral, natal source from which Seán's lineage emanates. The levelling force of the Big Wind, the catastrophic dimension to Irish history, renders aspects of his past resolutely foreign, sealed on the other side of an unbridgeable divide. In Brian Friel's memorable phrase, to try to remember everything, to reconstitute everything about this always fragmented and mutilated past, is another form of madness.

Yet such an inheritance is not necessarily debilitating, as Thomas Kinsella's eloquent description of his complicated association with past generations, first cited in relation to Crichton Smith, testifies. 'If the function of tradition is to link us living with a significant past, this is done as well by a broken tradition as by a whole one—however painful it may be humanly speaking. I am certain that a great part of my own past, as I try to write my poetry, is that the past is mutilated.'[106] The perfect availability of the past is not necessarily a feature of a historical continuum; the mere existence of discontinuities is no logical impediment to a sensible narrative that accounts for the immemorial experience of the nation. Corcoran described Bolger's earlier work as a way 'of defiantly locating contemporary experience in a historical continuum'; but in this continuum, the most consistent and regular feature is the persistent reappearance of this mutilated element.[107] In *A Second Life*, however, Bolger aggressively pursues a cognitive and social space outside any continuum that does not arrive at Seán's present status. No prior cultural moment is analogous or comparable to the experience chronicled, and no organizational model except the state guarantees and underwrites the private individual universe that ends the novel. Despite the narrative's legion of place names, Ireland conspicuously never coheres into a substantive unit. It is not territory that denominates Bolger's region but people. What is named and valorized is not a geographical region but an ethnic formation, one that is Irish and exceptional, historical but part of a continuum that has never known existence before this moment. Bolger dismantles the myth of

---

[106] 'The Irish Writer', in *Davis, Mangan, Ferguson? Tradition and the Irish Writer* (Dublin: Dolmen, 1970), 57.
[107] *After Yeats and Joyce*, 126.

Irish unity by attempting to step outside any incarnation it has previously enjoyed.

Seán's son Benedict is throughout the novel the focus for the desire to return to Dublin, part of a longing for *algos*. Benedict's name alludes to a specifically Catholic inheritance reformulated through the city, and at a soccer match a neighbour remarks on the child's likeness to Seán's adopted father. Having failed to discover roots, Seán can choose from those elements the city hosts. Watching Shelbourne achieve improbable glory in the European Cup, from the terrace on which his adopted father stood, is an example of Bolger's displacement of metaphors of authenticity. Soccer is an English game, concentrated mostly in the cities, while the Gaelic Athletic Association (GAA), part of the priest's world, nurtured a rural cultural nationalism. Demonized by some elements of the GAA as foreign, for many years members of the association were banned from playing this 'English' game.[108] The recent success of the Republic's national team, it has been claimed, promoted 'an Ireland that was universally recognizable, yet at the same time deeply personal. None of the team of 1994 [the team that campaigned in the 1994 World Cup held in the USA] lived in Ireland, all of them had Irish roots, they worked overseas—their absence from Ireland was a measure of successful Irishness in a competitive sport and a mark of the nation's long history of famine, emigration and exile.'[109] And in a similar vein, the name of Seán's son is finally made real when it does not try to inscribe an essence, when Benedict is seen as the culmination of a lineage that is not immemorially posited but is continually recreating itself in its own private universe:

We had baptised Benedict for the sake of Geraldine's family. For me it had been an empty experience. But now this passing of a name seemed real and wonderful as I walked towards the wire fence. I wanted my father to know that it was his name which Benedict was carrying, and that, through all my grief for my real mother, it was being carried with pride . . . I reached the goalmouth and lifted Benedict up like a trophy for his grandfather to see. (*ASL*, 295)

---

[108] 'Places: Town and Country', in Tom Humphries, *Green Fields: Gaelic Sport in Ireland* (London: Weidenfeld & Nicolson, 1995), 52–64.

[109] In the section entitled 'Jack Charlton and the New Nationalism', in Mike Cronin, *Sport and Nationalism in Ireland: Gaelic Games, Soccer and Irish Identity Since 1884* (Dublin: Four Courts Press, 1999), 129–42, at 139.

Seán finally enters the frame of his life by accepting the compromises involved in an adopted, non-essential identity. The reproduction of his own image through his father's camera, with Benedict as photographer, is a pleasingly complex assertion of Thomas Kinsella's belief that what 'links us living with a significant past, this is done as well by a broken tradition as by a whole one'. However unlikely a prospect it is, a third goal, 'scored by Izzi, a young Italian who worked by day in his uncle's fish and chip shop' (*ASL*, 293) is, perhaps, Shelbourne's first ever entry into the ideology of post-nationalism, as Seán realizes 'I had this one life to lead now, this one name that I would pass on to my children' (*ASL*, 296). The principle of apostolic succession is accepted, but this lineage within the state is primarily urban and private and indicative of the 'collapse of a value system based on exclusive, (exclusionary) national identities'.[110] For in one sense 'Izzi' personifies the nation as much as Kiberd's Kathleen Ní Houlihán, but one with a chameleon, cosmopolitan content that does not seek the ratification of a rural ethnic past, an idea explored most fully in Bolger's play *In High Germany*. Set during the 1988 European Soccer Championships the Republic emerges as a 'blessedly bastardised' nation, one whose multiracial line-up asks, as Shaun Richards puts it, 'what meaning is now carried by the signifier "Ireland"?'[111] The play celebrates the demise of history and ethnicity as markers in Irish life, but, in an irony Bolger never remarks upon, eleven Orange men from Holland (the country that gave Ireland William of Orange) defeats this symbol of liberalism. In the 1994 World Cup, as the Republic played Italy, the Ulster Volunteer Force massacred six men watching the game in a pub in the Catholic town of Loughinisland. They claimed that those watching were part of a Republican gathering. Bolger's version of Ireland would be a wonderful thing if it could be true, but as Thomas McCarthy's work will show, any escape from and abjection of the past is more difficult than Bolger would have us believe.

---

[110] Willy Maley, Chris Morash, and Shaun Richards, 'The Triple Play of Irish History', *Irish Review*, 20 (Winter/Spring 1997), 23–46.
[111] Ibid. 39.

VI   BOLGERISM?

What, then, is 'Bolgerism'? Is the cumulative effect of these
novels and collections still the absence of a civic discourse, a
mawkish sentimentality that legitimates the state even as it perceives itself to be 'a persecuted modernity'?[112] There is no doubt
that Bolger's political and ideological project (a term he would
probably disavow) is interested almost exclusively in discontinuities and ruptures, the aporia in the nation's narrative, and
pays scant attention to continuities. And there is no doubt his
monolithic account of Fianna Fáil's political tradition in *The
Journey Home* is schematic, an exaggerated account that cannot
pass for historical reality. The only kind of otherness Bolger
allows is internal, within the self; Ireland can never enjoy the
cultural specificity he claims for his own beleaguered constituency. He is for differences that make a difference as they affect
the private constituency of each writer in his anthology; he is
against defining difference as it emerges from the shared story
any anthology entails. Such collectives are not capable of being
reconstructed to meet the rigours of changing circumstances;
instead they're simply obsolete, more or less wholly irrelevant to
a society in which the traditional agencies of historic change have
collapsed. There is an actual decomposition of the idea of Ireland
in an age that is categorically different from what has gone
before, a perspective implacably opposed to Kiberd's historiciz-
ing of identity, his belief in the past as a reservoir of meaning.
Bolger submits everything to the discipline of present reality,
accepting the transformation of the world as it is and fully inserting the self into it. There is no genealogy of the nation that can
account for the present reality of Shelbourne and north Dublin,
a site that signals the emergence of new areas of contestation and
leaves Kiberd's notion of 'the people' struggling to catch up. But
submitting everything to the discipline of the present is inevitably
to traduce the past in some way, and the moral equivalence
drawn between the shoes and religion in *Emily's Shoes* might be
seen as one oversized example of this. The steadfast opposition
to developing any collective theory of these decentred forms,
these private universes, of considering them as part of any total-

---

[112] Kiberd, *Inventing Ireland*, 609.

ity, ensures they will be represented as completely fantastic in order to establish their irreducible individuality.

The political project, then, impacts adversely on his aesthetic, but it is also seen through his aesthetic. Seamus Deane claims that the return of the Northern crisis since 1968 (the year Bolger starts his anthology of Irish fiction) has exposed the lack of 'any system of cultural consent that would effectively legitimise and secure the existing political arrangements of the island. There has rarely been in Ireland any sustained coordination between prevailing cultural and political systems.'[113] It is difficult to view Bolger's introduction to the Picador anthology as anything other than the legitimation of one political arrangement, the Republic, while the constant insertion of all experience into the present accommodates the one time frame the state understands.

This is also apparent through one other important feature. Luke Gibbons claims, 'If there is a recurrent motif in discussions of narrative forms in Irish culture, it is that "closure" and "strict emplotment" are, to say the least, rare achievements indeed.'[114] The orderly procession of seamlessly connected events, the cumulatively growing organic history of the great English tradition, was always unavailable in an Irish culture marked by regular catastrophe. The end of *A Second Life*, however, is just such a point of closure, as the passing of the name signifies the end of Seán's Sweenyesque wanderings and a reconciliation with a mutilated tradition; the very use of the Sweeney myth is an indication of this. We have moved from Elizabeth's termination of her pregnancy in *Night Shift* to the adopted Benedict inaugurating a new, non-essential, civic conception of citizenship. The union of mother and child is a model of aestheticized human relations, and in Irish (and Scottish) literature, has often represented an allegorical configuration of an idealized union between colonized and the imperial power.[115] In this context, Elizabeth's

[113] 'Introduction', in id. (gen. ed.), *Field Day Anthology of Irish Writing*, vol. i, p. xx.

[114] 'Dialogue without the Other?: A Reply to Francis Mulhern', *Radical Philosophy*, 67 (Summer 1994), 29.

[115] See Katie Trumpener, *Bardic Nationalism: The Romantic Novel and the British Empire* (Princeton: Princeton University Press, 1997), 137. Trumpener describes 'crosscultural marriage as a form of countercolonization: when the English fall in love with the natives of Ireland, their courtship and union become occasions for proselytising and revelation'.

termination aborts any possibility of a coherent, continuous, national tale, for the ideals of marriage—balance, compromise, equality, shared affection—are impossible to discover in the *polis* she shares with Donal. Their separation reflects the unavoidable impact of divisions in the public sphere upon individuals. By *A Second Life*, these divisions have not been erased or confronted but avoided and domesticated. The quest narrative desacralizes and decodes the older forms of identity as the urban present is no longer haunted by the shadowy aura of an ethnic past. Reconciled with his wife in north Dublin, the micropolitics of the present and the category of the individual both repudiate the possibility of any contact with a totalizing history. But this liberation from a totality defines citizenship in strictly legal terms, as something entitled to protection from the public sphere. No element of his identity is realized through identification with the *polis*, the *respublica*, a fact which prematurely disallows any common recognition of a collective form of identification. As long as the possessor-class are in full possession of their self-identity, no chain of equivalence is acknowledged with regions outside his north Dublin home. Both *Emily's Shoes* and *A Second Life* are strictly emplotted in order to arrive at this private zone in the present moment, in a universe which is private to the extent that it cannot be shared with, altered by, or answerable to any wider, politicized conception of the public sphere.

4

Between the Falls Road and Kildare Street: Thomas McCarthy and the Location of Memory

Literature has always been a form of socialisation for ex-republicans, a way of recognising the court. Reading the fiction of Gerry Adams and listening to his voice, I was reminded of the fateful words of de Valera on August 12 1927: 'I am prepared to put my name down in this book in order to get permission to go into the Dáil'.[1]

Poetry is never provincial, only criticism can be provincial.[2]

I PARTY ANIMAL

IN ONE key episode from Thomas McCarthy's 1991 novel *Without Power*, rival Fianna Fáil and Coalition workers, campaigning in the presidential election of 1981, wander lost in thick fog in their west-Waterford constituency. The Coalition workers have destroyed Fianna Fáil election posters, but retribution is suspended as a swirling mist envelops both factions. The Fianna Fáil workers become 'one eye, one ear . . . as if the cold ghosts of the mountain's memory had taken over, and were now directing the progress of their minibus' (*WP*, 117). Their progress takes them over a cliff. The factions finally return home by following some sheep, where the local political calculus determines that, because the Coalition followed Fianna Fáil following the

---

[1] 'Streetwise: From the Falls Road to Kildare Street? Thomas McCarthy met Gerry Adams', *STET: The National Literary and Arts Newspaper*, 12 (Winter, 1993), 4.
[2] Thomas McCarthy, 'Poet as Librarian', *Poetry Ireland Review*, 29 (Summer, 1990), 54.

sheep, the Soldiers of Destiny, the Republican Party, the Party, emerge victorious. In the absence of any other distinguishing characteristic, voting in the presidential election is determined by local atavisms and intrigue, 'the cold ghost of the mountain's memory', and some electorally ineligible sheep.

The modern state, according to one of its most eminent historians, 'is the possessor of sovereignty over a given territory'.[3] Sovereignty is indivisible, limited internally only by the distinction between the private and public sphere, and the state's function is to provide rational rules governing the behaviour between groups, rules which can, if necessary, be enforced when broken. The state, as Breuilly explains, has universal aspirations. There should be no area or person either within the state or, theoretically, around the globe, that is not subject to the rule of a state; this is why a stateless person becomes, in theory and practice, a sort of non-person,[4] and why the geography of the state should form one coherent administrative unit.

The State survives and prospers as long as it can hold together the territorial coalition of places that gives it geographical form. The State is dependent on places for support as they are dependent on it for political influence. The political parties and local-central links it provides a locus for are in turn their main channels of political expression.[5]

Breuilly's understanding of the modern state helps illuminate the fog scene in *Without Power*. The Fianna Fáil workers, campaigning to win the presidency, the constitutional head of the state, become non-persons, non-individuals ('one eye, one ear') because the state has no sovereignty over mountain territory loaded with the Party's tribal memories; the 'rational rules governing the behaviour between groups' are abruptly suspended as a series of motives never reducible to a single or rational definition determine the election outcome. The Fianna Fáil workers are, to apply Denis Donoghue's terms, already inscribed by a mythology they have no choice but to inherit.[6] Although the Party workers aim to secure the leadership of the

³ John Breuilly, *Nationalism and the State* (Manchester: Manchester University Press, 1982), 355.
⁴ Ibid. 355.
⁵ John A. Agnew, *Place and Politics: The Geographical Mediation of State and Society* (Boston: Allen & Unwin, 1987), 40.
⁶ 'Being Irish Together', *Sewanee Review*, 84/1 (Winter 1976), 133.

state, their premature affiliation to a local index of tribal rivalries undermines, in John Agnew's phrase, the territorial coalition of places that gives the state geographical form. If the state is modern to the extent that it creates social conformity, 'a uniformity or universality to life within its borders',[7] Fianna Fáil undermines its theoretical commitment to this rational space by grounding a substantial portion of its own identity in 'the cold ghosts of the mountain's memory', in regions that contain a chthonic, immemorial, nationalist tradition that propels them over a cliff. The state may be shared with fellow citizens, but certain recognizable territories belong not to the world of ideas but to a premature mythology Party workers automatically inherit. The state may lay claim to the collective identity of the nation, and offers the nation the chance of being free through the universal concept of a sovereign state,[8] but for Fianna Fáil, the Republican Party, the twenty-six counties it helped usher into being is, perforce, an artificial entity. The nation, in other words, must at some level be protected from the state.[9]

This scene contains many of McCarthy's preoccupations: the obstinate myopia of the Republic's politics enables a spurious progress; the parties' campaigns, separate but dependent, belonging both to the modernizing world of ordered politics and a millenialism rooted in the rural peasantry.[10] The slim partition between the zero-sum logic of a modern presidential election and an apocalyptic, purposeless politics, in which sheep symbolically provide leadership, is a constant tension in McCarthy's work. To adapt the title of his interview with Gerry Adams, one road links the present-centred time of the state with the immemorial presence of the nation. In Irish Republican politics, the Falls

[7] Joel S. Migdal, 'Studying the State', in Mark Irving Lichbach and Alan S. Zuckerman (eds.), *Comparative Politics: Rationality, Culture, Structure* (Cambridge: Cambridge University Press, 1997), 209. See also Gopal Balakrishnan, 'The National Imagination', *New Left Review*, 211 (1995), 66: 'The State then stirs the national imagination merely by giving territorial shape to the language of public life.'

[8] Migdal, 'Studying the State', 228.

[9] 'Artificial entity' is a phrase used by Charles Haughey to describe Northern Ireland.

[10] R. V. Comerford, 'Nation, Nationalism, and the Irish Language', in T. E. Hachey and L. J. McCaffrey (eds.), *Perspectives on Irish Nationalism* (Lexington: University of Kentucky Press, 1989), 22. See also Tom Garvin, 'A Quiet Revolution: The Remaking of Irish Political Culture', in Ray Ryan (ed.), *Writing in the Irish Republic: Literature, Culture, Politics 1949–1999* (Basingstoke: Macmillan, 2000), 187–203.

Road and Kildare Street are opposite ends of the same route, and part of Gerald Dawe's description of McCarthy's basic theme: 'the repossession of the past—his family's and his country's—and the need to prove the artistic and imaginative viability of this project'.[11] Fianna Fáil's ambivalent, occasionally contradictory journey between ethnic and civic nationalism since Independence (an opposition in which McCarthy discovers an intimate connection) are explored throughout his work in a sustained examination of the Republic as a cultural entity.

After partition, Fianna Fáil's rhetoric of unity struggled to cope with the sensation of difference inevitably fostered by the 1920 Government of Ireland Act. Under de Valera, the Party defended symbols and used a political rhetoric which implied the supremacy within the island of an ethno-cultural rather than a civic identity. This ethnic nationalism proved remarkably resilient, even as the Party moved after de Valera towards a civic dimension, and established a virtual monopoly over the memory of Irish nationalism. And for all its well-documented faults, de Valera's kitsch but sincere vision established the ideal of community as an essential feature of the Irish political landscape. Hugh Kearney notes how the tensions between civic and ethnic identity are an inescapable part of our modern world, a point McCarthy's work implicitly endorses. In *Without Power*, the fog partly symbolizes the myopic intensity of a local politics that never completely concedes its autonomy to the rationally ordered space of the state. Galvanized and retarded by the lingering potency of memories and myths that simultaneously define and obscure their political vision, the Party workers occupy this fraught terrain between state and nation, the Republic and Republicanism, memory and destiny. This is how McCarthy acknowledges Kearney's point that 'To deny the pull of ethnic identity is to deny history. To allow a full play is to deny choice'.[12] McCarthy has said that 'poetry demands attention in a way that defeats comparison, it draws attention to the uniqueness of each poetic territory',[13] a phrase which echoes the

---

[11] 'The Suburban Night: Boland, Durcan and McCarthy', in *Against Piety* (Belfast: Lagan Press, 1995), 192.
[12] 'Contested Ideas of Nationhood', *Irish Review*, 20 (Winter/Spring 1997), 1–22.
[13] 'Thomas McCarthy Reviews . . .', *Poetry Ireland Review*, 40 (Winter 1993/4), 63.

micro-politics of Bolger's 'private fictional universes'. Yet the uniqueness of McCarthy's west-Waterford territorial region is inextricably entwined with the imaginative impact of Fianna Fáil's nationalism, and its response to an increasingly civic twenty-six-county state. The uniqueness of his poetic territory has to accommodate the state, the homogeneous space the Party now administers.[14]

The political dimension to the production of space differs quite fundamentally from Heaney's. John Kerrigan describes Heaney's tropes of territorial self-expression as 'a tribal welling-up which will green over the planet's earth-writing of "demenses" and "bawns"'. Though Heaney claims an ostensible pluralism for this constellation of place names, for Kerrigan they inevitably foster 'a language of at-homeness, dwelling, and proper naming of the fatherland remininscent (for all its Horatian elegance) of Lüneberg heath'.[15] McCarthy's geo-politics, the poetic territory and space produced through his writing, is not tied to the nostalgia of soil or a philological re-possession of place; his geographical imagination is instead bound to the idea of the *polis* as it manifests itself within his community.[16] For Eavan Boland, McCarthy's movement beyond 'a language of at-homeness', of dwelling, is exemplary: 'McCarthy's lines . . . hint at the fact that a recognizable project in this generation of poets is the de-romanticizing of place and a consequent re-statement of the Irish pastoral.'[17] This is a tradition of civic republicanism in which citizenship is never conceived as independent of the individual's insertion into a political community; but nor does McCarthy dissociate citizenship from nationality (as Bolger does), even as the dangers in this relationship for the poet are frankly acknowledged: 'Irish politics constantly demands an all-embracing anthology, a single canon,

---

[14] Lefebvre, *The Production of Space*, trans. Donald Nicholson-Smith (Oxford: Blackwell, 1991), 341.

[15] 'Earth Writing: Seamus Heaney and Ciaran Carson', *Essays in Criticism: A Quarterly Journal of Literary Criticism*, 47/2 (Apr. 1998), 149.

[16] See Seamus Heaney, 'The Sense of Place', in *Preoccupations: Selected Prose 1968–1978* (London: Faber and Faber, 1980), 131–2, for a different emphasis on the meaning and comprehension of place.

[17] 'New Wave 2: Born in the 50s; Irish Poets of the Global Village', in Theo Dorgan (ed.), *Irish Poetry since Kavanagh: The Thomas Davis Lectures* (Dublin: Four Courts Press, 1996), 140.

whereas every artistic life rebuffs that demand.'[18] McCarthy's scrupulous exploration of Fianna Fáil, the rural Catholic tradition that spawned the Plunkett brothers in Bolger, is in large part responsible for the uniqueness of his poetic territory, his *polis*, and it provides the subject of this chapter.

There is no sustained analysis of McCarthy's imaginative affiliation to Fianna Fáil,[19] though the development of a major part of McCarthy's career can be traced through his responses to the Party.[20] It is a history of complex successions of love and hate, or what Freud called 'ambivalence': 'the direction towards the same person of contrary—affectionate and hostile—feelings'.[21] Fianna Fáil's most recent historian claims it has 'probably done more than any other institution to shape the society of the Republic of Ireland'.[22] Its self-image is that of the party of 'the men of no property':[23] a phrase first used by Wolfe Tone to describe the rural, Catholic poor for ever estranged from the mechanisms of the state under British rule. Described by Sean Lemass as late as 1928 as 'a slightly constitutional party',[24] a phrase which captures the ambivalence of its irredentist flank towards the state, it boasts of being a national movement, not a mere party, an expression of the spirit of the nation, not an ideological faction. Fianna Fáil's dominance of the Republic

[18] 'Documents of Exclusion', *Irish Review*, 4 (Winter 1987), 141–2.

[19] The only substantial criticism of McCarthy's work is Catriona Clutterbuck's unpublished MA thesis, 'Place, Time, and the Possibility of Connection in Contemporary Irish Poetry' (University College Dublin, 1990), which offers an impressive number of readings of individual poems. I am very grateful to Dr Clutterbuck for making available her MA thesis to me. See also Thomas Dillon Redshaw, '*Teach Beag Nó Bungaló*: The Hidden Ireland of Thomas McCarthy', *Nua: Studies in Contemporary Irish Writing*, 1/1 (Autumn 1997), 1–14.

[20] Thomas McCarthy, 'Five Summer Afternoons', *Eire-Ireland*, 26/1 (Spring 1991), 7–18.

[21] Lecture 26, *Introductory Lectures on Psychoanalysis* (1917), in *The Standard Edition of the Complete Psychological Works of Sigmund Freud*, ed. James Strachey, 24 vols. (London: Hogarth Press, 1953–74), xvi. 428.

[22] Keiran Allen, *Fianna Fáil and Irish Labour: 1926 to the Present* (London: Pluto Press, 1997), 1.

[23] 'My life is of little consequence . . . Our independence must be had at all hazards, if the men of property will not support us, they must fall: we can support ourselves by the aid of that numerous and respectable class of the community, *the men of no property*.' Quoted in Jim Smyth, *The Men of No Property* (Basingstoke: Macmillan, 1994), p. ix.

[24] J. J. Lee, *Ireland 1912–1985: Politics and Society* (Cambridge: Cambridge University Press, 1988), 167.

since Independence is unique in European politics.[25] It does not offer an explicit social basis to its policies. Traditionally it has been pro-Catholic, pro-nationalist, anti-intellectual, prone to authoritarianism, and unashamedly populist. Analysts of Fianna Fáil stress this ability to touch this 'spirit of the nation'; Dick Walsh, for example, described the Party as possessing a 'blazing mystique [without] social content': it 'looked neither left nor right but steadfastly to the past and drew on the spirit of the nation, almost but not quite as Thomas Davis and the Young Irelanders had dreamed of it'.[26] Eamon de Valera, the founder of Fianna Fáil, created a party whose strength 'lay in the fact that it drew on much of what was beyond the rational'.[27] Twenty years after de Valera's death, he remains enigmatically, frustratingly immune from professional research: the bulk of his voluminous papers lie secure but inaccessible in a Franciscan house in south Dublin, a wonderful image for 'the Chief', 'the Long Fellow', the great national patriarch who, in Edna Longley's terms, 'managed to fuse the aura of father as paterfamilias and father as priest'.[28] McCarthy offers a unique insight into this 'aura', a window on a nationalist tradition that is often traduced but whose influence is not disputed. For as Tom Garvin notes, 'In a sense, much of the real politics of the Republic takes place, usually in camera, within the Fianna Fáil party or between Fianna Fáil and the major social institutions and interest groups of the Republic, rather than between the three main parties in the political system'.[29]

Garvin's pioneering work on Fianna Fáil emphasizes its success in transposing a political culture primarily devised for the needs of 'detribalised and stateless peasants' from the western periphery to the cities.[30] This sense of two temporal continuums

[25] Tom Garvin, 'The Destiny of the Soldiers: Tradition and Modernity in the Politics of de Valera's Ireland', *Irish Political Studies*, 26 (1978), 328–47.

[26] *The Party: Inside Fianna Fáil* (Dublin: Gill and Macmillan, 1986), 32, 42.

[27] J. P. O'Carroll, 'Eamon de Valera: Charisma and Politcal Development', in id. and J. A. Murphy (eds.), *De Valera and his Times* (Cork: Cork University Press, 1983), 208.

[28] *The Living Stream: Literature and Revisionism in Ireland* (Newcastle-upon-Tyne: Bloodaxe, 1994), 154.

[29] 'Theory, Culture and Fianna Fáil: A Review', in Mary Kelly, Liam O'Dowd, and James Wickham (eds.), *Power, Conflict, and Inequality* (Dublin: Turoe, 1982), 171–85, at 173.

[30] 'Political Cleavages, Party Politics and Urbanisation in Ireland: The Case of a Periphery-Dominated Centre', *European Journal of Political Research*, 6/1 (1974),

and two spatial arrangements that are not mutually exclusive but complementary—each of which contains the other—these two strands operating simultaneously within Fianna Fáil create the persistent ambivalences in McCarthy's work, ambivalences conveyed by such juxtapositions as light–dark, son–father, election–apocalypse. After partition, the consolidation of the new state required the mobilization of memories based on, to use Donoghue's term, a premature mythology, a nationalist narrative of a golden age, a fall, and, through the new state, a process of rebirth. Hence the first element in the above series is always haunted by the second.[31] The Party's troubled transposition from narratives of nation to state ironically reactivates a lingering attachment to those myths of rootedness, authenticity, and ethnicity, myths which the universal aspirations of the state were supposed to displace. This phenomenon Tom Nairn describes as the 'curse of rurality': 'many traits of the abandoned world may continue to "haunt" an existence in other ways apparently broken in to city existence and civic conditions . . . there is another term for such a haunting: ethnic nationalism. Ethnic nationalism is in essence a peasantry transmuted, at least in ideal terms, into a nation.'[32] Fianna Fáil is a powerful, enigmatic, ruthlessly efficient vote-getting institution that somehow masks its bureaucratic structure to draw on 'what is beyond the rational'. John Waters's autobiographical odyssey into the Party, *Jiving at the Crossroads*, an instant classic on publication in 1991,[33] and even Bolger's unrelentingly critical portrait, is testimony to the enduring charisma and importance of Fianna Fáil. McCarthy's ambivalent poetic journey with and into the Party is no less interesting.

In one sense, de Valera's own career is marked by a similar kind of ambivalence—contrary feelings, affectionate and hostile, are directed towards the same object (in Dev's case, the state).

27–44. 'Spirit of the nation' is also the title of Charles Haughey's collected speeches. For a stinging critique of this ideology see Fintan O'Toole, 'The Southern Question', in Dermot Bolger (ed.), *Letters from the New Island* (Dublin: Raven Arts Press, 1991), 15–44.

[31] See Joseph Ruane and Jennifer Todd, *The Dynamics of Conflict in Northern Ireland: Power, Conflict and Emancipation* (Cambridge: Cambridge University Press, 1996), 87.

[32] *Faces of Nationalism: Janus Revisited* (London: Verso, 1997), 91.

[33] (Belfast: Blackstaff Press, 1991).

After his Party finally 'shuffled'[34] into Dáil Eireann in 1927, it began the slow process of accommodating the twenty-six-county state to its nationalist rhetoric. Faced with the militarism of his erstwhile nationalist comrades, de Valera often brutally defended the previously denigrated partition. Because McCarthy's father was part of this process, he does not have the same latitude as Bolger to invent an alternative political or literary persona. For if, as Edna Longley says, it is through the parent motif that the 'individual locates himself or herself in history, and Irish history remains in many respects a family affair',[35] Bolger's use of adoption as trope, with all its emphasis on displacement, indeterminacy, the necessarily precarious and unstable basis to personal identity, contrasts with the omnipresent father figure in McCarthy's poetry, a constant reminder of the poet's own immersion in the Party's history. Or as McCarthy puts it in 'I think of fathers I've invented, and marvel that the earth is calm', a poem from the collection *The Lost Province,*

> I think of the terrible mistake poets made
> who attached themselves
> to Marx instead of their fathers
>
> . . . and nothing so puritan, or man-made
> as dialectical secateurs
> can sever the bond with the dead.
>
> (*TLP*, 66)

Writing, on this account, does not just reflect the reality of social division. As a social institution itself, it organizes the symbolic order of a community and provides the models for the personalities within it. McCarthy mocks his heroic aspirations, marvels 'that the earth is calm' despite his poetic broadsides. But the creative aspiration to match the social impact of the polity is a serious one, and the imaginative inspiration is always drawn from the history of southern Republicans like his father. McCarthy's location in this rural parliamentary Republicanism emerges fully in an interview with Gerry Adams, to which we will return. But as in Bolger, the gap between his immediate, local position as an individual and the totality of the island—for

---

[34] Lee, *Ireland: 1912–1985*, 155.
[35] ' "When Did You Last See Your Father?": Perceptions of the Past in Northern Irish Writing 1965–1985', in *Living Stream*, 152.

nationalists, the absolute forum within which Irish meaning and politics evolves—is frankly acknowledged. McCarthy's reluctance, even his inability, to cognitively map what lies beyond the territory of the state desacralizes the physical geography of the island. Or, as 'Mick Hannigan's Berlin Wall' puts it, 'as our divided island is a just thing: I perfect image of the spirit unwilling' (*TLP*, 49). McCarthy, however, can still embrace the idea of an individual identity realized through a political community: 'I recall Bloody Sunday. You recall I Enniskillen. Corpses lie on our flowers I while we think and talk and watch' (*TLP*, 65). Here he incorporates the dominant characteristic of Irish social ideology, a communalism founded on religion, nationality, locality, and the folk memory of common experience. This communalism, as Liam O'Dowd explains, is both a constructive and defensive strategy, a way of building the material specificity of the region and resisting its incorporation into the abstract, homogenized space of global capitalism:

The political boundaries of 'nation' and 'State' have been continually contested in Ireland—they are not 'above politics' as they are in other western European countries, rather they are the very stuff of party politics. Communalism is a strategy, therefore, for dealing with the great uncertainty about the economic, political and cultural parameters of modern Ireland—whether, for example, these parameters should be the 26-county State, Northern Ireland, the whole of Ireland, the British Isles, Anglo-America or the EEC.[36]

McCarthy's wariness of 'dialectical secateurs' results not from any aversion towards global political themes, or some residual fondness for a rooted dwelling. Instead, he recognizes the lingering potency of 'place' within the idea of the *polis*, and he responds to the challenge of creating a literature founded on this aspect of the Republic's cultural memory.

II SPECTRES OF DEV

McCarthy's first collection *The First Convention* received high praise for its depiction of the Republic's political and social life.

---

[36] 'Town and Country in Irish Ideology', *Canadian Journal of Irish Studies*, 12/2 (1987), 45.

For Eavan Boland, it was 'that rare and long-awaited advent in Irish poetry: a glimpse of de Valera's Ireland through the eyes of a poet born into the officially declared Irish Republic. Here is the scrutiny of the dream in the punishing light of reality.'[37] McCarthy's major themes were announced in such poems as 'State Funeral', where de Valera's burial releases a series of memories within the son that illuminate the psychological and political, private and public cleavages separating him from his father's generation.[38] The impact of public events, McCarthy consistently demonstrates, is also felt privately, so that the psychic and political are never entirely divorced:

> My father recited prayers of memory,
> Of monster meetings, blazing tar-barrels
> Planted outside Free-State homes, the Broy
> -Harriers pushing through a crowd,
>
> Blueshirts; and, after the war,
> De Valera's words
> Making Churchill's imperial palette blur.
>
> What I remember is one decade of darkness,
> A mind stifling boredom; long summers
> for blackberry picking and churning cream,
> Winters for saving timber or setting lines
>
> and snares: none of the joys of the here and now
> With its instant jam, instant heat and cream.
>
> It was a landscape for old men.
>
> (*TFC*, 10)

Anchored in a rural nationalism, the father's memories enable individual and communal self-definition; his son recalls only the lack of recollection, his preoccupation with a distant future, and detachment from the present moment, 'the here and now'. These dull and dark recollections resist representation—the 'lines' (poetic or physical?) spill over into the next line, into 'snares'— as they struggle for imaginative space beside de Valera's political rhetoric, packed with names and colour and light. The Yeatsian

---

[37] 'A New Voice in Poetry', quoted in Gerald Dawe, 'Suburban Night', 189.

[38] Garvin says 'it might be useful to know that the strongest differences in the Irish political elite have been generational rather than partisan' ('Theory, Culture and Fianna Fáil', 183).

echoes of 'a landscape for old men' ('That is no country for old men') are an ironic inversion of Yeats's fears of de Valera's partisan politics. Sexual, emotional, and poetic energies are hoarded, with subterranean snares awaiting any visible sign of spontaneous desire, any 'instant jam, instant heat and cream'. The change in metre here works to emphasize the stale present the boy is forced to inhabit. The nation defined through his father's memories becomes part of the boy's biological and emotional history, aiding self-definition but alienating him from the present. Social context and childhood trauma, 'Foucault and Freud',[39] always mingle in McCarthy in an ambivalent combination of personal and political memory that redounds throughout his work. De Valera may now be a television spectacle, as the family gather to watch his burial; but this private ritual, this 'native *déja-vu*', is made possible by the presence of the tribal culture of Fianna Fáil in the 'living-room', the latter phrase neatly capturing the way de Valera's rhetoric was internalized in the Republic. Public events have a dramatic and private impact, certainly; but the rhetoric used in politics itself emerges from a context which is, in the first instance, intensely private, a fact which accounts for the persistent ambiguities between private and public spheres in Irish civic life. In mourning de Valera, the poem implies, 'public' history is experienced privately, and yet that experience is simultaneously acknowledged to be communal. Thus no single memory presides in the poem: the commemoration of the father and the imaginative freedom of the 'here and now' are neither insolubly linked nor inalienably separate. An enduring admiration for de Valera—'De Valera's words | Making Churchill's imperial palette blur'; 'his austere grandeur'; 'Taut sadness'—ensures that frustration never becomes total renunciation. De Valera haunts the verse, perhaps even offers a rhetorical model for a truly effective political poetry, but he does not haunt McCarthy. At some level he is distant from the events described, so that he re-enters the communal experience of those events through the poem.

The act of writing, is, like de Valera's taking of the oath, a means of representing the nation. But representing the Republic,

<hr />

[39] A phrase used by Roy Foster in his commentary on Yeats's description of his childhood home. See 'Yeats: Love, Magic and Politics', *Independent on Sunday* (7 Mar. 1997), 28.

the twenty-six-county state, as the nation has, at least for the Party's nationalist flank, the aura of inauthenticity; like de Valera's signature, the Republic is a forgery, an inscription which does not correspond with a deeper, 'truer' reality. This deep ambivalence surrounds McCarthy's writing. The yearning for 'instant jam, instant heat and cream', for example, is partly ironic: immediate gratification of personal appetites is liberating because it is so much at odds with the austere historical and communal goals de Valera set; but this contrast also throws into new perspective the present. The contemporary Republic can never fully realize the aspirations for the Irish nation envisaged by the Party's founders, and for McCarthy, this is a source of guilty relief.

III   THE BLAZING MYSTIQUE OF WEST WATERFORD

Without Power, one of two novels centred on the Glenville family's west-Waterford political dynasty, develops this 'bonding with the dead'. This political constituency is McCarthy's poetic community, his theoretical location, the point from which his analysis of the ambiguous relationship between state and nation, civic and ethnic identity in Independent Ireland proceeds. For though the state's sovereignty depends on a uniform territorial coalition of places, its remit never extends unequivocally across Party territory. In one reading, the fog surrounding Party workers in *Without Power* suggests the state's persistent struggle to penetrate the physical and emotional source of the Party's 'blazing mystique', its 'slightly constitutional' communal origins. Defiance and dispossession galvanize Party workers in the novel, even as an instinctual attachment to their emotionally satisfying myths propels them towards the cliff's edge. The Party's capacity for extending its self-definition is endlessly inclusive and crassly reductive. Whatever it encounters becomes part of its all-embracing mythology as it ceases to differentiate between its own survival and the sovereignty of the state. Thus the O'Hara twins—the insane, under-age sons of a loyal Party supporter, plucked from the mountain fog to join the Party minibus, chanting their mantra 'uh Egg', or 'up Dev'—do not only exemplify de Valera's grip on the Irish psyche, the 'living room' of Irish lives.

The twins' irrational loyalty is also a form of participatory agency in the polity, a space supposedly organized on 'rational rules governing the behaviour between groups'.[40] Compare this to Bolger's use of incest with Sandra in *The Woman's Daughter*, a trope deployed against de Valera's rhetoric of the 'people united as a family—a nation of brothers'.[41] There, the identical likeness Sandra seeks through a sexual partner is a form of self-absorption, isolating her from any larger notion of community. The Party's expanded definition of the polity may include the O'Hara twins but it never individuates them. An effective, illegitimate form of political agency is offered to the O'Hara twins, a peculiarly difficult gift to unequivocally condemn. In one sense, of course, the twins are a lurid example of the exhaustion of the Party's Republican ideology, as political discourse is replaced by their reflexive chanting. They exemplify the instinctive but hardly inspiring bond that sustains the Party in crises, as the workers return home by deferring to the sheep. McCarthy's sympathetically critical representation allows, indeed enables, such negative readings; but these scenes do probe much more deeply into Fianna Fáil's fierce loyalties than Bolger's flatly oppositional stance.[42]

McCarthy's work in this way reveals his absolute, questioning loyalty to the Party, a position well described by the title of his second collection, *The Non-Aligned Storyteller*. 'For a writer', McCarthy claims, 'the beginning is always in the heart and its feeling rather than in the head and its techniques',[43] a priority that generates such characters as Eamon, a young, talented scientist whose rousing, calculated assessment of Fianna Fáil's *raison d'être* is unimaginable in Bolger's determined assault on the principle of tradition. Reading a British peer's comments on Ireland, Eamon concludes:

---

[40] Breuilly, *Nationalism and the State*, 355.

[41] Quoted in O'Carroll, 'Eamon de Valera: Charisma and Political Development', 208.

[42] See Thomas McCarthy, 'Golden Notebook of Dorgan's World', in *Gardens of Remembrance* (Dublin: New Island Books, 1998), 167–73, at 168: '[L]iterature fails the working class by its very nature. Literature communicates and makes connections like a borough politician. Being poor is not a social experience, it is private and unique to each family. It is something that each poor family has no wish to communicate, while retaining the right that their past struggles be honoured'.

[43] *Poetry Ireland Review* 42 (1994), 77.

The peer's words were a reminder of the political necessity of The Party, a reminder that The Party's chauvinism was a response to such blind racism. So long as there was political tension between England and Ireland the English would hate the Irish. When all the political tensions passed away the English would begin to love Ireland in the patronising perhaps doting way they loved other little countries like little Belgium. (*WP*, 257)

McCarthy's work similarly negotiates between impulses of the head and heart, rationality and feeling. For Eamon here propounds a series of beliefs which T. W. Moody, in a 1977 lecture, famously characterized as an opposition between science and myth. Historical revisionism has frequently turned to an opposition between 'scientific' and 'mythical' acounts of Irish history, elevating the former and deprecating the latter in hugely influential formulation.

> But nations derive their consciousness of their past not only—and not mainly from historians. They also derive it from popular traditions, transmitted orally, in writing, and through institutions. I am using the word myth to signify received views of this kind as contrasted with the knowledge that the historian seeks to extract by the application of scientific methods to his evidence.[44]

Avowedly rational, Moody's aspiration is to write 'value-free' history. Historical investigation, he claims, can be equated with the methods of empirical science, a philosophical movement known as historicism. Moody's concentration on social and economic themes has led to accusations of intellectual elitism; nowhere can such a methodology register the history of the dispossessed and the colonized, the history of those without power.[45] McCarthy repudiates a rationalism that marginalizes the O'Hara twins, even as he shuffles ever closer to it. Fianna Fáil's conservative, Catholic culture rarely elicits a sympathetic response from Irish novelists, as Bolger demonstrates. Aisling Foster's *Safe in the Kitchen*,[46] for example, has post-Independence Ireland represented by a joyless, hopelessly pious

---

[44] 'Irish History and Irish Mythology', reprod. in Ciarán Brady (ed.), *Interpreting Irish History: The Debate on Historical Revisionism* (Dublin: Four Courts Press, 1994), 71. See also Richard J. Evans, *In Defence of History* (London: Granta, 1997).
[45] Brendan Bradshaw, 'Nationalism and Historical Scholarship in Modern Ireland', reprod. in Brady (ed.), *Interpreting Irish History*, 191–216.
[46] (Harmondsworth: Penguin, 1993).

Fianna Fáil deputy incapable of adapting rural habits to urban life. McCarthy's affiliation and representation is more complex. The poetry must balance memory and aspiration, memorialize a nationalism within the boundaries of a state which the Party politically rejects.

To this end, McCarthy is preoccupied with moments that clarify the mutually dependent, shifting relationship between private and public. In *Without Power*, for example, the public status of the Chairman and Senator depends on their private virtues as citizens, so that the Party is never entirely externalized or construed exclusively as an ideological discourse, as a 'dialectical secateur'. Hence the appropriateness of the Glenville family as a setting for McCarthy's exploration of the rural power base of Fianna Fáil. Set in 1973, before an election to decide the Republic's attitude towards the North and the EEC, its indigenous history and international future (issues of the heart and head), the novel chronicles the emotional trauma which besets provincial Party workers contemplating the loss of power. A conflict between an irredentist nationalist caucus and those who accept the legitimacy of the state is reactivated. Control of the Party's historical memory is thus a key contemporary issue. It is why local party secretary Condolences Dineen prefaces each meeting with a list of local funerals, recalling 'the bond with the dead' that no dialectical secateurs can sever. The Party absorbs contingencies and confers meaning onto events through a 'blazing mystique' that is never challenged or changed by mere circumstance. It observes history as it passes by and notes each time how close it comes to its own position. The recent death of Elizabeth Bowen, for example, never impinges on the private universe of Party Chairman Ned. 'I wouldn't know anything about the family—they're not in our constituency. Farahy is in Cork, you see. Not our constituency at all' (*WP*, 7). In *Synge and Anglo-Irish Literature*, Daniel Corkery observed a hurling final in Thurles and famously asked 'Who will speak for these people?'[47] This kind of scene in *Without Power* announces McCarthy's determinedly provincial subject matter, his willingness to create, in the demise of Anglo-Irish culture, a literature

---

[47] (1931; Cork: Mercier Press, 1966), 15. McCarthy completed an MA thesis on Corkery at UCC. See McCarthy, 'Five Summer Afternoons', 16; see also Seán Dunne (ed.), *The Cork Anthology* (Cork: Cork University Press, 1993), 6.

that answers without condescension or illusion for Corkery's question.[48]

Ned never ascribes a universality to his values and beliefs; they never possess the self-evident certainty and security of the centre, the metropolis. The Party is secure when it is the sole possessor of a certain version of Irish history. But for all its unquestioned sense of belonging, it is threatened by the actual residents of the island. It is incapable of imagining anything beyond the exemplary instance of the individuals who are its officers. Benedict Anderson reminds us that 'members of even the smallest nation will never know most of their fellow-members, meet them, or even hear of them, yet in the minds of each lives the image of their communion'.[49] As de Valera once famously remarked, this 'image of their communion' (so apt a phrase for the Party) is acquired by looking into his own heart and what is not there cannot, by definition, belong. Reality must change, not the Party, hence the necessary deception of de Valera's signature to enter the Dáil. De Valera's Fianna Fáil offered an unchanging image of Ireland's present and future condition. For Ned, the contemporary is a tiresome and temporary distraction that never undermines his tenacious adherence to the Party's self-image.[50] Ned's innocent remark—'No interest in books, I'm afraid. Driving buses and politics, they're the things I'm interested in' (*WP*, 7)—reveals the Party's grasp of the continuities underlying its own continued existence. Books utilize the past to interpret the present; buses repeat previous routes, becoming useful to the extent that they do not deviate from this prescribed path.

This emphasis on repetition as a structural principle of historical understanding relies on the existence of a self-evident

[48] 'One is enobled, ultimately, by the things one chooses to record . . . Recently I myself have been subjected to criticisms of my poetry that are entirely political. It amazes me that there are still people around who would censor poets for their choice of subject-matter. There is no such thing as "correct" subject-matter. No poet can choose his parents or the social milieu out of which he wrote' ('Documents of Exclusion', *The Irish Review*, no. 4 (Winter 1987), 141–2).

[49] *Imagined Communities: Reflections on the Origins and Spread of Nationalism* (London: Verso, 1983), 13.

[50] 'An Irish person . . . is continually and sometimes uncomfortably reminded of how local, idiosyncratic and perhaps philosophically questionable are his particular sets of inherited political assumptions' (Tom Garvin, 'The Politics of Denial and of Cultural Defence: The Referenda of 1983 and 1986 in Context', *Irish Review*, 3 (1988), 1).

pattern of meaning in which the loyal components of a national culture are unquestionably accepted. The pragmatic extension of daily routine into politics, however, is ruptured by economic modernization and the Northern Troubles, for both ensure that history and memory are no longer sealed from public view.[51] Inherited political assumptions are now philosophically questionable, porous, and contested; history is bypassing the routes the Party prescribed, a fact Condolences acknowledges when he laments the public's response to the Party's removal of the special position of the Catholic Church.

Sometimes, Mick, sometimes I worry about people. They have no memory, their minds are destroyed with television. People don't realise what The Party went through in the nineteenth Dáil. We lost three great ministers, justice, finance, agriculture all because of that misfortunate fuckin' country, the north (*WP*, 17).[52]

The Party's protocols and mythology exist to police this public memory, to record an inalienable order rather than inaugurate the kind of novel patterns we find in Bolger. In Moody's terms, the accepted narrative of Irish history corresponds to the Party's concept of itself, rendering it structurally incapable of inaugurating a narrative which might cope with the sectarianism of 'that misfortunate fuckin' country' (or, indeed, its own). But the need for a rhetoric that aspires to a vision of unity and wholeness, a totality, is something McCarthy implicitly tolerates, even accepts. The Party's real material relationship to the local political class structure is presented with poignancy, with the private impact of public events quietly emphasized: ' "A hobby," Condolences said. "With them people it's a kind of hobby. They don't need politics like we do. If you're a dentist you don't need protection, you can be sure of that . . . *we can't change the way we are*" ' (*WP*, 18; emphasis added).

The emotional impetus behind Fianna Fáil's self-presentation is a theme in McCarthy's collection *The Lost Province*. His poem 'Picnic' digs beneath the Party's studied provincialism:

[51] For a useful summary of the basis of the Fianna Fáil party structure, see Tom Gallagher, 'The Dimensions of Fianna Fáil Rule in Ireland', *West European Politics*, 4 (1980), 54–68.

[52] A remark that echoes the reputed comments of Reginald Maudling, newly appointed Tory British home secretary, after his first visit to Northern Ireland: 'What a bloody awful country'.

How easily we discard
the personal life of a whole generation.
This was the essential home of a big family
a priest in Martinique, and, at Cappoquin station
an uncle bound for the fire-service in LA.

Saver of money, cashier of Atlantic passages.
It is not myth, but sociology!
The poor here suffered an awful tetanu.
Today you offer me profiteroles and salmon paté.

(TLP, 14)

McCarthy's suspicion of an ironic cast of mind, which draws attention only to its own linguistic procedures, is housed in the pleasing double-edgedness of 'profit-e-roles'. Even as the Party is 'setting lines and snares' that impede the circulation of meaning, the cosmopolitan nature of language, its capacity for universalizing an 'essential home', is registered. Also registered is an implicit sense of guilt at the benefits brought by a poetry that incorporates this deprivation, the profitable role of documenting the poor. To adapt Walter Benjamin's perhaps over-quoted maxim, every aspect of the Republic's contemporary prosperity conceals a history of suffering.[53] The 'salmon paté' brings into coalition a trope of homecoming that for impoverished emigrants is a reality (the salmon always returns to its breeding ground to die), and the phonetic and social affectation of the word 'paté'. McCarthy's work continually tries to incorporate and balance such pairings as memory and aspiration, myth and sociology.

The O'Hara twins in *Without Power*, for instance, exemplify the indiscriminate absorption of Party lore: their mother 'had talked her memory into their memories until the Party became a magic healing influence' (*WP*, 109). The Party mobilizes these memories for its own ends, ends which it assumes to be indistinguishable from those of the twins. Like the skeletons beneath the modern, sterile apartment in Bolger's *Emily's Shoes*, the twins reflect the competition between two apparently contradictory value systems for primacy in public space: a model of state

---

[53] 'Theses on the Philosophy of History', in *Illuminations*, ed. Hannah Arendt (1968; London: Fontana, 1992), 248: 'There is no document of civilization which is not at the same time a document of barbarism . . . barbarism taints also the manner in which it was transmitted from one owner to another.'

development drawn from the Enlightenment, in which historical memory is transmitted through institutions, and a populist memory nourished on oral history, of the kind Moody deprecated. This attachment to an emotionally satisfying myth produces a crassly reductive politics through its very inclusiveness: the loyalty which makes the twins practical members of the polity debases the very idea of a polity. Inarticulate, under age, and indistinguishable as individuals, they are Party voters, a powerful indication of the truncated, compromised, and contradictory forms of agency and destiny the soldiers of Fianna Fáil offer.

Many of McCarthy's personal poems offer faintly audible reflections on the tensions contained in this complicated contract between the poet and his subject matter. Dawe describes McCarthy's poetry as 'the search for authority, a position that enables the poet to measure and judge', but it is exactly this kind of position that the Party abrogates to itself and denies to the individual.[54] In 'Combing your hair', the self-absorption of a woman before a mirror gradually recedes as her husband participates in the ritual; but it is the permanent distance between them—'the straight and perfect partings'—that is finally recognized, not any greater unity or harmony:

> At first you combed your hair by the mirror
> With your back to me, the sunlight
> Catching the henna where it strayed.
> It was a private meeting you were having there.
>
> Then I cut my hair to your liking. We talked.
> About my hair for instance, the way
> It's always weak and very thin
> Like tea-bag tea too early in the morning.
>
> Now you comb your hair while I look,
> While I direct your combing here and there.
> Toward the straight and perfect partings
> Where henna waits in ambush for us both.
>
> (*TNAS*, 45)

The progression from a 'private meeting' (a political and personal term), to compromise, to dialogue, and finally to imperfect

---

[54] 'Suburban Night', 191.

resolution ironically combines an intimately personal touch (the 'henna') with dramatic language ('ambush') drawn from the public world of events and history. For a poet of McCarthy's preoccupations, the process is self-consciously analogous to an admittedly perfected world of parliamentary politics. Applying henna dye masks greying hair, surely; but it also highlights the one thing all individuals share, approaching death. Hence no one memory speaks for each or both protagonists; the validity of each separate experience is acknowledged, even as that recognition is marked by melancholy. In the most blissful of human relationships, there is no individual wholeness that completely precedes or escapes division and strife. Again, in a poem entitled 'Honeymoon Portrait', the end note is one of wary irresolution, without guarantee that a more permanent, stronger wholeness will emerge from the union of man and wife, from the necessary concessions such bonding entails: 'She caught the look of a honeymoon in you: | how no intelligent woman could subdue | the loss of territory that a marriage means.' (*TLP*, 19)

This kind of recognition is beyond the Party, which remains committed to the concept of individual and territorial wholeness, resisting any attempt by the state to demystify this fundamental ideal.[55] It tries to provide a metaphor for every psychological and social state by reducing characters to abstractions (Chairman, Senator, Condolences) even as they attempt to remain individuals (Ned, Gerald, and, of course, Condolences, a man permanently locked into his Party function). As Ned's comments on Elizabeth Bowen demonstrate, the Party retains an ambiguous attitude towards equality, a principle that requires it to transcend its own intensely familial loyalties and tribal structure. It promotes not liberation or change but consolidation, even if this perpetuates the injustices that spawned the Party. The Party's instinctive response is defiance, its natural reaction cautionary, its long-term goal continuity, however narrowly conceived, as it ironically relies on residual forms of patronage and inequality for its self-identity.

Condolences's redundancy is distressing, for example, because it signals the gradual encroachment of an autonomous state into

---

[55] David Lloyd and Paul Thomas, *Culture and the State* (London: Routledge, 1998), 12: 'The concept [of wholeness] is prepolitical precisely insofar as the political stands for a division of the human into partialities'.

the Party's traditional territorial heartland. When Condolences's wife travels to a redundancy office in a neighbouring village, the scornful response of a young graduate, a Labour Party supporter, offers cruel confirmation of the importance of the Party's communalism. It is a constructive and regressive strategy, for as the Party Chairman organizes work for Condolences as a gardener to the Winslows, the contemporary equivalent of Big House residents, Condolences and his wife remain estranged from the state which the Party helped found, instinctually locked into a territorially defined caste system and a woefully inadequate conception of emancipation. The process of change is the process of self-erasure; all that guarantees the Party's continued existence is the status quo it was established to erase. Fianna Fáil's populism is fundamentally ironic, in that its promise of 'social ascent as a universal possibility' automatically excludes any individual example of that progress from the Party's self-image.[56] As Condolences watches the Senator and Julie mix socially with his employers, enjoying a social mobility the Party promised all its members, this treasonous participation in the Party's own version of social ascent elicits a bitter judgement: 'The Senator is really a big shot now, he thought, hobnobbing with rich people. He doesn't need The Party. It was as if he had been deliberately put there, in Mr Winslow's garden in order that his loss of faith in the Senator should be complete' (*WP*, 217). The Party defines class as caste, thereby answering psychological as well as social needs; but its emotional base constantly contracts as a result, eliminating even erstwhile supporters from its self-image. Ned's cancer, for example (a metaphor for the demise of a certain brand of parish politics), is immediately recognized as another bond with the dead for the Senator to deploy: 'The Party's instinct for nostalgia was all-powerful. The faithful would come just to meet Ned, to shake his dying hand: to save that handshake for future reference like spare coins. Ned dying was a powerful asset' (*WP*, 201). The Party remembers the need to cannibalize its own memories, to continually deflect the contemporary in order to refurbish the past.

The great strength and weakness of the Party is that, like Ned's

---

[56] Allen, *Fianna Fáil and Irish Labour*, 2.

bus routes, its responses are ordered, constant, and fixed in advance through their loyal attachment to the tyranny of precedent. The jealously guarded filial link with 1916, for example, contains the nationalist energy through which the Party continually renews itself. But this cannot conceal the contradictory attitudes towards the North or account for the sectarianism of Northern refugee children, the legacy of the history it would rather not face. McCarthy posits an irreconcilable distance between the historical memory of the Republic and the violent eruption of that history in the North. To apply Edna Longley's terms, there is no 'premature homogenisation' of South and North, no cognitive map that would embrace both polities as a totality.[57] Represented as, respectively, adult and child, both communities are without a language which can describe the experience of division rather than unity: 'Ulster was far away. It had become an abstraction, like God. No southern ear wanted to suffer that embarrassment. Like a child trying to tell someone about an incestuous rape, the Ulster child offered its experience to uninterested adult ears' (*WP*, 154).

Seamus Heaney's poem 'Act of Union' imagined the coupling of Ireland and England producing 'an obstinate fifth column', the 'heaving province' of Ulster that clings to the mother, Ireland, from which it cannot be geographically separated. For Elizabeth Cullingford, Heaney's lyric allegorically presented 'England as the "imperially male" seducer, Éire as the ruined maid, pregnant with disaster, and Northern Ireland as the bastard child conceived of the rape'.[58] Though the angry sibling Ulster punishes its mother from within and its father across the water, Cullingford criticized Heaney for being 'possessed by . . . the atavistic myth he deplores'. McCarthy adapts the same metaphor of rape to present a generational and ontological gap between the nationalist communities of North and South. This conflict lies not just in another domain. If Heaney's colonial relationship is part of a fundamentally different historical language and experience, for McCarthy, conflict is generated from within, the familiar is itself alien.[59] His work does not gesture towards a reconciliation of

[57] 'Poetic Forms and Social Malformations', in *Living Stream*, 200.
[58] 'Thinking of Her . . . as Ireland', *Textual Practice*, 4/1 (1990), 1–21.
[59] Eileán Ní Chuilleanáin, 'Borderlands of Irish Poetry', in Elmer Andrews (ed.), *Contemporary Irish Poetry: A Collection of Critical Essays* (Basingstoke: Macmillan,

differences or towards the attainment of a workable 'hybrid' culture. Rather, it looks to the difficulty of maintaining a political identity founded on division through participation in a community for whom the values of wholeness and unity retain an almost hypnotic aura. McCarthy shows the idea of a national culture embracing both North and South as actually impossible for the Party's provincial, centrifugal structure to imagine, despite its rhetorical commitment to unity. To adapt Bolger's term, the Party continually refines the scope of its private political universe in order to guarantee the essentially unchanging substance of memories it can cannibalize but never refurbish or reinvent. Beyond its own local political constituency, beyond the state it is forced to inhabit and administer, everything is contingent, questionable, so that the correlation between geography and history in McCarthy is never the island nation which Fianna Fáil, the Republican Party, aspired to govern. As Tom Garvin puts it, 'Fianna Fáil, the Soldiers of Destiny, came to preside over the making of an Ireland which had an enormous east coast—and no north east corner'.[60] Reviewing *The Lost Province*, Bernard O'Donoghue remarks: 'Rarely has Kavanagh's doctrine of the primacy of the parish been put so unapologetically to the test'.[61] McCarthy's subject matter, in other words, reflects the Party's instinctive suspicion of meaning produced outside the geographical, linguistic, and political boundaries it patrols.[62] The Party's candidate for the presidency, for example, brings the full range of the capital's media to the region: 'It was thought that they would be foreigners or Dubliners, people whose political outlook couldn't be clearly identified' (*WP*, 93). The relevant differences are no longer the imperial faultlines in Heaney's representation but the internal ones between the Irish themselves.[63]

1992), 34: 'Heaney's poems of prehistoric ritual killings—such as his "Act of Union", where Ireland is raped by England—may be seen as strategies to avoid the asking of certain harsh questions close to home, the ascription of particular blame, in a way which seems more possible in the North than in the Republic.' Of course, the contemporary realities of Ireland's colonial past may still actually be 'harsh questions close to home' in Heaney's Derry.

[60] 'Destiny of the Soldiers', 347.
[61] 'Who Speaks for These?', *The Times Literary Supplement* (7 Mar. 1997), 24.
[62] 'Fianna Fáil's central motor is its network of localist connections' (Tom Garvin, 'The Growth of Faction in the Fianna Fáil Party, 1966–1980', *Parliamentary Affairs*, 34 (1981), 110–11).
[63] 'We live in an interdependent Ireland. Unionists, who live in mortal fear of our

What the Party finally lacks, consequently, is the power to conceive of itself as an agent of change. Eamon is, potentially, the Party's future. Young, articulate, a scientist who understands the Party's transmission of the past through what Moody called 'popular traditions', he shines at the Fianna Fáil Ard Fheis. It is he who symbolically fetches Ned's heirloom, a picture of de Valera, from the graveyard to the Glenville home. He seems destined to lead. Julie, Condolences's daughter, is ambitious, multilingual and oriented towards Europe. Yet she decides not to marry the Senator, a man emotionally crippled by the need to secure the Party a Dáil seat. The Party's refusal or inability to acknowledge the integrity of the present, to recognize history as a process, ensures that characters like Julie and Eamon define Ireland as a place where change cannot occur. *Without Power* ends with Eamon driving from Ned's funeral flanked by a patronizing Canon and an apolitical father, devoid of any means of affiliating with the Party's original ideals. It is not simply that the Party is a conservative organization—adhering to what is known can, in a certain context, be a truly radical policy—rather, it is the Party's instinctive identification of change as something that is automatically alien and hostile, an intrusion from beyond the boundaries it patrols. It is, finally, much more comfortable with the language of the O'Hara twins than Eamon's mixture of rhetoric and rationality. In McCarthy's highly stylized ending, Ned's body is symbolically appropriated by the Party's irrendentist flank because of the accidental intervention of the Church. Eamon, born into the Fianna Fáil family, thus retreats into a personal space in which the Party can never again intervene as a carrier of meaning.[64]

Yet any act of affiliation involves an ambivalence and self-questioning which makes McCarthy understand, and at one level desire, this kind of retreat. This is why he can never be labelled a straightforwardly social or civic poet. The miscellaneous bits and pieces of the everyday possess a mystical or spiritual quality

dreams, really do exist and really do object strongly. Not to know this is to be perpetually without power in the real sense' (McCarthy, 'Celtic Tigers, Mad Cows and Exiles', in *Gardens of Remembrance* (Dublin: New Island Books, 1998), 58–71, at 64).

[64] Fintan O'Toole comments on this general retraction in Irish public life in *The Ex-Isle of Erin: Images of a Global Ireland* (Dublin: New Island Books, 1996), 178.

in his work normally reserved for the transcendental. But the practice of governing, as the most systematic response to the everyday, attracts a particularly intense allegiance. A sacred air surrounds secular public figures, as in 'The Health Minister', where 'Ministries' has a vocational and professional edge that recalls Edna Longley's description of de Valera's fusion of 'the aura of father as paterfamilias and father as priest'. But where Longley says that poetry and politics, like church and state, should separate, the combination for McCarthy is never necessarily debilitating. The Minister's public engagement with the people can also be an intimate and private one, so that politics becomes 'the balsam of care'. McCarthy constantly juggles with this idea of the imagination having moral priority over the needs of the community:

> Some who held Ministries were honest, even holy.
> The Health Minister, for instance, with his minuscule voice;
> as if poverty had taken his breath away.
> His hands stretched over the tenements of the ugly,
> the poor and tubercular.
> His plans tore through the landscape of suffering
> to deposit clinics, hospitals; the balsam of care.
>
> (*TNAS*, 19)

Where Longley's vivid aphorism suggests that freedom from politics is the poet's pre-eminent achievement, this poem achieves a form of freedom through politics; for the fundamental concept animating it is not liberty but justice. In fact, liberty, freedom of expression, is possible only through the necessary intervention of the state. The Minister, who represents his constituency, has a 'minuscule voice', has 'his breath taken away' by deprivation. The Minister's own agency, his individuating voice (crucial, of course, to the poet), is made possible by a politics founded, in the first instance, on the pursuit of the common good, not liberty. The apparent paradox the poem insists on is actually a fundamental tenet of civic republicanism. As Quentin Skinner explains this tenet, 'we can only hope to enjoy a maximum of our own individual liberty if we do not place that value above the pursuit of the common good'.[65] The sole route to

---

[65] 'On Justice, the Common Good, and Liberty', in Chantal Mouffe (ed.), *Dimensions of Radical Democracy: Pluralism, Citizenship, Community* (London: Verso, 1992), 221.

individual liberty and freedom of expression is through public service, and so the poem becomes a public participation in the representation of his community, a form of civic republicanism that does not see the intersection between poetry and politics as simply interference in the realm of the imagination. Where Heaney grounds his locale in language, in the place names that function as poem titles and thus distil elements of the *genius loci* into the poem, these civic republican principles animate both McCarthy's communalism and a poetry that records the gradual eclipse of these principles within the Party.

The title poem of *The First Convention,* for example, is a public elegy for this fading idealism. A young boy's initial exposure to the Party's protocols is part of a dawning awareness of his own political agency, an agency the Party will habitually try to control. The Party promises to enable the emergence of the boy's self, to blaze a path through the fog: 'I wanted to be up front where I could | see the headlights piercing the darkness, | where I could follow the curving line | of the road whitening before the lights; | where I could see the phantom patches | of fog, opening and rising upward' (*TFC*, 12). Hence the aspirational verbs—'I wanted', 'I could'—(repeated three times), and the emphasis on a clarity of vision ('I could see') that looks beyond the expediency and concessions of local politics—these are part of an idealism the second section deflates, where the 'I' disappears and a recidivist darkness re-envelops the mature man to disfigure the language available to politics and poetry:

> That scene returns in dream: rough-coated men
> waving white polling cards, shouting 'Yes' or
> 'No' as the questions ooze from the speakers;
> and the huge brown buttons on their over-
> coats scratching my face, closing me in: the
> thick smell of beer and sweat nauseating.
>
> Always I force an opening to the doorways,
> through the excited mass of polling cards.
> In my dream-garden I can hear their faded
> oratory, the dying crackle of applause;
> the force of national politics soft-
> ening in the huge quietness of the dark.

The interpretation available for any given event is curtailed by the Party, as experience is absorbed and defined within uniformly determined limits, and the language available for public discourse coarsens into 'a faded oratory'. McCarthy forces an 'opening to the doorway' in order to withdraw into the imagination and escape the suffocating smells and sweat of a politics denuded of idealism, where ritualistic shouts of Yes or No replace debate. Yet the scene is indelibly lodged in his subconscious, in his dreams, and so the poem remains rooted in the mythology it confronts, a testimony to the enduring impact of the Party on his poetry and the constant vigilance required to distinguish between the two.

In 'Daedalus, the Maker', McCarthy makes a similar point. Dactylos, inventor of a means of communicating in which the fingers are used to sign the different letters of the alphabet, is praised for creating a language without public posture or rhetoric, with the capacity to spiral into new, unannounced patterns, the very quality that makes impossible the sequential ordering of political discourse. In this poem about the production of art, language already contains 'circular passages and minotaurs | lurking in the most innocent lines'. The 'I' appears in the last two verses because the poet is ironically most secure when conscious of his poetic self rather than any inherited Party identity, when he has determined 'To place art *anonymously* at the earth's altar' (emphasis added). Language circulates as a volatile, productive cocktail and so meaning can never be limited to one source or place, a quality that makes poetry anti-mimetic, never content to simply reflect an external reality:

> Often I have abandoned an emerging form
> to argue with priests and poets—
> only to learn the wisdom of Dactylos:
> that words make the strongest labyrinth,
> with circular passages and minotaurs
> lurking in the most innocent lines.
>
> I will banish argument to work again
> with bronze. Words, I have found, are
> captured, not made: opinion alone is
> a kind of retreat. I shall become like
> Dactylos, a quiet maker; moving between
> poet and priest, keeping my pride secret.
>
> (*TFC*, 20)

This space 'between poet and priest' is, perhaps, where such figures as the Health Minister are to be found, those who hold ministries while representing their communities. Yet though 'capturing' words suggests an organic aesthetic that repudiates politics, the realm where words are 'made' into rhetoric, McCarthy cannot escape 'opinions', so he is content to be 'a quiet maker' who rejects the arguments of politicians while accepting the need to participate in the public sphere they inhabit. Whereas politics is directed towards a *telos* that is external and future-oriented, the freedom poetry makes possible occurs within an already observable self. A poetry based on a party politics, in which so much personal investment is made, is thus riven by a tension McCarthy claims is responsible for a basic fault in his first two collections: the use of an 'uncritical memory'.[66]

'Returning to De Valera's Cottage' exemplifies this point. 'Return' denotes a cognitive space already mapped within the poet's memory; a location where de Valera is an extension of a corporate Irish personality. Full of sorrow and frustration, de Valera's peasant, rural arcadia coincides with something lodged in the Irish psyche, instead of being seen for the romantic and improbable construct it was:

> In finding his cottage we found a life that was
> inside ourselves. A small
> moment of sorrow. A tear
> riding down the glass of
> our eyes like blood fall-
> ing from a bullet wound.
> We kicked the heap of weeds
> with our heels and cursed the narrowness of the path.

The path is narrow not misdirected, while the tear riding down the glass is an evocative justification of the pastoral paradigm through Christian, perhaps specifically Catholic, imagery. McCarthy's ambivalent and persistent negotiation of the demands of a rational, secular politics, and the instinctive loyalty de Valera's's nationalism provokes, orbits round a series of oppositions—global or local? neutral or engaged? affiliated or

---

[66] A remark by McCarthy in conversation with the late Seán Dunne. Quoted in James Naiden, ' "Orphaned Like Us": Memory in the Poetry of Thomas McCarthy', *Eire-Ireland*, 28/1 (Spring 1993), 113.

dominated?—that are best understood through his second novel, *Asya and Christine*.

IV A NEUTRAL STATE?

Beckett's return to France at the outbreak of World War II is usually seen as an instance of his alienation from the Catholic nationalist insularity of the Free State. Preferring France at war to Ireland at peace, as he later put it,[67] when subsequently asked if he was English Beckett famously replied 'Au contraire'. Beckett still defined his own identity in opposition to Englishness, even as a universal political commitment overrode any affiliations to family and home. Beckett, in other words, created his own political and cultural context, one where the commitment to a politics unfolding at a universal level did not completely neutralize the emotive effect of traditional demarcations. Irishness was still a difference that made a difference.

For similar reasons, de Valera's policy of neutrality during World War II marks a key moment in Independent Ireland. Through it de Valera asserted Irish sovereignty and independence, answering the psychological needs of recent Irish history by accommodating Ireland's aspirations to its own unique mode of existence. As Roy Foster puts it, 'the principle of neutrality was too closely bound up with Irish identity and Irish sovereignty to be easily relaxed'.[68] And, of course, de Valera's regularly quoted St Patrick's Day broadcast of 1943 famously offered an idyllic alternative to the 'imperial venture' of war. Neutrality ensured stability, cohesion, and security while assuaging the Anglophobic instincts of Fianna Fáil's Republican flank. Perhaps most importantly, it symbolically registered Ireland's right to determine its own future. As one civil servant bluntly (some might say

---

[67] Anthony Cronin, *Samuel Beckett: The Last Modernist* (London: Harper Collins, 1996), 310.

[68] *Modern Ireland: 1600–1972* (London: Allen Lane, 1989), 561. See also Declan Kiberd's somewhat defensive comments, which seem to credit de Valera with postwar, geopolitical foresight, in 'Eamon de Valera: The Image and Achievement', in Philip Hannon and Jackie Gallagher (eds.), *Taking the Long View: 70 Years of Fianna Fáil* (Belfast: Blackwater Press, 1996), 27: 'The maintenance of neutrality protected most of Ireland from terrible bombing in the Second World War and, subsequently, made the Irish acceptable as successful UN peace-keepers.'

obtusely) put it, 'Small nations like Ireland do not and cannot assume the role of defenders of just causes except their own.'[69] The chosen future seemed, unlike Beckett's, absolutely different from that of its neighbours. Ireland was not just independent, it was different, not just separate, but isolated, a policy that provoked F. S. L. Lyons's elegant scorn, which echoed Moody's distinction between myth and reason:

The tensions—and the liberations—of war, the shared experience, the comradeship in suffering, the new thinking about the future, all these things had passed her by. It was as if an entire people had been condemned to live in Plato's cave, backs to the fire of life and deriving their only knowledge of what went on outside from the flickering shadows thrown on the wall before the eyes by the men and women who passed to and fro behind them. When after six years they emerged from the cave into the light of day, it was to a new and vastly different world.[70]

McCarthy's second novel, *Asya and Christine* (1994), brings into coalition the global and the local by, in Lyons's terms, entering the cave of wartime Ireland. Set in 1943 in Cappoquin, County Waterford, political constituency of Deputy Glenville, scion of the family political dynasty which continues till 1972 and *Without Power,* it explores the space between Lyons's universal perspective and Beckett's flat assertion of difference. For what Lyons's rhetoric really asks is whether a categorical sense of difference makes 'Irishness' an honorific condition or one of philosophical and moral deficiency; whether Irish history must be continually obsessed with its antagonistic relationship to England, or must it at some point form part of a global history. As Robert Fisk wrote of neutrality, 'symbolically, it could not be misunderstood: Éire had not accepted the values of the warring nations and did not intend to do so in the future'.[71]

The prologue commences in 1924 and charts Fianna Fáil's slow acceptance of the Free State. Glenville, a man without any

---

[69] See the ch. 'In Time of War: Neutral Ireland, 1939–1945', in Dermot Keogh, *Twentieth-Century Ireland: Nation and State* (Dublin: Gill and Macmillan, 1994), 108; more generally, see 108–56. See also M. A. G. Ó Tuathaigh, 'De Valera and Sovereignty: A Note on the Development of a Political Idea', in J. P. O'Carroll and J. A. Murphy (eds.), *De Valera and His Times* (Cork: Cork University Press, 1983), 62–73.

[70] *Ireland since the Famine* (London: Fontana, 1985), 551.

[71] *In Time of War: Ireland, Ulster and the Price of Neutrality, 1939–1945* (London: Paladin, 1987), 209.

traceable past, seeks to suppress memories of the civil war by
embracing the Party, the new state, and capital; and principally,
through an unswerving commitment to de Valera: 'He spoke
about events he had witnessed, terrible things, but he spoke
about them as if they belonged to the distant past. The past had
been put aside. Apart from his abiding love for Dev, everything
else had been superseded' (*A&C*, 15). What Joe Lee describes as
the 'emotional resentment of the excluded underdog'[72] ties
Glenville to Fianna Fáil. An urgent need to invent a personal
history not only accelerates his acceptance of the state; it also
requires the state to be a reflection of his own self-image. The
Free State offers thrilling possibilities as well as a profound cultural dilemma. It provides political autonomy and individual
agency; but it also substitutes for a history too painful for
Glenville to directly confront, an act of substitution that ultimately proves more disabling than liberating. Throughout the
novel, Glenville continually faces his political and administrative
impotence as the state, by asking him to prosecute Republicans,
demands he help abolish the history that produced him, even as
Republicans continually remind him of his own nationalist past.
Emotionally and financially, the Republican past he must disavow is the guarantor of his present status. The capital underpinning his business belongs to the anti-treaty IRA—those who
would destroy the state that supports his family, his business, his
reinvented self.

What Glenville seeks is an unattainable, private neutral zone
in a war between past and future, maintaining his identity
only through the insertion of a distance between himself and a
broader history that continually intrudes upon this secret self, a
position perhaps analogous to the Free State in 1943 as it tried to
avoid the ravages of war. Hence rationing, the regulated alloca-
tion of available indigenous and imported resources, is the
novel's governing trope. The state cannot allow individuals free
choice; appetites and aspirations must remain secondary to what
Robert Fisk described as 'the rejection of the values of the
warring nations', both in wartime and in future. Glenville's strict
demarcation between private possessions and the public realm—
'what had once belonged to the State still belonged to the State'

---

[72] *Ireland: 1912–1985*, 183.

(*A&C*, 58)—is not simply a political creed. The most profound privation his family suffer is the portion of his self he withholds for the state.

This internal struggle is registered in private details which, when exposed to the public sphere, become alive with an immanent, politically charged meaning. Sitting in his living room (a space also utilized earlier in 'State Funeral'), Glenville recalls receiving a Republican ballad written in blood. His present-centred domestic zone, a space the state facilitates and guards, here encounters a subterranean yet still public past that his personal life continually attempts to deflect: 'The Deputy could only recall one stanza. He placed the unread novel on the table. A glass of water was disturbed on its small blue Wedgwood saucer. Drops of liquid fell on to the face of his second-best watch' (*A&C*, 65). Just as the orality displaces literacy, there is an intrusive, unruly public realm that violates the privacy of a sanitized literary culture, and, in a nicely timed touch, ensures that temporality is somehow second hand, 'second-best'. 'Disturbed' here perhaps suggests the way politics is never fully externalized—a civic present is haunted by the tremors of an ethnic past. The drops of liquid distorting time recall 'the tear riding down the glass of our eyes like bloodfall— | from a bullet wound' in 'Returning to De Valera's Cottage'. The conflict between orality and literacy occurs simultaneously within Glenville because the Party seeks a rapprochement between two opposing traditions each of which contains the other. Fianna Fáil was initially organized largely on the basis of local IRA commanders, and this inheritance of IRA power structures generated its legendary party discipline.[73] In the novel, one of Deputy Glenville's constituents, a close neighbour, is a young IRA member sentenced to be hanged for murdering a member of the Free State police force. This physical proximity, alongside impassioned arguments with his wife Adele within the home, shows how geographically and psychologically, morally as well as politically, the state and its enemies overlap and intersect. Political differences thus utilize a language that is, in the first instance, exclusively personal. It is not just that politics affects

---

[73] Richard Dunphy, 'The Soldiers Set Out: Reflections on The Formation of Fianna Fáil', in Philip Hannon and Jackie Gallagher (eds.), *Taking the Long View: 70 Years of Fianna Fáil*, 9.

the family; the family actually supplies the rhetoric and organizational forms that politics utilize. Ostensibly personal poems, in other words, contain the language and qualities required for the political realm. Or as McCarthy puts it in an essay entitled 'Memory, Childhood and the Party': 'It was through my grandmother that I learned the astonishing breadth of kinship and interdependence of country people . . . the politics of families fascinate me. It is the first politics we learn to abide by and survive.'[74]

And just as the political stands for the division of the human into partialities,[75] fissures within politics can rip individuals apart, as the highly symbolic death of Bobby, the Deputy's son, demonstrates. Bobby leaves the family home after a vicious row with his mother over her neighbourly sympathy for the condemned man's Republican family. Killed while riding a motorcycle too quickly along a narrow path, his decapitation, the symbolic and literal separation of head and heart, shows the consequences if one is always at war with one's self, and that some other context for political discourse besides the family has to be discovered. Bobby is killed on a path that is literally too narrow, but this also recalls the line in 'Return to De Valera's Cottage': 'We . . . cursed the narrowness of the path'. His exuberant individualism bridles under the constraints of the collective; disregarding the speed limit, rationing of petrol, and his father's public status, he reacts against a *polis* in which everything, especially his own sense of political agency, is rationed, constrained. Though Bobby is acutely interested in the war, he launches a fumbled attack on Asya, the young Jewish woman who is his only connection with a politics that is something more than rhetorical and symbolic. Singing at his father's political rally, Bobby celebrates the exclusion of any version of history that situates the region in a context other than its own, one where 'History' is comprehended as an innocent and fleeting passage of loosely connected moments.

Bobby cleared his throat and found his key. He sang 'In happy moments Day by Day' with terrific grace and sweetness. The little bell of the Protestant church . . . lent a dreamlike atmosphere to the passing

---

[74] In *Gardens of Remembrance*, 13–29, at 15.
[75] Lloyd and Thomas, *Culture and the State*, 12.

minutes. In the June afternoon, with the rest of the world at war, all were happy to be part of the song. A young man singing at the height of his power on a fair day reminded the audience that their own children didn't have to go to war. This was the happy moment that The Party promised. (*A&C*, 118)

The use of rationing as a trope in the novel conveys its actual use by the Party to limit knowledge of the external, and one consequence of this strategy is Bobby's limited understanding of Asya's plight as a Jew. Each character in the novel is acutely conscious of the divisions between Cork and Waterford, Cappoquin and its neighbouring towns, but this consciousness never generates additional moral knowledge. Asya's growing sense of her own Jewishness, by contrast, is grounded in the principles of difference, sovereignty and independence, the same principles underlying de Valera's policy of neutrality. Her self-identity is asserted by shedding her Irish name, facing towards Europe, and engaging with the war, an approach the narrative explicitly endorses:

The accounts that her father wrote stiffened her resolve. She was determined to get out of Ireland. Living in a neutral country tended to make citizens blasé about evil . . . Alice felt wasted in a small town . . . even her real name was still kept hidden from almost everyone . . . If she stayed put she would never become herself. (*A&C*, 127)

This kind of statement—'Living in a neutral country tended to make citizens blasé about evil'—recalls Lyons's criticism of de Valera's neutrality policy. Asya sheds her adopted Irish name in order to interact with a global context beyond Ireland. The Party sheds its original name, Sinn Féin, traditionally and inaccurately translated as 'ourselves alone' ('Ourselves' is more accurate), to become Fianna Fáil, the Soldiers of Destiny who now patrol the boundaries of the state it once rejected, who, in effect, seal the borders of a state whose existence guarantees that its original destiny remains unachieved. What Seamus Deane asked of Brian Friel's *Translations* (first posed in relation to Bolger's *The Journey Home*) is still apposite: if a place, Party, or person is renamed and relocated, is it in some sense the same place, Party, or person as it had been, or is it entirely, essentially, different?[76]

[76] Deane, 'Brian Friel: The Name of the Game', in Alan Peacock (ed.), *The Achievement of Brian Friel* (Gerrards Cross: Colin Smythe, 1993), 107.

By separating the Irish experience from any context other than
its own, neutrality inscribed partition as a psychological principle as well as a political fact: it made the cognitive map of the
Irish experience correspond directly with the state's borders.
Any abstract category that exceeds this—Europe, justice, geography—remains secondary to the project of state building, a
project which ensures that the only majority that matters is an
Irish one. Or as de Valera puts it in the novel:

The State is the descendant of Sinn Féin. This State and its sovereign
government elected by the majority of the Irish people are the legitimate
descendants of Sinn Féin. Anyone who attacks this State or its servants
is an enemy of the Irish majority, the historical majority that's been
there since the time of O'Connell. (*A&C*, 140)

This definition of the historical majority suggests why McCarthy
'cursed the narrowness of the path' in 'Return to De Valera's
Cottage'. The Jews, unionists, Republicans, and dissenters within the region must conform to O'Connell's legacy as defined by
de Valera. *Without Power* and *Asya and Christine* in this sense
function as historical allegories, selecting key moments from the
past in order to comment on and seal a connection with the
contemporary moment in which McCarthy writes. Everything
outside this definition of the Irish experience is, by definition,
exotic. The Deputy's exchange with a stranger reading *Ulysses*
shows that what this policy ultimately makes exotic and alien is
the local, the familiar. Or as McCarthy has claimed elsewhere,
literature is never provincial, only criticism can be provincial:

'Cappoquin on the Blackwater. That very town is mentioned in this
book'. 'No!' They all sat up on hearing that. 'Is it a local history?'
enquired the Deputy. 'I'm surprised the author hasn't been in touch
with me'. 'Oh, he's trapped, trapped on the continent. Come to think of
it,' Mr Hurley went on, 'he died a couple of years ago'. He went back to
his book. They watched him furtively, but he seemed completely
absorbed in what he was reading. (*A&C*, 194)

Geographical proximity becomes the definitive index of strangeness or familiarity. By bringing strangeness home, making
Cappoquin unfamiliar, Joyce is cut adrift from an Ireland the
Deputy, in both senses of this word, represents. The Deputy and
the Party are associated with the inertia that drove Joyce into
exile. He is alien and alienated because the style of belonging

through which he imagines Cappoquin makes it an inauthentic, mobile signifier which does not necessarily connote a 'real' place. A native Irish writer representing Ireland as part of, not in contradistinction to, the wider world subverts the whole project of state building.

The last verse of McCarthy's poem 'November in Boston' captures this theme:

Those long November evenings I was made to feel as special
as a kiwi, a small green species resurrected from
its island grave. 'Listen! He's Irish! From back there.'
It took an hour of words for expectations to dispel,
for them to find a space for one *Sweeney* gone all calm
and clean-cut, like a piece of superior export crystal.

(*TSG*, 50)

Subject to the sentimental expectations of ex-patriots, the poem ends with the poet representing Ireland without being representative. Unlike Bolger's Sweeney, McCarthy's poetic persona is comfortable with the concept of a historical, national identity; the reference to Waterford Crystal is an authentic and manufactured emblem of home, an irony that suggests his questioners should see through his transparently Irish status to find the individual beyond the category of Irishness, so that they will understand the absolute but ever-questioning loyalty he has to the Ireland they seek to discover within him. The presence in Boston of images that are 'calm', 'clean-cut', 'superior export crystal', images drawn from a zone of middle-class comfort, also hints at the exhaustion of colonial faultlines for the poet from the Republic. The memory of loss, the catastrophic dimension to Irish history, cannot be the continual signifier of Irish identity. Or as he put it, 'One never comes away from a collection of poems by a Waterford poet with ankles bleeding. All the frustration and anger seems spirited away. Poets from the North (Paulin, Muldoon) can play filthy games inside the poetic square . . . Our Waterford poetic heritage is a world of glass.'[77]

---

[77] 'Thomas McCarthy Reviews . . .', 63.

V   THE MEN OF SOME PROPERTY

Asya and Christine developed themes which were already apparent in McCarthy's third volume of poetry, *The Non-Aligned
Storyteller*. The book is divided in two sections, one explicitly
dealing with the politics of the Republic, the other a series of
personal meditations called 'Biographies' reflecting on the first
section. A now canonical moment in contemporary Irish writing
is Heaney's poem 'Digging', where the act of writing becomes an
extension of his father's agricultural labour, 'a process of making
contact with what is hidden, making palpable what was sensed
or raised'.[78] The metaphors and images in Heaney's search—
butter, bogs, turf, the soft squelching liquids—are without a
core. The only limit to the meaning available is the idea of
meaning or understanding itself. No other intellectual frame or
boundary curtails this inner quest, this excavation of meaning, as
the land's natural, ongoing bountifulness exceeds any contingent
political arrangements.

In 'Party Shrine', McCarthy hints at the exhaustion of this
imagery in the new dispensation of the state. The poem is pre-
faced by a quotation from Austin Clarke: 'Come back, poor
Twentysixer. Live in lack.'[79] The quotation implies that the
poetic material available to the Republic (or Free State as it
then was) is of a categorically different kind from the energies
exploited by Heaney's archaeological trope. Any immanent
meaning in the new state is circumscribed by a political boundary that sets a horizon for the imagination of the author and
reader. In McCarthy's poem, the celebrations surrounding the
fiftieth anniversary of the 1916 Rising cannot conceal the Party's
diminishing idealism. The aura of the Rising recedes as the Party
celebrates 'the spell of itself'; it replaces what it once reflected,
abrogating the right to define and commemorate a history that
references nothing besides its own procedures. The Party has
ceased to regard itself as a metaphor. It does not bring dissimilar

---

[78] Heaney, *Preoccupations*, 142. Edna Longley says 'Heaney's methods affirm the
presence of depths and layers whereby the past imprints individual and community'
('When Did You Last See Your Father?', 164).
[79] See 'The Poet on his High Bicycle: Austin Clarke and Our Free State Memory',
in McCarthy, *Gardens of Remembrance*, 189–99.

aspects of Irish experience together to create a new and distantly independent Irish form of being. No longer content to simply represent Irish individuals, it now determines and polices what is representative of the Irish experience.

McCarthy thus commemorates his father's rural politics by locating himself through the motif in a certain space in Irish history.[80] The Heaneyesque holding of 'the shovel for my father as he lovingly polishes The Party shrine' achieves this; but he also acknowledges the poetic dangers this kind of affiliation involves. For while Heaney's much-criticized simile 'snug as a gun' described the political energies nourishing his writing, the weeds surrounding the abandoned shell case in McCarthy gesture towards the 'lack' or absence of political vitality noted by Austin Clarke. The 'process of making contact with what is hidden, making palpable what was sensed or raised' is interrupted by a state that fails to correspond with the nation's 'immemorial' past, at least as construed by the Party. To reapply Benedict Anderson, the state cannot create in the minds of each citizen an image of communion with the nation imagined by the Party's founders. The Party's spectral, millenarian relationship to history generates a vocabulary—'spell', 'genie-like', 'shrine'—that yearns for sudden, magical, divine intervention to transform the existing order and make brass golden; an intervention which will, like the rebels of 1916, forego mundane compromises and transform colonial dullness into exhilarating freedom. The Party's first sin is the Beckettian one of being born; its existence testifies to a state of affairs that is not wholly natural, and so it yearns for a moment before its being was necessary. The poem's numerical repetitions—sixty-six, twenty-six, sixteen—establish this fundamentalist framework, the yearning for the kind of sudden, total transformation utterly foreign to the pragmatic compromises politics entails. Recalling a phrase from 'Daedalus, the Maker', 'I will banish argument to work again | with bronze', we see how the Party's gloriously impossible aspirations inspire McCarthy's absolute, always questioning loyalty.

This millenarian dimension accounts for words such as 'magic' and 'spell' throughout the volume. A poem with the title 'Shopkeepers at The Party Meeting' contains the line 'they are

---

[80] Longley, 'When Did You Last See Your Father?', 152.

owning the landscape briefly, with the magical deeds of speech',
a formulation that recalls John Montague's famous lines from 'A
Lost Tradition',

> The whole landscape a manuscript
> We had lost the skill to read.

The Party's inspirational past joins with a legal term, 'deeds',
drawn from the bourgeois present. But that speech is now a
deed, a heroic act in itself, illustrates the Party's exclusively
rhetorical repossession of history. The contractual metaphor,
and the very temporary repossession of the landscape it signifies,
illustrates the rupture between nature and culture, between
the state McCarthy inhabits and the immemorial nation to
which Montague's and Heaney's organic metaphors allude.
Montague's presentation resembles Heaney's in that the distinctiveness and value of Irish culture is at least partly related to its
ability to reflect this already existing state of affairs.[81] For
McCarthy, the Party's self-image as a national movement representing the 'historical majority' must account for the fact that it
now belongs to 'the men of some property', the aspiring bourgeoisie who view land firstly as a commodity and only secondly
as Irish.

   The Party has a troubled relationship to the present moment it
aspires to dominate, for the political power it craves never
extends into the past, the sacred zone that contains its most
cherished self-images. In 'The Folklore of The Party' the displacement of the Party's 'elders' (again, a term more commonly
applied to a cabal of tribal leaders) inspires a Yeatsian threnody,
'Gone is their significant | laughter and precision'. The elders
admonish 'the malevolent spinners of opinion' for portraying
them as 'mere news'. Effective power controls memory; yet
opinion and news are tied to the chaos of the present, the
extemporaneous, so that the Party has an antagonistic relationship to the power it craves: it is never wholly satisfied with power
that cannot be applied retrospectively, to what Moody called
'received views'. The elders' impact is continually personal—'I
felt the impact of their business | in my heart'—and public, and

---

[81] See David Lloyd's attack on Heaney in 'Pap for the Dispossessed', in
Anomalous States: Ireland and the Post-Colonial Movement (Dublin: Lilliput Press,
1992), 13–40.

throughout the volume these concerns dominate. The poem 'Question Time', set in a social gathering centred on family and community, refers to a formal parliamentary procedure. The mystique surrounding figures like Emmet, Kitty O'Shea, and Higgins binds the community by offering answers that are reliably uncertain:

> Who was Robert Emmet's mistress? Who was Kitty
> O'Shea?
> Which IRA man was shot on his own wedding-day?
> How many death-warrants did Kevin O'Higgins sign?
> So much to answer between the buffet meal and wine—
> But the prize is a week in Brussels, money for two,
> and kisses from two Euro-MPs just passing through.
>
> (*TNAS*, 22)

The ritualistic procession of unanswered, perhaps unanswerable questions is, paradoxically, the only reliable form of historical narrative: questions never answered delegate to the Party a semblance of control over the past; in the absence of a comprehensible, rational response, they generate the Party's 'blazing mystique'. But the future unfolds outside this zone, and the ribbon of names that binds the community is replaced by a language without any spectral element. The hyphenation and abbreviation of 'Euro-MP' introduces a precise, clinical term to Irish political discourse and McCarthy's poetics, one that envisages a completely different form of representation. The O'Hara twins' 'Uh Egg' is of course equally precise, but the untranslatable context in which that phrase operates is instinctively understood by McCarthy. For the elders enforce the location of memory in a *polis* founded on his communalism, and provide the regional history that inspires his civic republican emphasis on justice and the common good.

'Question Time', however, seems caught between several mutually exclusive options: between a past too easily bathed in nostalgia and an indeterminate future of complete transience; between a context inimical to artistic production and an unfettered creative environment. Yet these oppositions turn out to be close connections. 'Uh Egg' and 'Euro-MP' are both mechanical phrases, meaningless without a semantic context through which they can be understood. What the Party's populist myth-

ology offers is a utopian context in which this language retrospectively attains meaning; like the new Europe, it promises an
indeterminate future as its utopian goal, and it is in this future
that coded terms like 'Uh Egg' and 'Euro-MP' will magically
reveal their full, coded meaning. The local and the cosmopolitan,
then, are neither implacably opposed nor inalienably different,
and at first it seems impossible to insist on any smooth demarcation between each as creative sites. What McCarthy's work does,
and here he recalls Crichton Smith, is not to write out these
contradictions but live passionately through the dialectic the
questions raise without proposing any totalizing response.

The phrase 'between the buffet meal and wine' occupies just
this type of space. 'Question Time' is analytical and observant,
sympathizing with the rituals it describes until those rituals
expunge all trace of his father's beliefs. Though it tries to arrive
at a balance between the blazing mystique of Emmet and
Higgins, and a Europe in which discrete couples (the 'money for
two') are prized over a specifically Irish community, the past in
the poem is tolerated only when it is neither strained and obscure
nor an unmediated presence; neither limited to the tyranny of
fact nor simply invented. And the dialectic between what is,
might have been, and what might be always occurs within the
incubus of individual memory.

In 'Black Flags at a Party Meeting', for example, his father's
resistance to fascist aggression never enters conventional historical narratives:

> I want to hunt
> The anonymous historian. I want to chase
> him into a corner and say 'I'll not forget!'
>
> I know how they left you with scars—
> but there's no historian of the *might have been*
>
> An elbow on the nose, a baton in the mouth,
> a blue shirt or a green pushing through a crowd:
> come home to memory where these are understood.
>
> (*TNAS*, 24)

McCarthy's collection, *The Lost Province*, dedicates the
poem 'Them Historians' to the medieval historian Professor
Donnchadh Ó Corráin. The poet's horizon, his imaginative

reach, it suggests, is always tied to the available historical evidence: 'You store the meat and mead. | Poets only travel where the archives lead' (*TLP*, 48). 'Cataloguing Twelve Fenian Novels' is perhaps the most blatant example of this principle. As a librarian in Cork City library, McCarthy must discard or re-catalogue those novels no longer in demand by the Cork public.[82] The poet is professionally obliged to evaluate historical narratives according to the appetites of a present-day audience, a principle the Party could never endorse. McCarthy must determine whether historical narratives are now better read as anthropology, as political science, are now redundant, or remain fictional, despite, as Moody says, the professional historical knowledge we now have of their fictionality. McCarthy is born into the Party, The Soldiers of Destiny, for whom the exact nature of the pastness of the past, as well as its availability and implications for the present, is never disputed. The deracinated state which now employs him, however, insists that the past is not fixed but answerable to the shifting, unpredictable appetites of the present moment.[83] The different versions of history offered by the Party and the state do not arise out of confusion about what happened, but out of a desire to account for a different set of feelings towards the present arising out of the same events. The state allows the present its full integrity, and acknowledges the malleability of the past by refurbishing the narratives through which the present knows itself. For the Party, history has never been subordinate to the capricious appetite of the contemporary, and so one of the primary functions of Party lore is to protect Irish history from the state it was instrumental in establishing.

VI   THE ADAMS FAMILY

In *Strange Country: Modernity and Nationhood in Irish Writing since 1790*, in a critique of F. S. L. Lyons, Seamus Deane offers a useful formulation for understanding McCarthy's position.

---

[82] Thomas McCarthy, 'Poet as Librarian', 55.

[83] 'Our past is an embarrassment. What we must do is extend our present into the past so that everything is altered to fit in. Everything must dovetail into the needs of the present' (McCarthy, 'Celtic Tigers, Mad Cows and Exiles', in *Gardens of Remembrance*, 63).

Deane accuses Lyons of denying political agency to Irish nationalists by construing Irish history as relentlessly fuelled by myth
while British actions are held to be measured, defined, rational.
Lyons, Deane argues, fails to understand 'that element in history
that is not history'.[84] In other words, the historian's 'beautifully
prepared indices and themes' ('Counting the Dead on the Radio,
1972') never wholly account for the motivation driving Party
members through the fog in *Without Power*. An association with
a version of history that can never be ratified through simple
'fact' produces the emotional resentment of the excluded underdog, so that the fog is, in this sense, the mystique produced by the
accumulated memories of events and figures—Emmet, Kitty
O'Shea, Kevin Higgins—whose importance is independent of
their actual existence as 'real' lived history. The Party is galvanized and retarded by what Deane calls that portion of history
that is not history. Any form of information in the present is
always struggling to maintain parity with that element of its past,
whether labelled myth, nostalgia, magic, or fear, that exceeds the
conventions of reportage or narrative. As Clutterbuck remarks,
the order these narratives impose is as speculative and precarious
as the books that promise to domesticate nature:[85]

> Counting the Dead on the Radio, 1972
>
> All that winter we lined and limed the earth.
> We read books too, and ordered even more—
> History rested on the brown hall table
> beside the bird-guides and seed catalogues.
> We read books as hungrily as Edmund
> Burke, with more affection than any dauphiness.
> Chaos in hard covers broke in upon us
> with beautifully assembled themes, perfect
> indices . . .

All that is certain is that the transmission and reception of
meaning across Ireland is not uniform, and that in McCarthy's
southern rural constituency, the message is distorted at every
point.

   'Counting the Dead on the Radio, 1972' is a poem in response

---

[84] *Strange Country: Modernity and Nationhood in Irish Writing since 1790*
(Oxford: Clarendon Press, 1996), 196.
[85] 'Place, Time', 92.

to Bloody Sunday. A boy's parents offer conflicting advice. The father 'says we should only trust I the News. We'll read more books, my mother said. I Fatherless, the radio has plenty to say':

> *Mama, a whole regiment has been attacked*
> *by a Catholic priest waving a blood-stained*
> *handkerchief. That's what the radio says.*
> My brother, with rabbit blood on his arm, sips tea,
> puts his adolescent ear to the ill-tuned radio
> whose crackles could be gunfire or a mild electric storm.
> A household filled with books, a brother used to death:
> my mother coughs again. We retune the wireless set.
>
> (*TNAS*, 28)

The southern political register is categorically different, with the muffled thuds, grunts, and torture heard being that of his brother hunting rabbits. Mediating these events through an exclusively local context leaves 'southern ears, clogged by too much of this, I we can barely comprehend what the radio says— I something has happened up in the north'. McCarthy's southern constituency has no memory of these events as sociology rather than myth, so the reception is ambivalent, the information never fully absorbed because it cannot 'come home to a memory where these are understood' ('Black Flags at a Party Meeting'). The poem meditates as much on the horror of this ambivalence as on the event itself. Whatever way the news is transmitted, distortion remains, and so the poem ends on this note of irresolution, with the family unsure what they are being asked to respond to. The date and place of Bloody Sunday are inscribed on the boy's memory, but no deeper political affiliation emerges. The poem ends but never arrives at a conclusion, as the family presented here can only 'retune' the device that feeds them information.

Does this retuning suggest a negative or positive ending? A renunciation or a renewed affiliation? These polarities are too crude for McCarthy, and by the time of *The Lost Province*, the two possibilities are not alternatives or even complementary positions. These poems do not erase contradictions but live passionately, blazingly through the dialectic of the 'questions not answered'.[86] The hyphenated title of 'The New Euro-Road'

---

[86] 'The dialogue of politics is always polemical, one-sided, argumentative whereas the work of poetry feeds upon ambiguity; it presents both the argument and its rebut-

responds to a new dual affiliation, where geography is no longer
an index of association and the impossibility of returning to
Ned's repetitive routes or de Valera's peasant cottage is acknowledged:

> We can never get back to the first surface of home.
> From the new EC road—raised above flood-level
> with German money—I can see the river-side street
> where I was born. I can hear the church bells.
>
> The town cowers like an exhausted father.
> Everything has changed. We were ever closer to Bonn,
> or Milan or Cologne. We were never closer
> to a fairy tale. Heartbroken afternoons at home.
>
> (*TLP*, 39)

In *Ireland in Exile*,[87] Dermot Bolger claims that Irish writers no
longer go into exile, they simply commute. The foreign is no
longer foreign, and McCarthy's 'exhausted father' of a town
hints at the improbability of recovering one's origin in this new
dispensation. The poet, deeply alienated from his own biography, nevertheless acknowledges some gains:

> My past has the texture of an Italian film:
> to be seen fully certain blinds must be drawn down
> against the light, and talk kept to a minimum.
>
> Misfortune flooded my childhood so many times.
> It's good to see it now from a raised Europe-road.
> Would I go back? Would a donkey go back to the mines?
> Would a salmon return to a lake without food?
>
> (*TLP*, 39)

A salmon's return to its origins is instinctual not chosen, as
it swims against the tide to give birth and die. Similarly,
McCarthy's allegiance could never be just a matter of economic
calculation. There is no wholly transparent perspective on the
past—'to be seen fully certain blinds must be drawn down'—and
the Party's apocalyptic yearning for a sudden and total transformation is no longer viable. A new European context raises
him above the Party's fundamentalist imagery, the floods, sheep,

---

tal' (McCarthy, 'Memory, Childhood and the Party', in *Gardens of Remembrance*,
13–30, at 27).

[87] (Dublin: New Island Books, 1995), 7.

fog, and sudden descent over cliff-faces. The language of absolute difference—in Fisk's phrase, the rejection of the values of other nations—is abjured in favour of a more mundane, philosophically stable cohabitation, despite the recognition that this aspiration has all the allure, and reality, of 'a fairy tale'.

The last of the five sections, however, 'Talking to Gerry Adams, 1994', returns us to an exclusively Irish context. The poem was written after the IRA ceasefire of 31 August 1994, a moment in Irish history when the Party, and Sinn Féin, the contemporary legacy of Fianna Fáil's violent Republican past, suddenly seemed capable of sharing a public space in which reconciliation was possible. Suspended above the violence of the IRA campaign, McCarthy's nationalist proclivities are reasserted with a quite startling comparison of Adams's face and that of Sean Moylan's in Keating's famous painting, *Men of the South*, an unashamedly romantic portrayal of the flying columns in the War of Independence.

Standing before the same painting, Yeats was 'overwhelmed with emotion' finding an Ireland 'not as she is displayed in guide book or history, but, Ireland seen because of the magnificent vitality of her painters'.[88] Adams's 'magnificent vitality' makes McCarthy doubt if a poetry based on politics is the appropriate response to Irish affairs:

> We are three floors above your foot-soldiers,
> which is the right of those who exchange ideas.
> We know nothing about fuses:
> we detonate opinions and views.
> Your handsome face (the face of Sean Moylan
> in Keating's *Men of the South*), has no pain
> visible to me. It has absorbed politics,
> and flying columns of documents.
>
> Today it's the 'productive atmosphere of peace'
> after war. I find myself switching sides
> already. Maybe this is what poets are for
> in a destitute time. To stay apart
> from the Dáil. Thinking finds a Protestant in me;
> and Ulster, an autonomous region of the heart.
>
> (*TLP*, 54)

---

[88] See Brian P. Kennedy and Raymond Gillespie (eds.), *Ireland: Art into History* (Dublin: Town House, 1996), 151.

This attraction was prefigured in an interview with Adams in 1993. McCarthy then wrote:

There is a strong sense of *déja vu* about Mr Adams. I feel I know him well. He is a seventy-year old man who held my hand at a Fianna Fáil dinner-dance in 1967, he is an eighty-year old man who has learned Irish at Frongroch. Here is the man Dev picked to explain the Economic War to farmers of the border counties.[89]

The interview is a fascinating, highly self-conscious encounter between poetry and politics, and between two variants of Irish Republicanism. And yet, despite McCarthy's evident sarcasm, with Adams the revolutionary suddenly part of Fianna Fáil's Friday-night chicken-supper dinner-dance circuit, this 1993 interview does not demonize Sinn Féin's constituency. Put simply, the North is not a place apart 'up there'; a permanently disconnected, ostracized community which we 'down here' permanently mistrust and miscomprehend. The disagreements between McCarthy and Adams are fundamental but not irreconcilable, because, unlike Bolger, McCarthy does not retain a residual nostalgia for an imaginative world in which political and personal wholeness is possible. The disjunctures between Sinn Féin's past and present, between its inclusive rhetoric and divisive war, its deeply provincial base and metropolitan headquarters, even its resourcefulness 'as a community-based protest group'—these are all analogous to themes and divisions which McCarthy anatomizes in the Party. McCarthy does not endorse Sinn Féin's colonial analysis of the conflict in Ireland, a framework which assumes that meaning in Ireland is still fundamentally the product of a relationship with an external power, Britain. Rather, conflict is generated from within, as the North is shown to be both familiar and alien, of the nation and a crucial component in the state's self-definition. McCarthy is partitionist, in the sense that his work does not gesture towards a reconciliation of differences or towards the attainment of a utopian 'hybrid' culture, a solution that will transcend partition and division. As 'Mick Hannigan's Berlin Wall' puts it, in a line which seems to suggest division is almost a metaphysical principle, 'as our divided island is a just thing: | perfect image of the *spirit* unwilling' (emphasis added). But in the derogatory sense

---

[89] 'Streetwise: From the Falls Road to Kildare Street?', 4.

that that word—partitionist—is often used in Irish discourse, as shorthand for a disinterest, even hostility, to the 'whinging' of northern Catholics,[90] it is inapplicable here:

But this isn't the *thirties*, I kept saying to myself as I waited in the dismal *bookshop reading room* of the *Dublin* Sinn Féin headquarters. The room I waited in reeked of *kitsch Belfast* Republicanism. Even the *foreign* pop music of FM or Atlantic 252 that filled the room seemed to deepen the relentless iconography of a *Republic* invented by the most resourceful community based protest group in the *world*. If this was the *future*, obviously Radio na Gaeltachta was not to be part of it.[91]

As Sinn Féin transmuted into Fianna Fáil, now Gerry Adams seems ready to take the first steps down the Falls Road to Kildare Street. We return to Seamus Deane's question: 'If a place (or a Party or a person) is renamed and relocated, is it in some sense the same place (Party or person) as it had been or is it entirely, essentially, different?'[92] The italicized words contain the creative dialectic running throughout McCarthy's work, through Sinn Féin and the Party that succeeded it. McCarthy recognizes in Sinn Féin an essential element of his own political origins, the path that links the Falls Road and Kildare Street: 'This isn't the future our father's planned, but it's authentic working-class stuff'.[93] The attraction of Sinn Féin's politics, however, cannot disguise its diminished vision for the Republic. Again and again McCarthy returns to Adams's failure as a writer to engage with an *un*imagined Ireland, an Ireland that does not have implacable disputes resolved in an imaginary realm: 'Do you realise that almost the entire book-reading public in Ireland would be alienated from the world you create? . . . There are many Irish worlds, from Molly Keane to Roddy Doyle . . . But the difference between their world and yours is that your recreated world of heroes and occupiers is also a view of the future . . . a major fragment is missing from these stories, one you don't value. That's the Protestant fragment, the one million who don't wish to share your future.'[94]

Adams insists, in a manner strangely similar to the rhetoric of

[90] A phrase used by Colm Tóibín in a radio interview in Nov. 1993.
[91] 'Streetwise: From the Falls Road to Kildare Street?', 4.
[92] 'The Name of the Game', 107.
[93] 'Streetwise: From the Falls Road to Kildare Street?', 4.
[94] Ibid. 4.

the EEC and Fianna Fáil, on a future that has still to be determined. His writing stands for the open possibilities of nationhood rather than the closed reality of the state.[95] For McCarthy,
Adams is guilty of 'The terrible mistakes poets make | who
tie themselves | to Marx instead of their fathers'. Because the
dialectic Adams lives through organizes itself around a totalized
solution, the political geography of the unitary island state, it
actually enforces partition ever more firmly on the Irish map.
Adams might believe that the Irish are a written nation, but in
McCarthy's terms, they cannot be a risen nation if he does not
supply them with a 'memory to come home to'. And as
McCarthy's whole oeuvre demonstrates, however, there can be
no one memory that accounts for the whole of the Irish experience:

> I recall Bloody Sunday. You recall
> Enniskillen. Corpses lie on our flowers
> while we think and talk and watch.
>
> It is Stormont, it is the Dáil
> that makes awkward, distant Hell-
> place where swallows go to browse.
> Truth is only a kind of petal
> blown against the wall of each house.
> It is power, it is powerful men
> I've interiorised. They leave me troubled
> and uprooted in my father's garden.

Uprooted and troubled, but still part of his father's living
space—this is the only form of absolute, questioning loyalty
McCarthy's ambivalence allows. The simultaneous feelings of
affiliation and distrust a political jurisdiction commands are part
of the poet's private universe, 'the power and powerful men' he
has interiorized. But unlike Bolger, this private universe never
repudiates the principle of a subjectivity developed through a
political identity. The simple presence of irresolution is no
impediment to this process. And the political fact of partition
does not lead to any premature homogenization of a southern
political identity or a closure of the history both states share. Or
as Eiléan Ní Chuilleanáin beautifully puts it, 'A line is drawn

---

[95] James Livesey and Stuart Murray, 'Review Article: Post-Colonial Theory and
Irish Culture', *Irish Historical Studies*, 30/119 (May 1997), 454.

across our experience, by an event in history or a pattern of nature, and we instantly find ourselves in a double life, cut in two by a line of bars.'[96] Despite the lines drawn across the cognitive map of their experience, McCarthy's regional community may still participate in a civic republican dialogue. Wholeness has never been a spiritual or political prerequisite for an effective, participatory agency. His Republic may be comprised of thirty-two, twenty-six, or any number of counties as long as history is available to his evolving personal universe. McCarthy's regional space is, in this sense, deterritorial; it never forecloses an engagement with the conflict of state and nation through an aestheticism grounded in the ideal continuities of place. For the most developed effort amongst these three Irish writers to elaborate that form of regional aestheticism, we must turn to Colm Tóibín.

---

[96] 'Borderlands of Irish Poetry', 25.

5

Colm Tóibín, Partition, and the Ends of History

> It was the centre of power, our neo-gothic cathedral at the top of the main street . . . much grander than the town's Protestant church it was a sign of the great rich might of the Catholic church in the nineteenth century . . . There are certain things that I know about them [his rural ancestors], or can imagine, but before them I can imagine nothing and I know nothing. The Cathedral is the beginning of real imaginable time.
>
> *TSOTC*, 5

> He must have been up there on Vinegar Hill during the battle of 1798, and he must have been around for the slaughter afterwards. No one else was very interested in this plaque, or the sectarian legacy. The plaque was a memorial to a past we would not repeat. History had come to an end in Enniscorthy.
>
> *TSOTC*, 295

> In the post-historical period there will be neither art or philosophy, just the perpetual caretaking of the museum of human history.[1]

I   THE END OF HISTORY

COLM TÓIBÍN was born in Enniscorthy, County Wexford, in 1955. A former editor of *Magill*, an influential current affairs magazine in the Republic, his novels, journalism, and travel narratives have made him a visible and articulate participant in

---

[1] Francis Fukuyama, 'The End of History?', in Gearóid Ó Tuathail, Simon Dalby, and Paul Routledge (eds.), *The Geopolitics Reader* (London: Routledge, 1997), 115.

Irish cultural debate. Raised, like Thomas McCarthy, in a strongly Fianna Fáil family,[2] he is at varying times a cultural conservative and political modernist (and even these terms can occasionally be reversed). Fiercely anti-nationalist, he is also an advocate and incisive critic of the revisionist enterprise. Thomas Pakenham's *The Year of Liberty*, for example, is attacked for its condescension towards Tóibín's father's Catholic nationalist culture, especially the reductive portrayal of the 1798 Rebels as, simply, a 'mob': 'When I read Pakenham's book about the central event in the history of the place where I was brought up, I find the tone and the use of language offensive and hurtful. For a few seconds I become the man at the launch hectoring Pakenham.'[3]

Tóibín's imagination is haunted by the missed opportunities of 1798 and the loyalties and memories it inspired, but it is inhabited by the version of Catholic nationalism that succeeded the United Irishmen's secular libertarianism. His writing seeks a space between oppositions which are actually linkages: he can be a cultural (and cultured) nationalist, and a liberal who is not a Republican; a secular revisionist who acknowledges Catholicism as an enduring element of Irish society; and, I want to argue, a liberal whose attitude towards the North of Ireland is ultimately illiberal. Tóibín's review of Declan Kiberd's *Inventing Ireland: The Literature of the Modern Nation* provides a good summary of his attitude towards cultural nationalism. The rhetoric of cultural difference, Tóibín claims, made opaque the reality of economic and social division, and Kiberd's incorporation of history into the realm of textuality inevitably blurs the proper, indeed the only, moral response to the violence of 1916:

The invention of Ireland by Yeats and his friends seems to me to have had some dire consequences for the citizens of Ireland, for the people who occupy the country. In this invention it was possible by using poems and plays, rather than pamphlets and economic arguments, to create a vague consensus and rhetoric of classlessness: a nation rather than a set of clashing interests. By establishing that 'Ireland' existed as an entity, it was easier for governments after Independence to indulge in

---

[2] Nicky Furlong, 'A Co. Wexford Boy who is Making Good', *Wexford People* (7 Jan. 1993).
[3] Tóibín, 'New Ways of Killing Your Father', *London Review of Books* (18 Nov. 1993), 3.

self-justification while hundreds of thousands emigrated. Ireland is free, who dares complain? . . . Kiberd is prepared to treat the Rising in the terms that some of its leaders sought to present it. But it was not a text: it involved the burning of buildings, the shooting of soldiers, the murder of civilians. And it also used the idea of hatred and text—Kiberd calls it performance—to create a cult of violence. I loathe everything about it, every single moment of it . . . It is depressing to watch him treat de Valera as a text . . . He refuses to deal with the grubbiness of Irish politics after Independence, reading it as though it were a medieval illuminated manuscript rather than a politics rife with opportunism, hypocrisy and failure.[4]

Kiberd's rendering of history, Tóibín seems to say, would be a wonderful thing if it were true, but like any general doctrine of nationalism or revisionism, its theory is inevitably separate from the tangible realities that inspired it.[5] Tóibín's liberalism, then, seems a pragmatic and—with its attacks on de Valera, Roy Foster, and Thomas Pakenham—a genuinely radical, independent alternative to nationalist–revisionist dichotomies. Sebastian Barry's 'fragmentary map'[6] of the Republic is finally given ethical, aesthetic, and political elaboration; this is the moment when the Republic's post-nationalist liberalism appropriates a cultural space through which it will define itself.

Besides proclaiming the end of history within the Republic, however, Tóibín also nominates its origin. His writing continually returns to Enniscorthy, scene of some of the bloodiest fighting of 1798, that brief moment when, depending on your politics, Protestant, Catholic, and Dissenter united under the common name of Irishman against an English invader, or when a hopelessly idealistic Republican rebellion descended into sectarian slaughter, the remnants of which are still visible today in Northern Ireland. The bicentenary of 1798 and celebration of Wexford's prominent role in the Rising are inescapably political events that draw on important elements in Irish Republicanism's

    [4] Tóibín, 'New Ways of Killing Your Father', 3.
    [5] For a summary of the critiques Yeats has provoked in Irish Studies, see Jonathan Allison, 'The Attack on Yeats', *South Atlantic Review*, 55/4 (Nov. 1990), 61–73. See also Warwick Gould and Edna Longley (eds.), *Yeats Annual No. 12: That Accusing Eye: Yeats and his Irish Readers* (Basingstoke: Macmillan, 1996), esp. John Wilson Foster, 'Getting the North: Yeats and Modern Irish Nationalism', 180–212.
    [6] *The Inherited Boundaries: Younger Poets from the Republic of Ireland* (Dublin: Mercier Press, 1986), 17.

collective memory. For Gerry Adams, '98 is a foundational moment for a radicalism capable of uniting Presbyterians and Papists.[7] But though Wolfe Tone brilliantly captured the possibilities awaiting a genuinely united Ireland, his legacy is claimed almost exclusively by Republicans: the sectarian contours of Irish identity, in other words, solidified after the Rising which aspired to abolish them failed. After 1798, the Orange order strengthened, the Act of Union was put in place, and Robert Emmet's abortive rising occurred. In one reading, the practical legacy of 1798 is the solidification of British rule in Ireland and the polarization of two religious communities. Despite this, 1798 remains so imaginatively potent that, according to one of its most prominent historians, it has yet to pass from politics into history.[8] Each year at Wolfe Tone's grave in Bodenstown, Republicans led by Sinn Féin renew their commitment to Tone's ideals, an act which implicitly acknowledges the IRA as his legitimate political heirs.

The commemoration of 1798 is inevitably selective, designed to serve the political priorities of the present. Kevin Whelan, for example, urges a reconsideration of the Rebels' essential unity, modernity, and secular goals in order to 'reappropriate a profoundly democratic symbol and an inspiring example of an effort to construct a representative, secular and pluralist politics on the island of Ireland',[9] whereas for Thomas Pakenham, the Rebels were 'a half-disciplined mob with little idea beyond plunder . . . the disaffected had no serious political aims'. Pakenham's rebellion is 'spontaneous': a furious peasant *Jacquerie*, rooted in immemorial sectarian hatreds and emptied of politics.[10] Similarly, Roy Foster characterizes events in Wexford as 'curiously contingent and haphazard', 'local . . . rather than ideological', and 'improvised'.[11] But, launching the state's official 1798 commemorations, the Taoiseach and leader of Fianna Fáil,

---

[7] See Gerry Adams, *Before the Dawn: An Autobiography* (London: Mandarin, 1996), 73.

[8] Kevin Whelan, 'Reinterpreting the 1798 Rebellion in County Wexford', in Dáire Keogh and Nicholas Furlong (eds.), *The Mighty Wave: The 1798 Rebellion in Wexford* (Dublin: Four Courts Press, 1997), 9–38.

[9] Ibid. 36.

[10] See Jim Smyth, 'Interpreting the 1790s', *History Ireland*, 6/2 (Summer 1998), 54–8.

[11] *Modern Ireland: 1600–1972* (London: Allen Lane, 1989), 274–8.

Bertie Ahearn, claimed to speak on behalf of 'a sovereign Irish government' that 'can trace its political lineage back to 1798 when the first republics in Wexford and Connaught were declared'.[12] Such flatly contradictory interpretations demonstrate the continually contested legacy of 1798; they also show the enormous emotional significance the act of commemoration entails. For 1798 is a concentrated example of the politics of remembrance, involving nothing less than the construction of the Republic's collective memory. Rebuking Pakenham in 1993, Tóibín pointedly noted that 'the committee to celebrate the 200th anniversary is already in place'.[13] This is the agitated voice of the man at the launch hectoring Pakenham, Tóibín the novelist refusing to relinquish 1798 as a historical and imaginative resource,[14] and perhaps exemplifying Jim Smyth's larger point on 1798 that 'senses of the past shared by the culture at large filter through to the academy'. Commemoration binds Enniscorthy together as a real, knowable community. But what does it mean to say, alongside this, that history has originated and terminated in this same site? How can Enniscorthy remain an enduring locus of value, an almost mystical site throughout his work, if all that has historically defined it is erased? And what replaces history? Reviewing *The Field Day Anthology of Irish Writing*, Tóibín criticized its omissions and its focus on national rather than social issues, the rhetoric of difference over the reality of partition and the cultural, economic, and social changes this enshrined. The source of such omissions, he claimed, lay in the view that 'Southern Ireland is contemptible and complacent, and that the changes which have taken place here are nothing besides the great events which have rattled Northern Ireland'.[15] How is it possible to criticize the exclusion of the Southern state from history if history has ended? What is Tóibín's aesthetic and political response to the fact of violence, past and present, in Ireland? These tensions throughout Tóibín's writing make explicit the themes discussed previously in Bolger and McCarthy and confront the dichotomy and overlap between

---

[12] Quoted in Tom Dunne, 'Wexford's *Comoradh* '98: Politics, Heritage, and History', *History Ireland*, 6/2 (Summer 1998), 49.

[13] 'New Ways of Killing Your Father', 4.

[14] 'Introduction', in Jim Smyth (ed.), *Revolution, Counter-Revolution and Union* (Cambridge: Cambridge University Press, 2000), 18.

[15] *Canadian Journal of Irish Studies*, 18/2 (Dec. 1991), 122.

region, state, and nation. For as Todd and Ruane remind us, partition had a profound impact on the form of the new Southern state, giving it a 'distinct spatial, economic, demographic, religious and political profile, shaping its culture, identity, institutions and sense of community'.[16] These spatial and cultural coordinates become legible in Tóibín through attempts to mask or render invisible the impact of partition on the region, to make the writer's local universe irrevocably private, inalienably separate.

'The End of History' is of course Francis Fukuyama's term for the triumph of liberal democracy over all other conflictual forces of political and human organization. Fukuyama's post-historical consciousness celebrates 'the total exhaustion of viable systematic alternatives to Western liberalism'. Thus it is not a period or stage of history that ends but 'history as such: that is, the end point of man's ideological evolution and the universalisation of Western liberal democracy as the final form of human government'.[17] Only the nagging voices of irreconcilables remain, which Fukuyama names: Palestinians and Kurds, Sikhs and Tamils, Irish Catholics and Walloons, Armenians and Azeris. These groups 'will continue to have their unresolved grievances'. Meaning in the public sphere will be produced through the exclusion of groups and of issues which are irrational because they are irreducible to an economic calculus. These groups and issues are ghettoized as metaphysical, a condition politics can never penetrate, and any future conflict will be between those within and without history, between the historical and post-historical world. In the post-historical period, Fukuyama boasts, there will be neither art or philosophy, just the perpetual caretaking of the museum of human history. If ever there were a justification for comparative post-colonial theory, Fukuyama's list of irreconcilables is it.[18] But how does this museum of human history fit with Tóibín's liberalism? How is the 'end of history'

---

[16] 'The Republic of Ireland and the Conflict in Northern Ireland', in Joseph Ruane and Jennifer Todd, *The Dynamics of Conflict in Northern Ireland: Power, Conflict and Emancipation* (Cambridge: Cambridge University Press, 1997), 249.

[17] 'End of History?', 115.

[18] See 'Northern Irish Poetry and the End of History', in Edna Longley, *Poetry and Posterity* (Northumberland: Bloodaxe, 2000), 280–316, for an application of Fukuyama's thesis to Northern Irish cultural affairs.

manipulated so that the state categorizes certain groups as non-negotiable outcasts, irredeemably excluded from history?

In his magisterial critique of the 'end of history' thesis, Perry Anderson highlights Fukuyama's endorsement of Hegel's view of the state as the space in which history concludes. The present will, according to Hegel, 'cast aside of its barbarity', allowing 'true reconciliation, which reveals the state as the image and actuality of reason to become objective'.[19] The state is the space for Hegel in which 'the world spirit', Absolute Knowing, finally grasps itself as absolute, and 'the series of spiritual forms is therewith for the moment concluded'.[20] Hegel never explicitly mentions the 'End of history' but he does thematize the closure of the historical process. Lutz Niethammer's study *Posthistoire*, published soon after Fukuyama's essay, treated 'post-history' not as a formal theory but more 'a symptomatic sensibility', a structure of feeling. Niethammer claims:

In the wake of de-Stalinization and the events of May 1968—when French intellectuals distanced themselves from the Communist Party with which they had largely sympathised in the postwar period—the philosophy of history stemming from Marx and Hegel finally lost its hegemony, and it was denounced for its pretensions as an authoritarian language-game invented by master-thinkers.[21]

Fukuyama's imaginative and political geography is strictly conterminous with that of the state. Only those within a state's borders are within history, in theory and in practice endowed with a subjectivity and agency that enables them to affect history. And because the phenomenon of post-history anatomized in Niethammer emerges in 1968, the year in which Bolger commences his anthology of the Republic, the 'end of history', then, is somehow entangled with the emergence and crystallization of the Republic as a state, a mature cultural and geographical space that plays amiable host to the preoccupations of Bolger and Tóibín. The act of calling an end to history is, inevitably, an event within history, and Tóibín, I want to argue, derives the

---

[19] Anderson, *A Zone of Engagement* (London: Verso, 1992), 285.
[20] See the ch. 'The State: The Consciousness of Freedom', in Shlomo Avineri, *Hegel's Theory of the Modern State* (Cambridge: Cambridge University Press), 176–93.
[21] *Posthistoire: Has History Come to an End?*, trans. Patrick Camiller (London: Verso, 1992), 138.

authority to do this from the Republic's perceived maturity, its arrival at 'the end point of man's ideological evolution', as part of the universalization of Western liberal democracy Fukuyama lauded despite all the exclusions attached to this process.

The end of history in Fukuyama and Niethammer is not the arrival of a perfect system but the refusal to countenance any better alternatives to what is now available: 'we cannot picture to ourselves a world that is essentially different from the present one, and at the same time better'.[22] Fukuyama does not reject the idea of further political progress, but he does believe that liberal democracy provides a permanent solution to problems of equality and justice. Thus we no longer require idealist notions of what constitutes history or historical agency; this, as Fred Halliday's socialist critique of Fukuyama points out, is itself an idealistic notion. In positing economic and scientific development and human freedom as 'the motor of history', Halliday accuses Fukuyama of ignoring 'the main motor of human history, in this and previous centuries: namely, collective political action, action by groups, be these classes, nations, states'.[23] In Fukuyama's global coalition of liberal states, reason replaces religion, capitalist democracy supplants nationalist collectivity, universalization displaces localities, and the state supersedes the nation in the slowly concluding cadences of historical evolution.

Henri Lefebvre, in his enormously suggestive *The Production of Space*, describes this process as one in which the state's rational inscription of a geographical and historical space ironically terminates the very development of geography and history as variable coordinates of the polity. The state

plans and organises society 'rationally' . . . The state crushes time by reducing differences to repetitions and circularities . . . Space in its Hegelian form comes back into its own. The modern state promotes and imposes itself as the stable centre—definitively—of (national) societies and spaces. As both the end and the meaning of history—just as Hegel had forecast—it flattens the social and cultural spheres. It enforces a logic that puts an end to conflicts and contradictions. It neutralizes whatever resists it by castration or crushing.[24]

---

[22] Fukuyama, quoted in Anderson, *Zone of Engagement*, 46.
[23] 'An Encounter with Fukuyama', *New Left Review*, 193 (1992), 95.
[24] *The Production of Space*, trans. Donald Nicholson-Smith (Oxford: Blackwell, 1991), 23.

Though the exhaustion of nationalist ideology is a given for Tóibín ('I loathe everything about it [1916], every single moment'), the 1790s is arguably the pivotal decade in the evolution of modern Ireland, the states and the nation(s). The Wexford Republic, Boolavogue, Vinegar Hill, New Ross, Enniscorthy—these are the still resonant sites where the United Irishmen sought to plant the Tree of Liberty. The failure of 1798 does not diminish its continuing allure for the Republican imagination of Stewart Parker and Tom Paulin, for example, and no single event, including the Famine, has provoked such intense commemoration and debate in Ireland. But how does Tóibín's imaginative geography, his regionalism, intersect with the state's homogenization of space, its crushing of all that defines Enniscorthy as a unique cultural sphere? When Fukuyama proclaims 'it matters very little what strange thoughts occur to people in Albania or Burkino Faso',[25] geography becomes one of the conditions dictating entry into the public sphere, of deciding who is within and without history. How, then, in a context that treats certain geographical sites as irrelevant, can Tóibín proclaim the end of history in the precise location of Enniscorthy? How can a site saturated with that 'element in history that is not history', a Republican imagination of heroic resistance and rebellion, provide a 'rational' historical memory soldered to the historiography and geography of the twenty-six-county state? Through these questions, I want to argue, Tóibín's liberalism and regionalism collide.

II ONCE A CATHOLIC?

History for Tóibín commences not with Tone's idealism but with the immediate, physical reality of the institutional church and Catholic rural nationalism. The immediacy, complexity, and occasionally contradictory nature of this reality is a constant theme which his much-praised prose style conveys.[26] Yeats con-

---

[25] 'End of History?', 9.
[26] See D. J. Taylor, 'Just like Old Troubled Times', *Independent* (26 Sept. 1992); Bill Maxwell, 'One Blooming Good Yarn', *Irish Independent* (19 Sept. 1992); Frederic Lindsay, 'Against All Better Judgement', *Scotsman* (12 Sept. 1992); Linda Grant, 'A Sentence beyond Words', *Independent on Sunday* (13 Sept. 1992); John

vinced himself that the poet is never the bundle of accidents and incoherence that sits down to breakfast,[27] and his doctrine of the mask enabled a secondary self, far removed from the chaotic configuration of accidents and mishaps that comprise the quotidian world. There is no single central vision in Tóibín, no concept such as Yeats's 'unity of being' similarly capable of organizing the Irish experience into a whole. His imagination is inaugurated and impeded by 'the real imaginable time' of Catholic nationalism; a landscape devoid of these components is literally unimaginable, for it would involve erasing a part of his self.

The Cathedral in *The Sign of the Cross* is thus a site for becoming and for mourning, for an individual imagination and communal remembrance. As 'the beginning of real imaginable time', the Cathedral initiated the process by which Catholics such as his father become conscious agents in history. It made possible the narrative Tóibín now interrogates so that total abjection or transgression of that narrative is never an option. Certain things are not subject to the chaos of free choice for the citizens of Ireland, the people who sit down each day to breakfast in the Republic. Tóibín's prose style chronicles this reality in which no vague consensus or rhetoric of classlessness is possible. The point is not to see Ireland as a nation, an imagined community, but a set of clashing interests, to deal with the grubbiness of Irish politics after Independence and partition, to see it, to quote his criticism of Kiberd, as 'a politics rife with opportunism, hypocrisy and failure'.

The larger scheme of *The Sign of the Cross* enacts this complicated association. Each Easter during the nineties Tóibín left Ireland to tour Europe and report on Catholicism, mostly in Eastern European countries where the relationship between religion and the state was being renegotiated in the wake of communism. These tours are recounted in *The Sign of the Cross* (the analogy between Ireland and Eastern Europe is invited but never fully explored). Easter in Ireland, of course, entwines Catholicism and nationalism through the commemoration of

---

Lanchester, 'Justice of a Family Man', *Guardian* (10 Sept. 1992). Tóibín's most recent novel, *The Blackwater Lightship*, was nominated for the 2000 Booker prize.

[27] 'A General Introduction for my Work', in *Essays and Introductions* (Basingstoke: Macmillan, 1961), 509.

the 1916 Rising. The yearly flight from the commemoration of rebellion and blood sacrifice, martyrdom and regeneration, and the continuing relevance of 1916 to Northern politics, is the book's basic structural principle. Exploring Catholicism's relationship to Auschwitz and anti-Semitism in Poland, to socialism in Spain, the status of Catholics in Protestant England—an acquired, secular, and international knowledge now confronts inherited and local Catholic assumptions, as Easter is no longer a ritual invocation of a single, fixed historical event but a process dispersed across state boundaries. *The Sign of the Cross* physically demonstrates that such boundaries and histories are porous and intertwined, not immutable and separatist. The journeys perform a physical and symbolic erosion (a key metaphor for Tóibín) of the ideology of 1916 (at least as construed by him), which claimed the absolute sovereignty of the island as a forum for Irish meaning. They aim to demonstrate that ethnic affiliation no longer binds the individual to a single historical narrative, that it is possible to pick and mix promiscuously from a European Catholic heritage, and that there is a 'real imaginable time' beyond the annual commemoration of 1916 which does not negate the narrative inaugurated by Enniscorthy's Cathedral.

But tourism and travel in this fashion are inherently elitist. The mobility to pursue meaning across a range of European sites requires wealth and leisure time. What the yearly return to Enniscorthy acknowledges are the imaginative, political, economic, and territorial boundaries that still surround the individual and collective memories of the people, as he puts it, who actually live in the country. Irish Catholic identity emerges as a still very specific ethnic formation located in a given place and a given history.[28] Tóibín's intellectual and spiritual journey must orbit round Enniscorthy's enduring specificity; the grand narrative of Irish nationalist history that still operates in his birthplace. The meaning available to his family is not, as in Bolger, always entwined with placelessness (the actual and symbolic Coventry to which Sean Sweeney's mother was sent in *A Second Life*); his horizon of meaning is the 'truth' which his family

[28] Stuart Hall, 'The Local and the Global: Globalization and Ethnicity', in Anne McClinctock, Aamir Mufti, and Ella Shohat (eds.), *Dangerous Liaisons: Gender, Nation, and Postcolonial Perspectives* (Minnesota: University of Minnesota Press, 1997), 175.

extracts from history, even as he recognizes the implicit bias of the version manufactured. The destiny of form is conferred upon this 'truth' by its progressive transmission through generations, which is why, in one of Tóibín's wilier comments, 'there was no revisionism in Enniscorthy'. The form his destiny will take, then, is not finally a matter of discursive negotiation.

The Sign of the Cross is a progressive expansion of the Catholic narrative inaugurated by the Cathedral. In one sense it provides the equivalent of the international percussion of events across Europe that generated the 1798 Rising in Wexford: for if Tóibín as a post-nationalist is divorced from 1798's Republican politics, he wants to offer an alternative that is not Catholic and parochial but equally expansive and fraternal, a genuinely international inheritance. A major theme in Irish social life since the Famine has been the inexorable rise of the Catholic bourgeoisie and farming classes, a communal inheritance that now confronts a metropolitan and mostly secular present in which individualism demands primacy. The book's pivotal scene reflects this. An intensely emotional therapeutic session between Tóibín, a Protestant psychoanalyst, and a prostitute is organized through Tóibín's work with *Magill*. In other words, those elements of Irish society which challenge Enniscorthy's Catholic nationalist assumptions—Protestantism, prostitution, and Tóibín—combine to enable access to an unresolved trauma surrounding his father's death and burial in the Cathedral. The real imaginable communal time of the Cathedral cooperates with psychoanalysis, a clinical practice which emphasizes unconscious aspects of the individual. Tóibín's repeated blessings over his father's body are a symbolic reconciliation with these communal origins. 'I saw it now as the cross which the altar boy had carried in front of my father's coffin as it had wheeled down the centre aisle of Enniscorthy cathedral, but I was not sure' (*TSOTC*, 138).

'The sign of the cross' is taken from Beckett's short story 'The Expelled', and like Bolger, Tóibín warms to Beckett's scepticism towards Irish nationalism. Invited to read in Dublin at a government-sponsored commemorative ceremony of the seventy-fifth anniversary of 1916, his instinct is to read from 'First Love':

What constitutes the charm of our country, apart of course from its scant population, and this without the meanest help of any contraceptive, is that it is all derelict, with the sole exception of history's ancient faeces. These are ardently sought after, stuffed and carried in procession. Wherever nauseated time has dropped a nice fat turd you will find our patriots, sniffing it up on all fours, their faces on fire.[29]

This detachment escapes Tóibín. For what Beckett excoriates is never in Enniscorthy just a literary, intellectual, or political conviction. The droppings of 'nauseated time' are converted through the commemoration ceremonies into a narrative that is not endlessly without meaning; its procession produces and transmits a meaning that achieves the destiny of form and realizes itself as one of the continuities, the myths underpinning the idea of community. Declining the invitation to a metropolitan commemoration is an intellectual choice of little emotional consequence; refusing the Enniscorthy ritual, however, involves a profound spiritual and physical exile.

He asked me to join other descendants, mostly grandchildren, of the men who had fought in the Easter Rebellion in the town of Enniscorthy, where I was born and where my grandfather had fought . . . this was closer to home. There would be no quoting Beckett in Enniscorthy. No one at any of the meetings to plan the march, I was assured, had expressed the slightest doubt about the Rising; no one knew anything about revisionism; it had filtered from the universities to the middle classes in the cities, but not beyond. People in Enniscorthy were simply proud that their forebears had been involved in the Rising. I would love to have marched with them. I wandered around Seville that Easter wishing things were simpler, wishing that I was not in two minds about everything.[30]

The simultaneous desire to end and endure history, to participate in a historical narrative one knows to be bankrupt, renders contemporary time uninhabitable: the Cathedral, the inaugurator of real imaginable time, encourages the intrusion of 1916 into the present as politics rather than history, thereby evacuating the present of a meaning based on Ireland as a 'set of clashing

[29] Tóibín, 'New Ways of Killing Your Father', 6.
[30] Ibid. 6; see also Tóibín's *Homage to Barcelona* (London: Simon & Schuster, 1990).

interests'. The consensus to which Tóibín refers regarding the legitimacy of the Rising is anything but vague. But his flight from the commemoration is more than a political gesture. His father is the author of a historical narrative of 1798 which emphasized Catholic oppression,[31] so that the same value-laden narrative of tradition, continuity and particularism that fuels contemporary Republicanism underpins his own familial and communal history. The struggle with history is partly Oedipal; the oppositions of termination and prolongation, ending and enduring, are actually associates because, for Tóibín, nationalist history and the nationalist father are both connected to the idea of an authentic origin. The father, as the author of a certain value-laden narrative of that history, bequeaths a version against which Tóibín is fundamentally opposed. Tóibín possesses, then, a history he has not authored and which refuses to allow him to be the author, the agent of his own actions. The revision of his father's narrative is hence always a psychological as well as political process. Writing of his first visit to Barcelona, Tóibín 'saw it as a place where I could be free. But more than anything I saw it in black and white. Franco, the police and the apparatus of the state were evil: the dissidents were good. It would be easier than Ireland where these lines are never clear. I was looking for a mainland, somewhere whose narrative I could follow with respect and wonder.'

'Respect and wonder', arguably, are qualities conspicuously lacking in Pakenham's depiction of his father's history, but they are equally absent from those dissidents he admires like Beckett. This passage powerfully catalogues the confusion a post-nationalist landscape entails and points to his writing's larger project: to offer a sustained analysis of a post-nationalist, Catholic culture from the perspective of an affiliate, someone emotionally attached to its traditionally sustaining myths but eager to move beyond the remit such myths dictate. Like McCarthy, Tóibín is possessed by a myth he is content to explore. No Beckett exists in Enniscorthy, no scepticism of nationalist grand narratives, because that history is never straightforwardly externalized and objectified. The Rising never exists outside its embodiment in the forms of community it

---

[31] Published by Dermot Bolger's New Island Press: Michael Tóibín, *Enniscorthy: History and Heritage* (Dublin: New Island Books, 1998).

enables, hence it is not possible to rid Enniscorthy of what sustains it as an enduring, specific community.[32]

The last injunction of Ivor Brown, the Protestant psychiatrist, is to visit his father's grave and listen to jazz; that is, to combine a commemoration of his origins with a radically synchronic, spontaneous cultural form in which, as we saw in Crichton Smith, individual elements are never harmonized into a greater whole.[33] The parameters of Tóibín's individual consciousness and its associative hinterland are expanded, but they retain Enniscorthy's indelible print to reveal a narrative that, no matter how implicated in the lives of others, remains authored by his own consciousness. The Cathedral is thus no longer the exclusive inaugurator of his imagination; like the jazz, it has to concede and embrace an individuation that enables a corporate structure to flourish.

What ends in the last chapter, 'The Ends of History', then, is a narrative based exclusively on Enniscorthy's Cathedral. The key trope here is renovation. Because Enniscorthy can't be rid entirely of a narrative which is structuring its present, the best alternative is to renovate the structure we are forced to inhabit. The Cathedral, eroded by time, undergoes repair, and an ecumenical service in the local Protestant church offers Catholics the opportunity of worship. These renovations are a symbolic and actual admission of the Cathedral's inability to host all that Enniscorthy now contains. For so long a foundational site for Irish nationalism, Enniscorthy now confronts the moment when inherited forms and structures are no longer adequate to the Republic's predicaments. But this is not a post-Catholic landscape, and part of Tóibín's larger project is to cement the idea that renovation does not mean reinvention:

---

[32] See Gearóid Ó Crualaoich, 'Responding to the Rising', in Máirín Ní Dhonnchadha and Theo Dorgan (eds.), *Revising the Rising* (Derry: Field Day, 1991), 50–71.

[33] See Seán Healy, 'Interview with Michael Longley conducted by Dermot Healy', *Southern Review*, 31/3 (Summer 1995), 556: 'I've always enjoyed jazz, but I took to it in a big way the year I got married. It's important for a formalist like me to be reminded of the possibilities of improvisation. The spontaneity of jazz is one of the best anti-dotes against authoritarianism, totalitarianism. That's why its emergence in the century is of the greatest cultural importance. I would suggest that jazz is the twentieth-century's most significant contribution to the culture of the world. The Nazis hated it. They were frightened of swing. Syncopation is the opposite of the goose-step.'

Our Cathedral was built on a larger site at the top of the hill. It was a massive towering structure. When it opened in the 1840s, it must have been the first time that people had reason to pay attention to the clock, to arrive somewhere all at the same time, to remain quiet for long periods, to stand up together, sit down together, allow others to pass, to wait their turn. It was where a certain sort of civilisation began in the town. (*TSOTC*, 293)

Time, order, and social cohesion are synonymous with the Cathedral but do not disappear upon its demise. Nor does the local particularity of Enniscorthy depend entirely upon the Cathedral's continued existence in the same form. Tóibín's own provenance continues to be recognized—'My parents were married in this church. I was baptised here. I watched my father's coffin being wheeled down this church' (*TSOTC*, 293)—but it no longer requires a Protestant other as an essential element of its self-definition: the ecumenical service is intended to signal the end of a history predicated on these kinds of conflictual oppositions. Watching a plaque of a Protestant soldier from 1798, Tóibín delivers the epitaph for the historical narrative begun in 1846:

He must have been up there on Vinegar Hill during the battle of 1798, and he must have been around for the slaughter afterwards, which I heard so much about when I was a child. We were in his church now; we had been invited. Protestant service as well as Mass would be said here in the morning. No one else was very interested in this plaque, or this sectarian legacy. The plaque was a memorial to a past which we would not repeat. History had come to an end in Enniscorthy. (*TSOTC*, 295)

The narrative Tóibín seeks is finally discovered within a Republic liberated of a conflictual past ritually finding expression through commemoration and spectacle. The return from Europe each year reinforces the idea that Ireland, so long an island perched on the periphery of England and Europe, is now a mainland, a state, a cultural space which offers its citizens the opportunity to believe that they are at the centre of one's own world. Tóibín's liberalism would seem to have found its own authentic, secular and democratic home.

In its criss-crossing of national boundaries, its provision of a series of multiple texts with no single authentic experience, its resistance to any isolated or insular definition of Irish Catholicism, and its exposure of the constructed nature of boundaries, *The Sign of the Cross* is a quintessentially postmodern narrative. As Maxine Feifer notes in *Tourism and History*, the self-conscious contemporary traveller (what she calls the post-tourist) knows his non-tourist status, knows 'he cannot evade the condition of outsider'.[34] The post-tourist is alienated from all he briefly intersects with. He inevitably questions traditional forms of community and representation by transgressing geographical, political, and, through narratives of travel, textual limits. He is inevitably inscribed within new intellectual and cultural formations. This, in theory, is the postmodern condition of the traveller.

The continual return to Enniscorthy, however, demonstrates the permanence of certain boundaries. Enniscorthy is never straightforwardly equivalent to other European Catholic cultures. As the site for a new way of thinking about the way Ireland might be thought of, it does not just redraw the cultural map, it effects an alteration in the principle of mapping. A heightened consciousness of space and place, in a globalized system of shifting nation states, paradoxically involves denuding Enniscorthy of its most conspicuous historical element, the confrontations of 1798. The particularism of the region never makes it exceptional, even as the rhetoric of equality never erases the reality of difference. Hence the use of renovation as a trope: adaptation, not abjection, is Tóibín's aim. For it is pointless to affirm history in the light of contemporary 'new realities' when that history has rarely accepted the real as the ultimate index of value and truth. Part of the truth of Enniscorthy's history lies in what people believe to have happened, and this has no necessary correspondence with the sequentially ordered 'facts' of professional historical narratives. The different versions of history offered by his father and Pakenham do not arise out of confusion about what happened, but out of a desire to explain different sets of feelings arising out of the same events.

---

[34] *Tourism in History: From Imperial Rome to the Present Day* (New York: Stern & Day, 1986), 271.

III   BETWEEN THE FOUR COURTS AND BOOLAVOGUE

The personal and cultural reconstructions required in the wake of nationalism are embodied in Eamon Redmond, a Wexford-born, Dublin-based High Court judge at the centre of Tóibín's second novel, *The Heather Blazing*. The title is taken from 'Boolavogue', a ballad commemorating a slaughter at Vinegar Hill near Enniscorthy in 1798 where an estimated 20,000 people are thought to have been killed in two weeks.[35] Eamon Redmond oscillates physically and emotionally between Dublin and Cush, County Wexford, between the centre of the twenty-six-county state and a foundational site for a Republican memory focused on territory and the island. In this portrayal of a society 'where cherished ideals are now in a state of terminal collapse',[36] Eamon's service to the state—the classical neutral instrument of mediation between the various constituencies that make up the nation[37]—and defence of the constitution is always at odds with his nationalist heritage. He is emotionally maimed by his proximity to the nationalism which previously nourished him. Named after de Valera, his surname also evokes John Redmond, leader of the Home Rule party that accepted the twenty-six-county state.[38] The focus is on the tensions and ambivalences (in Freud's sense, the direction towards the same person of contrary—affectionate and hostile—feelings) within the Catholic culture of post-Independence Ireland, most of which Eamon Redmond's biography incorporates: his family trace their nationalist heritage through 1798, 1916, and the civil war, though he now works for a Fíanna Fáil party that has excised this nationalist legacy from its contemporary self-identity; he defends a Catholic constitution, though he no longer believes in God. Eamon no longer actually believes in the principle of belief,

[35] See Nicholas Furlong, 'Local or Cosmopolitan?: The Strategic Importance of Wexford in 1798' in Keogh and Furlong (eds.), *Mighty Wave*, 109–17.
[36] Neil Corcoran, *After Yeats and Joyce: Reading Modern Irish Literature* (Oxford: Oxford University Press, 1997), 98.
[37] Immanuel Wallerstein, *Geopolitics and Geoculture: Essays on the Changing World-System* (Cambridge: Cambridge University Press, 1991), 10.
[38] A point Tom Herron also notes in 'ContamiNation: Patrick McCabe and Colm Tóibín's Pathographies of the Republic', in Harte and Parker (eds.), *Contemporary Irish Fiction*, 189.

whether spiritual or political, but he remains deeply and silently marked by the complex apostolic heritage of Cush and the legacy of his father: 'The handwriting, when he wrote something quickly, had become exactly the same as his father's, a set of round squiggles, indecipherable to most others' (*THB*, 4).

Underlying judgements which aspire to be value-free—neither moral or subjective, but simply a reflection of what the Constitution requires—is this highly personal, hermetic world. The issues before Eamon are deeply moral but his judgements are not.[39] In one sense he inhabits the sanitized, apolitical, private space of Michael in Bolger's *Emily's Shoes*. But where the skeletal remains beneath that space signal a catastrophic dimension to Irish history, the memory of loss as an intrinsic, ineradicable element of the Irish public sphere, the term 'the heather blazing' rebukes any aspiration to contrive at a loss of such memory. On 26 May 1798, heather was set ablaze to indicate the gathering points for the rebels around Boolavogue, and the ballad of the same name supplies the novel's title with the necessary heritage that informs Eamon's judgements for the state:

He cited the facts of the case: the handicapped child who needs constant care and would need such care . . . for the rest of his life . . . He tried to set the case out clearly, factually, coldly . . . He now began to summarise the legal precedent governing the state's duties and the individual's rights. He cited a number of American cases (not intrinsically Irish) which had come up in the course of the hearing. He went on to explain that there was nothing in the constitution which either stated or implied that the citizen had an inalienable right to free hospital treatment. The state's functions and responsibilities had to cease at a certain point; the state had freedoms and rights as well as the citizen. As he read the judgement he became even more certain of the rightness of his judgement, and began to see as well that it might be important in the future as a lucid and direct analysis of the limit to the duties of the state. (*THB*, 6)

The deracinated accent of the state has no necessary connection with Irish activities—an American precedent is more relevant than Enniscorthy—and geographical and historical differences are unrecognizable in the placeless, present time of the state. In the novel, the state is the guarantor of and metaphor for a new public sphere in which citizenship replaces community,

---

[39] Herron, 'ContamiNation', 168.

the general the specific, the present the historical, the clarity of written judgements an oral history imbibed in Wexford. And most importantly, a twenty-six-county Republic replaces an Irish nationalism based on the ideal of a unitary island. The cumulative effect of such political and cultural transitions in Eamon is finally the replacement, or sacrifice, of a portion of the self, for we know Eamon primarily by what he sees and does, by the bundle of accidents that constitute his life. His judgements for the state demand an allegiance to a general principle of freedom that requires a suppression of the will. In Hobbesian terms, the state induces the citizen to decide to give up individual will and act freely having taken this decision not to disobey.[40] Only when the citizen is prepared to abdicate this right to disobey can he or she enjoy freedom, a principle flatly renounced by such ballads as 'Boolavogue', where a single rebel hand, the individual agent, acts alone to enable the emergence of a deeper form of communal resistance:

> *A rebel hand set the heather blazing*
> *and brought the neighbours from far and near*
>
> (*THB*, 74)

The emotional corrosion the state induces in Eamon proceeds from the suppression of this same will. He is required to advocate the state's rights on child and psychiatric care and imprison three suspected IRA members, public cases which register as profoundly personal issues—his daughter, wife, and family are affected by his judgements. Because the relationship between private and public in Ireland is inevitably porous, his son's query on a judgement against a pregnant schoolgirl expelled from a Catholic school is automatically converted into a subversive threat against the state: ' "Keep up the good work," Donal said to him as they shook hands. "The Four Courts will never fall again, you can be sure of that," he said in reply, smiling sourly' (*THB*, 123). Revolution, the violent eruption of history into the present, animated his predecessors; preserving the state as the terminus of his family's nationalist commitment now involves inoculating the present time, the only time the state

---

[40] Quentin Skinner, *Liberty before Liberalism* (Cambridge: Cambridge University Press, 1997), 8.

acknowledges, against all other processes. In other words, like Glenville in McCarthy's *Asya and Christine*, Eamon must protect the state from Irish history.

This is why coastal erosion is the novel's key trope. As each year the homes of Eamon's lifelong friends subside into the sea, the iconography of nationalist politics, the absolute sovereignty of the island, literally disappears along with (as in Bolger) the possibility of representing Irish society through stable topographical imagery. But unlike Bolger, whose narratives enact the disjuncture between a rural past and an increasingly urbanized present, Tóibín's is a straight line of historical development. The novel is a *Bildungsroman* for both Eamon and Ireland, where maturity involves a physical and political distance from at least some of what Enniscorthy's real imaginable time represents for Tóibín—the faith, soil, and nationalism of the Cathedral's traditional narrative. Eamon's annual return to Cush, however, is, as in *The Sign of the Cross*, part of an attempt to locate a fixed space beyond the process of erosion, despite (as the metaphor invites) the relentless tide of history. For what is under most pressure in the novel is the oral transmission of history indicated by the title. As a child, Eamon occupies a castle Spenser once lived in, symbolically reclaiming Ireland from one of the earliest systematic colonizers, and collects pikes used by the 1798 Rebels.[41] Both events are understood as part of a highly personal, tendentious narrative whose meaning has little to do with its relationship to 'facts':

Our grandmother now on our mother's side . . . she was brought here. It was the time of the evictions . . . she knew the men of 'Ninety-eight', the woman looked into the fire and then back at the two visitors. 'She would have been too young to remember it, but they told her about it, and it was she who always said that they came down this way and that was the end of them. That's all I remember now. There was a man who used to come here and they used to talk about it'. (*THB*, 23)

This is wonderfully informative and completely imprecise. It keeps all participants anonymous while inserting Eamon's family into a grand narrative of Irish liberation, and their historical agency is directly connected to their ability to voice this

---

[41] A theme also touched upon in Tóibín's first novel, *The South* (London: Picador, 1990).

rendition. Yet one key trope in the novel, which we also saw in Bolger, is the progressive loss of speech. Both his father and wife lose the power to speak, while Eamon's marriage fails primarily because of an inability to communicate openly.[42] These strokes are never just physical. His father, a teacher of history and geography, the classic ingredients of an Irish nationalist narrative, is no longer able to express history as a coherent and seamless entity:

But there was a day when his father got stuck in the story, when nothing came from him except vague sounds, and his whole face seemed drawn and twisted. (*THB*, 149)

For as long as he could remember, his father had made a speech at the final rally in the Market Square, but this time he would not be able, his voice was not clear enough. (*THB*, 159)

Eamon speaks for his father in front of Lemass and de Valera, and works as a speech writer for Fianna Fáil; but this present-centred rhetoric is an ironic inversion of the party's nationalist origins, as it colludes with what sanitizes history of its catastrophic dimension. The loss of memory and the loss of speech defeat the memory of loss. Questioned by a historian on a report that advised the Irish government to treat the North as a different society, a place apart, a report he helped prepare, Eamon

nodded and encouraged the historian to go on, all the time thinking back to the evening in his grandmother's house when he first heard the story. He kept listening, more and more sure that he should not mention the story about his father and Cathal Brugha, these men should consign it to silence, as his father had done with the names of the men who did the killings in Enniscorthy. (*THB*, 180)

For this guardian of the state the professional historian is a tame inquisitor. What is personally and politically destabilizing is a history not beholden to 'facts', but one in which the present has a dynamic relationship with a past that makes itself available for contemporary use; history as a force from which values might be derived instead of the sealed purity of a present-centred constitution. In this sense, *The Heather Blazing* anatomizes the radical potential of such historical memory which *The Sign of the Cross* tries to terminate.

---

[42] Herron, 'ContamiNation', 183–7, develops this aspect of the novel.

The key tropes in the novel, coastal erosion and swimming, combine around these same issues. Quizzed by Donal on the response of the *Irish Times* to his judgement against a pregnant schoolgirl at a Catholic school, Eamon responds: ' "It's a funny day when a newspaper starts asking legal judgements". He was suddenly angry. "But I don't think we can discuss the case, if you don't mind. I'd rather go back to discussing coastal erosion or the temperature of the Irish sea." ' (*THB*, 119). Again and again Eamon immerses himself in the waters off Cush. As a child, swimming with his father seemed to locate a point of profound but vague equilibrium:

His father was waving to him and swimming in a dog-paddle stroke towards the shore. He moved out until he, too, had to jump to avoid the waves. He wondered how you could get the courage to dive in: what would those first moments be like? 'don't throw me in' . . . 'let go my neck' his father said again. He waited for a moment then jumped as best he could into the water . . . He was out of his depth now, but able to keep himself up in the water without his father's help. When his father turned and floated, he floated too, with his head right back in the water, his body relaxed, but enough air in his lungs to keep him from sinking . . . Soon, they climbed up the cliff, each helping the other, taking his father's sandals when he needed both his hands to pull himself up. They were hungry now, and they *knew* that their dinner would be on the table for them when they got back to the Cullens's house. (*THB*, 54; emphasis in original)

This is a community still unselfconsciously organized around principles of allegiance and succession, hence the sea is not yet a corrosive force and the cliff is not eroding but solid. Somewhere between land and sea Eamon floats independently in a moment before history insisted that his public and private worlds irretrievably intersect. What is truly impressive in this presentation is that Eamon's attempts to recover this moment are never presented as simple nostalgia. The yearly migration to these waters, in search of that same point of equilibrium, is never fully explicated, because the point of Tóibín's language is not to explain, but through a series of active verbs convey what it is the protagonist feels:

He turned and walked slowly into the sea, ignoring the waves and wading without hesitation once the water was up to his waist. Without stopping, he dived in and swam out, lifting his head only to take in air,

trying to exercise his arms to relax the muscles in his neck . . . growing
tired rested his head on the water and floated. He closed his eyes, unsure
now whether he was floating in towards the shore or out towards the
horizon, but on opening them he found that he had let himself float a
good distance northwards and swam back until he was close to where
he had left his ruck-sack. (*THB*, 208)

The symbolic lack of moorings is associated with his work for a
state that denies his father's nationalism. And it is this indeterminate note, this unrelenting incommensurability, that ends the
novel. The father of his daughter's son is unknown, so that
Eamon's attempt to recapture this same equilibrium with his
grandchild inevitably fails. There is no one single lineage or
principle that can account for the future the family confronts.
Michael, Eamon's grandchild, possesses an incomplete knowledge of his origins; his refusal to submit to the rites Eamon
underwent, the relentless process of erosion and resistance of
Cush's nationalist past, signals the end of one kind of history.
Niamh's son does not internalize history as the search for a
surrogate father:

Eamon knew that the water would be a shock for Michael. He stood at
the edge for a while, drinking in the sun and watching Niamh as she
swam away from them. Then he began to wade out, talking quietly to
his grandson to soothe him. He jumped at each wave until Michael
began to watch for waves and laugh as each one approached. Eamon
held his grandson under the arms and lifted him high so that the sun was
on his back, and then he lowered him into the water until his legs were
wet, holding him firmly all the time. He ducked him down into the
water and out again, but it was too much for him. He was frightened.
Eamon began to carry him slowly in towards the shore. (*THB*, 245)

A striking feature of *The Heather Blazing* is the ordinariness of
the language. The focus is relentlessly forensic, comprehending
the external world via the tiniest details; the text does not
obscure or valorize these details, or make them representative
of any larger scheme, but instead reflects the persistence of the
mundane. Thus the exact same sentences—'Eamon Redmond
stood at the window looking down at the river which was deep
and brown after days of rain. He watched the colour, the mixture
of mud and water, and the small currents and pockets of movement within the flow' (*THB*, 1 and 177)—open sections one and
three. Eamon Redmond's complexity—the local 'currents and

pockets of movement' of his rather dull life within the general, dramatic flow of Irish history—is not lessened by the absence of political spectacle from his world, by the absence of the kind of tragic artifice that Yeats insisted, in his doctrine of the mask, was a prerequisite of the virtuous life:

> If we cannot imagine ourselves as different from what we are and assume that second self, we cannot impose a discipline upon ourselves, though we may accept one from others. Active virtue as distinguished from the passive acceptance of a current code is therefore theatrical, consciously dramatic, the wearing of a mask. It is the condition of arduous full life.[43]

This is an important theme for Tóibín, foregrounded in his review of Declan Kiberd's *Inventing Ireland*. Tóibín's refusal to participate in 'The Flaming Door', a government-sponsored commemoration of 1916 by literary and visual artists, not only rejects history as spectacle; it also rebukes the idea that culture should cooperate with or even sponsor political practice. Writers do not invent an imaginary realm in which individuals unconsciously interact; there is no parallel universe of a real and invented Ireland where, for example, Michael and Eamon might unite. Thus Gay Byrne, not Yeats, attracts Tóibín's considerable powers of analysis (and unusually fulsome praise). Chronicling daily life in the Republic reveals implacable ideological divisions in the public sphere which cannot be erased in the realm of culture:

> For the next twenty years 'The Late Late Show' would stage the drama of Irish life, the play between the established and the new whose intensity was only matched in the emerging countries of the third world . . . It was a drama called the Republic of Ireland, in five parts, with ads in between, relayed to every household in the country . . . middle Ireland entering its complex head . . . There is a war in Ireland which Gay Byrne has been dramatising for the past twenty years. Between reality and the perception of reality, between de Valera's vision of Ireland and Patrick Kavanagh's *The Great Hunger*.[44]

Cairns Craig has noted that an important element of the Kailyard was not just its stereotypical view of Scottishness but

---

[43] 'Per Amica Silentia Lunae', in *Mythologies* (London: Macmillan, 1962), 334.

[44] Colm Tóibín, *The Trial of the Generals: Selected Journalism* (Dublin: Raven Arts Press, 1990), 86–93.

the way it obscured Scotland's view of itself. The rhetoric of cultural difference made opaque the reality of economic and social division, and also Scotland's indigenous abilities to bring about actual change. Tóibín's criticism of the Irish revival echoes this same point. Any extrapolation of nationality from writing is deplored, any infatuation with general ideas that seek to penetrate through to an original cause of the Irish condition, like Kiberd's post-colonialism, is fatally flawed. Theory is always divorced from the tangible realities that inspire it, while Tóibín's own liberalism is, apparently, a clear-sighted and pragmatic reflection of the island's enduring divisions.

IV   THE MARCHING SEASON

The political consequences of this aesthetic distinction are at their most legible in *Bad Blood: A Walk along the Irish Border*, a travel narrative which documents some of the most obstinately tangible realities of Irish history. Here is where Tóibín's liberalism creaks under the weight of a sectarian history that refuses to end. The book enacts Tóibín's belief that history can be reflected and recorded but not transformed, for it skirts along the perimeter of one of the areas Fukuyama described as irretrievably outwith history. Mixing metaphysical exposition and sociological observation, *Bad Blood* details his journey along the Northern Irish border in the summer of 1985, several months after the signing of the Anglo-Irish agreement, a document which, by formally acknowledging the Republic's role in certain internal affairs of Northern Ireland, caused bitter resentment amongst Northern Unionists. The Republic as a state seemed willing to embroil itself in Irish nationalism, a strategy which offended many Irish liberals. Mary Robinson, for instance, resigned from the Irish Labour party in protest at its support for the agreement.[45] The premiss of the book, the political context it seeks to occupy, is an expansion of a phrase in Tóibín's review of

---

[45] See Garret Fitzgerald, 'The Origins and Rationale of the Anglo-Irish Agreement of 1985' and Paul Arthur, 'The Anglo-Irish Agreement: A Device for Territorial Management', in Dermot Keogh and Michael H. Haltzel (eds.), *Northern Ireland and the Politics of Reconciliation* (Cambridge: Cambridge University Press, 1993), 189–207 and 208–25 respectively.

Roy Foster's *Paddy and Mr Punch*: 'No one wants territory, merely a form of words ambiguous enough to make them feel at home . . . when I read a book like this, or Thomas Pakenham's *The Year of Liberty*, I know that I am not part of the consensus of which books like these are part'.[46]

Joe Cleary has pointed to the 'discursive invisibility' of partition in Irish cultural discourse, the various modes of 'censorship, including self-censorship, [that] have generated elaborate circumlocutions or forms of doublespeak that express positions on the partition question even when they appear to sidestep that uncomfortable topic altogether'.[47] *Bad Blood* aims to discover 'a form of words' ambiguous enough to manoeuvre between nationalism and unionism, Protestantism and Catholicism, revisionism and traditionalism. The journey cannot contest or transform territorial boundaries already established by the Boundary Commission formed in 1921. Tóibín's route has already been decided by history, so that complete volition or agency is neither possible nor necessary because, in Hobbes's terms, the freedom to undertake this journey arises only when he accepts the limitations imposed upon him by both states. The book thus contains a psychology, a history, and a politics.[48] In this limited sense, history has ended; the journey's beginning, route, and end is predicated on the notion that history is indelibly inscribed on the landscape and therefore exhausted as a dialectical process. The individual agency celebrated in ballads like 'Boolavogue' is profoundly diluted as he is condemned to repeat what has already been decided. There is no attempt to make the Yeatsian distinction between active and passive virtue, that key word in classical republicanism, merely an acceptance of the current code. The terrain cannot be transformed, and the only available challenge is to procure a form of words that will enable him to endure the journey. This, then, in post-Independence Irish liberalism, is 'the condition of the arduous full life', this is the conclusion of history as Yeats and Irish cultural nationalists have traditionally understood it. But how does this museum of human history fit with Tóibín's liberalism? How can the 'end of history' be

---

[46] 'New Ways of Killing Your Father', 6.

[47] 'Partition and the Politics of Form in Contemporary Narratives of Northern Ireland', *Ireland and Cultural Studies*, special issue of *South Atlantic Quarterly*, 95/1 (Winter 1996), 227, 228. [48] See Anderson, *Zone of Engagement*, 345.

manipulated by the state to exclude certain groups as non-negotiable?

The only formal resource supporting Tóibín's trip is the Tyrone Guthrie Arts centre in Annaghmakerrig. This is a centre set up by Sir Tyrone Guthrie to give artists and writers free board during projects. Other than this practical support, he is alone. The larger scheme of the book thus becomes: how can the category of the aesthetic and the category of the individual, as a discrete subject, survive in a sectarian landscape that recognizes only the most polarized communal oppositions? The walk is full of moments which Mary Louise Pratt describes as 'contact zones': spaces in which peoples geographically and historically separate come into contact with each other and establish ongoing relationships.[49] Travel writing as a genre engages a narrator's individual consciousness with what is deemed to be alien, exotic, or other, and in Ireland this has traditionally meant the West.[50] For Tóibín, the southern, secular post-nationalist intellectual, the north is culturally and constitutionally set apart from 'the South' (perhaps explaining Seamus Deane's pithy dismissal of the book as 'futile').[51] Like Bolger's and Barry's anthologies, the genre implicitly acknowledges a separate reality for the North not so much by land, as by its inability to be incorporated into the 'real imaginable time' of the narrative initiated by the Cathedral in Enniscorthy. Travel writing, as Tim Youngs reminds us, can reveal much more of the society journeyed from than of the country apparently written about.[52] Bringing the Catholic baggage of Enniscorthy along the route ensures that the border is rendered, to adapt Joe Cleary's remarks on *The Crying Game*, invisible as a political construct. All issues ultimately relate back to a fixed register of identity, the Cathedral, which is structurally incapable of diagnosing the border in terms of politics and power.[53]

[49] *Imperial Eyes: Travel Writing and Transculturation* (London: Routledge, 1992), 1–10.
[50] Barbara O'Connor and Michael Cronin (eds.), *Tourism in Ireland: A Cultural Analysis* (Cork: Cork University Press, 1992).
[51] Dympna O'Callaghan, 'An Interview with Seamus Deane', *Social Text*, 38 (1994), 40.
[52] 'Buttons and Souls: Some Thoughts on Commodities and Identity in Women's Travel Writing', *Studies in Travel Writing*, 1 (Spring 1997), 117–40.
[53] Cleary, 'Partition and the Politics of Form', 263.

This is how Toibin's much-praised, simple, forensic prose style should be viewed. The tone is always non-judgemental, non-evaluative, for there is no possibility of Tóibín imagining ourselves as different from what we are. The active virtue Yeats endorsed is part of the project of imagining a nation, an entity called Ireland; this passive acceptance of the current code is part of the project of naturalizing the state, North and South. The style chronicles the inalienable separateness of both states. The facts, it would seem, speak for themselves, as the narrative naturalizes the religious, cultural, and ethnic divisions under observation and the political states that accord with them.[54] The separate states are a symptom of a reality which is, a priori, irretrievably split along sectarian lines, and thus no further comment is necessary on differences incubated over centuries, no intrusive narrative evaluation need take place.[55] The solitary act of writing is thus analogous to the isolation of his journey. Writing provides a space that is somehow part of but removed from the complicated mesh of national boundaries and political borders he must physically inhabit. Tim Youngs's comments are suggestive here:

This intense concentration on literary travel as an individual, imaginative and creative phenomenon is profoundly indicative of the 'post-colonial' shift towards a deceptively democratic form of peregrination. Writing one's way out of position becomes the very marker of one's place . . . the concentration on writing as a process through which identity is realised may be a distraction from the political and cultural factors on which identity in fact depend.[56]

The state is a symptom, never a cause of the divisions he encounters, an inalienable element in the given order of things which his continually mobile, continually displaced status as a traveller cannot confront or change. Such a methodology has deep ideological implications, for Brendan Bradshaw's primary criticism of revisionist history is of the myopia of its professionalism, its

---

[54] See Thomas M. Wilson and Hastings Donnan, 'Nation, State and Identity at International Borders', in eid. (eds.), *Border Identities: Nation and State in International Frontiers* (Cambridge: Cambridge University Press, 1998), 1–31.

[55] Cleary, 'Partition and the Politics of Form', 267.

[56] 'Punctuating Travel: Paul Theroux and Bruce Chatwin', *Literature and History*, 6/2 (Autumn 1997), 79–81. For an evocative and commendably sceptical view of contemporary Ireland through a travel narrative, see Rebecca Solnit, *A Book of Migrations: Some Passages in Ireland* (London: Verso, 1997).

obsession with a value-free narrative that 'denies historians recourse to value judgements and, therefore, access to the kind of moral and emotional register necessary to respond to human tragedy'.[57] It lacks any tragic dimension, any capacity for registering the memory of loss, or in Bradshaw's phrase, the catastrophic dimension to Irish history. As Carol Kaplan puts it, the 'nomad represents a subject position that offers an idealised model of movement based on perpetual displacement', a strategy that prematurely disallows the possibility of Tóibín becoming an agent in his own history.[58] His progress along the border is, like Fukuyama's conception of history, relentlessly progressive: there is a determined refusal to engage with or be sidetracked by any idealistic theory of the irrational, of imperialism, or of nationalism, those elements which fuel the history that actually created the border. The route taken possesses a gravitational, teleological pull that implies the solution to any problems encountered are known in advance. Perry Anderson's claim that in Fukuyama's thesis, 'progress towards freedom now has only one path'[59] is a charge equally applied to Tóibín: any narrative not insolubly linked to the local and the real as they are encountered daily in the world is implicitly and explicity, consciously and unconsciously, rejected.

The commemoration of any historical event is inevitably selective, but by commencing history in *The Sign of the Cross* in the mid-1840s, just before the rise of a Catholic rural bourgeoisie (the same strategy that fuelled F. S. L. Lyons's *Ireland since the Famine*), Tóibín's narrative siphons the transformative potential of '98 from the body politic. The catastrophic dimension to Irish history, '98 and the Famine, is extinguished; the only narrative acknowledged is the narrative inaugurated by the Cathedral.[60] No other inspirational model can intrude, ensuring that all oppositional politics must be directed against unmasking the myths

---

[57] 'Nationalism and Historical Scholarship in Modern Ireland', reprod. in Ciarán Brady (ed.), *Interpreting Irish History: The Debate on Historical Revisionism* (Dublin: Four Courts Press, 1994), 204.

[58] Quoted in Youngs, 'Punctuating Travel', 83.

[59] *Zone of Engagement*, 282.

[60] 'The "pre-modern" quality puts the Famine beyond the reach of writers who came after it; and the speed with which society transformed itself . . . made the history of 1846, 1847 and 1848 in Ireland a set of erasures rather than a set of reminders' (Colm Tóibín, *The Irish Famine* (London: Profile Books, 1999), 66).

that Catholic nationalism has imposed on Irish life. Those radical themes that might challenge this scenario, like 1798, are excluded. In Hobbes's terms, Tóibín has abdicated his right to enjoy a complete historical consciousness in order to act freely within the confines of an unchanging state.

Tóibín's phrase, the 'form of words', taken from his review of Roy Foster's *Paddy and Mr Punch*, introduces the role of the aesthetic in state formation. In 1985 the Republic was convulsed by a series of highly fractious referendums on divorce, and it is this context that surrounds the aesthetic.

The result of the divorce referendum was made known the following Friday morning. It was clear and overwhelming: the country had voted no. I was in Monaghan, at Annaghmakerrig, the house which Sir Tyrone Guthrie had left to the Irish nation as a retreat for artists . . . He specified in his will, when leaving the house to the nation, that the artists should eat together in the evening. The house was supported by the Arts Councils, North and South; people came from both sides of the border. The area around the house was still a mixed society, with thriving Church of Ireland, Presbyterian and Catholic congregations. (*BB*, 49)

The artist's immediate context is the oppressive Catholic legislation of the Republic; the Guthrie centre provides a possible context, one in which religious difference is not synonymous with cultural and ethnic division. The Guthrie centre is of history, but because it contains and sponsors the aesthetic, it is not destined to repeat history as politics: it does not funnel historic divisions into the present moment. This presents culture as an ostensibly autonomous zone, but the disinterested autonomy of the aesthetic, the mythic solution it opposes to the surrounding sectarianism, not only leaves the role of the state in all this unchallenged, it also works as a set of border controls, actively sealing the Republic from contamination by a historical narrative in the North that shows no sign of ending.

The impact of the aesthetic is never fully explained, just glimpsed at irregular intervals when Tóibín has trouble with maps or travels down roads that end nowhere, have been abandoned, closed, or in some way become redundant. The map that points the way towards feeling at home does not rely on the accumulation of empirical detail. The aesthetic is disinterested in any form of knowledge that is oppositional, as Tóibín's exchange with a British soldier demonstrates. For if topography is no longer an adequate or stable symbol for the contemporary Irish condition, as the coastal erosion in *The Heather Blazing* symbolizes, cartography can no longer unproblematically reflect and represent that landscape. In other words, only the aesthetic can point the way towards feeling at home.

I saw the soldiers straight ahead . . . He showed me his map . . . The map was incredibly detailed, every house, every field, every road, carefully denoted and described. It would be impossible to go wrong with such a map. Different colours made everything clear. He laughed when I explained my plight with maps. I showed him my Michelin and my Ordnance, and he shook his head in wonder at how out-of-date they were. His was the map I should have, he said. (*BB*, 163)

The 'real imaginable time' of Enniscorthy, the wonderful imprecision of oral history, is replaced by militaristic facts and precision which make everything cognitively clear but imaginatively opaque. The soldier's laughter stems from the epistemological, even ontological gulf between his and Tóibín's map.[61] Faced with roads closed or controlled by the British military or Northern nationalism, Tóibín's map has to be created by transcending the immediate tangible realities of the conflict and trusting the aesthetic to ensure he avoids danger spots. 'None of the roads the soldier suggested was marked on my map . . . I had abandoned the Ordnance Survey map on the basis that it was better to carry a map with a few roads marked than a map with too many, some of which didn't exist' (*BB*, 170).

The Guthrie centre and the aesthetic thus offer the only realistic route through Irish history and politics. Tóibín has to map what Bolger called a 'private fictional universe' in order to negotiate this terrain. There is no possibility of changing the historical route he must take, just interpreting it as an inalienable element in the given order of things and avoiding any confrontation with it. The imagination that chronicles partition thus seals partition, finally accommodating its own segregation within inviolable state borders. For maps, as J. B. Hartley explains, are a major example of the interaction between a state polity and military technology.

---

[61] See J. B. Hartley, 'Maps, Knowledge, Power', in Denis Cosgrove and Stephen Daniels (eds.), *The Iconography of Landscape* (Cambridge: Cambridge University Press, 1988), 277–312.

Military maps are a small but vital cog in the technical infrastructure of the army in the field . . . Map knowledge allows the conduct of warfare by remote control so that, we may speculate, killing is more easily contemplated. Military maps not only facilitate the technical conduct of warfare, but also palliate the sense of guilt which arises from its conduct: the silent lines of the paper landscape foster the notion of a socially empty space.[62]

This 'socially empty space' (so similar to Lefebvre's view of the state as the space that flattens or crushes conflicts and contradictions in the social and cultural spheres) is given tacit assent by Tóibín's determination to adhere to already permanently inscribed, immutable borders between the Northern and Southern states. 'Works of art necessarily evolve in a dialectic of interests and disinterestedness', claims Adorno in *Aesthetic Theory*. Tóibín appropriates the aesthetic to enable him to stick unerringly to the state's border, to a space whose only rational interest is in preserving its disinterest in everything except the present moment in which its own being is comprehended. This is the impoverished dialectical space Tóibín's aesthetic wilfully occupies.[63] The cognitive map his aesthetic creates abdicates any possibility of a political agency that could deviate from this pre-programmed historical route. As David Harvey notes, 'Mapping is a discursive activity that incorporates power. The power to map the world in one way rather than another is a crucial tool in political struggles. Power struggles over mapping . . . are therefore fundamental moments in the production of discourses.'[64]

The passage on the Guthrie Centre occurs in the chapter entitled 'The Road to Darkley', scene of a sectarian massacre by the Irish National Liberation Army in 1985, and immediately afterwards in the narrative Tóibín comes across Swift's entry in the guest book at an eighteenth-century guesthouse:

> Glaslough with rows of books upon its shelves
> written by the Leslies all about themselves.
>
> (*BB*, 165)

[62] Ibid. 284.

[63] Theodore W. Adorno, *Aesthetic Theory*, trans. C. Lenhardt and ed. Gretel Adorno and Rolf Tiedemann (London: Routledge & Kegan Paul, 1984), 17.

[64] *Justice, Nature and the Geography of Difference* (Oxford: Blackwell, 1996), 112.

Swift is part of a cognitive map that enables Tóibín to confront and evade a militarized public space. Even on the road to Darkley, the aesthetic is glimpsed, inescapably caught up with politics but never necessarily political. For on both occasions, at the Guthrie centre and this guesthouse, the aesthetic offers sanctuary from the route Tóibín negotiates. It is not the representation of place that determines whether the aesthetic comes into existence but the place that is being represented: only those areas that fall within the remit of the narrative inaugurated by the Cathedral have the sanction of the aesthetic bestowed upon them.

The final effect of representing partition is the segregation of the imagination within the state that accords with its perceived originary moment. The last episode of 'The Road to Darkley' has Tóibín, and the pastor of the Darkley church where the massacre took place, point in opposite, completely incommensurate political and spiritual directions:

When Bob Bain came out we walked around the hall until we faced north towards Armagh. I pointed to the Catholic Cathedral jutting up out of the town. 'Would you like to have a church as big as that?' I asked him. He wouldn't, he said; what he had here was stronger and better, he was sure of that. (*BB*, 182)

The implicit point of the exchange, which utilizes the symbolic power of the Armagh Cathedral, home of the Catholic primate of all Ireland, is that each belongs to fundamentally different, absolutely irreconcilable historical narratives.

V   A PAPER LANDSCAPE

Brian Friel's *Translations*,[65] of course, famously mobilized cartography as a metaphor through which Ireland's colonial past might be addressed. In that play, the Donnelly twins kill Lieutenant Yolland, the British officer responsible for constructing a map in English of Irish place names, the stable system all imperial powers need to characterize people within certain fixed limits. The Donnelly twins never enter the text of *Translations*; they are in this sense uniquely untranslatable. If they signal the

[65] (Derry: Field Day, 1985).

IRA's association with a tradition of millenarian violence stemming from the eighteenth century, they point to the unfinished
nature of the conflict. The Donnellys represent the possibility of
change, violent change. They are the twins across the water, a
revolutionary duo whose liminal presence ensures that wherever
state boundaries are imposed, one untranslatable element of
Ireland still intuitively corresponds with an original landscape,
an essential fixed idea that can't be cancelled or erased by the
process of naming.[66]

The Donnelly twins personify the conflict in 'Boolavogue', the
kind of agency that sets the heather blazing. They remain outside
the text, unseen and unavoidable, but they inevitably vitiate the
public space the text purports to represent: as long as the
Donnelly twins are potential entrants into the text, they threaten
the stability of any system, especially a system of relational references like a map which the military can use to rigidly designate
and demarcate terrain. Epistemologically and politically, then,
the Donnellys threaten to shatter the apparatus of the state, the
British state, in Ireland.

In the context supplied by Fukuyama's definition of the end of
history, the Donnelly twins will always wait across the water,
separated by an unbridgeable divide from a consumerist culture
which is incapable of recognizing their historical or ideological
grievances. For Bolger, Barry, and Tóibín, the Donnelly twins
could never cross the border and apply for citizenship of the
Republic their anthologies reflect. If they did, they would probably be candidates for political internment, certainly be candidates for imaginative extradition, and it is most likely, to reapply
Hobbes, that their lives would be nasty, British, and very short.

Tóibín's version of the 'End of History' in *The Sign of the
Cross* relegates conflict to the 'perpetual caretaking of the

---

[66] See Seamus Deane, 'Brian Friel: The Name of the Game', in Alan Peacock (ed.),
The Achievement of Brian Friel (Gerrards Cross: Colin Smythe, 1993). See also Mary
Hamer, 'Putting Ireland On the Map', *Textual Practice*, 3/2 (1989), 184–201, at 184:
'Maps, no less than any other text, are agents of change. They create sites for contestation of meaning. No more than classic realism can a map reproduce the material
reality of the terrain that is its subject; it can only represent. And in that act, meaning
is constructed and disputed, power relations engaged. Mapping conventions, their
signifying practices, though apparently rigorously co-ordinated with material reality,
cannot deliver cartographers from their inherent commitment to the creation of a
new fiction'.

museum of human history'. Inside the Protestant church, facing a memorial to a soldier of the crown forces in 1798, he comments 'No one was very interested in this plaque, or the sectarian legacy. The plaque was a memorial to a past we would not repeat' (*TSOTC*, 295). Wherever sectarianism occurs, then, is still part of the ghetto of history. The north of Ireland is a metaphysical condition that politics can never enter, while the Republic occupies a space that is post-historical. *Bad Blood* does not so much explore the impact of partition as enact the segregation of issues and figures like the Donnelly twins that still feel subject to and responsive to history as politics. 'The end of history', then, is not just an acceptance of history. It purposefully establishes a frame for what ought to occur within the inviolable state formations on the island. If we understand legitimacy as a quality derived not from formal laws or decrees, 'but from the social acceptance (or acceptability) and appropriateness of norms that the governed accord assent',[67] Tóibín legitimizes the state so long as it does not adjust the predetermined course of his journey through history, or more accurately, through this *post-*historical landscape. In Yeats's terms, this is the passive acceptance of a current code; there is no space in which the state could be the active seeker of virtue. And to again deploy Yeats's terms, it is also theatrical, as the aesthetic seals the individual from the messy reality of any history which does not correspond with the territory of the state. 'We cannot picture a world that is essentially different from the present one, and at the same time better' is Fukuyama's claim. In aligning this credo with the state, Tóibín settles for the grim logic of sectarian arithmetic enshrined by partition. Enniscorthy, and any other place within this post-historical frame, ceases to belong just to geography; it is a depoliticized space exhausted of history, of catastrophe. The memory of loss, in other words, is curtailed by a strategic loss of memory. This is what Edna Longley means, I think, when she says that the Republic should 'cease to talk so glibly about "accommodating diversity" and face up to difference and division'.[68] But it is also the point where post-nationalism becomes

---

[67] John Coakley, 'Competing Conceptions of Legitmacy and the Creation of the New State', *Études irlandaises*, 21 (Winter 1995), 55–65, at 55.

[68] *The Living Stream: Literature and Revisionism in Ireland*, (Newcastle-upon-Tyne: Bloodaxe, 1994), 195.

post-liberal, where certain non-negotiable criteria for entry into the public sphere are established. The cognitive map produced by his aesthetic robs Enniscorthy of classical, civic republican principles in order to distance the Republic from the North. Though *The Blackwater Lightship*, his latest novel, can place the pain of a young man dying of aids in this same Wexford setting, *Bad Blood* allows no such contact. As a self-conscious, self-policing fiction, it patrols its own borders, mapping the abstract space of the Republic, the state, and removing it from any imaginative engagement with the history of the nation that produced it.

In Habermas, the public sphere is a realm in which individuals gather to participate in open dialogue. Potentially everyone has access to it, and all enter on equal terms, as the bundle of accidents that confront breakfast each day. Habermas saw the literary sphere, which dealt with issues of cultural rather than governmental concern, prefiguring the political public sphere, in which, obviously, there could be no space for any Yeatsian hierarchy.[69] The constitution of Tóibín's literary sphere, the aesthetic that constructs his 'fragmentary map' of the Republic, denies the Republic's obligation to speak to or for the Donnelly twins. The Donnellys will never be cross-border bodies. A rhetoric of difference founded on the incommensurable narratives of Presbyterianism and Catholicism overrides the possibility of a historical identity based on 1798 forming the basis of the public sphere. Ironically, the secular post-nationalist still seems solidly wedded to fundamentalist religious identities for his dramatic 'other' to ensure the southern state endures. A more abrasive critique of the connection between private and public realm, and the eligibility of individuals who might query the power relations between the two, is prematurely interned in the museum of human history by 'elaborate forms of doublespeak that expresses positions on partition while appearing to side-step that uncomfortable topic altogether'.[70]

But this is not in itself an indictable (or extraditable) offence. It is plausible and probably necessary to identify certain beliefs as

[69] See Robert C. Holub, *Jurgen Habermas: Critic in the Public Sphere* (London: Routledge, 1991), 3; Bruce Robbins, 'Introduction', in id. (ed.), *The Phantom Public Sphere* (Minneapolis: University of Minneapolis Press, 1993), pp. i–xxi.

[70] Cleary, 'Partition and the Politics of Form', 227.

metaphysical and therefore impervious to the dialogue a polity entails. Tóibín's elegy for the history of 1798, however, is, in the context of contemporary Irish politics, an elegy for the secular, democratic politics with which the United Irishmen sought to replace sectarianism. Tóibín's anti-nationalism causes him to flee from any historical memory potentially contaminated by association with contemporary Republicanism. It is a peculiarly undiscriminating tactic, embracing 1798, 1916, 1991, and the open-ended future in which the north of Ireland remains for ever locked outside history. It is almost commonplace now for critics to invoke Walter Benjamin's famous dictum 'to brush against the grain of history' in instances, like this, where a blatantly partisan historiography attempts to rewrite the past in the light of the present. But Tóibín actually removes a species of grain from the past. 'The 1790s remain as a vision and an inspiration for the 1990s', claims Kevin Whelan, a Wexford historian.[71] Tóibín terminates any dialogue between past and present that might keep a *certain form* of history alive. 'Forgetting', said Nietzsche, in 'On the uses and disadvantages of history for life', 'is essential to action of any kind':

A man who wanted to feel historically through and through would be like one forcibly deprived of sleep, or an animal that had to live only by rumination and ever repeated rumination. Thus: it is possible to live almost without memory, and to live happily moreover, as the animal demonstrates; but it is altogether impossible to live at all without forgetting . . . there is a degree of sleeplessness, of rumination, of the historical sense, which is harmful and ultimately fateful to the living thing, whether this living thing be a man or a people or a culture.[72]

The form of destiny Enniscorthy achieves in Tóibín is not simply untouched by revisionist history. Because it now acts as a foundational site for the state, it is absolved from contact with any history. In Nietzsche's formulation, it must forcibly forget any past that does not unequivocally endorse the state's relentless submission to the present moment. Lefebvre says that the state 'crushes time by reducing differences to repetitions and

---

[71] 'The Politics of Memory', in Mary Cullen (ed.), *1798: 200 Years of Remembrance* (Dublin: Irish Reporter Publications, 1998), 160.
[72] *Untimely Meditations*, trans. R. J. Hollindale (Cambridge: Cambridge University Press, 1983), 62.

circularities'.[73] But if time and history are crushed by the state, Tóibín's aesthetic accommodation of the state's non-historical dimension is actually an inversion of the trans-historical aesthetic he derided in Yeats and his friends. Tóibín's visceral reluctance—inability is not too strong a word—to acknowledge that nationalism has been one of the motors of constructive change in Irish history is responsible for an aesthetic that is wholly geared to accommodating Fukuyama's insistence that 'we cannot picture to ourselves a world that is essentially different from the present one, and at the same time better'.[74]

This is a world in which people do not live. They simply exist. The form of equilibrium Eamon discovers in *The Heather Blazing* is part of a liberal doctrine in which citizenship is a purely legalistic term which tries to minimize the exigencies of social responsibility. Tóibín responds to Yeats's invention of a nation by imagining a state in which change, the hope that fired the Republican imagination in Wexford 1798, is unimaginable. This is a republic drained of republicanism, replaced by a liberalism that, as Quentin Skinner puts it, 'is in danger of sweeping the public arena bare of any concepts save those of self-interest and individual rights'.[75] The disappearance of antagonism and division from this politics is another symptom of the end of history: the perennial contest between equality and liberty is foreclosed as the aesthetic is conscripted to help seal the state's borders and eliminate the political, a scenario that is the very antithesis of the Republican ethos. In Quentin Skinner's interpretation, this ethos says that 'unless we act to prevent this kind of political corruption by giving our civic duties priority over our individual rights, we must expect to find our individual rights, themselves undermined'.[76] The proud Wexford association with 1798 is now just one of those elements confined to a vague consensus, a museum of human history, in which the slowly concluding cadences of Enniscorthy's history are subordinate to a new politics rife with the old opportunism, failures, and hypocrisy.

[73] *Production of Space*, 23.

[74] Quoted in Anderson, *Zones of Engagement*, 46.

[75] 'On Justice, the Common Good and Liberty', in Chantal Mouffe (ed.), *Dimensions of Radical Democracy: Pluralism, Citizenship, Community* (London: Verso, 1992), 222.

[76] Ibid. 223.

Conclusion

Travelling in Space

AT FIRST GLANCE, the dominant theme in this book appears to be travel, not space. The two, though, are intertwined. McIlvanney's Laidlaw is forever travelling back towards the birthplace of Tam Docherty, the source of the difference that makes *the* difference for Scotland: the regional space that contains the nationalist aspiration towards independence. For Crichton Smith, travel is part of a composite self which never reaches a determinate, stable location. Hector McCleod and Trevor, for example, are marked by the translations and exchanges that come from encountering multiple cultures as both colonizer and colonized. Because there is no one single location that accommodates the form of selfhood in Crichton Smith's characters, freedom emerges through the occupation of this indeterminate physical and psychological space. And this ambivalence—what post-colonial theory labels 'liminality'[1]— also effectively works against the form of representational space and time in McIlvanney's republicanism and his allegory 'Scott': the transparent rational agency he assumes seems unavailable in Crichton Smith's Highland region.

Within the Republic of Ireland, Seán Blake in Bolger's *A Second Life* migrates from country to city; from the rural world of a mother he never knew towards the private, urban space of citizenship in his adopted north Dublin home, a space in which the 'otherness' of his rural past is fully visible but remains incomprehensible and distant from the present moment. As with Crichton Smith, Bolger's repeated use of doubling signals a composite self marked by multiple allegiances and translations: the slim partition between Donal and Dan, Francie and Hano, Kate and Cáit, Sean Blake and Paudi Sweeney never completely

[1] Homi Bhabha, 'Freedom's Basis in the Indeterminate', in John Rachman (ed.), *The Identity in Question* (London: Routledge, 1995), 49–61.

unifies their separate but connected biographies. Because there is no common context or memory these characters can be assumed to share, Bolger's urban space accords individual freedom priority over any public aspiration to the good: justice is construed as the absence of any impediment to the realization of this private individuality. Throughout his novels, Bolger's characters are oppressed by any formulations of justice that are communal. By separating citizenship from nationality, the city provides a measure of anonymity and freedom, and the absence of public virtue is not, ultimately, a sufficient reason for Bolger to forego this inviolable privacy. Compare this to McIlvanney, where the detective Laidlaw, the public servant and seeker of virtue, pieces together the scattered scraps of evidence the city hosts to recover a justice that insists on the interconnection between private and public morality. In Dublin and Glasgow, 'Bolgerism' and 'Dochertyism' use the same themes and spaces to construct different visions of justice for the state and the nation.

Thomas McCarthy is forever travelling between the Falls Road and Kildare Street, between the competing claims of the Party and its violent origins in Sinn Féin. The chthonic nationalism that propels Fianna Fáil forward and over a cliff haunts Bolger, but for McCarthy, de Valera's Republicanism is one possible construction of the common good. For better or for worse, Fianna Fáil is the community through which McCarthy's individual freedom is realized. Tóibín's travels along the border symbolically inscribe a narrow liberal space. Inaugurated and guaranteed by the existence of the state, this space is connected to but separate from the competing claims of nationalism and loyalism, Catholicism and Protestantism; and the present time of the state insulates Tóibín from these adversarial historical forces.

But are these public forces really in unrelenting opposition to a private individualism? Like Bolger and McCarthy, Tóibín's individual identity is constructed partly through the nationalism he rejects. To return to Ferdia Mac Anna's essay cited in the Introduction, 'The Dublin Renaissance: An Essay on Modern Dublin and Dublin Writers', the GPO may now be regarded as a beleaguered spectacle; but its very mention means that it does have a meaning, a meaning Mac Anna polemically chooses not to revere: it cannot be erased from the political and geographical space these writers occupy. When an attempt is made to cleanse the landscape of nationalism, as in Tóibín's post-historical Enniscorthy, it is hard not to view the process as the psychological equivalent of blowing up Nelson's column: removing the visible indications of an oppressive past is no guarantee that liberty can mean liberation. Indeed, the vehemence of Bolger's portrayal of the Plunketts may show the endurance and potency of the nationalist tradition he excoriates. Why, otherwise, despite the evident sarcasm, could Mac Anna go for 'an exciting afternoon . . . down to the G.P.O. in O'Connell Street to look for bullet holes left over from the 1916 Rising'?[2] And Joyce would of course recognize a number of shop fronts in modern Dublin—certainly in central Dublin (and definitely some of the pubs). Like Bolger's portrayal of the Plunkett brothers, Mac Anna exaggerates the place of Joyce as an 'official' literary icon in order to accentuate the radical newness of his own literary constituency, to establish every manifestation of tradition as outmoded. In fact, Joyce would have shared his suspicion of nationalist shrines, and in this way, Mac Anna thus remains ironically wedded to the tradition he excoriates. Scarred, disfigured, ridiculed—the GPO and 1916 still fascinate, despite the competing attraction of Mac Anna's soft-porn lesbian vampire films. This small incident highlights a common concern for the writers examined here: what terms are available from the past to describe present conditions in the Republic? What form of liberalism is offered by these prominent proponents of a separate 'southern' culture, and what does the Scottish example prove?

In *Liberalism and the Limits of Justice*, Michael J. Sandel touches on some of the issues at stake here, using language that has, in an Irish context, an additional resonance. Sandel comments on John Rawls's distinction between the right and the good, a distinction in which Rawls claims

we are free and independent selves, unbound by antecedent moral ties, capable of choosing our ends for ourselves. This is the conception of the person that finds expression in the ideal of the state as a neutral framework. It is precisely because we are free and independent selves, capable of choosing our own ends, that we need a framework of rights that is neutral among ends. To base rights on some conception of the good

---

[2] Ferdia Mac Anna, 'The Dublin Renaissance: An Essay on Modern Dublin and Dublin Writers', *Irish Review*, 10 (Spring 1991), 14.

would impose on some the values of others and so fail to respect each person's capacity to choose his or her own ends.[3]

Is the free and independent Republic a state in which the self retains some shared conception of the good? Does an adversarial past that is, as Mac Anna's imagery illustrates, still stubbornly visible in the present, disable any attempt to make the state something more than a neutral framework? And what role does the aesthetic play in this process? I have criticized Tóibín for disassociating the North from any possible conception of the good in the Republic; the act of calling an end to history is, of course, an act in history, not the inevitable terminus of natural, geological trends. The criticism is not that Tóibín's diagnosis is wrong or that liberalism is structurally incapable of addressing the issues his work makes visible; Tóibín's is, of course, only one of the many varieties of liberalism, and I have argued that his antinationalism is actually post-liberal. Rather, it is that the conscription of the aesthetic into his writing works to conceal the inadequacy of his political vision. In his writing, the aesthetic and the political are different aspects of the same things, braided together to avoid any possible contact with a history beyond the state's borders. Like Bolger, Tóibín seems to construe justice by its distance from any order that is antecedent to us. Neither allows for the possibility of a public culture in which the past has the potential to provide a shared fund of commonly recognized ideas. Tóibín's end of history, Bolger's private citizenship and tortuously complicated narratives, Mac Anna's array of suburban prose, poems, and memoirs—these all posit disagreement on aims and goals as the reason for rejecting any philosophical underpinning that could provide aims or goals. The political life their aesthetic describes leaves little room for the kind of public deliberation necessary to test the plausibility of contending moralities—to persuade others of the merits of nationalist or Catholic or Protestant ideals. In Tóibín's post-historical universe, in Bolger's sanitized north Dublin spaces, in Mac Anna's airport customs area: no one can be persuaded of the merits of, for example, Brendan Bradshaw's nationalism and catastrophic dimension.

---

[3] Sandel, *Liberalism and the Limits of Justice* (2nd edn.; Cambridge: Cambridge University Press, 1998), 187.

Again, it is not that Tóibín, Bolger, and Mac Anna are wrong in disputing Bradshaw's Catholic nationalism: it is that they envisage a *polis* in which citizens may not introduce into political discourse their comprehensive moral and religious convictions, at least when debating matters of justice and rights, especially in the North.[4] Enniscorthy and north Dublin are spaces that should not invoke any philosophical foundations for the new liberal arrangements within the state, other than that they must remain distant from a nationalist past. If literary anthologies are hypothetical images of social diversity,[5] the variety of private fictional universes in Tóibín's and Bolger's anthologies offers a form of pluralism that allows no substantive judgements on issues that might query the underlying assumptions of the role of the state, its potential for defining a justice that is not inalienably separated from the communal history of nation. The fact of reasonable pluralism about the good is a form of postmodern relativism that establishes the priority of rights; there can be no social cooperation among these various adherents of incompatible but reasonable moral and religious convictions, except if they are cooperating to validate the state as a neutral space in which, to quote Tóibín's introduction to *Soho Square: New Writing from Ireland*, there are 'no responsibilities'.[6] This affirmation of difference within the state is now the same as the affirmation of sameness with the nation: the very same conceptual framework of difference and sameness, opposition and affirmation, is replayed.

'Modern Irish politics', says Denis Donoghue, is 'a politics of the same, not a politics of difference'.

Many Irish people have grown tired of being told that they are interesting beyond their numbers or that the trajectory from race through nation to state has made them distinguished among their European associates. They want to be the same as everyone else, the same as England to begin with and as the United States later on. It is their right.[7]

To claim the right to have 'no responsibilities', not even the

---

[4] Ibid. 211.

[5] John Guillory, *Cultural Capital: The Problem of Literary Canon Formation* (Chicago: University of Chicago Press, 1993), 7.

[6] (London: Bloomsbury, 1993), 9.

[7] *The Parnell Lecture 1997–1998: Ireland: Race, Nation, State* (Cambridge: Magdalene College Occasional Papers, 1998), 27.

responsibility to confront and evaluate Darkley, a slaughter which threatens the very basis of meaning and liberty, is to ensure that this brand of liberalism will never do more than facilitate two communities who point in incommensurate directions. Ireland will thus never be 'the same'; rather it will remain disfigured by differences which the state thinks it is its duty to genially accommodate. In Tóibín's presentation, the state will designate as an alien 'other' anyone who suggests its political duties exceed its territorial remit.

This form of liberal detachment is unduly severe. It affirms the virtues of political liberalism only for political purposes, for their role in supporting a constitutional regime, a state, that protects people's rights. But as Sandel notes, 'Whether and to what extent these virtues should figure in people's moral lives generally is a question political liberalism does not figure to answer.'[8] A liberalism that adapts Fukuyama's 'end of history' thesis to terminate Enniscorthy's Republican heritage is not a liberalism worth having. It is abstract and decorous. In Ireland of all spaces, it is not possible to be neutral on every issue. And it is here that Declan Kiberd's criticism of Bolger and Tóibín, their failure to imagine a resilient civic discourse, is relevant.[9] Impartiality does not always serve justice; it can, in certain instances, simply mask oppression.[10] In *The Heather Blazing*, Eamon Redmond may read his Catholicism into the constitution; but in *Bad Blood*, Colm Tóibín's 'liberalism' imaginatively insulates the state from the history of the nation from which it derives. This is what Sandel calls the restrictive nature of liberal public reason: the belief that politics should avoid rather than express substantive moral judgements.[11]

As should be evident from the criticism in this book, I think that Irish liberals like Tóibín should face this issue. Liberalism must offer some substantive and coherent conception of what is good, not withdraw to the post-historical spaces of Enniscorthy

---

[8] *Liberalism and the Limits of Justice*, 195.

[9] *Inventing Ireland: The Literature of the Modern Nation* (London: Jonathan Cape, 1997), 610.

[10] Chandran Kukathas, 'Liberalism, Multiculturalism and Oppression', in Andrew Vincent (ed.), *Political Theory: Tradition and Diversity* (Cambridge: Cambridge University Press, 1997), 132–53.

[11] See Alasdair MacIntyre's *After Virtue* (Notre Dame, Ind.: Notre Dame University Press, 1981), for an incisive critique of this aspect of liberal thought.

and north Dublin in defence of the right not to be assaulted by
tradition and history. In Ireland, our conception of our selves as
private citizens is not, after all, completely divorced from the
public identity we establish through cultural practice. And it is
not feasible for a claim to carry weight simply because it is made
by us as private citizens: what critical response do Mac Anna's
soft-porn lesbian vampire films require compared to, say,
Bradshaw's catastrophic dimension? Are these films part of the
rich plurality a liberalism would sponsor, a defiant counterblast
to Bradshaw and Kiberd's formulation of 'the people', a term
which subsumes the individual's fate to that of the collective? Or
are they symptomatic of the impoverished vision of the post-
nationalist imagination, of what Kiberd claims is this 'generation's inability to achieve a truly civic discourse'.[12] I hope the
humourlessness of the contrast does not detract from the underlying issue. As McCarthy's work shows, fundamentalists rush in
where liberals fear to tread, in the space between the incommensurate identities Tóibín's studiously non-judgemental prose
describes but never evaluates.

Declan Kiberd concludes *Irish Classics* with some typically
provocative claims for the intersection between culture and politics in Ireland: 'The seeds of the Belfast Agreement were sown in
the works of Irish literature.' Now, he argues, 'identity is rooted
less in the relation between persons and territory than in the
relations of persons to one another . . . The Belfast Agreement
sounds the death-knell for old style constitutions.' The language
of the agreement, he claims, shows it possible to be creatively
ambiguous, one thing and another, both Irish and modern. An
'unprecedented knowledge' is possible in zones where cultures
collide, and so the agreement, endorsed by an overwhelming
majority (94 per cent) of the state's voters, sacrificed the
Republic's territorial claim on the north so that citizens, North
and South, might be Irish, or British, or both: 'The Belfast agreement gives everyone the chance to start again.'[13]

[12] 'The Children of Modernity', *Irish Times*, 22 June 1991, p. 9. See also Fionnula
O'Connor's ch. 'The South: I don't like their attitudes', in *In Search of a State:
Catholics in Northern Ireland* (Belfast: Blackstaff Press, 1993), 223–72: 'Brought
up to yearn for the greater part of their nation on the other side of an imaginary,
arbitrary line on the map, they now feel little more than lack of sympathy with the
inhabitants of another country.'
[13] *Irish Classics* (London: Granta, 2000), 630–2.

In *Bad Blood*, writing after the 1985 Anglo-Irish agreement, does Colm Tóibín offer the likes of the Donnelly twins the chance 'to start again', the chance to realize their Irishness outside the British state? Is soldering the imagination so strictly to the state's geography a humane, practical response to violence motivated by territory? Is it, in effect, an imaginative anticipation of the deletion of articles 2 and 3 from the Republic's self-definition? Or does a language beholden to the present-centred fact of the state's border permanently remain one thing and never part of the 'other'? Does the conscription of the aesthetic by Bolger and Tóibín, to ensure that the narrative of the state never intersects with the nation, escape the thematics of territory or simply suppress them? What territorial limits, what *ne plus ultra* do Bolgerism, Tóibínism, and Dochertyism set to the practice of citizenship in the culture and society of their nations? By looking to Scotland and McIlvanney's work, by seeing what is excluded by his national allegory, perhaps some insights into the thematics of Irish post-nationalism become available.

The whole basis of my chapter on Crichton Smith has recently been questioned by some of the most exciting revisionist historiography to appear in Scotland. In *Scotland after Enlightenment*, Craig Beveridge and Ronnie Turnbull dispute the notion that Calvinism was an inherently unproductive aspect of Scottish cultural history and query whether Walter Scott and Jacobitism offered merely an aestheticised version of a 'real' history. Scott, they claim, talked to survivors of 1745 and incorporated their stories into his narratives. In the survival of Jacobitism 'was sustained a powerful expression of Scottish identity, a symbol of ideals and aspirations which though once defeated, cannot be forgotten or erased, and which constituted the paradigm for an ever-possible Rising'.[14] The bullet holes on the GPO eloquently express the material and psychological scars of Ireland's 'ever-possible Rising'; Mac Anna's almost voyeuristic fascination with them stems from the way they curtail his rights as an individual in the present. But Scotland offers a fascinating example of the pursuit of the public culture Irish liberals seem intent to move beyond.[15] In McIlvanney's work, his honourable republican

---

[14] *Scotland after Enlightenment* (Edinburgh: Polygon, 1997), 79.
[15] Cairns Craig, 'Twentieth Century Scottish Literature: An Introduction', in id. (ed. and gen. ed.), *The History of Scottish Literature*, iv. *Twentieth Century*

legacy eventually assimilates all differences into one homogeneous bloc and swaps liberty for liberation. But like Crichton
Smith, he insists that Scottish citizens confront the existence
of an indigenous tradition in all its occasional incoherence and
contradictions. The mere existence of difference within Scotland
does not make evaluation impossible; the presence of a variety of
options does not invalidate any agreement on what might be
worth pursuing, as Beveridge and Turnbull's reclamation of
Jacobitism *and* Calvinism attempts to demonstrate. The catastrophic dimension to Scottish history does not make unavailable terms from the nation's past to describe Scotland's present,
stateless predicament.

Bolger's private universe or Tóibín's post-historical Enniscorthy cannot claim the right to ask the state to concede that
certain issues which connect the Republic to the nation's past,
such as its attitude to the North, are simply not subject to choice.
The inscription of regional spaces within the state is a form of
pluralism, certainly; but it cannot dictate that the territory
beyond the state is no concern of these regions. For that is the
severest stricture of liberal public reason. The differences that
make the difference should be available to every region of the
island in which the state exists; whether that region be Belfast,
Dublin, Enniscorthy, or Waterford.

(Aberdeen: Aberdeen University Press, 1987), 13: 'Why should Scottish literature
have retained and indeed asserted its independence in a context where the Scottish
people—unlike the Irish, for instance—have seemed deeply resistant or apathetic
about other forms of independence? In part, it is that Scotland has, despite both
internal and external pressures, never been integrated into the cultural values of the
British state. The texture of Scottish life, in its religious, educational, legal, linguistic
forms, remains distinct from that of England to an extent which is little recognised in
England, let alone the outside world.'

Select Bibliography

PRIMARY WORKS

Bolger, Dermot, *Night Shift* (1985; London: Penguin, 1991).
—— *Internal Exile* (Dublin: Raven Arts Press, 1986).
—— *The Woman's Daughter* (1987; London: Penguin, 1991).
—— *The Journey Home* (London: Viking, 1990).
—— *The Lament for Arthur Cleary*, in *A Dublin Quartet* (Harmondsworth: Penguin, 1992).
—— *Emily's Shoes* (London: Penguin, 1992).
—— *A Second Life* (London: Penguin, 1994).
—— 'The Woman's Daughter', in *Finglas Lilies* (Dublin: Raven Arts Press, 1981).
—— and O'Loughlin, Michael, *A New Primer for Irish Schools* (Dublin: Raven Arts Press, 1985).
—— (ed.), *The Bright Wave/An Tonn Gheal: Poetry in Irish Now* (Dublin: Raven Arts Press, 1986).
—— *Invisible Dublin: A Journey through Dublin's Suburbs* (Dublin: Raven Arts Press, 1991).
—— (ed.), *The Picador Book of Contemporary Irish Fiction* (1993; rev. and expanded edn., London: Picador, 1994).
—— *Ireland in Exile* (Dublin: New Island Books, 1995).
—— 'Who'd be a Northside Playwright?', interview with Dermot Bolger, *Irish Press* (20 Sept. 1989), 22.
—— 'Speaking with . . . Dermot Bolger', *In Cognito*, 1 (1997), 13–14.
—— Unpublished interview with Dermot Bolger by Alexander Downes.
Crichton Smith, Iain, *Thistle and Roses* (London: Eyre & Spottiswoode, 1961).
—— *Deer on the High Hill* (Edinburgh: Giles Gordon, 1962).
—— *The Last Summer* (London: Victor Gollancz, 1969).
—— *My Last Duchess* (London: Victor Gollancz, 1971).
—— *Goodbye Mr Dixon* (London: Victor Gollancz, 1974).
—— *An End to Autumn* (Basingstoke: Macmillan, 1978).
—— 'Between Sea and Moor', in Karl Miller (ed.), *Memoirs of a Modern Scotland* (London: Faber and Faber, 1970).
—— *On the Island* (London: Macmillan, 1979).
—— *Towards the Human: Selected Essays* (Edinburgh: Macdonald, 1986).

Crichton Smith, Iain, *Consider the Lilies* (1968; Edinburgh: Cannongate, 1987).

—— *An Honourable Death* (London: Macmillan, 1992).

—— 'The Double Man', in R. P. Draper (ed.), *The Literature of Region and Nation* (Basingstoke: Macmillan, 1989).

—— Longley, Michael, and Tebb, Barry, *Three Regional Poets* (London: Poet and Printer, 1968).

McCarthy, Thomas, *The First Convention* (Brandon: Dolmen Press, 1978).

—— *The Non-Aligned Storyteller* (London: Anvil Press, 1984).

—— *Without Power* (Brandon: Dolmen Press, 1991).

—— 'Five Summer Afternoons', *Eire-Ireland*, 26/1 (Spring 1991), 7–18.

—— 'Streetwise: From the Falls Road to Kildare Street? Thomas McCarthy met Gerry Adams', *STET: The National Literary and Arts Newspaper*, 12 (Winter 1993), 3–4.

—— *Asya and Christine* (Dublin: Brandon, 1994).

—— *The Lost Province* (London: Anvil, 1997).

—— *Garden of Remembrance* (Dublin: New Island Books, 1998).

—— 'Documents of Exclusion', *Irish Review*, 4 (Winter 1987), 141–2.

—— 'Poet as Librarian', *Poetry Ireland Review*, 29 (Summer 1990), 54.

—— Thomas McCarthy Reviews . . . , *Poetry Ireland Review*, 40 (Winter 1993/4), 63.

McIlvanney, William, *Remedy is None* (1966; Glasgow: Richard Drew Publishing, 1989).

—— *Docherty* (1975; London: Sceptre, 1987).

—— *A Gift from Nessus* (1968; Edinburgh: Mainstream, 1990).

—— *Laidlaw* (1977; London: Hodder and Stoughton, 1983).

—— *The Papers of Tony Veitch* (1983; London: Sceptre, 1992).

—— *The Big Man* (1985; London: Sceptre, 1990).

—— *Strange Loyalties* (1991; London: Sceptre, 1992).

—— *Surviving the Shipwreck* (Edinburgh: Polygon, 1991).

—— *The Kiln* (London: Sceptre, 1996).

—— 'Growing up in the West', in Karl Miller (ed.), *Memoirs of a Modern Scotland* (London: Faber and Faber, 1970).

—— 'The Cowardly Lion', *Radical Scotland*, 11 (Oct./Nov. 1984), 12.

—— 'Digging Deep to Save a Nation's Culture', *Guardian* (29 Aug. 1985).

—— *The Official History of Celtic Football Club 1888–1988*, written and narrated by William McIlvanney (BBC Enterprises Ltd, 1988).

Tóibín, Colm, *Bad Blood: A Walk along the Irish Border* (1987; London: Vintage, 1995).

—— *The Trial of the Generals: Selected Journalism* (Dublin: Raven Arts Press, 1990).

—— *Homage to Barcelona* (London: Simon & Schuster, 1990).

—— Review of *The Field Day Anthology of Irish Writing*, *Canadian Journal of Irish Studies*, 18/2 (Dec. 1991), 122.

—— *The South* (London: Picador, 1990).

—— *The Heather Blazing* (London: Picador, 1992).

—— 'New Ways of Killing Your Father', *London Review of Books* (18 Nov. 1993), 1–6.

—— *The Sign of the Cross: Travels in Catholic Europe* (London: Vintage, 1995).

—— *The Story of the Night* (London: Picador, 1997).

—— *The Blackwater Lightship* (London: Picador, 1999).

—— (ed.), *Soho Square: New Writing from Ireland* (London: Bloomsbury, 1993).

—— (ed.), *The Penguin Book of Irish Fiction* (Harmondsworth: Penguin, 1999).

—— *The Irish Famine* (London: Profile Books, 1999).

SECONDARY WORKS

Adams, Gerry, *Before the Dawn: An Autobiography* (London: Mandarin, 1996).

Adams, Ian H., *The Making of Urban Scotland* (London: Croom Helm, 1976).

Agnew, John A., *Place and Politics: The Geographical Mediation of State and Society* (Boston: Allen & Unwin, 1987).

—— 'The Devaluation of Place in Social Science', in id. and James S. Duncan (eds.), *The Power of Place: Bringing Together Geographical and Sociological Imaginations* (Boston: Unwin Hyman, 1989).

Ahmad, Aijaz, *In Theory: Classes, Nations, Literatures* (London: Verso, 1992).

Allan, David, *Virtue, Learning and the Scottish Enlightenment* (Edinburgh: Edinburgh University Press, 1993).

Allen, Keiran, *Fianna Fáil and Irish Labour: 1926 to the Present* (London: Pluto Press, 1997).

Allison, Jonathan, 'The Attack on Yeats', *South Atlantic Review*, 55/4 (Nov. 1990), 61–73.

—— (ed.), *Yeats's Political Identities* (Ann Arbor: Michigan, 1996).

Anderson, Benedict, *Imagined Communities: Reflections on the Origins and Spread of Nationalism* (London: Verso, 1983).

Anderson, Carol, and Norquay, Glenda, 'Superiorism', *Cencrastus* 15 (1994), 8–10.

Anderson, Perry, *A Zone of Engagement* (London: Verso, 1992).

Andrews, J. H., 'Land and People, *c.*1780', in T. W. Moody and W. E. Vaughan (eds.), *A New History Of Ireland*, iv. *Eighteenth Century Ireland 1691–1800* (Oxford: Clarendon, 1986).

Arnold, Matthew, *On the Study of Celtic Literature* (London: Smith, Elder, 1867).

Arthur, Paul, 'The Anglo-Irish Agreement: A Device for Territorial Management', in Dermot Keogh and Michael H. Haltzel (eds.), *Northern Ireland and the Politics of Reconciliation* (Cambridge: Cambridge University Press, 1993).

Ascherson, Neal, 'Don't Be Afraid—and Don't Steal!', lecture to the annual conference of the SNP, repr. in *Games with Shadows* (London: Radius, 1988).

—— 'Scottish Contradictions', in *Games with Shadows*.

Ash, Marinell, *The Strange Death of Scottish History* (Edinburgh: The Ramsay Head Press, 1980).

Ashcroft, Bill, Griffiths, Gareth, and Tiffin, Helen, *The Empire Writes Back: Theory and Practice in Post-Colonial Literatures* (London: Routledge, 1989).

Bakhtin, M. M., *The Dialogic Imagination: Four Essays*, trans. Caryl Emerson and Michael Holquist, ed. Michael Holquist (Austin: University of Texas Press, 1981).

Balakrishnan, Gopal, 'The National Imagination', *New Left Review*, 211 (May–June 1995), 56–70.

Barker, Rodney, *Political Legitimacy and the State* (Oxford: Clarendon Press, 1990).

Barry, Kevin, 'Representing Insurgency: A Critique of Post-Colonial Aesthetic Theory', *Études irlandaises*, 19 (1994), 10–16.

Barry, Sebastian, *The Inherited Boundaries: Younger Poets from the Republic of Ireland* (Dublin: Mercier Press, 1986).

Bartlett, Thomas, 'Ulster: 1600–2000: Posing the Question', *Bullán: An Irish Studies Journal* 4/1 (Spring 2000), 1–16.

Beer, Gillian, *Forging The Missing Link: Interdisciplinary Stories*, Inaugural Lecture delivered 18 Nov. 1991 (Cambridge: Cambridge University Press, 1992).

Bell, Catherine, *Ritual Theory, Ritual Practice* (New York and Oxford: Oxford University Press, 1992).

Bell, Desmond, 'Cultural Studies in Ireland and the Postmodernist Debate', *Irish Journal of Sociology*, 1 (1991), 83–95.

Bell, Ian, 'McIlvanney: Hunting for Morality in Scotland's Myths', *Scotsman* (16 Apr. 1983).

Benjamin, Walter, 'Theses on the Philosophy of History', in *Illuminations*, ed. Hannah Arendt (1968; London: Fontana, 1992).

Berlin, Isaiah, 'The Originality of Machiavelli', in *Against the Current:*

Essays in the History of Ideas (Oxford: Oxford University Press, 1981).

Beveridge, Craig, and Turnbull, Ronald, *The Eclipse of Scottish Culture* (Edinburgh: Polygon, 1989).

—— 'Inferiorism', *Cencrastus*, 89 (Spring 1982), 4–5.

—— *Scotland after Enlightenment* (Edinburgh: Polygon, 1997).

Bhabha, Homi K., *The Location of Culture* (London: Routledge, 1994).

'Big Bill and the Wee Man in the Portaloo', *Aberdeen Press and Journal* (11 Oct. 1991), 12–14.

Blackie, John Stuart, *The Language and Literature of the Scottish Highlands* (Edinburgh: Edmonston & Douglas, 1976).

Bock, Gisela, Skinner, Quentin, and Viroli, Maurizio, *Machiavelli and Republicanism* (Cambridge: Cambridge University Press, 1993).

Boland, Eavan, *Object Lessons* (Manchester: Carcanet, 1995).

Bradbury, Richard, 'Sexuality, Guilt and Detection: Tension between History and Suspense', in Brian Docherty (ed.), *American Crime Fiction: Studies in Genre* (Basingstoke: Macmillan, 1988).

Bradshaw, Brendan, 'Nationalism and Historical Scholarship in Modern Ireland', reprod. in Ciarán Brady (ed.), *Interpreting Irish History: The Debate on Historical Revisionism* (Dublin: Four Courts Press, 1994).

—— 'Nationalism in Ireland: An Historical Overview', *Bullán: An Irish Studies Journal*, 5/1 (Summer–Fall 2000), 5–23.

—— and Morrill, John (eds.), *The British Problem, c.1534–1707* (Basingstoke: Macmillan, 1996).

—— and Roberts, Peter (eds.), *British Consciousness and Identity* (Cambridge: Cambridge University Press, 1998).

Brennan, Timothy, 'The National Longing for Form', in Homi K. Bhabha (ed.), *Nation and Narration* (London: Routledge, 1990).

Breuilly, John, *Nationalism and the State* (Manchester: Manchester University Press, 1982).

Brewer, John D., 'Conjectural History, Sociology and Social Change in Eighteenth-Century Scotland: Adam Ferguson and the Division of Labour', in McCrone, Kendrick, and Straw (eds.), *The Making of Scotland*, 13–30.

Brown, Calum, *The Social History of Religion in Scotland since 1730* (London: Methuen, 1987).

Brown, Terence, 'The Dublin of Dubliners', in Bernard Benstock (ed.), *James Joyce: An International Perspective* (Gerrards Cross: Colin Smythe, 1982).

—— *Ireland: A Social and Cultural History* (London: Fontana, 1985).

—— 'Letters from Nowhere', *Irish Review*, 3 (Spring 1987), 10–17.

Brown, Terence, 'Poetry and Partition: A Personal View', *Krino*, 12 (Spring 1986), 17–23.

—— 'Review Article: New Literary Histories', *Irish Historical Studies*, 30/119 (May 1997), 462–70.

Butlin, R. A., 'Land and People *c.* 1600', in T. W. Moody, F. X. Martin, and F. J. Byrne (eds.), *A New History of Ireland Volume*, iii. (Oxford: Clarendon Press, 1976).

Calder, Angus, *Revolving Culture: Notes from the Scottish Republic* (London: I. B. Taurus, 1994).

—— 'A Descriptive Model of Scottish Culture', *Scotlands*, 2/1 (1995), 1–14.

Campbell, James, 'Toughs and Moralists', *The Times Literary Supplement*, 8 July 1993, 24.

Campbell, T. D., 'Francis Hutcheson: "Father" of the Scottish Enlightenment', in R. H. Cambell and A. S. Skinner (eds.), *The Origins and Nature of the Scottish Enlightenment* (Edinburgh: John Donald Publishers, 1982).

Canny, Nicholas, 'The Formation of the Irish Mind: Religion, Politics and Gaelic Irish Literature, 1589–1750', in C. H. E. Philpin (ed.), *Nationalism and Popular Protest in Ireland* (London: Past and Present Society, 1987).

Carey, John, *The Intellectuals and the Masses: Pride and Prejudice among the Literary Intelligentsia, 1880–1939* (London: Faber and Faber, 1992).

Chambers, Ian, 'Cities without Maps', in John Bird, Barry Curtis, Tim Putnam, George Robertson, and Lisa Tickner (eds.), *Mapping the Futures: Local Cultures, Global Changes* (London: Routledge, 1993).

Chapman, Malcolm, *The Gaelic Vision In Scottish Culture* (London: Routledge, 1978).

Chitnis, Anand, *The Scottish Enlightenment* (London: Croon Helm, 1976).

Cleary, Joe, *Literature, Partition and the Nation State: Culture and Conflict in Ireland, Israel and Palestine* (Cambridge: Cambridge University Press, 2002).

—— 'Partition and the Politics of Form in Contemporary Narratives of Northern Ireland', *Ireland and Cultural Studies*, special issue of *The South Atlantic Quarterly*, 95/1 (Winter 1996), 225–76.

—— 'Colonial/Post-Colonial Studies and Ireland: A Project in the Making', unpublished paper.

Clutterbuck, Catriona, 'Place, Time, and the Possibility of Connection in Contemporary Irish Poetry', University College Dublin MA thesis, 1990.

Comerford, R. V., 'Nation, Nationalism, and the Irish Language', in Hachey and McCaffrey (eds.), *Perspectives on Irish Nationalism* (Lexington: University of Kentucky Press, 1989).

Corcoran, Neil, *After Yeats and Joyce: Reading Modern Irish Literature* (Oxford: Oxford University Press, 1997).

Corkery, Daniel, *Synge and Anglo-Irish Literature* (1931; Cork: Mercier Press, 1966).

Coroneos, Con, 'History, the Boundary, and *The Third Man*', in Rosa González (ed.), *Culture and Power: Institutions* (Barcelona: Promociones Publicaciones Universitarias, SA, 1996).

Craig, Cairns, 'Myths against History: Tartanry and Kailyard in 19th Century Scottish Literature', in Colin McArthur (ed.), *Scotch Reels: Scotland in Cinema and Television* (London: British Film Institute, 1982).

—— 'Resisting Arrest: James Kelman', in Gavin Wallace and Randall Stevenson (eds.), *The Scottish Novel since the Seventies* (Edinburgh: Edinburgh University Press, 1993).

—— *Out of History: Narrative Paradigms in Scottish and British Culture* (Edinburgh: Polygon, 1996).

—— 'Scotland and the Regional Novel', in K. D. M. Snell (ed.), *The Regional Novel in Britain and Ireland, 1780–1990* (Cambridge: Cambridge University Press, 1998).

Craig, David, *Scottish Literature and the Scottish People* (London: John Donald, 1961).

Crawford, Robert, *Devolving English Literature* (Oxford: Clarendon Press, 1992).

—— *Identifying Poets: Self and Territory in Twentieth-Century Poetry* (Edinburgh: Edinburgh University Press, 1993).

—— 'Defining Scotland', in Susan Bassnet (ed.), *Defining British Cultures: An Introduction* (London: Routledge, 1997).

Crualaoich, Gearóid Ó, 'Responding to the Rising', in Máirín Ní Dhonnchadha and Theo Dorgan (eds.), *Revising the Rising* (Derry: Field Day, 1991).

Cullen, L. M., *The Emergence of Modern Ireland* (London: Batsford, 1981).

—— 'Economic Development, 1691–1750', in T. W. Moody and W. E. Vaughan (eds.), *A New History of Ireland* (Oxford: Clarendon Press, 1986).

—— and Smout, T. C. (eds.), *Comparative Aspects of Economic and Social History 1600–1900* (Edinburgh: John Donald Publishers, 1977).

Cullingford, Elizabeth, 'Thinking of Her . . . as Ireland', *Textual Practice*, 4/1 (1990), 1–21.

Curtin, Nancy, *The United Irishmen: Popular Politics in Ulster and Dublin 1791–1798* (Oxford: Clarendon Press, 1994).

Daiches, David, *The Paradox of Scottish Culture* (London: McMaster University Press, 1964).

Damer, Sean, *Glasgow: Going for a Song* (London: Wishart, 1990).

Davie, George, *The Democratic Intellect: Scotland and her Universities in the Nineteenth Century* (Edinburgh: Edinburgh University Press, 1961).

Dawe, Gerald, 'Thomas McCarthy', *The Honest Ulsterman*, 100 (Winter 1995), 133–4.

Deane, Seamus, 'Heroic Styles: The Tradition of an Idea', in *Ireland's Field Day* (Notre Dame, Ind.: University of Notre Dame Press, 1984).

—— 'Arnold, Burke, and the Celts', in *Celtic Revivals* (London: Faber and Faber, 1985).

—— (gen. ed.), *The Field Day Anthology of Irish Writing*, 3 vols. (Derry: Field Day, 1991).

—— 'Introduction' in id. (ed.), *Nationalism, Colonialism, and Literature* (Minneapolis: University of Minnesota Press, 1990).

—— 'Canon Fodder: Literary Mythologies in Ireland', in Jean Lundy and Aodán Mac Pólín (eds.), *Styles of Belonging: Culture and Ideology in Ireland* (Belfast: Lagan Press, 1992).

—— 'Brian Friel: The Name of the Game', in Peacock (ed.), *Achievement of Brian Friel*.

—— 'Land & Soil: A Territorial Rhetoric', *History Ireland*, 2/1 (Spring 1994), 31–4.

—— 'The Production of Cultural Space in Irish Writing', *boundary 2/21* (Fall 1994), 117–44.

—— *Strange Country: Modernity and Nationhood in Irish Writing since 1790* (Oxford: Clarendon Press, 1997).

Devine, T. M., and Dickson, David (eds.), *Ireland and Scotland 1600–1850* (Edinburgh: John Donald Publishers, 1983).

Dickson, David, 'The Place of Dublin in the 18th Century Economy', in Devine and Dickson (eds.), *Ireland and Scotland 1600–1850*.

'Disaffected McIlvanney Switches Allegiance from Labour for "Pragmatism" of Nationalists: Writer turns to SNP for Socialist Values', *Herald* (6 Apr. 1996), 5.

Docker, John, *Postmodernism and Popular Culture: A Cultural History* (Cambridge: Cambridge University Press, 1994).

Donaldson, W., 'Bonny Highland Laddie: The Making of a Myth', *Scottish Literary Journal*, 3/2 (Dec. 1976), 30–50.

—— *The Jacobite Song* (Aberdeen: Aberdeen University Press, 1988).

Donnelly, James S., Jun., *The Land and the People of Nineteenth-*

Century Cork: The Rural Economy and the Land Question (London: Routledge & Kegan Paul, 1975).

Donoghue, Denis, 'Being Irish Together', *Sewanee Review*, 44/1 (Winter 1976), 133.

—— *We Irish* (Berkeley and Los Angeles: University of California Press, 1986).

Dunbar, William, *The Poems of William Dunbar* ed. W. Mackay Mackenzie (London: Faber and Faber, 1970).

Dunn, Douglas, 'Divergent Scottishness: The Novel of Damaged Identity', in Gavin Wallace and Randall Stevenson (eds.), *The Scottish Novel since the Seventies* (Edinburgh: Edinburgh University Press, 1993).

—— 'Introduction' in id. (ed.), *The Faber Book of Twentieth-Century Scottish Poetry* (London: Faber and Faber, 1992).

Dunn, John, 'Political Obligation', in David Held (ed.), *Political Theory Today* (Stanford: Stanford University Press, 1991).

Dunne, Tom, 'New Histories: Beyond Revisionism', *Irish Review*, 12 (Spring/Summer 1992), 1–12.

Durkacz, Victor Edward, *The Decline of the Celtic Languages* (Edinburgh: John Donald Publishers, 1983).

Eagleton, Terry, 'The End of English', *Textual Practice,* 1/1 (Spring 1987), 1–9.

—— 'Nationalism, Irony and Commitment', in Deane (ed.), *Nationalism, Colonialism and Literature:* (Field Day Pamphlet No. 13; Derry: Field Day 1988).

—— *The Ideology of the Aesthetic* (Oxford: Blackwell, 1990).

—— *Heathcliff and the Great Hunger* (London: Verso, 1995).

—— *Crazy John and the Bishop and Other Essays on Irish Culture* (Cork: Cork University Press, 1998).

—— 'Form and Ideology in the Anglo-Irish Novel', *Bullán: A Journal of Irish Studies,* 1/1 (Spring 1994), 17–26.

Edwards, Owen Dudley, *A Claim of Right for Scotland* (Edinburgh: Polygon, 1989).

Ellis, Stephen, *Tudor Ireland: Crown, Community and the Conflict of Cultures 1470–1603* (London: Longman, 1985).

English, Richard, and Walker, Graham (eds.), *Unionism in Modern Ireland* (Basingstoke: Macmillan, 1996).

Feifer, Maxine, *Tourism in History: From Imperial Rome to the Present Day* (New York: Stern & Day, 1986).

Ferguson, Adam, *Essays on the Intellectual Powers, Moral Sentiments, Happiness and National Felicity* (Paris: Parsons and Galignoi, 1805).

—— *An Essay on the History of the Civil Society*, ed. Duncan Forbes (Edinburgh: Edinburgh University Press, 1966).

Ferguson, Paul, and Whelan, Kevin (eds.), *Rural Ireland, 1600–1900* (Cork: Cork University Press, 1987).

Ferguson, William, *Scotland 1689 to the Present: The Edinburgh History of Scotland* (Edinburgh and London: Oliver & Boyd, 1968).

Fink, Z. S., *The Classical Republicans An Essay in the Recovery of a Pattern of Thought in Seventeenth Century England* (1945; Evanston, Ill.: Northwestern University Press, 1962).

Finlay, Richard, 'National Identity in Crisis: Politicians, Intellectuals and the "End of Scotland", 1920–1939', *History*, 79/256 (June 1994), 242–59.

Fisk, Robert, *In Time of War: Ireland, Ulster and the Price of Neutrality, 1939–1945* (London: Paladin, 1987).

' "Fist-Fights and Metaphors for Kilmarnock": D J Taylor on William McIlvanney, a Scottish Storyteller Launching Guerilla Attacks from the Front Line', *Independent* (28 Jan. 1989), 11–12.

Fitzgerald, Garret, 'The Origins and Rationale of the Anglo-Irish Agreement of 1985', in Dermot Keogh and Michael H. Haltzel (eds.), *Northern Ireland and the Politics of Reconciliation* (Cambridge: Cambridge University Press, 1993), 189–207.

Fogarty, Michael, Ryan, Liam and Lee, Joseph (eds.), *Irish Values and Attitudes: The Irish Report of the European Value Systems Study* (Dublin: Dominican Press, 1984).

Foster, Aisling, *Safe in the Kitchen* (Harmondsworth: Penguin, 1993).

Foster, John Wilson, 'The Geography of Irish Fiction', in Patrick Rafroidi and Maurice Harmon (eds.), *The Irish Novel in Our Time* (Lille: Centre d'Études irlandaises de l'Université de Lille, 1976), 89–102.

—— (ed.), *Arguments in Favour of the Union* (Belcouver: Belcouver Press, 1995).

Foster, R. F., *Modern Ireland 1600–1972* (London: Allen Lane, 1989).

—— 'History and the Irish Question', in Ciarán Brady (ed.), *Interpreting Irish History: The Debate on Historical Revisionism* (Dublin: Four Courts Press, 1994).

—— 'Yeats: Love, Magic and Politics', *Independent on Sunday* (7 Mar. 1997), 28.

Foucault, Michel, 'Questions on Geography', trans. Colin Gordan from the interview in *Hérodote*, 1 (1976), repr. in *Michel Foucault: Power/Knowledge: Selected Interviews and Other Writings 1972–1977* (Hemel Hempstead: Harvester, 1980).

—— 'Space, Knowledge and Power', in id. *The Foucault Reader*, ed. Paul Rabinow (London: Peregrine, 1987).

Frampton, Kenneth, 'Towards a Critical Regionalism', in Hal Foster (ed.), *Post-Modern Culture* (London: Pluto Press, 1983).

—— *Modern Architecture* (London: Thames & Hudson, 1992).

Freeman, T. W., *Pre-Famine Ireland: A Study in Historical Geography* (London, 1957).

Freud, Sigmund, *Introductory Lectures on Psychoanalysis* (1917), in id., *The Standard Edition of the Complete Psychological Works of Sigmund Freud*, ed. James Stachey, 24 vols. (London: Hogarth Press, 1953–74), vol. xvi.

Friel, Brian, *Translations* (Derry: Field Day, 1985).

Fukuyama, Francis, 'The End of History?', in Gearóid Ó Tuathail, Simon Dalby, and Paul Routledge (eds.), *The Geopolitics Reader* (London: Routledge, 1997).

Furlong, Nicky, 'A Co. Wexford Boy who is Making Good', *Wexford People* (17 Jan. 1993), 10.

—— '1798 in Wexford', in Dermot Keogh and Nicky Furlong (eds.), *The Mighty Wave: The 1798 Rebellion in Wexford* (Dublin: Four Courts Press, 1997).

Gallagher, Tom, 'The Dimensions of Fianna Fáil Rule in Ireland', *West European Politics*, 4 (1980), 54–68.

Gardner, Patrick, *Kierkegaard* (Oxford: Oxford University Press, 1988).

Garvin, Tom, 'Political Cleavages, Party Politics and Urbanisation in Ireland: The Case of a Periphery-Dominated Centre', *European Journal of Political Research*, 6/1 (1974), 27–44.

—— 'The Growth of Faction in the Fianna Fáil Party, 1966–1980', *Parliamentary Affairs*, 34 (1981), 105–12.

—— 'The Politics of Denial and of Cultural Defence: The Referenda of 1983 and 1986 in Context', *Irish Review*, 3 (1988), 1–8.

—— 'The Destiny of the Soldiers: Tradition and Modernity in the Politics of de Valera's Ireland', *Irish Political Studies*, 26 (1978), 328–47.

—— 'The North and the Rest', in Charles Townshend (ed.), *Consensus in Ireland: Approaches and Recessions* (Oxford: Clarendon Press, 1988), 95–109.

—— 'Theory, Culture and Fianna Fáil: A Review', in Mary Kelly, Liam O'Dowd, and James Wickham (eds.), *Power, Conflict, and Inequality* (Dublin: Turoe, 1982), 171–85.

Gates, Henry Louis, jr, *Loose Canons: Notes on the Culture Wars* (New York: Oxford University Press, 1992).

Gibbons, Luke, 'Constructing the Canon: Versions of National Identity', in Deane (gen. ed.), *The Field Day Anthology of Irish Writing* (Derry: Field Day, 1991), 567–72.

—— 'Identity without a Centre: Allegory, History and Irish Nationalism', *Oxford Literary Review*, 4 (1992), 358–75.

Gibbons, Luke, 'Dialogue without the Other?: A Reply to Francis Mulhern', *Radical Philosophy*, 67 (Summer 1994), 29.

—— *Transformations in Irish Culture* (Cork: Cork University Press, 1996).

Giddens, Anthony, 'Action, Subjectivity, and the Constitution of Meaning', in Murray Krieger (ed.), *The Aims of Representation Subject/Text/History* (Stanford: Stanford University Press, 1994).

Gifford, Douglas, 'Scottish Fiction since 1945', in Norman Wilson (ed.), *Scottish Writing and Writers* (Edinburgh: The Ramsay Head Press, 1977).

—— *The Dear Green Place? The Novel in the West of Scotland* (Glasgow: Third Eye Center, 1985).

—— 'Bleeding from All that's Best: The Fiction of Iain Crichton Smith', in Gavin Wallace and Randall Stevenson (eds.), *The Scottish Novel since The Seventies* (Edinburgh: Edinburgh University Press, 1993).

Glassock, R. E., 'Land and People *c.* 1300', in Art Cosgrove (ed.), *A New History of Ireland*, ii. *Medieval Ireland 1169–1534* (Oxford: Oxford University Press, 1987).

Gow, Carol, 'An Interview with Iain Crichton Smith', *Scottish Literary Journal*, 17/2 (Nov. 1990), 56.

—— *The Mirror and the Marble: The Poetry of Iain Crichton Smith* (Edinburgh: Saltire Society, 1992).

Gould, Warwick, and Longley, Edna (eds.), *Yeats Annual No. 12: That Accusing Eye: Yeats and his Irish Readers* (Basingstoke: Macmillan, 1996).

Graham, Brian J., 'No Place of the Mind: Contested Protestant Representations of Ulster', *Ecumene*, 1/3 (July 1994), 257–82.

Graham, Colin, 'Post-Colonial Theory and Kiberd's "Ireland"', *Irish Review*, 13 (Winter 1992/3), 62–7.

—— '"Liminal Spaces": Post-Colonial Theories and Irish Culture', *Irish Review*, 16 (Autumn/Winter 1994), 29–43.

Grant, Linda, 'A Sentence beyond Words', *Independent on Sunday* (13 Sept. 1992), 22.

Gray, Alasdair, *Lanark, A Life in Four Books* (London: Paladin, 1987).

—— *Why Scots Should Rule Scotland* (Edinburgh: Polygon, 1992).

Guillory, John, *Cultural Capital: The Problem of Literary Canon Formation* (Chicago: University of Chicago Press, 1993).

Hachey, T. E., and McCaffrey, L. J. (eds.), *Perspectives on Irish Nationalism* (Lexington: University of Kentucky Press, 1989).

Hall, Stuart, 'The Local and the Global: Globalization and Ethnicity', in Anne McClinctock, Aamir Mufti, and Ella Shohat (eds.), *Dangerous Liaisons: Gender, Nation, and Postcolonial Perspectives* (Minnesota: University of Minnesota Press, 1997).

Halliday, Fred, 'An Encounter with Fukuyama', *New Left Review*, 193 (1992), 95.

Hanham, H. J., *Scottish Nationalism* (London: Faber and Faber, 1969).

Hartley, J. B., 'Maps, Knowledge, Power', in Dennis Cosgrove and Stephen Daniels (eds.), *The Iconography of Landscape* (Cambridge: Cambridge University Press, 1988).

Harvey, David, *The Condition of Postmodernity* (Oxford: Blackwell, 1989).

——*Justice, Nature, and the Geography of Difference* (Oxford: Blackwell, 1996).

Harvie, Christopher, *No Gods and Precious Few Heroes: Scotland since 1914* (1981; Edinburgh: Edinburgh University Press, 1987).

—— *Cultural Weapons: Scotland and Survival in a New Europe* (Edinburgh: Polygon, 1992).

—— *Scotland and Nationalism: Scottish Society and Politics 1707–1994* (London: Routledge, 1994).

—— *Regions and Regionalism* (London: Routledge, 1994).

Haycraft, Howard, *Murder for Pleasure: The Life and Times of the Detective Story* (London: Peter Davies, 1942).

Healy, Seán, 'Interview with Michael Longley conducted by Dermot Healy', *Southern Review*, 31/3 (Summer 1995), 554–9.

Heaney, Seamus, *Preoccupations: Selected Prose 1968–1978* (London: Faber and Faber, 1980).

—— 'Open Letter', in *Ireland's Field Day* (Notre Dame, Ind.: University of Notre Dame Press, 1984), 23–32.

—— *The Redress of Poetry: An Inaugural lecture Delivered before the University of Oxford on 24 October 1989* (Oxford: Clarendon Press, 1989).

—— 'The Regional Forecast', in R. P. Draper (ed.), *The Literature of Region and Nation* (Basingstoke: Macmillan, 1989).

—— 'Frontiers of Writing', *Bullán: An Irish Studies Journal*, 1/1 (Spring 1994), 1–15.

Heidegger, Martin, 'The Origins of the Work of Art', in *Basic Writings*, ed. David Farell Krell (London: Routledge, 1978).

Heise, Ursula, *Chronoschisms: Time, Narrative, and Postmodernism* (Cambridge: Cambridge University Press, 1996).

Hewitt, John, 'Regionalism: The Last Chance', in *Ancestral Voices: The Selected Prose of John Hewitt*, ed. Tom Clyde (Belfast: Blackstaff, 1987).

Hogg, James, *The Jacobite Relics of Scotland*, 2 vols. (Edinburgh, 1819–21).

Holquist, Michael, 'Whodunit and Other Questions: Metaphysical

Detective Stories in Post-War Fiction', *New Literary History*, 3/1 (Autumn 1971), 141–9.

Holub, Robert C., *Jurgen Habermas; Critic in the Public Sphere* (London: Routledge, 1991).

Hook, Andrew, 'Scotland and Romanticism: The International Scene', in id. (ed.), *The History of Scottish Literature,* ii. *1660–1800*, (gen. ed. Cairns Craig) (Aberdeen: Aberdeen University Press, 1987).

Horner, Arnold, 'From City to City-Region: Dublin from the 1930s to 1990s', in Kevin Whelan (ed.), *Dublin* (Dublin: Geography Publications, 1992).

Horton, Patricia, ' "Bagpipe Music": Some Intersections in Scottish and Irish Writing', *Scotlands*, 4/2 (1997), 66–80.

Houghton, J. P., 'Irish Local Newspapers: A Geographical Study', *Irish Geography*, 2/2 (1950), 56.

Houston, R. A., 'The Demographic Regime', in T. M. Devine and R. Mitchinson (eds.), *People and Society in Scotland 1760–1830* (Edinburgh: Edinburgh University Press, 1988).

Howes, Marjorie, *Yeats's Nations: Gender, Class, and Irishness* (Cambridge: Cambridge University Press, 1997).

Hume, John, 'Europe of the Regions', in Richard Kearney (ed.), *Across the Frontiers: Ireland in the 90s* (Dublin: Wolfhound, 1988).

Humphries, Tom, 'Places: Town and Country', in *Green Fields: Gaelic Sport in Ireland* (London: Weidenfeld & Nicolson, 1995).

Hunter, James, 'The Emergence of the Crofting Community: The Religious Contribution, 1789–1843', *Scottish Studies*, 18 (1974), 110.

—— *The Making of the Crofting Community* (Edinburgh: Edinburgh University Press, 1976).

—— 'The Gaelic Academy: The Cultural Commitment of the Highland Society of Scotland', *Scottish Studies,* 18 (1974), 98–110.

Huyssens, A., 'Mapping the Post-Modern', *New German Critique*, 33 (Fall 1984), 5–52.

Ivison, Duncan, 'Postcolonialism and Political Theory', in Andrew Vincent (ed.), *Political Theory: Tradition and Diversity* (Cambridge: Cambridge University Press, 1997) 154–71.

Jameson, Fredric, 'On Raymond Chandler', *Southern Review*, 6 (1970), 624–50.

—— *Marxism and Form* (Princeton: Princeton University Press, 1971).

—— 'Cognitive Mapping', in *Marxism and the Interpretation of Culture* (Basingstoke: Macmillan, 1988).

—— *Postmodernism, or The Cultural Logic of Late Capitalism* (London: Verso, 1991).

Jenkins, Alan, *The Social Theory of Claude Lévi-Strauss* (London and Basingstoke: Macmillan, 1979).

Johnson, Samuel, and Boswell, James, *A Journey to the Western Islands of Scotland and The Journal of a Tour to the Hebrides* (1772; Harmondsworth: Penguin, 1984).

Jordan, David M., *New World Regionalism: Literature in the Americas* (Toronto: University of Toronto Press, 1994).

Kearney, Colbert, 'Dermot Bolger and the Dual Carriageway', *Études irlandaises* (Autumn 1994), 25–39.

Kearney, Hugh, *The British Isles: A History of Four Nations* (Cambridge: Cambridge University Press, 1989).

Kearney, Richard, 'Culture—The Price You Pay', interview with George Steiner, in id. (ed.), *Visions of Europe* (Dublin: Wolfhound Press, 1992).

—— *Postnationalist Ireland: Politics, Culture and Philosophy* (London: Routledge, 1996).

Kedourie, Elie, *Nationalism* (London: Hutchinson, 1966).

Kelly, John, 'Introduction to James Joyce', *Dubliners* (Oxford: Blackwell, 1993).

Kelman, James, *Some Recent Attacks: Essays Cultural and Political* (Stirling: AK Press, 1992).

Kennedy, Brian P., and Gillespie, Raymond (eds.), *Ireland: Art into History* (Dublin: Town House, 1996).

Kennedy, Liam, 'Modern Ireland: Post-Colonial Society or Post-Colonial Pretensions?', *Irish Review*, 13 (Winter 1992/3), 107–21.

Kermode, Frank, *The Sense of an Ending* (London: Oxford University Press, 1967).

Kerrigan, John, 'Earth Writing: Seamus Heaney and Ciaran Carson', *Essays in Criticism*, 48 (1998), 144–68 (repr. in *Twentieth-Century Literature Criticism* (Farmington Hills, Miss.: Gale, 2001)).

—— 'Hidden Ireland: Eiléan Ní Chuilleanáin and Munster Poetry', *Critical Quarterly*, 40/4 (Winter, 1998), 76–100.

Kiberd, Declan, 'The Elephantine of Revolutionary Forgetfulness', in Máirín Ní Dhonnchadha and Theo Dorgan (eds.), *Revising the Rising* (Derry: Field Day, 1991).

—— 'The Children of Modernity', *Irish Times* (22 June 1991), 9.

—— 'Establishment Shots', *Graph: Irish Literary Review 13* (Winter 1992–Spring 1993), 5–8.

—— 'Post-Colonial Ireland: Being Different', in Daltún Ó Ceallaigh (ed.), *Reconsiderations of Irish History and Culture* (Dublin: Léirmheas, 1994).

—— *Inventing Ireland: The Literature of the Modern Nation* (London: Jonathan Cape, 1997).

—— 'James Joyce and Mythic Realism', in Keith Snell (ed.), *The Regional Novel in Britain and Ireland* (Cambridge: Cambridge University Press, 1998), 136–63.

Kidd, Colin, *Subverting Scotland's Past* (Cambridge: Cambridge University Press, 1993).

—— 'The Canon of Patriotic Landmarks in Scottish History', *Scotlands*, 1/1 (1994), 1–18.

Kierkegaard, Soren, *The Point of View of My Work as an Author*, trans. Walter Lowrie (London: Oxford University Press, 1939).

—— *Concluding Unscientific Postscript*, trans. David F. Swanson and Walter Lowrie (Princeton: Princeton University Press, 1941).

—— *Journals and Papers*, ii. F–K, ed. and trans. Howard V. Hong and Edna H. Hong (Bloomington, Ind., and London: Indiana University Press, 1963).

—— *Either/Or*, ii. trans. Walter Lowrie (Princeton: Princeton University Press, 1971).

—— *The Concept of Dread*, trans. Walter Lowrie (Princeton: Princeton University Press, 1973).

Kinsella, Thomas, 'The Irish Writer', in *Davis, Mangan, Ferguson? Tradition and the Irish Writer* (Dublin: Dolmen, 1970).

Kirkland, Richard, *Literature and Culture in Northern Ireland since 1965: Moments of Danger* (Harlow: Longman, 1996).

Lanchester, John, 'Justice of a Family Man', *Guardian* (10 Sept. 1992).

Lee, J. J., *Ireland 1912–1985: Politics and Society* (Cambridge: Cambridge University Press, 1989).

Leerssen, Joep, 'Theory, History, Ireland', *Irish Review*, 17/18 (Winter 1995), 1–8.

—— *Remembrance and Imagination: Patterns in the Historical and Literary Representation of Ireland in the Nineteenth Century* (Cork: Cork University Press, 1996).

Lefebvre, Henri, *The Production of Space*, trans. Donald Nicholson-Smith (Oxford: Blackwell, 1991).

Leonard, Tom (ed.), *Radical Renfrew: Poetry from the French Revolution to the First World War* (Edinburgh: Polygon, 1990).

Lincoln, Bruce, *Discourse and the Construction of Society: Comparative studies of Myth Ritual, and Classification* (New York, Oxford: Oxford University Press, 1989).

Lincoln, Colm, 'City of Culture: Dublin and the Discovery of Heritage', in Barbara O'Connor and Michael Cronin (eds.), *Tourism in Ireland: A Critical Analysis* (Cork: Cork University Press, 1992).

Lindsay, Fredric, 'The Glasgow Novel: Myths and Directions', *Books in Scotland*, 21 (Summer 1986), 24.

—— 'Against All Better Judgement', *Scotsman* (12 Sept. 1992), 22.

Livesey, James, and Murray, Stuart, 'Review Article: Post-Colonial Theory and Irish Culture', *Irish Historical Studies*, 30/119 (May 1997), 452–61.

Lloyd, David, *Anomalous States: Ireland and the Post-Colonial Moment* (Dublin: Lilliput Press, 1992).

Longley, Edna, *The Living Stream: Literature and Revisionism in Ireland* (Newcastle-upon-Tyne: Bloodaxe, 1994).

—— 'Northern Irish Poetry: Literature of Region(s) or Nation(s)', in James A. Davies and Glyn Pursglove (eds.), *Writing Region and Nation*, special issue of *Swansea Review* (Swansea: Swansea University Press, 1994).

—— Review Article, 'What do Protestants Want?', *Irish Review*, 20 (Winter/Spring 1997), 104–20.

Lucas, John, 'The Idea of the Provincial', in *Romantic to Modern Literature: Essays and Ideas of Culture 1750–1900* (Brighton: Harvester Press, 1982).

—— *England and Englishness: Ideas of Nationhood in English Poetry, 1688–1900* (London: Hogarth Press, 1991).

Lukacs, George, *Realism in Our Time: Literature and the Class Struggle* (New York: Harper and Row, 1964).

Lydon, James, 'The Expansion and Consolidation of the Colony, 1215–1254', in T. W. Moody, F. X. Martin, and F. J. Byrne (eds.), *A New History of Ireland*, ii. *Early Modern Ireland 1534–1691* (Oxford: Clarendon Press, 1976).

Lynch, Michael, *Scotland: A New History* (London: Pimlico, 1992).

—— 'Scottish Culture in its Historical Perspective', in Paul H. Scott (ed.), *Scotland: A Concise Cultural History* (Edinburgh and London: Mainstream, 1993).

Lyons, F. S. L., *Ireland since the Famine* (London: Fontana, 1985).

Lythe, S. G. E., and Butt, J., *An Economic History of Scotland, 1100–1939* (Glasgow: John Donaldson, 1975).

Mac Anna, Ferdia, 'The Dublin Renaissance: An Essay on Modern Dublin and Dublin Writers', *Irish Review*, 10 (Spring 1991), 14–30.

McBride, Ian, ' "The School of Virtue": Francis Hutcheson, Irish Presbyterianism and the Scottish Enlightenment', in D. George Boyce, Robert Eccleshall, and Vincent Geogheegan (eds.), *Political Thought in Ireland since the Seventeenth Century* (London: Routledge, 1992).

MacCarthy, Conor, 'Ideology and Geography in Dermot Bolger's *The Journey Home*', *Irish University Review: A Journal of Irish Studies*, 27/1 (Spring/Summer 1997), 99–106.

McCrone, David, *Understanding Scotland: The Sociology of a Stateless Nation* (London: Routledge, 1993).

MacDiarmid, Hugh, 'Contemporary Scottish Literature and the National Question', in *Selected Essays of Hugh MacDiarmid*, ed. and introd. Duncan Glen (London: Jonathon Cape, 1969).

McDonagh, Oliver, *States of Mind: A Study of Anglo-Irish Conflict 1780–1980* (London: Allen & Unwin, 1985).

McDonald, Peter, 'History and Poetry: Derek Mahon and Paul Muldoon', in Elmer Andrews (ed.), *Contemporary Irish Poetry* (London: Macmillan, 1992).

—— *Mistaken Identities: Poetry and Northern Ireland* (Oxford: Clarendon Press, 1997).

McNeil, Kirsty, 'An Interview with James Kelman', *Chapman*, 57 (Summer 1989), 1–9.

Malantschuk, Gregor, *Kierkegaard's Thought*, ed. and trans. Howard V. Hong and Edna H. Hong (Princeton: Princeton University Press, 1971).

Maley, Willy, Morash, Chris, and Richards, Shaun, 'The Triple Play of Irish History', *Irish Review*, 20 (Winter/Spring 1997), 23–46.

Malzahn, Manfred, 'The Industrial Novel', in Cairns Craig (gen. ed.), *The History of Scottish Literature* (Aberdeen: Aberdeen University Press, 1987).

Mandel, Ernest, *Delightful Murder: A Social History of the Crime Story* (London: Pluto Press, 1984).

Martin, Augustine, 'Novelist and City: The Technical Challenge', in id. (ed.), *The Genius of Irish Prose* (Dublin: Gill and Macmillan, 1972).

Masden, Deborah L., *Rereading Allegory: A Narrative Approach to Genre* (Basingstoke: Macmillan, 1995).

Massey, Doreen, 'The Possibilities of a Politics of Place', in Linda McDowell (ed.), *Undoing Place: A Geographical Reader* (London: Arnold, 1998).

Maxwell, Bill, 'One Blooming Good Yarn', *Irish Independent* (19 Sept. 1992), 22.

Migdal, Joel S., 'Studying the State', in Mark Irving Lichbach and Alan S. Zuckerman (eds.), *Comparative Politics: Rationality, Culture, Structure* (Cambridge: Cambridge University Press, 1997).

Miller, William L., *The End of British Politics? Scots and English Political Behaviour in the Seventies* (Oxford: Clarendon Press, 1981).

Milton, Colin, 'Contemporary Scottish Fiction', in Peter Zenzinger (ed.), *Anglistik & Englischunterricht Scotland: Literature, Culture, Politics* (Heidelberg: Carl Winter Universitatsverlag, 1989).

Mitchinson, Rosalind, and Roebuck, Peter, (eds.), *Economy and Society in Scotland and Ireland 1500–1939* (Edinburgh: John Donald, 1988).

Moi, Toril, *Sexual/Textual Politics: Feminist Literary Theory* (London and New York: Routledge, 1988).

Moody, T. W., 'Irish History and Irish Mythology', reprod. in Ciarán

Brady (ed.), *Interpreting Irish History: The Debate on Historical Revisionism* (Dublin: Four Courts Press, 1994).

Moorhouse, H. F., ' "We're off to Wembley!" The History of a Scottish Event and the Sociology of Football Hooliganism', in David McCrone, Stephen Kendrick, and Pat Straw (eds.), *The Making of Scotland: Culture & Social Change* (Edinburgh: Edinburgh University Press, 1989).

Morgan, Edwin, 'The Beatnik in the Kailyard', in *Essays* (Manchester: Carcanet New Press Ltd, 1974).

Morris, Christopher W., *An Essay on the Modern State* (Cambridge: Cambridge University Press, 1998).

Morrison, Blake, and Motion, Andrew, (eds.), *The Penguin Anthology of British Verse* (Harmondsworth: Penguin, 1982).

Mouffe, Chantal, 'Democratic Politics Today', in ead. (ed.), *Dimensions of Radical Democracy: Pluralism, Citizenship, Community* (London: Verso, 1992).

Murphet, Julian, *Literature and Race in Los Angeles* (Cambridge: Cambridge University Press, 2001).

Murray, Isobel, 'Breaking Out of Crime Writer's Prison', *Glasgow Herald* (23 Apr. 1983), 26.

—— and Tait, Bob, *Ten Modern Scottish Novels* (Aberdeen: Aberdeen University Press, 1984).

Naiden, James, ' "Orphaned like Us": Memory in the Poetry of Thomas McCarthy', *Eire-Ireland*, 28/1 (Spring 1993), 10–18.

Nairn, Tom, *Faces of Nationalism: Janus Revisited* (London: Verso, 1997).

—— *Auld Enemies: Essays from the Nairn on Monday Column in* the Scotsman (Glasgow: Common Cause, 1991).

Nash, Catherine, 'Embodying the Nation: The West of Ireland Landscape and Irish Identity', in Barbara O'Connor and Michael Cronin (eds.), *Tourism in Ireland: A Critical Analysis* (Cork: Cork University Press, 1993).

'New Chapter as McIlvanney Endorses Nationalists', *Herald* (6 Apr. 1996).

Niethammer, Lutz, *Posthistoire: Has History Come to an End?,* trans. Patrick Camiller (London: Verso, 1992).

Nietzsche, Friedrich, 'On the Uses & Disadvantages of History for Life', in *Untimely Meditations*, trans. R. J. Hollindale (Cambridge: Cambridge University Press, 1983).

O'Brien, Sean, *The Deregulated Muse* (Newcastle-upon-Tyne: Bloodaxe, 1998).

O'Callaghan, Dympna, 'An Interview with Seamus Deane', *Social Text*, 38 (1994), 36–44.

O'Carroll, J. P., 'Eamon de Valera, Charisma and Political Development', in id. and J. A. Murphy (eds.), *De Valera and his Times* (Cork:
Cork University Press, 1983).

O'Connor, Fionnula, *In Search of a State: Catholics in Northern
Ireland* (Belfast: Blackstaff Press, 1993).

O'Donoghue, Bernard, 'An Interview with Bernard O'Donoghue',
College Green 1/2, (1989), 11–13.

—— *Seamus Heaney and the Language of Poetry* (Hemel Hempstead:
Harvester Wheatsheaf, 1994).

—— ' "The Half-Said Thing is Dearest": Paul Muldoon', in Michael
Kenneally (ed.), *Poetry in Contemporary Irish Literature* (Gerrards
Cross: Colin Smythe, 1995).

—— 'Who Speaks for These', *The Times Literary Supplement*, (7 Mar.
1997), 180.

O'Dowd, Liam, 'The States of Ireland: Some Reflections on Research',
Irish Journal of Sociology, 1 (1991), 96–106.

Ó Gráda, Cormac, 'New Perspectives on the Irish Famine', *Bullán: An
Irish Studies Journal*, 3/2 (Winter 1997–Spring 1998), 103–16.

Oldfield, Adrian, *Citizenship and Commmunity: Civic Republicanism
and the Modern World* (London and New York: Routledge, 1990).

O'Toole, Fintan, 'Going West: The Country and the City in Irish
Writing', in Mark Hederman and Richard Kearney (eds.), *The Crane
Bag* , ix. (Dublin, 1985).

—— 'The Southern Question', in Dermot Bolger (ed.), *Letters from the
New Island* (Dublin: Raven Arts Press, 1991), 15–44.

—— *Meanwhile Back at the Ranch: The Politics of Irish Beef* (London:
Vintage, 1995).

—— *The Ex-Isle of Erin: Images of a Global Ireland* (Dublin: New
Island Books, 1996).

—— *Green Card Black Hole* (Dublin: New Island Books, 1996).

Ó Tuama, Seán, 'Stability and Ambivalence: Aspects of the Sense
of Place and Religion in Irish Literature', in Joseph Lee (ed.),
Ireland: Towards a Sense of Place (Cork: Cork University Press,
1985).

Ó Tuathaigh, Gearóid, 'Decolonization, Identity and State-Formation:
The Irish Experience', in Rosa González (ed.), *Culture and Power:
Institutions* (Barcelona: Promociones y Publicaciones Universitarias,
SA, 1996).

Paulin, Tom, 'Northern Protestant Oratory and Writing 1791–1985',
in Seamus Deane (gen. ed.), *The Field Day Anthology of Irish
Writing*, iii. (Derry: Field Day Publications, 1991).

—— *Minotaur: Poetry and the Nation State* (London: Faber and Faber,
1992).

Peacock, Alan (ed.), *The Achievement of Brian Friel* (Gerrards Cross: Colin Smythe, 1994).

Pittock, Murray, *The Invention of Scotland: The Stuart Myth and Scottish Identity, 1638 to the Present* (London: Routledge, 1991).

Pocock, J. G. A., 'British History: A Plea for a New Subject', *Journal of Modern History*, 47 (Dec. 1975), 601–21.

—— 'Contingency, Identity, Sovereignty', in Alexander Grant and Keith J. Stringer (eds.), *Uniting the Kingdom?: The Making of British History* (London: Routledge, 1995), 292–302.

—— *The Machiavellian Moment: Florentine Political Thought and the Atlantic Republican Tradition* (Princeton: Princeton University Press, 1975).

—— *Virtue, Commerce, and History: Essays on Political Thought and History, Chiefly in the Eighteenth Century* (Cambridge: Cambridge University Press, 1985).

Pollak, Andy (ed.), *A Citizen's Inquiry: The Opsahl Report on Northern Ireland* (Dublin: Lilliput Press for Initiative '92, 1993).

Porter, Dennis, *The Pursuit of Crime: Art and Ideology in Detective Fiction* (New Haven and London: Yale University Press, 1981).

Pratt, Mary Louise, *Imperial Eyes: Travel Writing and Transculturation* (London: Routledge, 1992).

Pred, Alan, 'Place as Historically Contingent Process: Structuration and the Time-Geography of Becoming Places', *Annals of the Association of American Geographers*, 74/2 (1984), 279–97.

Radhakrishnan, R., 'Nationalism, Gender, and the Narrative of Identity', in Andrew Parker (ed.), *Nationalism and Sexualities* (London: Routledge, 1992).

Rappaport, Roy, 'The Obvious Aspects of Ritual', in *Ecology, Meaning, and Religion* (Richmond, Calif.: North Atlantic Books, 1979).

Reizbaum, Marilyn, 'Canonical Double-Cross: Scottish and Irish Women's Writing', in Karen Lawrence (ed.), *Decolonizing Tradition: New Views of Twentieth-Century 'British' Literary Canons* (Chicago: University of Illinois Press, 1992).

Richards, Eric, *A History of The Highland Clearances*, ii. *Emigration, Protest, Reasons* (London: Croom Helm, 1985).

Richards, Shaun, 'Northside Realism and the Twilight's Last Gleaming', *Irish Studies Review*, 2 (Winter 1992), 18–20.

—— 'The Triple Place of Irish History: Progressive Regression in Contemporary Irish Culture', *Irish Review*, 20 (Winter/Spring 1997), 36–43.

Richardson, Thomas C., 'Reinventing Indentity: Nationalism in Modern Scottish Literature', in Horts W. Drescher and Hermann

Volkel (eds.), *Nationalism in Literature* (Frankurt am Main: Verlag Peter Lang, 1989).

Robbins, Bruce, 'Introduction', in id. (ed.), *The Phantom Public Sphere* (Minneapolis: University of Minneapolis Press, 1993).

Robbins, Caroline, *The Eighteenth-Century Commonwealthman: Studies in the Transmission, Development and Circumstances of English Liberal thought from the Restoration of Charles II until the War with the Thirteen Colonies* (Cambridge, Mass.: Harvard University Press, 1956).

Rorty, Richard, *Irony, Contingency, Solidarity* (Cambridge: Cambridge University Press, 1989).

Rose, Margaret, *The Post-Modern & the Post-Industrial* (Cambridge: Cambridge University Press, 1992).

Royle, Trevor, *The Macmillan Companion to Scottish Culture* (London: Macmillan, 1984).

—— 'Man of the People', *Scotland on Sunday* (21 Sept. 1985).

Ruane, Joseph, and Todd, Jennifer, *The Dynamics of Conflict in Northern Ireland: Power, Conflict and Emancipation* (Cambridge: Cambridge University Press, 1996).

Rushdie, Salman, *Imaginary Homelands* (London: Granta, 1992).

Said, W. Edward, *Orientalism* (1978; Harmondsworth: Penguin, 1985).

Salmond, Alex, 'Influences', *New Statesman and Society* (10 Mar. 1995).

—— Keynote Address, Annual Conference of the Scottish National Party, 27 Sept. 1996.

—— 'Irish Show Scots Road to Success', *Irish Times* (1 May 1997).

—— 'Way to Unleash the True Potential of Scotland', *Glasgow Herald* (23 Apr. 1997).

Schoene, Berthold, 'A Passage to Scotland: Scottish Literature and the Postcolonial British Condition', *Scotlands*, 2/1 (1995), 107–21.

Scott, Paul, 'The End of Britishness', *Cencrastus*, 46 (Autumn 1993), 7–10.

Scott, Tom (ed.), *The Penguin Book of Scottish Verse* (Harmondsworth: Penguin, 1970).

Scott, Sir Walter, *Waverley* (1815; Harmondsworth: Penguin, 1985).

Sher, Richard B., 'From Troglodytes to Amerians: Montesquieu and the Scottish Enlightenment on Liberty, Virtue and Commerce', in Wooton (ed.), *Republicanism*.

—— *Church and University in the Scottish Enlightenment: The Moderate Literati of Edinburgh* (Edinburgh: Edinburgh University Press, 1985).

Shields, Alexander, *A Hind Let Loose, or An Historical Representation* of *The Testimonies, Of The Church of Scotland, for the Interest of Christ* (Edinburgh, 1687).

Shils, Edward, 'Nation, Nationality, Nationalism and Civil Society', *Nations and Nationalism*, 1/1 (1995), 93–118.

Sillars, Jim, *The Case for Optimism* (Edinburgh: Polygon, 1986).

Skinner, Quentin, *The Foundations of Modern Political Thought*, i. *The Renaissance* (Cambridge: Cambridge University Press, 1978).

—— *Liberty before Liberalism* (Cambridge: Cambridge University Press, 1997).

Slaven, Anthony, *The Development of the West of Scotland: 1750–1960* (London and Boston: Routledge and Kegan Paul, 1975).

Smith, Anthony D., *National Identity* (Harmondsworth: Penguin, 1991).

Smith, David, *Socialist Propaganda in the Twentieth-Century British Novel* (London and Basingstoke: Macmillan, 1978).

Smith, Neil, 'Homeless/Global', in John Bird, Barry Curtis, Tim Putnam, George Robertson, and Lisa Tickner (eds.), *Mapping the Futures: Local Cultures, Global Changes* (London: Routledge, 1993).

Smith, Olivia, *The Politics of Language 1791–1819* (Oxford: Oxford University Press, 1984).

Smout, T. C., *A History of the Scottish People 1560–1830* (1969; London: Fontana, 1982).

—— 'Patterns of Culture', in A. Dickson and J. H. Treble (eds.), *People and Society in Scotland*, iii. *1914 to the Present* (Edinburgh: John Donald Publishers Ltd in association with the Economic and Social History Society of Scotland, 1991).

Smyth, Gerry, *The Novel and the Nation: Studies in the New Irish Fiction* (London: Pluto Press, 1997).

Smyth, Jim, *The Men of No Property* (Basingstoke: Macmillan, 1994).

Soja, Edward, *Postmodern Geographies: The Reassertion of Space in Critical Social Theory* (London: Verso, 1989).

Somerville-Arjat, Gillean, and Wilson, Rebecca E. (eds.), *Sleeping with Monsters: Conversations with Scottish and Irish Women Poets* (Dublin: Wolfhound Press, 1990).

Sperber, Dan, 'Claude Lévi-Strauss', in John Sturrock (ed.), *Structuralism and Since from Lévi-Strauss to Derrida* (Oxford: Oxford University Press, 1979).

Spring, Ian, *Phantom Village. The Myth of the New Glasgow* (Edinburgh: Polygon, 1990).

Stewart, A. T. Q., *The Narrow Ground* (Belfast: Blackstaff, 1977).

Stewart, Colonel David, *Sketches of the Character, Manners and Present State of the Highlands of Scotland* (Edinburgh, 1822).

Tani, J. Stefano, *The Doomed Detective: The Contribution of the Detective Novel to Postmodern American and Italian Fiction* (Carbondale, Ill.: Southern Illinois University Press, 1984).

Taylor, Charles, 'The Politics of Recognition', in Amy Guttmann (ed.), *Multiculturalism: Examining the Politics of Recognition* (Princeton: Princeton University Press, 1994).

Taylor, D. J., 'Just like Old Troubled Times', *Independent* (26 Sept. 1992).

Taylor, Mark C., *Kierkegaard's Pseudonymous Authorship: A Study of Time and the Self* (Princeton: Princeton University Press, 1975).

Todorov, Tveztan, *The Typology of Detective Fiction* (Cambridge: Cambridge University Press, 1989).

Trotsky, Leon, *Literature and Revolution* (London: Redwords, 1991).

Trumpener, Katie, *Bardic Nationalism: The Romantic Novel and the British Empire* (Princeton: Princeton University Press, 1997).

Turner, Victor, 'Liminal to Liminoid in Play, Flow, and Ritual: An Essay in Comparative Symbology', in *From Ritual to Theater.*

——*From Ritual to Theater: The Human Seriousness of Play* (New York: Performing Arts Journal Publications, 1982).

Turnock, David, *The Historical Geography of Scotland since 1707* (Cambridge: Cambridge University Press, 1982).

Wallace, Gavin, 'Introduction', in id. and Randall Stevenson (eds.), *The Scottish Novel since the Seventies* (Edinburgh: Edinburgh University Press, 1993).

Wallerstein, Immanuel, *Geopolitics and Geoculture: Essays on the Changing World-System* (Cambridge: Cambridge University Press, 1991).

Walsh, Dick, *The Party: Inside Fianna Fáil* (Dublin: Gill and Macmillan, 1986).

Waters, John, *Jiving at the Crossroads* (Belfast: Blackstaff Press, 1991).

——*A Race of Angels: The Genesis of U2* (Belfast: Blackstaff Press, 1994).

Watson, George, 'Scottish Culture and the Lost Past', *Irish Review*, 9 (Spring 1991), 34–44.

——'A Culloden of the Spirit', in Colin Nicholson (ed.), *Iain Crichton Smith: Critical Essays* (Edinburgh: Edinburgh University Press, 1994), 37–50.

Whelan, Kevin, 'The Catholic Parish, the Catholic Chapel and Village Development in Ireland', in *Irish Geography,* xvi (Dublin: Geographical Society Of Ireland, 1983).

——'Reinterpreting the 1798 Rebellion in County Wexford', in Dáire Keogh and Nicholas Furlong (eds.), *The Mighty Wave: The 1798 Rebellion in Wexford* (Dublin: Four Courts Press, 1997).

—— 'The Power of Place', *Irish Review*, 12 (Spring/Summer 1992), 13–20.

—— 'The Bases of Regionalism', in Prionsiás Ó Drisceoil (ed.), *Culture in Ireland: Regions, Identity and Power* (Belfast: The Institute of Irish Studies, 1993).

—— 'An Underground Gentry?', in *The Tree of Liberty: Radicalism, Catholicism, and the Construction of Irish Identity, 1760–1830* (Cork: Cork University Press, 1996).

—— 'The Intellectual and the Region', in Liam O'Dowd (ed.), *On Intellectuals and Intellectual Life in Ireland* (Belfast: Institute of Irish Studies, 1996).

—— 'The Politics of Memory', in Mary Cullen (ed.), *1798: 200 Years of Remembrance* (Dublin: Irish Reporter Publications, 1998).

Williams, Raymond, 'Region and Class in the Novel', in Douglas Jefferson and Graham Martin (eds.), *The Uses of Fiction: Essays on the Modern Novel in Honour of Arnold Kettle* (Milton Keynes: Open University, 1982).

Wilson, Thomas M., and Hastings, Donnan, 'Nation, State and Identity at International Borders', in eid., *Border Identities: Nation and State in International Frontiers* (Cambridge: Cambridge University Press, 1998).

Winks, Robin (ed.), *Detective Fiction: A Collection of Critical Essays* (Eaglewood Cliffs, NJ: Prentice Hall, 1980).

Withers, C. J., 'The Geographical Extent of Gaelic in Scotland 1698–1806', *Scottish Geographical Magazine*, 97/3 (Dec. 1981), 12–18.

Wooton, David (ed.), *Republicanism, Liberty, and Commercial Society 1649–1776* (Stanford: Stanford University Press, 1995).

Young, G. M., 'Scott and the Historians', *Sir Walter Scott Lectures, 1940–1948* (Edinburgh: University of Edinburgh Press, 1946).

Youngs, Tim, 'Buttons and Souls: Some Thoughts on Commodities and Identity in Women's Travel Writing', *Studies in Travel Writing*, 1 (Spring 1997), 117–40.

—— 'Punctuating Travel: Paul Theroux and Bruce Chatwin', *Literature and History*, 6/2 (Autumn 1997), 79–81.

Index

Printed in the United Kingdom
by Lightning Source UK Ltd.
121156UK00001B/16